The Monk's Tale

Kathleen Hughes, R.S.C.J.

The Monk's Tale

A Biography of Godfrey Diekmann, O.S.B.

THE LITURGICAL PRESS • Collegeville, Minnesota

Cover design by Ann Blattner.

Photo credits: page 57, Bob Hasse; page 128 (bottom right), The Archives of the University of Notre Dame; pages 173, 280, 306, Rohn Engh; page 297 (bottom), Placid Stuckenschneider, O.S.B.; pages 302, 309, 310, Robin Pierzina, O.S.B.; back cover, Penny Gill.

Poem entitled "Forthcoming Moontime," page vii, copyright © 1988 by Eva Hooker, C.S.C. All rights reserved.

Printed in the United States of America.

Library of Congress Cataloging-in-Publication Data

Hughes, Kathleen, 1942–
   The monk's tale : a biography of Godfrey Diekmann, O.S.B. /
  Kathleen Hughes.
      p.   cm.
   "Bibliography of Godfrey Diekmann, O.S.B.": p.
   Includes bibliographical references and index.
   ISBN 0-8146-1984-3
   1. Diekmann, Godfrey.   2. Benedictines—United States—Biography.
 I. Title.
 BX4705.D515H84   1991
 271'.102—dc20   91-10516
  [B]   CIP

CONTENTS

Foreword ix

Preface xv

Chapter 1 1

Chapter 2 26

Chapter 3 51

Chapter 4 86

Chapter 5 111

Chapter 6 148

Chapter 7 183

Chapter 8 221

Chapter 9 252

Chapter 10 277

Appendix: Honors Received. 321

Bibliography of Godfrey Diekmann, O.S.B. 345

Index 367

Forthcoming Moontime

For Godfrey Diekmann, O.S.B.

"All good discourse must, like forward motion, know resistance."
James Merrill, *The Changing Light at Sandover*

Your forthcoming moontime
            bursts on summer
            circling in high gear:

                       the dark-light
                       cadence breaking words
                       into another season
                       of fitful truth;

                       unnamed and named
                       misgivings, lit up
                       like falling jets,
                       split and vanish;

                       a moon so full we no
                       longer sleepwalk
                       and one could say
                       good-bye to dark!

                       and sing!
                              yes!   sing!

Your fierce words
assume the disciplined
routine of a summer day:

                       that light
                       will burn our ungodly
                       muteness
                       into slow motion and
                       silence, into
                       reason
                       fiery-eyed and dazzling.

Eva Hooker, C.S.C.
July 15, 1988

FOREWORD

THE TASK of a prefacer or presenter or writer of forewords is twofold—at least in the case of a biography like *The Monk's Tale,* the story of Dom Godfrey Diekmann, O.S.B. It is to introduce and commend the book itself, as I most certainly do, and to offer some supplementary observations about the subject of the biographical study.

The first part of the task is simple enough. Kathleen Hughes has done an exacting job of research, using voluminous correspondence and journals, interviews with Godfrey and those associated with him over several decades, as well as selective analysis of events, themes, and immense contributions made to the twentieth-century liturgical renewal.

The best thing to be said about a biographical study is that it is worthy of its subject, surely a cliché come true in this book. The author has told the tale well indeed, in an account that is serious enough in dealing with Godfrey's massive accomplishments and influence, yet engaging and lively in anecdote and quotation.

The several years of diligent work by Kathleen Hughes are completed at an opportune time. The liturgical review *Worship,* which owes its very character to Godfrey, will soon celebrate its sixty-fifth birthday. It is just over fifty years since the first Liturgical Week was celebrated in Chicago, with Godfrey as a major speaker. The Constitution on the Liturgy, promulgated on December 4, 1963, and the International Commission on English in the Liturgy (ICEL), born on October 17, 1963, will soon observe their thirtieth anniversaries. In both of them Dom Godfrey played a distinctive role from the beginning—and happily continues to play a role in ICEL to this day.

Perhaps more important, as postconciliar liturgical renewal catches its second wind in the 1990s, thoughtful members of the American Church, lay and ordained, are taking another look at the origins and development of the liturgical movement over the past seven decades and more. The signs of this very profitable exercise are several. Biographies of Martin Hellriegel, parish priest, and Paul Hallinan, archbishop—both closely associated with Godfrey, although in rather different ways—have recently been published. Two volumes entitled *How Firm a Foundation* have also appeared: one, edited by Kathleen Hughes, offers a sampling of writings of liturgical pioneers; the second, edited by Robert Tuzik, provides brief accounts of liturgical leaders, American and European. And even a videotape of oral history, from Liturgy Training Publications, reminds a new generation of what can be learned from an exciting past. All this contributes to an instructive, stimulating record of the pastoral enterprise within the Church community that goes by the name of liturgical renewal.

This brings me to the second purpose of this foreword—my own appraisal and personal testimony to the greatness of Godfrey Diekmann. It is a difficult task, not at all because of any peril of exaggeration—quite the contrary—but because of constraints of space, and I must not indulge in triumphalistic nostalgia.

As will be evident in this book, my own association with Godfrey spans more than four decades, specifically in relation to his editorship of *Worship,* in which position he was my early mentor; in the promotional days and "Weeks" of the Liturgical Conference; and in preconciliar, conciliar, and postconciliar undertakings, the latter including the ICEL program from 1963 to the present. Because it has been a close personal friendship grounded in common liturgical, ecclesial, and gospel concerns, I can only try to be objective and choose for mention two or three marks of his life and Christian character.

"Holistic" is the jargon adjective of today to refer to integrity, wholeness, and breadth. There is a sense in which Godfrey has been single-minded. No aspect of his theological and patristic scholarship, his pastoral and liturgical insight, his preaching and teaching and editing, his liturgical, ecclesial, and social activism falls outside what has been a life of commitment to the gospel of Jesus and to God's People, the Church. This commitment has been wonderful to see in the volumes of *Worship* he edited, in conferences and published papers, in the personal interchanges of Roman, ICEL, and other meetings. It comes down, in Godfrey's case, to unity of purpose coupled with unrivaled openness and enthusiasm.

This is not a *positio* for canonization, and so I will not dwell on the goodness of the man and the evident signs of his monastic spirituality and his Christian love for his sisters and brothers in faith. Unquestionably this is the reason for vast numbers of friendships, for much deep affection and respect. But Godfrey's warmth and enthusiasm deserve some enlargement in these comments.

No promoter of the liturgical renewal has maintained an unswerving comprehension and commitment more steadfastly than Godfrey Diekmann. In his eighties—and may he have many more years—he is young in ideas, young in hopes. This is not by any means a characteristic of those who have fought the good liturgical fight, seen the compromises or the aberrations—of course, far fewer liturgical aberrations than instances of apathy.

With age, it seems, some have narrowed their horizons; some few have regressed into gloom and reaction. It is just the opposite with Godfrey. He is as open today to the breath of the Spirit and all the potential of liturgical growth as when he was a young monk venturing upon patristic and theological studies, next accepting the mantle of Virgil Michel, and then moving far beyond his own mentor.

I could give chapter and verse for many facets of Godfrey's life, from the days when we worked together in the trying but exhilarating conciliar endeavors or from personal conversation and exchange. A single example will suffice. At the most recent meeting of the ICEL advisory committee, in October 1990, Godfrey was as full of ideas, as responsive and dynamic in his reactions, as concerned with the prayer of the praying community as the youngest and most zealous participant in those sessions.

Because his contribution to the Church at large, and especially to the Church in the English-speaking world, has been "liturgical," it is important to add quickly—as these pages will record—that Godfrey's concerns have never been the least sanctuary-limited or chancel-confined. Quite the contrary, he has shared with other American liturgical greats—Michel, Reinhold, Hillenbrand, Hallinan, Hovda, Sloyan, and the "Boston group" (especially Mary Perkins Ryan, Thomas Carroll, Shawn Sheehan, and William Leonard)—the deepest concern for justice, peace, and fairness within and outside the Catholic community.

As soon as the Constitution on the Liturgy was published in 1963, Godfrey (and I) regretted how few are its direct references to the total mission of the Church in its context of Christian communal holiness and worship. In a way *Sacrosanctum Concilium* is a "churchy" document, perhaps inevitably so because of its explicit goal of Roman liturgical reform within the life of the Catholic people. It is necessary to hunt down the few mentions of the apostolic and social dimension of the celebration of the mysteries as these are part of the total life of the Church, part of the liturgical commitment of faith that is made in text and rite.

As is obvious enough, this limitation of the Constitution on the Liturgy is a formal one. Even the more expansive (and original) definition and exposition of the Church's nature in the Dogmatic Constitution on the Church *(Lumen Gentium)* had to be supplemented by the reflective Pastoral Constitution on the Church in the Modern World *(Gaudium et Spes)*. My point is only that Godfrey Diekmann, certainly as much as any liturgical promoter and more than almost all, has been acutely conscious that the holy liturgy does not by any means exhaust the Church's evangelical mission and ministry.

Adversity he has seen, and probably disappointments enough, including the misunderstandings of those colleagues whose liturgical perceptions and visions were meager. The most absurd but grievous affronts came, I regret to say, from my own university, the Catholic University of America, where the course of academic freedom has been a bumpy road. He was among the distinguished group of banned speakers in the days of the Second Vatican Council and, more seriously, was disinvited from his regular summer lectureship. The *amende honorable* was later made by way of an honorary degree and repeated opportunities to teach at this university, to the satisfaction and pride of his students.

It is trite enough to hold out the subject of biography as model and exemplar, even if in this case it is hardly likely that the ongoing liturgical renewal will find another leader of Godfrey's breadth and courage, style and temperament. Again, it is not original, if true and sound, to hope that our contemporaries and the next generation will reflect upon his life and learn from it. But there is something particularly appropriate in one of the many parts played by Godfrey in a long ecclesial career. Along with another American scholar of German ancestry, John Quasten, Godfrey prepared the first draft of the conciliar affirmation of liturgical inculturation, ultimately pronounced in *Sacrosanctum Concilium,* nos. 37–40, all in the most open-ended fashion.

This single instance of inculturation, simply called liturgical adaptation in the 1960s, is a key to the whole renewal of Christian worship. There is recovery of the best traditions lost several centuries back, especially the tradition of organic growth within the Spirit-filled community of worshipers. The signs of the times are embraced, as the human arts and the human sciences strengthen, in the most diverse ways, the cultic life of the Church and its response to the action of the Spirit of God. The horizons are enlarged, and the liturgical freedom of the People of God within the communion of the Churches is affirmed with balance and insight and inner dedication, that most traditional "faith and devotion" of the first Roman anaphora. These fine and happy words do not do justice to what can be learned from Godfrey Diekmann, but they do say that no doors or windows were closed by him as he moved us forward to liturgical and much larger reform and Christian growth.

FREDERICK R. McMANUS

The Catholic University of America
Washington, D. C.

January 1991

THE IDEA FOR THIS BIOGRAPHY was born at a Sunday dinner in the spring of 1980. During the academic year 1979–1980 I was in residence at the Institute for Ecumenical and Cultural Research at St. John's Abbey and University at Collegeville, Minnesota, working on my doctoral dissertation for the University of Notre Dame. I had met Father Godfrey Diekmann, O.S.B., two years earlier when I was a guest participant at a meeting of the advisory committee of the International Commission on English in the Liturgy (ICEL) in Edinburgh, Scotland. While still a graduate student at Notre Dame, I was both delighted and a bit awed to be invited to an ICEL meeting. As I walked into the conference room for the opening of that meeting, Father Diekmann motioned to me to take the chair beside him. Before I knew it, Godfrey had made a date with me to visit the Edinburgh castle over the lunch break while participants half his age would be napping.

In the course of that meeting in Scotland, Godfrey tutored me in ICEL's *disciplina arcani* during the sessions and engaged me often in flying side trips at the breaks. But most fascinating for me were the dinners at which Godfrey would regale all at table—and sometimes the whole restaurant—with endless anecdotes of the early liturgical movement and the personalities involved; of his travels, adventures, and latest acquisitions either for his hat collection or for the monastic microfilm library at St. John's (both equally important); of the architectural brilliance of such and such a building that we should not miss; of the Second Vatican Council, its cast of characters, its agenda, its high and low moments; of his being "fired" from the Catholic University (this was always recounted with a certain pride at the company he kept at that time—and continues to keep); of the civil rights marches in Selma and Washington; of the great European liturgical scholars whom he met during his student days at Sant' Anselmo and Maria Laach. The list could go on and on.

Godfrey's interests are catholic, his zest for storytelling boundless. He has never been without good stories of people and events that most of us have only read about and wondered about. And he is at his best at the head of a dinner table. Godfrey once described himself to me as "a maître d'," one who likes to seat friends together at table. It is an image that serves well to characterize this man who delights in nothing more than good conversation over a meal with friends he has assembled for the occasion.

So it was, in the spring of 1980 at Collegeville, that the "maître d'" arranged for me to join him at table for Sunday dinner at the home of his sister Marie. Particularly voluble on that day, Godfrey entertained us with recollections of Vatican II—some of the more homely, inside stories that made the people and issues very much alive for me. I remember saying to Godfrey on that occasion that it would be a great loss when he died, because so many stories would die with him. Then I blurted out, "Really, we ought to pickle your brain!"

Not a very nice thing to say, but it made me pause to realize that Godfrey's death would mark the end of an era. I liken it in my own mind to the end of the Apostolic Age. With Godfrey's death we would lose a vital narrator of the liturgical movement in the United States. And anyone who knows Godfrey knows that it is not premature to speak of his mortality, since he seems to have a brush with death about every two years, though only lately (as he would tell it) has he taken them seriously enough to summon a pious thought.

Capturing Godfrey's words seems particularly important because he has not left a great corpus of writings. Once he actually apologized to me for having written so little. Though his bibliography fills many pages, nearly all the major pieces in this corpus of writings were public addresses that were later published. Godfrey was an editor for twenty-five years, a renowned teacher, a much sought-after speaker, but not a writer. How important, then, to dialogue with the man and capture the stories and the vision in his own words!

This project was launched in the fall of 1987 when, with the assistance of grants from the Association of Theological Schools and the Society of the Sacred Heart, I began a sabbatical from the Catholic Theological Union. Originally I was interested in concentrating on two particular facets of Godfrey's life. Through his eyes I hoped to capture the history and the spirit of the liturgical movement in the United States and to attempt to recover the vision of liturgy articulated at Vatican II. The former has always intrigued me, for I believe that we cannot really understand our present without knowing our past. The latter has served as inspiration for my teaching of liturgy and sacraments at the Catholic Theological Union and the impetus for my work with the International Commission on English in the Liturgy, an association that has continued since that meeting in Edinburgh. Yet I have a nagging fear that the vision of Vatican II is slowly being eroded on both sides of the Atlantic—by us, in not appreciating that the reform of the books was only a preliminary to the real liturgical renewal; by Rome, in their timorous retrenchment from that vision. So at first it seemed important to look at the liturgical movement and Vatican II through Godfrey's life and work for their mutual illumination.

Yet Godfrey is a man larger than life. Once the project was launched, it took on a life of its own. I recognized that I could not limit myself to these two facets but that I needed to do a biography which would communicate the breadth of his interests and a hint of his escapades, as well as the circumstances which made the liturgical movement in the United States a movement unique in the Church and which prepared so well for the reforms that Vatican II would introduce. The success of that movement is due to many, many people, some of whose names will crop up in these pages. But surely in great measure Godfrey played a central role, both as editor of *Orate Fratres,* which was the chief organ of the liturgical movement in the crucial years prior to the Council, and more importantly as the indefatigable speaker who took the message of the liturgical movement and made it available to crowds both great and small all across our country.

Because Godfrey's influence extends beyond editing and speaking, we will also need to understand Godfrey the patristics scholar and educator of several generations of students; Godfrey the retreat master for vast numbers of priests and women religious; Godfrey the monk with a vow of stability who became a world traveler; Godfrey the ecumenist; Godfrey the man immersed in social action; Godfrey the *peritus* at the Council; Godfrey the entertainer, yet an exceptionally private person whom few in or out of the monastery claim to know very well; Godfrey the man overwhelmed by feelings of hopeless inadequacy when asked to replace Virgil Michel! And yet, replace him he did. It would be interesting to speculate in these pages about whether the liturgical movement as we know it in retrospect would have taken the same twists and turns had Virgil Michel lived beyond his forty-eight years and Godfrey remained tucked in a classroom. But that is to get ahead of the story.

So many people have helped me to tell this story. Godfrey spent endless hours answering questions—sometimes my questions, but often the questions he wanted me to ask. He also gave me a list of family and friends whom I should contact. It is an index of the love and esteem which Godfrey commands that I was so graciously assisted by his numerous colleagues and friends.

I am grateful to the following persons for their willingness to be interviewed or to send me taped reflections about Godfrey:

MISS MARIE DIEKMANN, Godfrey's younger sister, who also made available family letters and keepsakes;

MR. PAUL DIEKMANN AND MRS. DORIS DIEKMANN, Godfrey's younger brother and sister-in-law;

MRS. LEMAY BECHTOLD, an editor at the Liturgical Press, alumna of St. Benedict's College, where she first met Godfrey;

MISS ADE BETHUNE, artist, founder of St. Leo Shop, writer for *Orate Fratres,* colleague in the early liturgical movement;

DR. ROBERT BILHEIMER, Presbyterian minister, retired Executive Director of the Institute for Ecumenical and Cultural Research, former Associate General Secretary and Director of the Division of Studies of the World Council of Churches;

FATHER PASCHAL BOTZ, O.S.B., classmate of Godfrey's at St. John's and Sant' Anselmo, and traveling companion during their student days in Europe;

FATHER ALLAN BOULEY, O.S.B., Associate Professor of Theology and Liturgy at St. John's University;

FATHER ALBERIC CULHANE, O.S.B., Assistant to the President for University Relations at St. John's, student of Godfrey's, and collaborator with him on the Scriptural Institute at St. John's;

FATHER JOSEPH CUNNINGHAM, Rector of St. Vincent de Paul Seminary, Boynton Beach, Florida, fellow member of the International Commission on English in the Liturgy, and sometimes traveling companion;

FATHER ALFRED DEUTSCH, O.S.B., now deceased, former Professor of English, St. John's University;

ABBOT BALDWIN DWORSCHAK, O.S.B., sixth Abbot of St. John's Abbey (1950–1971);

MONSIGNOR JOHN J. EGAN, priest of the Archdiocese of Chicago, Assistant to the President, Office of Community Affairs at De Paul University, formerly Assistant to the President and Director of the Center for Pastoral and Social Ministry at the University of Notre Dame;

ABBOT JOHN EIDENSCHINK, O.S.B, seventh Abbot of St. John's Abbey (1971–1979);

MONSIGNOR JOHN TRACY ELLIS, Professor of Church History, Catholic University of America, academic colleague of Godfrey's both at the Catholic University of America and the University of San Francisco;

DR. DANIEL FINN, Associate Professor of Theology, St. John's University;

GRADUATE STUDENTS, St. John's University School of Theology;

FATHER ANDREW GREELEY, priest of the Archdiocese of Chicago, Director of the National Opinion Research Center, author;

MRS. PATRICIA JOYCE AND MR. THOMAS JOYCE, graduates of the College of St. Benedict and St. John's University respectively, friends of Godfrey's;

BROTHER FRANK KACMARCIK, OBL.S.B., artist, consultant, designer, collaborator on *Orate Fratres/Worship;*

FATHER EMERIC LAWRENCE, O.S.B., monk of St. John's, close friend and collaborator of Godfrey's;

FATHER WILLIAM LEONARD, S.J., retired Professor at Boston College and founder of its Liturgical Library Collection, "Liturgy and Life," colleague in National Liturgical Weeks;

DR. MARTIN MARTY, historian of modern Christianity, University of Chicago, member of the press at Vatican II;

FATHER MICHAEL MARX, O.S.B., who worked with Godfrey in editing *Worship;*

MRS. ABIGAIL McCARTHY, Benedictine Oblate, author, friend of Godfrey's;

THE HONORABLE EUGENE McCARTHY, former Senator from Minnesota, friend and student of Godfrey's;

FATHER KILIAN McDONNELL, O.S.B., member of the theology faculty of St. John's University, founder of the Institute for Ecumenical and Cultural Research;

FATHER GILBERT OSTDIEK, O.F.M., Professor of Liturgy at the Catholic Theological Union, Chicago, collaborator on the International Commission on English in the Liturgy, and Godfrey's traveling companion on one of his many "last" trips to Europe;

MR. JOHN PAGE, Executive Secretary of the International Commission on English in the Liturgy;

MRS. MARY PERKINS RYAN, author, contributor to *Orate Fratres/Worship,* friend and colleague of Godfrey's in the early liturgical movement, in National Liturgical Weeks, and at the Assisi Congress;

FATHER KEVIN SEASOLTZ, O.S.B., Rector of St. John's Seminary, Professor of Theology and Liturgy, canonist, General Editor of *Worship;*

FATHER SHAWN SHEEHAN, now deceased, priest of the Archdiocese of Boston, colleague in National Liturgical Weeks, friend;

DR. ROBERT SPAETH, Professor of Liberal Studies, St. John's University, student of Godfrey's;

BROTHER PLACID STUCKENSCHNEIDER, O.S.B., artist with The Liturgical Press, monk of St. John's;

ABBOT JEROME THEISEN, O.S.B., eighth Abbot of St. John's Abbey;

FATHER HILARY THIMMESH, O.S.B., President of St. John's University from 1982 to 1991, student of Godfrey's;

SISTER MARY ANTHONY WAGNER, O.S.B., Professor of Theology at the College of St. Benedict, friend and academic colleague;

MONSIGNOR VINCENT A. YZERMANS, priest of the Diocese of St. Cloud, author, formerly editor of the diocesan newspaper, journalist at the Second Vatican Council.

The following offered their reflections about Godfrey in writing:

FATHER FRANCIS J. BUCKLEY, S.J., University of San Francisco, friend and academic colleague;

BISHOP CHARLES BUSWELL, retired Bishop of Pueblo, Colorado, colleague during Vatican II;

MR. WILLIAM COFELL, Collegeville, retired Professor of Education at St. John's, student and friend of Godfrey's and the Diekmann family;

SISTER MARIETTA CRAHAN, O.S.B., St. Louis, Missouri, student, friend and correspondent of Godfrey's;

DR. ROBERT CUSHMAN, Professor of Theology, Duke University, colleague at Vatican II, in the ecumenical movement, and in the Institute at Tantur;

BISHOP REMI DE ROO, Bishop of Victoria, Canada, friend and colleague during Vatican II;

SISTER MARY DOLORES DOWLING, O.S.B, San Diego, California, student of Godfrey's;

REVEREND DR. C. JACK EICHHORST, Lutheran Bible Institute of Seattle, colleague in the early ecumenical movement;

FATHER BALTHASAR FISCHER, priest of the Diocese of Trier, West Germany, colleague during Vatican II;

GORDON JOSEPH CARDINAL GRAY, retired Cardinal Archbishop of St. Andrews and Edinburgh, Scotland, colleague at Vatican II and on the International Commission on English in the Liturgy;

PROFESSOR G. B. HARRISON, Palmerston North, New Zealand, Professor of Shakespeare, colleague on the International Commission on English in the Liturgy;

FATHER ROBERT HOVDA, writer for *Worship,* author in the field of liturgy, student and fellow traveler of Godfrey's;

SISTER AUDREY JONES, O.S.B., Clyde, Missouri, student of Godfrey's;

SISTER GEORGETTA LOXTERKAMP, O.S.B., first cousin of Godfrey's;

MONSIGNOR JOHN J. McENEANEY, priest of Sioux Falls, South Dakota, colleague in National Liturgical Weeks;

FATHER CLEMENT J. McNASPY, S.J., musician, National Liturgical Weeks colleague, promoter of the vernacular in *Worship* prior to Vatican II;

FATHER PETER MONOPOLI, priest of South Australia, student, loaned tapes of an interview with Godfrey;

SISTER JOSEPHINE MORGAN, R.S.C.J., retired Professor of Music, Pius X School of Liturgical Music, Manhattanville College, collaborator in National Liturgical Weeks;

DRS. FRANZ AND THERESE MUELLER, German friends of Godfrey's, writers for *Orate Fratres;*

FATHER BURKHARD NEUNHEUSER, O.S.B., monk of Maria Laach, Germany, fellow student with Godfrey at Sant' Anselmo, lifelong friend;

MONSIGNOR JOHN M. OESTERREICHER, Seton Hall University/Seminary, colleague during and after Vatican II in the ecumenical movement;

REVEREND ROBERT D. PELTON, Director General, Priests of Madonna House, Canada, correspondent of Godfrey's;

FATHER PETER SAMMON, priest of the Archdiocese of San Francisco, student, participant in National Liturgical Weeks, and academic colleague;

FATHER WILLIAM SKUDLAREK, O.S.B., Associate Professor of Theology, St. John's University, student and fellow monk of Godfrey's;

FATHER GERARD SLOYAN, Professor of Theology, Temple University, colleague in National Liturgical Weeks and academic colleague at the Catholic University of America, wrote a regular feature on catechesis for *Worship;*

BISHOP GEORGE H. SPELTZ, former Bishop of St. Cloud, the diocese in which St. John's Abbey is located, colleague at Vatican II;

DR. DOUGLAS STEERE, Professor Emeritus of Philosophy at Haverford College, Chairman of the Friends World Committee, colleague at Vatican II and in the post-Vatican Ecumenical Spiritual Institute;

MOTHER KATHRYN SULLIVAN, R.S.C.J., retired Professor of Scripture, Manhattanville College, writer for *Worship,* colleague in National Liturgical Weeks;

DR. SYLVESTER THEISEN, Professor of Sociology at St. John's University, student of Godfrey's;

SISTER MARY PAULA THOMPSON, O.S.B., Tucson, Arizona, student of Godfrey's;

MR. WILLMAR THORKELSON, former religion editor for the *Minneapolis Star* during and after Vatican II;

SISTER MAUREEN TRULAND, O.S.B, Osage Monastery, Oklahoma, student of Godfrey's;

FATHER ROBERT TUZIK, priest of the Archdiocese of Chicago, who opened to me some of his Ph.D. research on Reynold Hillenbrand;

MONSIGNOR ALOYSIUS WILMES, priest of the Archdiocese of St. Louis, colleague in National Liturgical Weeks and at the International Congress on the Liturgy at Assisi;

ARCHBISHOP GUILFORD C. YOUNG, of Hobart, Tasmania, Australia, colleague during Vatican II and in the beginnings of the International Commission on English in the Liturgy.

This material was supplemented by access to the monastic and university archives at St. John's through the kindness of FATHER VINCENT TEGEDER, O.S.B., abbey and university archivist; also by SISTER ELEANOR BERNSTEIN, Center for Pastoral Liturgy, University of Notre Dame; FATHER CHRISTIAN CEPLECHA, O.S.B., archivist, Illinois Benedictine College (formerly St. Procopius College); FATHER DANIEL DURKEN, O.S.B., Director of the Liturgical Press when this project was launched, who assisted with editorial directives; MS. EILEEN EGAN, associate of Dorothy Day on the *Catholic Worker;* FATHER ZACHARY HAYES, O.F.M., Professor of Theology, Catholic Theological Union, who made translations of German and gave valuable technical assistance; MS. ECHO LEWIS, archivist, Madonna House, Combermere, Ontario, Canada; MS. MARGARET J. THOMAS, Executive Director of the Minnesota Council of Churches; MS. KATHARINE TEMPLE, archivist for the *Catholic Worker.* The entire library staff at Catholic Theological Union were consistently patient and helpful colleagues in this project.

In addition, the International Commission on English in the Liturgy, the Bishops' Committee on the Liturgy, and the Liturgical Conference were most gracious in allowing me access to their archives. I thank MR. JOHN PAGE, FATHER JOHN GURRIERI, and MS. RACHEL REEDER, respective Executive Directors of these organizations, for the courtesies that they and their staffs extended to me.

I regret that most of the photographs appearing in this volume are lacking proper credit and here express my thanks to all those anonymous photographers over the years who captured Godfrey's life and work.

The drawing of Godfrey on page 320, a reproduction of a previously unpublished sketch made during Vatican Council II, is the work of DR. FREDERICK FRANCK, an artist and author whose illustrations made during the Council have been collected in *Outsider in the Vatican* (New York: Macmillan, 1965). My gratitude to Dr. Franck for allowing me to use his work. I am also grateful to EVA HOOKER, C.S.C., Vice-President for Academic Affairs at St. John's University and my friend for many years, for allowing me to reprint her poem "Forthcoming Moontime," written in honor of Godfrey Diekmann (page vii).

At various stages of this project, the manuscript was read and critiqued by family and friends, who have rescued me from repetition, grammatical errors, and factual inaccuracies. Particularly helpful have been the suggestions of FATHER FREDERICK R. McMANUS, colleague and close personal friend of Godfrey's since the forties, whose memory for dates and places is legendary. I am also grateful to Fred for writing the Foreword. As for the last word, I thank FATHER KENNETH O'MALLEY, C.P., librarian of the Catholic Theological Union, for his painstaking work on the Index.

The research for this book was accomplished with the assistance of JAMES DONOHUE, C.R., a graduate student at Catholic Theological Union, and, above all, with the untiring energy and encouragement of FRANCES KRUMPELMAN, S.C.N., who set up interviews, transcribed tapes, sorted and labeled photographs, tracked down and organized the bibliography and honors sections, contacted archivists around the country, and performed the countless editorial tasks without which this project would never have been completed. And it would never have been published without the wise and thorough assistance of MR. JOHN SCHNEIDER of the Liturgical Press, a superb editor and a very gracious collaborator.

Finally, of course, I must express my gratitude to Godfrey for trusting me to tell his story.

IT IS NOT INSIGNIFICANT that Godfrey Leo Diekmann grew up in Stearns County, Minnesota, close to Lake Wobegon, "where all the women are strong, the men are good-looking, and the children are above average." The culture, principles, values, and enduring charm of those mythical townspeople, made famous by Garrison Keillor, are the same forces that shaped Godfrey's childhood. They are the stuff of his growing up.

Leo Diekmann, who would receive the name Godfrey when he entered the monastery, was born on April 7, 1908, in Roscoe, Minnesota, the sixth of eight children born to John Conrad Diekmann and Rosalie Loxterkamp. Although both Conrad and Rosalie had been raised in the Westphalian region of Germany, in villages only about twenty miles apart, they never met until after they had come to the United States. Both came from traditional farm families and were steeped in traditional German Catholicism, a heritage that would pervade the atmosphere of their home.

Conrad Diekmann, a schoolteacher in Germany, was a pacifist who chose to emigrate to the United States rather than be inducted into the military. Like so many others from his homeland, he settled in central Minnesota. After a year spent in perfecting his English at the school run by the Benedictine monks at Collegeville, he started teaching—primarily English, French, and music—in the small villages nearby. Teaching was a vocation he would continue for thirty-five years. He also served as church organist and music director.

Diekmann was a man of principle, an outstanding teacher, a stern disciplinarian, an excellent musician, and a great storyteller. To this

1

day, those who remember him speak of him with reverence and respect, and just a bit of awe.

Rosalie Loxterkamp emigrated to the United States as a young girl and grew into a remarkably beautiful woman. Known as "die schoene Rose" (the lovely rose), she was also described as elegant in her appearance and her manner, prim and proper, attractive, delightful, outgoing, and all her life a woman of prodigious energy. One daughter–in–law characterized shopping expeditions with Mrs. Diekmann as "thoroughly exhausting," prompting the conjecture that Rosalie would have appreciated the adage "Shop till you drop."

After her marriage to Conrad, Rosalie began to organize her household as befitted the local schoolteacher's family. While she did not have the book learning of her husband, she was an excellent cook and a clever seamstress—altogether a fine homemaker.

Conrad and Rosalie's children appeared with a certain regularity about every two years: first Hubert, then Julia, Clara, Conrad, Boniface, and Leo. When two more years passed without the appearance of another Diekmann, that was that. A formal portrait was taken. Then Marie turned up after a four-year interval, followed by Paul. In many ways Marie and Paul formed a second family. The Diekmanns were a small clan by the standards of those days. Ten, twelve, and even eighteen children were not uncommon among their neighbors.

At the turn of the century in Stearns County, public education was thoroughly Catholic. The schoolteacher rather than the pastor was responsible for teaching catechism, along with other subjects. Teachers were a class apart, highly educated, cultured, held in a place of honor after the pastor—in some instances even on the same plane as the pastor.

Herr Lehrer and *Herr Priester* worked in tandem, with sometimes the merest hint of rivalry. After early Mass on Sunday, the pastor examined the children on what they had learned during the week. The story is told of the Sunday when the pastor was quizzing the children on their catechism and one child knew no answers. The pastor blamed Mr. Diekmann and shouted at him up in the choir. Mr. Diekmann shouted back that the child had not been in school all week! Perhaps it was from his father that Leo developed his strong sense of justice as well as a certain facility with the quick retort.

Conrad Diekmann took learning for granted in his home. He taught his children the German language and insisted that they speak it correctly. He had a library of German classics, which he urged his children to read. Leo had worked through his father's library by the age of twelve. In fact, the child read everything in sight. One day he picked up his father's book *The Robbers,* which was about the Thirty Years' War, including a description of an attack on a convent and the raping of nuns. When his father discovered Leo with the book, he scolded him and gave him a licking. This was no book for a child his age! After absorbing this, Leo retrieved the book to see what he had missed.

Leo thought that his father's method of discipline was harsh. He suspected that his father punished his own children more frequently than he did others, perhaps to give an example of a well-disciplined family. In the classroom Conrad Diekmann would use a willow branch for punishment, chosen and cut by the culprit in question, lending his own knife for the selection. Once Leo pretended to have lost the knife in order to avoid punishment. It didn't work.

Rosalie took care of the lesser infractions, punishing more quickly than her husband, who was "all moderation" and whose punishments, while harsh, were not that frequent.

Discipline aside, the Diekmann home was a happy one, as relaxed and low-keyed as the regimen for that number of children would permit. The table was a place where the family liked to congregate and loved to talk—there were seldom arguments or raised voices. Mr. Diekmann always used language with care and never used profanity. His strongest words were "thunderation" and "godesey."

Conrad Diekmann's storytelling ability was legendary. One could listen time and again and never hear the same story repeated or, if repeated, always with a new twist, a different ending. When Mr. Diekmann had friends in to play cards, his children would lean over the banister to monitor his storytelling. Leo, later to be known as a dinner-table raconteur, began his lessons at an early age in the company of his father.

Leo describes his family as having been "desperately poor," a judgment not borne out by other accounts. Although the family suffered the same shortages and deprivations as their neighbors, there was always something special about the food and the care with which Rosalie presented it. It is true that a schoolteacher's salary was never more than about ninety dollars a month, meager earnings to provide food and clothing for the Diekmann brood. But because *Herr Lehrer* was also the parish organist and choir director, the Diekmanns received more invitations than most to the local "swell affairs," and Conrad sometimes also received material gratuities for his services. Moreover, what food they could raise was supplemented by the bounty from occasional hunting forays led by Conrad Diekmann, an avid hunter, who would allow his children one long weekend for hunting each fall. Hunting, in fact, was the only possible excuse for missing school—not even sickness was permitted to interrupt the educational process.

Rosalie was a very proud woman, particularly attentive to her status as spouse of *Herr Lehrer*. She was extremely proper and demanded proper behavior of her children. When Leo was ready to graduate from high school, his mother took him to a store in St. Cloud to buy his first pair of long trousers. But Leo, too embarrassed to wear the unfamiliar long pants, appeared at the graduation ceremony in his knickers. Rosalie was "mortified" by his behavior.

Appearances were important; presentation was worth endless care. It is said that the seams in Rosalie's stockings were *always* straight and that she never wore the same hat twice. She would buy a new hat, and after wearing it once, she would take to her sewing machine and completely remodel it. Her fondness for headwear must have been part of the genetic make-up of her son Leo, who developed a special liking for hats in his adult years. Rarely would he return from a trip without an addition to his collection: a British beefeater's hat, a Turkish fez, a deerstalker's cap à la Sherlock Holmes, an Arab kaffiyeh, a Peruvian stocking cap, an Ethiopian monastic headdress, a variety of embroidered yarmulkes—the assortment is quite remarkable, and each hat has a story.

While maintaining a happy home, the Diekmanns rarely displayed affection openly. Overt affection was not deemed appropriate; feelings were neither demonstrated nor discussed. One day Leo surprised his mother while she was ironing and discovered that she was weeping quietly as she worked. He presumed that she was weeping over the death of Julia, the daughter she had loved so deeply, but they never talked about the incident.

Such reserved behavior was not unique to the Diekmanns. Stearns County boys who joined the military were warned about the public

John Conrad and Rosalie Diekmann with their six oldest children: (back row) Hubert, Leo (Godfrey), Clara; (front row) Boniface, Conrad, and Julia (1911)

displays of affection they would encounter when they went overseas. Leo recalls that he first consciously kissed his mother when they met after his father's death. It was an awkward gesture he would not often repeat with her.

Leo's family nickname was "Pechvogel," the bad-luck bird! This name was given him because he was such a risktaker, with an attitude that he could do anything and surpass anyone else's accomplishments. "Accident prone" would not accurately describe Leo, since he quite deliberately chose to be a daredevil. He was a show-off and liked to play to an audience. "Do now and think later" was his motto.

Leo was always first—he had to be first. He had the tallest stilts; he could throw a firecracker the highest; in skiing he would be the one to break the trail, to take the first jump, although he once fell through glazed ice and skinned his face badly. As a child he almost blew himself up with a Belgian gun that took a smaller shell than he had used. In school he went out for football "whole hog" and broke several bones. These early escapades had their counterpart in eight or so brushes with death in his adult years.

5

Though never an outstanding athlete, Leo did enjoy many sports. He recalls learning to ski on barrel staves whose tips had been bent in hot water. "Primitive but adequate" was how he regarded these poverty skis fashioned by a neighbor. He was not too bad at tennis, occasionally beating the reigning champion. His winter love was sail-skating, a sport that allowed him to move at lightning speed across the ice. As for the summer, he wrote once of a "passionate fondness" for boating and swimming. His lifelong desire was to learn to ride well, to be so identified with a horse, close to the earth, feeling unparalleled strength and speed.

In his later adult years "Pechvogel" would take long walks in the woods in quest of wild mushrooms, chokecherries, and watercress. This was decidedly not a habit acquired in his youth. As a boy, Leo never helped pick chokecherries, wild grapes, dandelions, whiskey cherries, or wild gall. He never worked in the garden or picked potato bugs. He was the only Diekmann child who never learned to milk the cow, and when it was time to make hay, he would disappear. Recalls his younger brother Paul: "You couldn't find him; he was under the bed reading." While his siblings may have resented his absence, his father excused him. Leo was, after all, doing something constructive.

A few years later Leo would have second thoughts about such behavior and urge his younger brother to take a different approach. In a letter to his family he wrote:

> I suppose Paul is still working on the neighbor's farm. It'll do you no end of good, I think. There really isn't enough to do at home to keep you steadily occupied, and I know that if you're not busy, you'll be in some mischief or other. Now don't say that you wouldn't be! You know better than that yourself. And in more than one way I envy you. I never was very strong on the work stuff myself when I was home (was I, Dad?) but I wish now I had done more in that line. After all, studying and studying all your lifetime [this at the age of 21!], gives a somewhat restricted outlook on life. And it isn't good for the liver either. In order to get some exercise here, I swing two big iron dumbbells around morning and evening. The little bit of walking we get otherwise, isn't quite enough for me.[1]

Music could always be heard coming from the Diekmann home. In addition to being an accomplished organist, Mr. Diekmann played the trumpet and the violin and was an outstanding tenor. He encouraged his children's musical development. Mrs. Diekmann would often hum to herself as she went about her work. Conrad was a fine trumpet player. Clara had the makings of a concert pianist and practiced four or five hours a day.

Leo began flute lessons as a young boy, then picked up the piccolo and the clarinet in turn. Next he mastered the oboe and learned how to make his own reeds. When the oboe began to give him headaches, he switched to the English horn, an alto instrument. Leo was fascinated by all the wind instruments, and later, during his travels, he would be drawn to similar instruments with unusual sounds. He recalls, for example, hearing an orchestra in Greece and being curious about the sound coming from a double-reed instrument, so he went to examine it. It was a handmade tenor oboe, and since the holes were not scientifically placed, the sound it produced was "weird but lovely." Leo asked to replace the oboist and began to play with the orchestra, accompanying dancing in the square for the next hour.

His first instrument remained his first love, and for twenty-five or thirty years he was first-chair flute in the St. John's community and student orchestra. Slight paralysis on the right side of his mouth, the result of a stroke, prevents him from playing any wind instrument now. That void is partially filled by recording and listening to music, mostly of the Renaissance and Baroque periods.

What was Leo's relationship to his brothers and sisters as they were growing up? "Not particularly close" is his own estimate. His brother Hubert was too much older than he to have been close. His sister Julia died at the age of seventeen, when Leo was still quite young. His brother Conrad (Coonie) had preceded him into the monastery before they were old enough to appreciate each other, although Coonie would prove to be a wonderful steadying influence on Leo, and their loyalty to each other would deepen over time. Boniface (Bony) was probably the odd man out in the family, the child of a schoolmaster who did not take to education and eventually joined the service—again before Leo could form an adult relationship with him. Leo had profound respect for Clara, who later would shoulder the burden of caring for the family after their father's death, but they never were particularly close. Marie and Paul were still young children when Leo left home for boarding school at St. John's. In his correspondence

Leo Diekmann at age 5

Boniface, Conrad, and Leo swimming with their father in the Sauk River (1916)

Leo (third from left) and his brothers with their rattles on Easter Monday

Leo on his high school graduation day (1923)

from Europe to his family, there is a tenderness for his parents, but for his brothers and sisters there is mostly a good deal of advice from a brother growing worldly wise and wishing to share his newly acquired wisdom.

Growing up in a German Catholic household in Stearns County entailed certain religious practices that were unquestioned. These included morning and evening prayer, prayer before and after meals, and the family rosary during Lent. Participation in Sunday Vespers in the parish church was as common as going to Sunday Mass. In fact, in Stearns County, Vespers would remain a popular parish devotion well into the fifties.

Leo found Vespers boring and regarded Father Leo Winter, O.S.B., the pastor in Roscoe, after whom he was named, a folk hero because he would occasionally cancel Vespers in the summertime. There was no such relief during the winter. The parish was the center of activity on Sunday, with people staying on until milking time. If the pastor preached less then an hour, the community complained, "What is he getting paid for?" It was a kind of entertainment.

So, too, were the music and the hymn singing. Nearly everyone had a copy of *Catholic Song and Prayer Book* by Hillesbusch, a book that contained five different Mass settings and many hymns. Every congregation was capable of singing at least three Masses as well as hymns for the principal seasons. The book contained many Latin hymn texts, such as the *Vidi aquam,* as well as a fine collection of German hymns. A number of the older German priests at St. John's make singing some of these hymns part of their Christmas celebration to this day.

Another popular book was Leonard Goffine's *Devout Instructions,* a book of explanations of the epistles and gospels for the Sundays and holy days of the Church year. It could be found in most Stearns County homes, and in the Diekmann home it was sometimes read aloud. Leo remembers it as a kind of primitive version of Pius Parsch's *Church's Year of Grace.* He liked it.

Leo's experience of "Church" as he grew up included occasional skirmishes between the Germans and the Irish. In the neighboring village of Melrose, for example, the place where his mother had lived, most people were Germans, but a railroad workhouse attracted a number of Irish to the town. So there were two churches: the *Catholic* church and the smaller *Irish* church. Monsignor Richter, the pastor of the

Catholic church, thundered against "mixed marriages" between Germans and Irish, a situation he regarded as more serious than marriage to a Protestant. In the town of St. Martin, where the Diekmanns lived for a number of years, Leo heard sermons that equated losing one's German language with losing the faith. It was the role of the Church to keep both the German Catholic faith and German culture alive.

During his childhood Leo was fascinated by a unique liturgical practice—the celebrant's use of snuff as part of the Mass. A box of snuff was placed on the right side of the tabernacle, and another was put in the pulpit. Just before the *Lavabo* the priest would dip snuff and then wash his hands. After the postcommunion prayer he would again dip a bit of snuff. This was called the clergyman's tobacco and was particularly useful in longer services when the clergy could not smoke. In time the practice spread from the clergy to the laity, but eventually, even without the aid of the liturgical movement, it disappeared without a trace.

Prayer at school and at home, regular attendance at Mass and Vespers, singing of the Proper of the Mass and of the great hymn texts in Latin and German, spiritual reading oriented to the liturgical year—this was the raw material of Leo Diekmann's spiritual life. It was supplemented by *The Following of Christ,* a book which he received as a gift when he graduated from high school and which pleased him because he regarded it as marking his passage into "spiritual maturity." He read it faithfully every day for several years, including his year of novitiate. Only later would it be reckoned a spiritual classic. Such spiritual riches at Leo's disposal! Yet he had no personal copy of the Scriptures and would not be drawn to them until a stroke in the late sixties allowed him leisure for prolonged study and prayer.

Leo does not have happy memories of the parish or of the role of the pastor and visiting priests in his spiritual awakening. The parish priest was a man generally regarded with dread; he was harsh and unyielding, a man Leo remembers as communicating more the fear of God than God's love. It never occurred to Leo that he was expected to love the man. Once, in the novitiate, he heard a story of another novice who had been spanked by this same pastor but struggled loose and bit the man on the calf of his leg. It was a story

Leo would long relish for the little bit of vicarious vengeance it afforded him.

A turning point in Leo's religious history occurred at the age of ten when he developed "a very strange notion of God." A parish mission that he attended with his family had a profoundly negative effect on his spiritual development. The mission preacher was a Redemptorist, "all gaunt, all blood and thunder," a man notorious throughout the Order for a style of preaching that could scare the living daylights out of his listeners. It worked its effect on ten-year-old Leo, dredging up memories of his first confession at the age of six.

The day before Leo was to make his first confession, his mother sent him to his room to examine his conscience and prepare for confession. It was a beautiful day, and Leo became distracted by neighbor children playing outside. He leaned out the window, longing to be with his playmates, too beguiled by them to examine his conscience. When marched to the confessional the next day, he realized that he was unprepared, so he simply made up a list of likely sins on the spur of the moment and walked out perfectly satisfied, giving no further thought to the confession. Now here was a priest whose preaching convinced Leo that his first confession had been a "bad" confession and that all subsequent confessions had therefore been bad confessions—four years of bad confessions! He had to set things right.

The parish had one of those old-fashioned confessionals with a wooden grill—not even a cloth to cover the grill and protect the anonymity of the penitent. The confessor had to have realized that Leo was just a little boy kneeling there, but he treated the child as a long-lost sinner and gave him a penance to fit the gravity of his sins, a rosary a day for the next four months. That was the beginning of a period of scrupulosity in Leo's life. Daily he became more afraid of God's wrath.

He remembers now that for three years he was terrified of walking to and from school in the dark of fall and winter. These daily journeys involved passing through a woods where every step echoed as if someone were walking behind him, trying to catch up. Trees would snap and break with the cold; owls would hoot. For three years Leo ran this gauntlet filled with fear, shouting acts of contrition, convinced that he was already damned to hell and that God was simply biding time before pouncing! Apparently Leo was unable to hide his fears at home. His father, and sometimes his younger brother Paul, would meet him halfway. His brother attributed Leo's fear to the howling of wolves, not the fear of God's judgment.

Leo was especially afraid of the dark and what the psalmist calls "the terrors of the night." Visiting the outhouse before bedtime produced the same panic as walking through the woods alone. It was a short trip, perhaps only fifty yards at most, but even a flashlight didn't help. Leo was morally certain he would be killed one of those nights, and his outhouse visits were often followed by horrible nightmares—vivid dreams of hell, fire, and a clock ticking "ever-never, ever-never." Years of scrupulosity and fear of God followed that parish mission.

Such was Leo's earliest concept of God, a concept unrelieved by his father's catechism lessons or by the religion classes once he began studying at St. John's. As a result of those high school religion classes, he became convinced that those who couldn't do anything else were assigned to teach religion. Particularly dreadful was his senior course in religion, taught by an occasional tippler whose method was memorization of the catechism, including the punctuation. The entire class consisted of rote repetition: "God made me to know Him, *comma,* to love Him, *comma,* and to serve Him in this life, *comma,* and to be happy with Him for ever in the next, *period,*" with little or no explanation. Leo wryly summarized that experience: "There wasn't much in the way of getting a grasp of the Christian realities."

Despite what he remembers as less than adequate formal study of religion, Leo's theological intuitions were coming alive. One impetus for this awakening was the cemetery next door to his childhood home. In St. Martin, where he lived for about seven years, the Diekmann house and garden bordered the cemetery, an ideal place to play "hide-and-seek" among the headstones. The cemetery was blessed ground surrounded by a stone wall. Outside the wall were earth mounds. The significance of the wall began to trouble Leo: "We children knew the large earth mound was a suicide; the smaller ones were all unbaptized children. It was heartrending. I could never understand this—buried like animals!"[2] Limbo was a theological construct he would publicly challenge as a mature theologian, but even as a child Leo had the instinct to question this teaching and to try to work it out. Quite possibly such interior confusion about basic Church teaching contributed to Leo's "very strange notion of God." It would take several more years and the care of a kindly novice master to relieve Leo of this burden.

It may well have been his parents' concern for their fearful child that persuaded them to send him as a boarding student to St. John's halfway through high school. Having begun his education at home with his father, Leo had started grammar school very early and had skipped some grades. He was only eleven—very young to begin high school, and especially to live away from home.

Although tortured interiorly by scrupulosity and fear, Leo projected another side of his personality to others. There was and would remain throughout his adult life a boyishness about him, an attractiveness, an exuberance, an ability to make friends easily. People were drawn to him. A classmate recalls that Leo was "an easily met person," a tall, blond, very handsome young man, seemingly quite unaware of his physical charm. It was a surprise to him, several years later while studying in Rome, to be selected as an artist's model for a painting of St. Sebastian—but with his abbot's proviso that he could strip only to the waist for the sessions. He never saw the finished product, to his great regret!

Yet another Roman encounter with another artist served to keep him humble about his good looks. In a letter to Abbot Alcuin Deutsch, he describes how the artist approached him and whispered excitedly:

> "Do you know whom you remind me of?" I surely didn't, but expected great things: perhaps the czar or the crown prince of so-and-so, all of whose portraits he claims to have painted. On receiving my negative reply, he buttonholed me, took me over into the next room, and with a triumphant flourish pointed to the picture of the court fool of Philip IV of Spain, painted by Velasquez. And what a visage! Prominent protruding jaw and lower lip, a bulbous nose, and bleary eyes! . . . He insisted: "You are young yet: but you can't fool an artist's eye. When you get to be about twenty years older, you will look exactly like that." I do hope his "artistic eye" *squinted* that time.[3]

Leo's boyish good looks would mature far more gracefully than this encounter prophesied, to say nothing of his boyish charm, which is characteristic of him to this day.

Daily life at St. John's was nearly as cloistered for the students as for the monks. Students kept the monastic horarium, rising early,

Leo at age 19, when he applied for a Rhodes scholarship (1927)

attending Mass and Vespers, dining at the same hours as the monks. Students were surrounded by monks; the latter served as teachers, coaches, advisors—a constant presence. It was the most natural transition from high school into St. John's two-year junior college program. At the end of those two years a student either left the campus to continue college elsewhere or remained at St. John's to attend the diocesan seminary or to enter the Benedictine novitiate.

Leo chose to stay and to become a monk, despite the fact that he had two girls picked out. One was a beautiful redhead by the name of Helen, whom he had fancied for her looks, and the other a plainer girl but with a reputation as a fine cook, especially of fudge and other candies. In describing his decision years later, Godfrey claims he simply "drifted into the monastery," not that it was an unreflected decision but that it was a natural development after discovering in St. John's a second home.

Priesthood was highly regarded in the Diekmann home. Once Leo decided to become a priest, he took it for granted that he would be a Benedictine, the only priests known to the family. Whether Leo was influenced in this decision by his brother Coonie, who had preceded him to the monastery, is not clear. What is clear is that this impetuous young man made a decision which pleased his father and made him very proud but which made his mother laugh out loud. "Too scatterbrained," she said.

Leo was seventeen when he crossed the threshold from junior college to monastery. During his years of monastic formation, three monks would influence him profoundly. They were Father Athanasius Meyer, novice master for thirty-two years at St. John's; Father Virgil Michel, wunderkind monk just back from his European adventures, who would be Leo's philosophy teacher and junior prefect; and Abbot Alcuin Deutsch, a man who would identify intelligence and talent in Leo and challenge him in ways the young monk otherwise might not have chosen.

"Novitiate was wonderful," Godfrey said one day with less than total recall, "because we had a very, very good novice master, Father Athanasius." In fact, Godfrey's year of novitiate, by the assessment of both family and community members, was extremely difficult. One of his contemporaries speculated that he was probably going faster than he should have and wore himself out. He was sick a good deal of the time and became very thin. Father Athanasius used to beat cream and eggs together and give Godfrey the drink to build up his strength. Godfrey detested this daily drink and found another way, once his novitiate was over, to supplement his monastic diet. He would visit his mother's kitchen, keeping one foot outside the door to observe the letter of the law while reaching inside for one of her sweets.

When Leo Diekmann entered St. John's Abbey, he was almost three years younger than the others in his class and long remained an overgrown kid, leaning heavily on anyone who was willing to spend time with him. He liked fun and was very carefree, the youngster among his classmates, and didn't really mature with the others. He was a large boy, and his rapid physical growth continued during the novitiate. Every two months or so an inch had to be added to his habit. He was noticeably brighter than the others but less mature emotionally, preferring the activities of the younger boys. Part of his difficulty in adjusting to novitiate life was due to his continued growth; part was due to his inability to assume the discipline and pressure of that year, to adapt to the diet, to rise so early—and this despite the self-discipline he had learned in a fairly strict German home and despite his quasi-monastic experience in boarding school. His contemporaries recall that during that first year Coonie quietly fended for his brother and protected him from the criticism of others. All in all, this difficult adjustment to monastic life was alleviated only by the gentleness of Father Athanasius, whom Leo loved as a second father.

Father Athanasius was the first person to open the world of the liturgy to his charges. Prior to Virgil Michel's study abroad, Athanasius's interest in liturgy had been sharpened by such publications as Romano Guardini's *The Spirit of the Liturgy* and by conversation with like-minded people such as Father William Busch, a professor of liturgy in nearby St. Paul. Athanasius welcomed Virgil Michel's return from Europe and delighted in learning more about the rudiments of the liturgical movement as Michel expounded them on his return.

In 1924 Virgil Michel had been sent to Europe for the study of philosophy, but it was the wave of liturgical renewal sweeping across the continent that captivated him. He visited Maria Laach in Germany, St. André in Belgium, and Klosterneuburg in Austria, all of

Profession of simple vows, July 11, 1926

Godfrey and his mother during his clericate years

Godfrey in his clericate years (1926–28)

Godfrey with his brothers Paul and Boniface (1928)

17

them abbeys where the pastoral liturgical movement was developing. H. A. Reinhold, himself schooled in the European liturgical movement before immigrating to the United States, described the profound effect of Virgil's travels on his future course:

> It is almost beyond human comprehension to grasp the completeness with which he absorbed everything that Austria, Belgium, and Germany had to offer. But greater yet was what he did with it. Instead of dragging his find across the border as an exotic museum piece, he made it as American as only an American mind can make it. He had seen the high sweep of German ecclesiology and sacramentalism; he had admired the Belgians for their clear grasp of a new spirituality and their critical awareness of all that stood in the way of liturgical, ecclesiastical piety from traditional carry-overs; he had learned in Austria what the common people could gather from the Church's treasure without fright, but he did not come back to force these foreign and incoherent molds on the American church. Besides, his clear realism and his burning apostle's heart had one urge none of the great masters in Europe seemed to see: the connection of social justice with a new social spirituality. For Virgil Michel the labor encyclicals of Leo XIII and the liturgical reforms of Pius X did not just by accident happen within one generation, but were responses to cries of the masses for Christ who had power and gave the good tidings. They belonged together.[4]

It was particularly from St. André's Lambert Beauduin, whom history would name the undisputed founder of the pastoral liturgical movement of the twentieth century, that Virgil took his inspiration and reshaped it for an American context. It was Beauduin's vision of integral Christianity that Michel was able to bring home, Beauduin's recognition that a true understanding of liturgy implied a social movement as well, Beauduin's pastoral liturgical principles for the promotion of the participation of all in the one Sacrifice. Virgil Michel recognized that Lambert Beauduin's vision was difficult to implement in Europe, where the liturgical movement was characterized by its devotional aspects and was largely confined to the rites. But what Beauduin could not carry out in Europe *was* possible in the United States. The vision of Lambert Beauduin became the inspiration of Virgil Michel's life.

Those must have been heady days at St. John's when Michel returned full of ideas for the promotion of the liturgical movement.

One can only guess at the discussions, the liturgical ferment, the chapter deliberations, the sense of adventure that permeated the monastery and touched the consciousness even of fledgling monks. During Godfrey's first year in the abbey (1926–1927) *Orate Fratres* was founded and the Liturgical Press began the publication of its Popular Liturgical Library.

It was their novice master, and only later Virgil Michel, who drew the novices into this new world of ideas. Though already an old man, Father Athanasius was completely open and was enthusiastic about furthering Virgil Michel's ideas and projects. "So," Godfrey recalls, "we got Virgil Michel through the lips of Athanasius Meyer." Father Athanasius taught with a great sense of history, which ignited Godfrey's interest in historical sources. But more importantly, Athanasius introduced his novices to the concept of the Mystical Body of Christ. As Godfrey's appreciation for this concept deepened, he would regard its effect on him as a turning point, "a major event in my life and understanding." He was enthralled by this teaching and continued to probe its meaning. In Godfrey's last year of college Virgil Michel challenged him to write an essay on the Mystical Body, supplying as reference Anger's *The Mystical Body According to St. Thomas*. The essay of six or seven pages, "perfect for a pamphlet" in the author's estimation, was not accepted by Michel for publication.

Years later, on hearing of the death of Father Athanasius, Godfrey attempted to capture what the man had meant to him:

> His departure seems to cause such a void, that it is almost impossible to think of St. John's as the same place without him. I know that all his novices, past and present, will grieve his loss, for he was a real Father Master to all. But I feel that I owe him a debt of gratitude far beyond the ordinary, not only for what he did for me during my year of novitiate, but more especially, for all the trouble and care I caused him during my two years of clericate. He was, in truth, my *"zuflucht"* [recourse, shelter, refuge, sanctuary]. Were it not for him, I don't know where I'd be at present. Certainly not here at Maria Laach, and most likely not in the Order.[5]

One must stand back and marvel at the transformation that took place in Leo Diekmann in his formative years. Arriving at St. John's as a terrified child, scrupulous and fearful of an angry God, he became, first as student and then as monk, a young adult captivated by a sense of the Mystical Body, Christ and members. It was fitting that Leo should receive the monastic name Godfrey, meaning "the peace of God," to mark the beginning of this interior transformation and the serenity that filled him, thanks in large measure to the extraordinary kindness of Father Athanasius.[6]

A second influence during Godfrey's formation was Virgil Michel. Dom Virgil was Godfrey's junior prefect, one of the two or three geniuses that Godfrey claims to have met in his lifetime, a man whose character and temperament were very different from Athanasius Meyer's. The latter had inspired enormous affection in his novices; Virgil Michel inspired admiration but rarely affection. He was a distant man and one whom Godfrey regarded as something of a robot.

As clerics, Godfrey and his classmates studied philosophy under Father Virgil. In his course on the history of philosophy, Virgil developed one idea after another, concept after concept, with great rapidity. Godfrey was critical of Virgil's teaching:

> His ideas seemed to be on a level quite removed. There was hardly any relationship, as far as we could see, between the reality of our life problems and these classes. They all seemed remote. Perhaps I shouldn't generalize, but the impression I received was that he seemed cold.[7]

As junior prefect, Virgil Michel was also responsible for giving weekly conferences. One conference that stands out in Godfrey's mind concerned the use of time. "Don't waste time," Virgil urged them. "Never lose a moment." And he used himself as an example: he had learned French by having a list of French words pasted on his mirror so that when he shaved, he could learn them by heart. Virgil's obsession with the use of time extended to every spare moment. Even while he was brushing his teeth, his eyes were riveted to a periodical. His astounding energy and drive only intimidated his charges. Godfrey notes laconically, "We weren't quite up to that sort of thing!"

It is not surprising, then, that Virgil never seems to have won the fraternal affection of the juniors nor of some of his confreres:

> While much loved by most of his fellow monks, a few thought of him as a dehumanized intellect. Because he was somewhat unimaginative and almost completely unsentimental, some of his brethren considered him cold, heartless, even mechanistic, as he went about plan-

ning his day's work to the minute. He seemed aware of his cold exterior. Once when others were impressed and he remained unmoved, he recorded the situation in his Diary, adding, "Am I really so inhuman?"[8]

As Godfrey thought of his early encounters with his junior prefect, he wondered out loud about Virgil's temperament and his way of relating to others:

> We didn't consider him with our heart but with our heads. And I suspect that this was his life problem. Later on when I came back from Europe I was assigned to assist him . . . and he sometimes shared his problems with me, and I began to realize that the man was suffering. And I think one of the main reasons why he was suffering was the fact that he realized that he gave the impression of being cold and being an automaton. He lacked certain human dimensions as far as outside was concerned. I think he felt very deeply and he craved affection and he wasn't able to give it. And he couldn't receive it either.[9]

Virgil Michel was probably never regarded by any of his charges as a *"zuflucht."* He may well have longed for someone to play that role in his own life.

It would be logical to speculate that Virgil Michel's role in Godfrey's life was decisive in initiating him into the liturgical movement. At the same time, the spiritual lineage from Virgil to Godfrey was bridged, perhaps unwittingly, by people like Father Athanasius Meyer. After that time, Godfrey claims, he never again had to shift directions. Father Athanasius provided a very basic direction in liturgy, a simple and elementary foundation, and the rest, says Godfrey, was there implicitly: "For the rest of my life it was more or less an evolving of what I learned there—and sometimes, too, an explosion when I realized the import of things." This liturgical awakening in Godfrey was possible because Virgil reached a person like Father Athanasius, who was responsible for the spiritual formation of the novices and who had both the temperament and the teaching ability to inspire others with his insights.

Godfrey's first abbot was also an important influence in his development. Abbot Alcuin Deutsch was a man whom Godfrey revered and respected, perhaps even occasionally feared. Godfrey likens Abbot Alcuin affectionately to a medieval ruler: "Abbot Alcuin was a great man. . . . In many ways he was a prince-bishop of medieval times. If he lived today, the whole place would explode in two weeks. We couldn't take it. In many ways he was a dictator.''[10] Apparently Abbot Alcuin rather enjoyed that reputation: ''He thought the term 'Lord Abbot' was just right, the way it should be, and he insisted on that. . . . ''[11] Some years ago one of his monks attempted to explain Lord Abbot Alcuin's approach to governance in this way:

> If you want something and just ask the abbot for it, you may get an outright refusal. The way to approach the abbot is to hem and haw and say, ''Father Abbot, you wouldn't have the authority to permit me to take a Caribbean cruise, would you?'' He will say, ''Young man, I order you hereby to take a Caribbean cruise.''[12]

Despite his reputation as an authoritarian, Abbot Alcuin could also be a kindly man. He might publicly reduce one of his monks to tears, and then, just as publicly, repent of his severity and apologize.

Abbot Alcuin was a remarkably farsighted and courageous man. Godfrey recalls:

> He had a vision of the Church, a vision of the greatness of the Church and the needs of the Church, and they always took precedence over our own needs. And he gave us a sense of that greatness, that vision. And he had a great sense of faith. After the Second World War, we gave ten percent of our total income to European relief. . . . At a time when no Catholic institution in the United States dared to send anybody for higher education except to Catholic University, Notre Dame, or Rome, we had all sorts at universities all over the United States and Europe. . . . Now that gives you a sense of [his] vision.[13]

Alcuin believed that the greatest danger of the Benedictine situation was ingrown Pelagianism, which Godfrey defines as misplaced loyalty: a mistaken sense that the abbey is self-sufficient and is in possession of the truth. In Godfrey's judgment, it was Alcuin's courage and vision in sending scholars to be trained in such a wide spectrum of disciplines in so many different places which have, in the long run, given St. John's its remarkable reputation and character.

Godfrey eulogized Alcuin as one of the great abbots of modern times, a man of authority, a man of generosity, a founder, even a father. Surely it was from personal experience of Alcuin's paternal side that Godfrey said:

> The burdens of his office were heavy. The projects he undertook were varied and vast. Yet he had time for the ''details'' too. Under the stress

Virgil Michel, O.S.B.

Abbot Alcuin Deutsch, O.S.B.

of work, he was apt at times to bark a sharp "Come in!" As soon, however, as he saw that one had a personal problem, of whatever sort, he gave his unstinting and fatherly attention. One never felt that one intruded on his time. He had no office hours. He was always accessible. No one visited the sick more frequently than he. No one was a more faithful correspondent, and his letters were not just matter-of-fact business but usually full of news and friendliness. It has often been remarked, too, that one could not wish for a better, more jovial companion on a trip.[14]

Godfrey occasionally speculates about the relationship of Alcuin Deutsch and Virgil Michel, and here we see yet another side of Abbot Alcuin:

[Abbot Alcuin] had to stay on top. And so he was proud of Virgil Michel, but he wanted to be the boss. And he wanted to take all the credit, if you wish. I think that Virgil Michel could not submit completely to this, should I say, this domination by Alcuin. . . . Putting it another way, Abbot Alcuin had to have a protégé whom he would encourage and he could be proud of, but Virgil Michel was too big a man to be just a protégé.[15]

23

Whether Godfrey realized it at the time or not, Abbot Alcuin had a number of protégés, and Godfrey himself could be counted among them. It was Alcuin who selected Godfrey and his classmate Paschal Botz to go to Sant' Anselmo, the international Benedictine college in Rome, for graduate degrees and who, through a lively correspondence with Godfrey over the next four years, would continue to exercise a profound influence on his development in matters great and small. For his part, Godfrey grew in affection for his "Lord Abbot" even as he discovered the wiles of approach if one wanted to take a Caribbean cruise.

Godfrey looks back on his years in formation as providing the foundation of all that would follow. "The foundations were good," he mused one day. "There were great flashes of insight where I saw the implications of things. They all fitted into the picture. The picture was established, was outlined, in those years."[16]

NOTES TO CHAPTER 1

1. GLD, letter to "Dearest Folks," Rome, July 5, 1929.

2. GLD, taped interview, November 1987.

3. GLD, letter to Abbot Alcuin Deutsch, Rome, March 6, 1932.

4. H. A. Reinhold, "The Liturgical Movement to Date," in *Christ's Sacrifice and Ours,* National Liturgical Week, 1947 (Boston: The Liturgical Conference, 1948) 11.

5. GLD, letter to Abbot Alcuin Deutsch, Maria Laach, September 8, 1931.

6. Abbot Alcuin prided himself on being a genius at giving appropriate names. In selecting the name Godfrey, Abbot Alcuin ignored all three names that Leo had submitted. During the naming ceremony Abbot Alcuin must have noted that Leo was not overjoyed with his new name, because afterward Alcuin told him he might want to take the name Geoffrey, another form of the name. Godfrey thought this over briefly, but because Mutt and Jeff were currently popular comic strip characters, he feared that students would "ring the changes" on the name Geoffrey. Godfrey it would remain, a name he has grown to like over the years.

7. GLD, taped interview, April 1987.

8. Paul Marx, O.S.B., *Virgil Michel and the Liturgical Movement* (Collegeville, Minn.: The Liturgical Press, 1957) 386–387.

9. GLD, taped interview, April 1987.

10. Ibid.

11. Father Paschal Botz, O.S.B., taped interview, October 19, 1987.

12. Story of Father Angelo as recounted by Father Paschal Botz, taped interview, October 19, 1987.

13. GLD, taped interview, April 1987. Godfrey's estimate of Abbot Alcuin Deutsch needs to be tempered by that of others. Father Emeric Lawrence noted: "There were and are a few of us [monks] who still think of him [Abbot Alcuin] as a very stubborn and prejudiced man. He did not want the college to grow, and the flood of GIs after the war pained him considerably." Letter of Emeric Lawrence, O.S.B., to the author, May 8, 1988.

14. GLD, editorial, *Orate Fratres* 25 (June 1951) 291–292.

15. GLD, taped interview, April 1987.

16. Ibid.

CHAPTER *2*

Abbot Alcuin said, "I'm going to send you to Rome."

I'm not exactly crazy about the idea, but it has its compensations, not the least of which is the traveling and "taking in" of art museums and the like in Rome and, during vacation, in other cities.[1]

So saying, Godfrey registered his ambivalence about studies abroad. It was the summer of 1928, a first threshold moment in the young monk's life.

During the academic year 1928–1929, Godfrey took his maiden voyage abroad, started graduate studies in Rome, and made his solemn profession as a Benedictine monk at Monte Cassino. He began to mature rapidly through all the challenges of living in another culture, discovering a larger world, and growing in self-knowledge and self-possession in the midst of it all.

Curiously, Godfrey's entrance into the monastery had not proven to be a significant "rite of passage," because his early experience of monastic life at St. John's Abbey was radically continuous with his growing up and schooling. True, certain notable developments had taken place during his first three years in the monastery: he had experienced an intellectual awakening under the tutelage of Father Athanasius Meyer; he had developed a more congenial notion of God; he had been challenged by a new ecclesiology; he had been swept along in the liturgical ferment upon Virgil Michel's return from Europe. At the same time, he was still in the midst of his own adolescent development with its attendant lack of focus. He was, after all, only eighteen years of age when he made his triennial vows at St. John's and only twenty when he finished his course in philosophy.

This Stearns County native had never been outside Minnesota and had been to the Twin Cities only twice—once on a school outing and more recently with his classmate, Paschal Botz, O.S.B., to be examined for a Rhodes scholarship. He was attached to his family and enjoyed the stability of the monastery. To this point, his life was "all of a piece."

It should not be surprising, then, that Godfrey had mixed emotions, at least at first, about the opportunity for study in Europe. The idea of a graduate degree from Sant' Anselmo interested him less than the prospects, only vaguely imagined, of discovering another world. Godfrey, together with Paschal Botz, began the journey to Rome on October 1, 1928. His farewell to his confreres at St. John's, as recorded in his diary, sounds almost jaunty: "Goodbye to home and St. John's. The clerics gave us a fine, heartening sendoff. They turned out *en masse* and even accompanied us to the bus, altho (or perhaps because of it) it was time for classes to begin. Thank you!"[2]

The separation from his parents appears to have been much more difficult. An eyewitness remembered Mr. Diekmann running along next to the train until he could no longer keep up and then shouting: "Goodbye, Godfrey, goodbye." Godfrey wrote of this leave-taking:

> It was very hard to say goodbye to Dad and Mother. My dear, dear parents, you smiled bravely through the farewell and tried to make it as easy for me as possible. But it is you who suffer most. God grant that we see each other again in a joyous reunion. It won't be an eternity, only four long years.[3]

The tone of this diary entry, a bit overwrought and melodramatic, is unlike anything Godfrey will write again, either in his diaries or his correspondence. It could have been that he was beginning his travel diary with a certain rhetorical flourish. On the other hand, there may have been some premonition on his part that he would not see one or the other of his parents again, and such proved to be the case. His father died seventeen months later.

The journey to Rome was made in three stages: bus and train travel to the East coast, an ocean voyage, and some days spent sightseeing through France and Germany before the start of classes. At every stage, adventures awaited the young students.

Godfrey's diary provides a charming record of two neophyte travelers, babes in the woods really, who probably experienced something analogous to the *tremendum et fascinans*—emotions generally associated with one's encounter with the Holy: "Arrived in Chicago. Boys oh boys; two poor innocents from the country let loose in the big bandit burgh. We clung together like twins in the immense station."[4]

In Chicago, Godfrey and Paschal were joined by a monk named Benno from St. Procopius Abbey in Lisle, Illinois. Of this new traveling companion Godfrey recalls only that he never smiled, but apparently Benno's more sober approach to life did not lessen Godfrey's wonder or enthusiasm, as the following excerpts from his diary will attest:

> Left for N.Y.C. Got a fast train to boot, for which we ordinarily would have had to pay six dollars extra, but a kind policeman showed us how to get out of that. He came up, introduced himself, and said "You know, I'm a K. of C. and you priests and us got to stick together. Now, Father, you take . . . . " I could have kissed his florid, moustachioed, Irish face. Got out of six hours of wearisome train travel and avoided the "extra" at that. Climbed into a Pullman. First in my life. Had an awful time undressing and slipping into my nightie, due in great part to the fact that the 300 bucks burnt in my pockets and I didn't feel safe. . . . Train crawls on the bank of a river and on both sides rise beautiful heights. But my appreciation for scenery was nil just then, for a woman in a seat kitty-corner from mine was telling her neighbor crony in a catty voice that pierced thru one's marrow: "Then I says to him, and he says, says he, and then I says to him again"— etc. *ad infinitum* till I was ready to choke her. . . . Arrived in *the* Metropolis [New York]. . . . Rolled down Fifth Avenue as if it belonged to us. What would the old Dutchmen have thot, had they seen us from their graves. . . . What a city is this New York. Almost as much a city underground as on the surface. . . . In the afternoon, we went to Bronx park to see the show. A great collection of all manner of beasts and birds and reptiles (And monkeys). The latter were most interesting. They wisely blinked at us, whispered an edifying whisper into their neighbor's ear, and then seemingly laughed at us. Oh man, foolisher by far, why resent the theory of descent from such noble stock. . . . We took a big Friday supper at a restaurant, close by a theatre. Some of the Follie Girls were also there. They didn't look so good away from the stage. Looked jaded.[4]

Godfrey's diary is filled with people met, places visited, scenery enjoyed, and food sampled. As would prove true all of his life, *every-*

*Paschal Botz
and Godfrey
leaving
for studies
in Rome (1928)*

American students at Sant' Anselmo, 1928–29; Godfrey standing, second from left

thing captured his attention, nothing escaped him. He constantly evaluated, sometimes rushing to judgment, sometimes recording fleeting impressions. By and large Godfrey delighted in each new experience, but occasionally a bit of pique comes through. One finds, for example, in the pages of his diary an unbecoming youthful intolerance of what he perceived as dirty people, unaccustomed odors, various public displays, and the annoyances and discomforts of travel. He did not "suffer fools" easily and expressed irritation when such crossed his path. On the other hand, numerous kindnesses are noted with appreciation. In these initial diary entries Godfrey demonstrated that he was his father's son, having inherited the fine art of storytelling.

After such satisfying adventures on the trip from Collegeville to *the* Metropolis, the next leg of their trip was a disappointment, as Godfrey wrote some weeks later to Abbot Alcuin:

> The trip across was not so pleasant. It was rather stormy most of the way. The tables and chairs were all chained to the floor, and special retainers for the dishes were placed on the table, but even so, we occasionally had our entire dinner or supper upon our laps before we were quite prepared to receive it. Seasickness bothered me only one day, but on none of the other days did I feel quite sure of myself, or rather, of my stomach. Besides, the weather was decidedly chilly, and the passengers few, and those few, mostly Frenchmen. So that part of the trip which I had anticipated with the greatest amount of pleasure, turned out somewhat of a "fizzle."[6]

Unfortunately, this letter to the abbot is supplemented only by one cryptic and intriguing diary entry: "Paschal. Saloon. Poker."[7] Perhaps the voyage was not quite as dismal as his letter made it sound.

Godfrey also told his abbot about his shipboard apostolate:

> It was a most surprising experience for me to see how many on board came up to us and wanted to "talk religion" and have their difficulties explained. Not that they wanted a controversy, though there was one like that, but they seemed very earnestly to be seeking for some light and information.[8]

Here marks the beginning of Godfrey's astonishing "travel ministry"! Everyone who has ever journeyed with him will corroborate that such a ministry is second nature to him. All his life this "easily met" person has quite quickly entered into conversations of substance:

straightening out marriages, reconciling individuals, encouraging the fainthearted along the way. "Travel ministry" is a regular part of Godfrey's apostolic life, and has been well honed over the years.

Joe Cunningham, one of Godfrey's frequent traveling companions in conjunction with meetings of the International Commission on English in the Liturgy, delights in telling a story of traveling with Godfrey in England. One day they checked into a hotel and put their bags in their rooms before meeting in the lobby for dinner. Godfrey returned to the lobby first and, as Joe approached, was in deep conversation with the husband of the woman who had registered them. Although they had not registered as priests, Godfrey had already met this Irishman and discovered that he was a "renegade Catholic." Joe marvels: "Even his wife did not know he was a Catholic, but in ten minutes Godfrey knew it. . . . Godfrey could not hide either his priesthood or his love of people."[9]

Paschal and Godfrey stepped off the ship on French soil and spent several weeks as tourists before settling down at Sant' Anselmo. Their travel was concentrated around Paris and Munich. Now Godfrey was able to begin the "taking in" of museums that he had eagerly anticipated as the compensation of study abroad. An entry in his diary after a visit to Versailles is wonderfully instructive of his approach:

> Wonderful paintings, many I suppose very famous, but we didn't know. Afterward we'll kick ourselves for not having paid attention, or, for not knowing what to pay attention to. *But we shouldn't look thru other people's eyes.* Enjoy it yourself.[10] [Emphasis added.]

From the beginning Godfrey chose to be his own tutor and tour guide, examining, evaluating, exploring. He would be his own "taste-fashioner," not being a slave to others' interests or preoccupations. His eye became all important in this evaluative project. Over the years he added to his store of wisdom, learning the history of the art or architecture he visited, filling in details of events and circumstances surrounding an object's creation or ruin, building a collection of stories to accompany his running commentary. Sixty years later there would be no one more knowledgable or delightful with whom to tour. And it had all begun with this flash of insight at Versailles.

During his sojourn in Paris, Godfrey recorded his impressions with a smattering of newly discovered French expressions, demonstrating a special fondness for the all-purpose *"beau."* At the Sainte Chapelle he noted: "Peek hole of Louis XI for Mass. *Petit mais plus beau.* Rose window in back— modern, *pas beau."* At Notre Dame: "Outside. *Très beau. Les statuettes,* little, big, funny, etc. Wise old gargoyles." At Montmartre: "Some new style stained glass windows. (Too flashy, not as subdued and *beau* as old.).'' At the Madeleine: "Swell church, frequented by swells." And he concluded: *"Paris* more beautiful than N.Y. or Chi. Crooked streets, Charm. Buildings have character. Ancient. Quaint."[11]

From France Godfrey and Paschal traveled to Munich for a twelve-day visit with Coonie Diekmann, who had preceded his brother to Europe for graduate study. Godfrey reported this visit to the abbot:

> Munich with Conrad, the dachshunds, the Löwenbräu and Andechser, the museums, and picture galleries, furnished us enough material of interest for our stay there. The first mentioned was delighted that we came, though, to be sure, a certain "dachel" also seemed to take a decided fancy to us. The above juxtaposition of subjects is, I suppose, rather unfraternal, but I don't mean it that way. To see Conrad again and to be with him, made Munich feel absolutely like home, and the twelve days thus passed much too soon. He is well and happy, though his plumpness is of the "nil" quality.[12]

It was during this sojourn with Conrad in Germany that Godfrey experienced the opera for the first time. He and Paschal were able to get tickets for Wagner's *Siegfried.* Knowing the plot, they expected a young man to play the lead, but to their chagrin an old man took the part, a man whose voice cracked, who lumbered about the stage, who missed the dragon when he thrust his sword. They found the performance terrible and were surprised when the audience applauded loudly. Then they discovered that the lead was a famous tenor giving his last performance before retirement—just one of hundreds of instances of Godfrey's charmed existence! They became more generous in their assessment of the performance after that.

That was the first of many operas Godfrey would attend in Europe, a taste he cultivated while he traveled. He likes to tell a story about attending *Tannhäuser* a number of years later in Paris. At that time clergy attendance at the opera was frowned upon. Since Godfrey had no appropriate garb apart from his habit, he decided to wear his overcoat to cover up the rabat [a backless, vestlike garment worn by clerics] over his undershirt. At the entrance a woman insisted on taking his overcoat despite his frantic protests that he had a cold. He was thoroughly embarrassed. When chorus girls filled the stage, one of his companions put his head down and said, "Let's get out of here," to which another replied in a stage whisper, "You damn fool, we paid good money for this; close your eyes." They stayed for the whole performance. It was only the next day that Godfrey saw a sign in a sacristy that put priests on notice: any priest, native or foreign, who attended the opera was suspended from offering Mass. The sign didn't stop Godfrey from celebrating Mass, but he had the good grace to do so "with some hesitation."

Time was running out before classes were to begin. Paschal and Godfrey made their way to Rome by train, a trip Godfrey found exceedingly tiresome and unpleasant. Sleep proved impossible in the third-class car, and even their dozing was interrupted at midnight when they had an unexpected six-hour layover in Bologna—something the ticket agent had assured them would not happen. Godfrey later wrote to Abbot Alcuin: ". . . when we arrived at St. Anselm's next day at 4:00 P.M., it appeared to us, not like a school, but like a wonderful big dormitory, plus a few rest rooms."[13]

Immediately they were thrust into a three-day retreat. Godfrey wrote to Abbot Alcuin that they had arrived "safe in soul and body"—at least so he had judged—but Sant' Anselmo was taking no chances as far as the soul was concerned. They "derived much benefit" from the retreat, despite the fact that they understood only about half of the Italian conferences.

Before concluding his first letter home to Abbot Alcuin, Godfrey provided a scrupulous accounting of the monies spent along the way:

Train fare (including excursion to Andechs)	$ 51.33
Meals, drinks, etc.	7.07
Baggage	10.40
Taxi and Trams	2.44
Tips to ship's stewards and Pourboires	4.35
Visits to Museums, etc.	1.75
Opera (in Munich)	2.00
Donation to St. Mary's	3.35
Fountain Pen	3.55
	86.09[14]

It doesn't add up exactly, but no matter. Godfrey's accounts tended to be detailed and meticulous. He is very careful, to this day, about what he spends and will return money, even small change, which he has not used for that for which he requested it.

Orientation to life at Sant' Anselmo was necessarily hurried, since classes began almost at once, and with them, the end of the leisurely transition that Paschal and Godfrey had enjoyed. Godfrey adjusted quickly and easily. Just as Munich with Conrad had felt "absolutely like home," so now Godfrey could describe Sant' Anselmo as "not at all as stonily massive and repelling as the pictures I've seen of it. On the contrary, its warm, cream colored brick exterior make it appear friendly, and *almost* homelike."[15]

Godfrey never experienced any of the illnesses sometimes associated with travel or adjustment—a good thing! The brother nurse at Sant' Anselmo, in Godfrey's judgment, knew more about butchering pigs than medicine. No matter whether one had a headache, a cut finger, a broken leg, or sore eyes, the nurse had the same remedy—a "purga." Not until Christmas would Godfrey express any homesickness at all, and this he did in characteristic German fashion: "Christmas is drawing closer and closer. I get a funny empty feeling around my stomach whenever I think of it, for I can only think of it in terms of home. But then I'll have to celebrate it more in the right way, in the spirit, this year."[16]

The course of study for the first year included five hours of Fundamental Theology, five hours of Dogma, five hours of Moral Theology, three hours of Exegesis, three hours of Liturgy, two hours of Biblical Greek, one hour of Archeology, and two hours of "sermons by superiors." Godfrey found the course "pretty stiff climbing at first when everything is flung at a fellow in Latin. It's quite easy to understand, but, the moment I try to take notes, I forget the train of thought in 'fishing' for the right Latin word to use. But it'll soon be better, I hope."[17]

So the year began. Godfrey found the studies more challenging than any to date. He admitted as much to Abbot Alcuin:

> I thought I had a load last year, but then many an hour was free in which I could read magazines and often do even less useful things than that. This year, the studies are always *pressing,* urging, piling up in threatening bulk if I don't tackle them with vim.[18]

After about a month of classes Godfrey wrote home about one of his professors: "Our Dogma professor is what the students at home would call 'a whiz.' He is just a young priest yet, called Anselm.''[19] Dom Anselm Stolz, Godfrey's professor of systematics, was an attractive teacher who developed a following among his students. His influence on Godfrey would become one of the most important in Godfrey's theological development, for Anselm introduced Godfrey to a sense of mystery and to what Godfrey refers to as ''the theology of the heart.'' From Anselm, Godfrey formed the conviction that the effort to grasp speculative theology would be successful to the extent that it was accomplished with reverence and awe—not a bad lesson at the beginning of his studies, and one that would form the foundation of Godfrey's own enormous success as a teacher.

Studies that first year proved arduous:

> Honestly, if you could see us, the way we're "plugging" over *De relationibus in divinis,* and what Isaias said and what he didn't say, and *De censuris, quid dicendum,* etc. ETC., I do believe you could be heartless enough to laugh and say, "It'll do you good." In other words, we're working hard to get through the exams without going under, and I hope it'll be with flying colors (the getting through, of course), if for no other reason than to fulfill the trust you placed in us by sending us here. Paschal and I have been spouting theses at one another every day now for some time, during the noon hour, so that we will be able to handle the Latin a little better when the show-down comes, and also that we get used to hearing ourselves speak, so that we won't get stage-struck.[20]

The work of that first year was rewarded. Godfrey received two *eminenters*, two *summa cum laudes*, and one *magna cum laude*. About the latter he offered Abbot Alcuin that timeworn scholastic explanation: "I was rather at a disadvantage when the P. Professor started quizzing me on matter that I hadn't thought was for the exam, and so hadn't studied as thoroughly as the rest. But then I passed all the same, and that is the essential point anyway."[21] Alcuin was delighted with Godfrey's "justifiable joy in your splendid notes," but of his good beginning Alcuin warned, "Don't let it breed over-confidence. I congratulate you on the result, but beg you to remember that human results hang by a slender thread, which may be broken by even a slight adverse wind."[22]

Students from Sant' Anselmo marching in annual procession in the Testaccio area of Rome; Godfrey fifth on right

While Godfrey applied himself to his studies, "all work and no play" was *not* his experience during this transition year. His letters and his diary record numerous adventures as he began to find his way around Rome and its environs. "Rome, with all its ruins . . . plus a number of fine old churches, is intensely interesting. Every stone seems to have its history, and the people prosaically, I almost said sacrilegiously, pass by and take it all as a matter of course."[23]

So Godfrey, having found the city "intensely interesting," set out to discover yet more. He went "down, down, down the steps to the catacombs" and sang a Mass there "with ardor" in memory of the early Christians. He stood on the rostrum where Cicero spoke and thought of him as "an old friend." He paused in wonder before a grave inscription: "To my husband, with whom I never quarreled." He visited a walled fortress from the Middle Ages and expected, in that setting, "to see a company of knights coming around every corner." He examined the medallions of all the popes at St. Paul's and found that "some look terribly goofy," but Paul's statue did him justice—"makes him a tough old fighter." Godfrey's powers of observation continued unabated.[24]

*A day
at the beach
at Ostia (1930);
Godfrey
second
from left*

Climbing the Titlis mountain near Engelberg (1930); Godfrey in the lead at far left

37

As time permitted there were excursions outside the city, to Frascati, Grottaferrata, and Viterbo, the latter a place of "medieval cobblestone streets, so crooked and narrow, spanned by stone arches overhead, the ancient stone buildings, the little two-wheeled carts drawn by pot-bellied little donkeys, and the absence of every modern vehicle, the quaint garb of the people, etc., all were things to fascinate a modern sophisticated animal."[25]

Hard as it may have been for him, that "modern sophisticated animal" was always scrupulously honest about his impressions. He recorded his first visit to the Sistine Chapel with wistful regret:

> I tried to kid myself along, tried to make myself believe that I liked it, that it was wonderful and all that, but such is the perversity of human nature, I couldn't quite succeed. Some individual figures and groups I like, but the effect of the whole, —. I am now in that stage where I got myself believing that it is "growing" on me. I'm afraid it'll need a whole lot of tender nursing and care before it manages to "grow" to anything resembling full stature.[26]

Unmoved by the Sistine Chapel, Godfrey was nevertheless touched to the core at St. Peter's, particularly on the occasion of the fiftieth sacerdotal jubilee of Pius XI, December 20, 1928:

> Church crowded. Heard silver trumpets herald approach. Everybody strains to see. Finally see Pope, sitting high, blessing slowly and solemnly on all sides. Big red cape, white cap (first saw tips of helmets and spears of Swiss guards). Clapping and much cheering among lay people. Mass. . . . Silver trumpets during elevation. Sends tingle all thru one and one bows down and says "My Lord and My God" much more ardently. . . . After Mass ran to back of Church to get a better glimpse as he is carried out. . . . He comes slowly blessing. Fierce ardor of cries. Loud, *waves* rolling and swelling as he comes closer. I choked and trembled. Fierce loyalty. . . . Cries and I cried fiercely. Viva il Papa. Silver trumpets. [And there follows a very rare glimpse of his interior life.] So much for the representative of God, I felt. Why so cold to Jesus?[27]

Of less interest to Godfrey during this first year in Rome was the growing ferment surrounding Mussolini. He would become fascinated with the political situation in Europe once he was more at home there, and in his later adult years he would develop a lively interest in the politics of Church and state, a fact to which all recipients of his Christmas letters can attest. But during his first months abroad, he only occasionally mentioned rumors he had heard about the solution to the "Roman question" or signs he had seen posted for a Fascist rally or the size of the demonstration for *Il Duce*—and generally when he noted the latter it was for the purpose of comparing the skimpy crowds that gathered around *Il Duce* with the throngs surrounding the Pope. Godfrey was similarly apolitical with regard to events in the United States in the months following his departure. However, if politics were "on hold" for the moment, patriotism flourished. His first Fourth of July outside the United States included

> . . . flauntingly displaying the American flag on the outside of my door, getting the Bro. to serve "second wine" at table, going to Ostia for a swim in the afternoon, and guzzling down three big steins of dunkler Löwenbräu to America's health; long may she live! Now if that isn't enough patriotism, even if it was rather moist, I don't know. Of course I tried to get a few firecrackers also, but failing that, attempted a home made bomb, but the blasted thing refused to function.[28]

Not every outing in Rome was serious, as is clear from one of Godfrey's descriptions, this one of a return trip from Frascati:

> On the way home we got the cramp of three months dignity out of our limbs. There were six of us: Paschal, four other Americans, and myself; and so we could run down steep slopes, "peg" snowballs, and shout and sing to our hearts' content without fear of scandalizing anybody up there in the open, uninhabited hills. It felt great.[29]

And why not? "Augustine," noted Godfrey in his diary, "got started running down a very steep slope!"[30]

At Sant' Anselmo with Godfrey was a deacon from Downside Abbey in England, a man who had great mechanical skill. At that time radio was just coming in and was "forbidden fruit" for students. This deacon made a crystal set and headphones for each of the Americans and the English. The problem was where to hide it. Godfrey was convinced that a lot of snooping went on. Ah ha! Beside each bed was a wooden cabinet containing a chamber pot. Others used the pot at night and marched in solemn procession carrying them to the washroom in the morning, but the Americans never used them and so decided on the chamber pots as the best place to hide the crystal sets.

Cardboard was put in the pot, then the radio, then more cardboard. All were certain that no one would lift the cover to examine the pot— and they were right. The sets picked up only one station, but to Godfrey's delight it was a classical station, so he listened to classical music and many operas. By his own account, "I could not get enough of it."[31]

This story was replicated some years later when television was relatively new. Godfrey went to visit his brother Paul in Dayton, and discovering the TV set, said: "I'm going to saturate myself with this." And he did. Said Paul of his brother: "Godfrey never takes a dipperful or a pailful, but the whole barrel at one time and gets it out of the way."[32]

Godfrey's letters and diary entries are filled with a lively interest in food: in cakes soaked in liqueur ("something to tell one's grandchildren about!"); in fine, tarty cakes ("hurrah"); in the quality of the spaghetti, served sometimes with Frascati wine ("m-m-m"); in discovering breads ("the shape and size of mamma's round cinnamon kuchen"). He was also fascinated by the fasting discipline of monasteries he visited, and described it, sometimes with frank incredulity: "three sardines and a bit of fruit!" or "just one spud—beastly skimpy!"

As Godfrey delighted in new cuisine, so too did he revel in the opportunity to continue developing his musical tastes with new "dishes." He described hearing the *Benedictus* and the *Miserere* sung in polyphony by Casimiri's choir at the Basilica of St. John Lateran:

> It's wonderful. Of course there are no women in it, but the soprano part is taken by a number of trained boys, whose voices, clear and strong, perfect soft and fortissimo, are much better than women's voices for such occasions. It's a perfect *one,* a beautiful, rounded whole. One almost imagines that heaven must be something like that.[33]

He visited the Russian church and there discovered music that was "very peculiar but piercingly beautiful": "It sounds primitive; a *'plaintive wail'* would perhaps describe it best. Their intervals are not full steps and half steps, but *quarter steps,* and it gives a most striking effect, especially as they sing it in their guttural Slavic tongue."[34]

Meanwhile, back at Sant' Anselmo studies continued apace. In the course of their first semester Godfrey and Paschal had discovered their need for a typewriter, and this became the occasion for a very interesting exchange between Godfrey and Abbot Alcuin. Their machine was hopelessly antiquated and in ill repair. Rather than ask for a typewriter directly, or, for that matter, rather than writing, "We don't suppose you have the authority to give us a typewriter. . . !" Godfrey wrote a lengthy fairy tale: "Once upon a time, there used to be a typewriter. . . . " The tale goes on to tell of numerous owners, lengthy and faithful service, and now, despite tender nursing by Godfrey and Paschal, their diagnosis is serious: the machine is *in extremis*.

The story took up three pages of a letter, after which Godfrey concluded:

> This is the story, and although it's a lot of foolishness, still it serves to break the news *gently* to you that we are minus a useable typewriter. And that is why I inflicted [the story] on you, for a blunt asking for such a big item as a typewriter might seem a little presumptuous, especially since we have been here only for such a short time.[35]

The letter was written and mailed in December, and time passed without any response from the abbot. Godfrey became a bit anxious as the weeks passed, and finally, in the middle of February, broke down and addressed the topic again:

> There is a quasi-modern song, the exact words of which I have forgotten, but their sense is something like this: Too long waiting for an answer engenders doubt in one's mind. So also now! The letter I sent to you for Christmas was perhaps not exactly what it should have been, and I owe you an apology. I had a vague kind of fear at the time that it was somewhat "fresh"; but then I thought, you must so often get such cut and dried, stiffly correct letters, that something foolish would perhaps be welcome. Well, I suppose you agree it was foolish enough. I do always succeed in making such an ass out of myself when I try to be funny.
>
> In plain words then: Paschal and I very respectfully (and hopefully) ask your permission to buy a typewriter for ourselves.[36]

Godfrey was afraid he had made a dreadful fool of himself. Abbot Alcuin responded warmly to the contrary:

> Once or twice you expressed the fear—in previous letter[s]—that you may have been "flippant." Don't fear; I will not misinterpret your letters. I will sense whether you have intended to be flippant—I don't

> think you ever will intend to be so. An affectionate familiarity I do
> not resent.[37]

Nor, apparently, legitimate need. Permission was granted to purchase
a brand new Olivetti.

Such "affectionate familiarity" continued to develop between Godfrey and Abbot Alcuin, particularly as Godfrey faced the prospect
of taking solemn vows.

> July 11 is drawing closer rapidly. I have no doubts whatsoever about
> my vocation. In fact, so confident am I and so much do I look for-
> ward to the day without any hesitation, that sometimes I really pause
> and wonder whether the going isn't too smooth, whether I don't take
> it too much as a matter of course. It seems to me that there should
> be more of a weighing of balances, that the devil should put up more
> of a fight. Instead, the step doesn't seem so momentous to me at all,
> but rather like a casual step forward, as if I simply was made for the
> life and there could be no question of anything else. I wonder if such
> a state can be a natural one, or whether it is simply a deceiving calm,
> with the big struggle only coming after I have bound myself for ever.[38]

The same letter included a glimpse of his reticence and his sensitivity
in matters of the inner world:

> It is so much easier to write these things than it would be to speak
> them face to face. I can feel sure in writing that I have expressed my
> exact meaning, whereas in speaking one naturally feels some hesitancy
> in uttering one's inner feelings, and so, when finished, often doesn't
> even know whether the hearer has understood perfectly.[39]

The one concern that troubled Godfrey as he faced solemn profession was the possibility that his family would have need of him for
their support. He turned to Clara, stalwart among those still at home,
and confided his concern to her:

> You know, Clara, I'm supposed to make my Solemn Vows this sum-
> mer, on July 11. I am anxiously and joyfully looking forward to the
> day when I can pledge myself solemnly to God's service for the rest
> of my life. Only one thing troubles me somewhat: Dad is getting quite
> old, and what if anything should happen to him? Who would then
> earn the money for the upkeep of a home? Of course, this is only an
> hypothesis, but one that troubles me not a little. After I will have made
> my Solemn Vows, I will *ipso facto* not be able ever to help out finan-

cially. So it seems to me now that in making Solemn Vows, I'm shirking my share of responsibility and laying it all on you, for you would then be, after all, the one that would have the whole load on yourself almost. Bony I don't think could be depended on very much, and Paul and Marie are young yet. Of course, this is looking at things quite pessimistically, but I feel that I should take all things into consideration before making the final step.[40]

Godfrey knew that the abbey would help out if that were absolutely necessary, but he hoped it would never come to that point. He confided to Clara: "I wouldn't like the idea of my folks being dependent on the Abbey, and I don't think you would either."[41] He begged her to write as soon as possible, and in the meantime to keep the matter confidential.

Godfrey voiced the same financial concerns to the abbot, who decided to settle the matter by calling the Diekmanns to St. John's and discussing the question openly with Godfrey's parents and Clara. They assured the abbot that Godfrey could go ahead. With that question settled, Alcuin wrote:

> So you may go on with a peaceful conscience to make your holocaust. I hope you will never regret it, but let the "Suscipe me, Domine" ever ring in your ears when the troubles and trials of life, which will come to you as they do to all, make you feel heavy and dejected. Rest assured that only an abiding sacrificial spirit will make you happy; dejection comes only when self-love has been hurt and when we do not give ourselves fully to God.[42]

With these assurances, Godfrey proceeded to make his plans with serenity. He and Paschal would spend the summer at Monte Cassino, and there they would make their vows. Godfrey anticipated what it would be like:

> We are leaving for Monte Cassino this noon. Most likely we shall have to make our Solemn Vows to His Lordship early in the morning, quite privately in the crypt, for the Cardinal of Naples will celebrate the Pontifical later in the morning, and then, of course, we couldn't be bothered with. It is indeed a great privilege to be able to vow oneself to God's service forever in the monastic life, at the tomb of our Holy Father, and in the very place hallowed by his former presence and labors. You may be sure that I shall pray there earnestly for you, dear Father Abbot, and for my confreres who are making the momentous

step with me, in particular, and for all back home in general. This letter will reach you much too late for the 11th, but I am certain it is not necessary to have written and asked in order to be assured that you will remember us in the Holy Sacrifice on that day, and that you will pray that we may always receive the grace to be your obedient and devoted sons.[43]

But they did not have to make their vows in private early in the morning. Instead, their ceremony was quite spectacular, as Godfrey narrated to his folks:

> We had expected that we would make our vows rather privately to the Abbot-bishop of Monte Cassino, since we knew that the Cardinal of Naples would celebrate the Pontifical Mass on that day, and therefore we didn't think it possible to pronounce them during Mass. But when we arrived here we were told that the Abbot would receive our Vows during the Pontifical Mass of the Cardinal. . . . Present in the sanctuary were 17 bishops, four abbots, about 200 priests, and the community of the abbey. The Church was crowded with people. You see, Monte Cassino is celebrating the 1400th anniversary of the founding of the abbey by our Holy Father St. Benedict, and so there are big celebrations all the year. Consequently also, there was such a big celebration on the 11th, the Solemnity of St. Benedict.
>
> . . . First of all the dignitaries and priests went down into the crypt, where they vested. Then followed a procession with the relics of St. Benedict and St. Scholastica, the Cardinal, each bishop and abbot (all dressed in cope and mitre) carrying one of the reliquaries. The Pontifical Mass that followed was carried out with grandiose ceremonies. At the Offertory, the Cardinal and the Assistants at Mass took their places on the Pontifical throne, while a seat for the Abbot of Monte Cassino was placed on the altar platform. Then we came out and pronounced our Solemn Vows, then signed the parchment on which we had written them, with a pen of gold that is only used for that purpose. The parchments were then placed on the altar where they remained all during the Mass. Thereupon we sang the "Suscipe me Domine" etc., were invested with the cuculla, and received the Pax from the Abbot, the Cardinal, bishops, abbots, and the whole community. Then we were led into the main part of the church among the people, where a place had been prepared, laid down, were covered with the black funeral cloth, candles placed at both sides; there we remained lying during the whole Mass, until the Communion. It was

Godfrey (second from left) and Paschal (fourth from left) on the day of their profession of solemn vows at Monte Cassino, July 11, 1929

*Godfrey
and Don Paulo
after making
solemn
profession
at Monte Cassino*

frightfully hot, clothed as we were with our heavy habit and cuculla, and then covered yet with the heavy velvet black funeral cloth. Then also, I got cramped pretty badly, lying rigidly and uncomfortably on the stone floor for about ¾ of an hour. But it made me realize all the more vividly what I had just done: died to the world and all it offers and promised myself to God's service for ever. So this first little uncomfortableness was a good beginning of offering everything up to God's honor and glory. I hope I shall always receive the grace of God to realize that all troubles and difficulties are to be borne for God's glory and for one's own sanctification.[44]

Godfrey remained at Monte Cassino for the rest of that summer, living in the shadow of "our Holy Father Benedict" and trying to imbibe his spirit. His remarkable year of transition was capped by an insight about the ordinary, day-to-day nature of sanctity, and this he disclosed to Abbot Alcuin:

We've been here just about two months now. I must say that I am somewhat disappointed, and I shall try to explain why. Before I came, I expected I don't know what of Monte Cassino. It seems foolish to myself now, when I look back upon it, but that doesn't change matters. Somehow or other, I had an impossible ideal in my head; I thought it must be *the* place of all places, picturing it as if surrounded and pervaded by some palpable cloud of sanctity, so that just staying here would work wonders.

Naturally, however, I found no such place. There is, instead, the same daily routine, the same hundred and one trifles as everywhere. Even at the tomb of Our Holy Father, I am barely filled with that sense of inspiration, "in the harbor" kind of feeling that I imagined should be inevitably connected with any Benedictine's visit to this holy place. It seems to be all a matter of cold will power. Only occasionally, when I make my meditation there, something akin to the above is granted to me. But I hope my prayer at his tomb will be heard, that I be filled with a true Benedictine spirit, and that I will be a true monk according to his heart. And then, I suppose, unconsciously one does imbibe something here, just by trying to do one's duty every day.[45]

Again, a characteristically German note, and on this note Godfrey's first full year in Rome came to an end. The first threshold of his life had been crossed, the first rite of passage successfully negotiated. And, as with any rite of passage, the familiar had been left behind.

Abbot Alcuin visiting with Godfrey and Paschal at Sant' Anselmo (1929)

"Sophisticated animal" was the way Godfrey referred to himself at one point during this year of transition, but "cocky" might more adequately describe this monk whose world had been exploded by travel and study, by observing and recording, by comparing and evaluating constantly.

Rome, the city of the martyrs, the city of the Latin Fathers, had started to work its magic on him, broadening his vision, affecting his philosophy of life, and opening him to a variety of relationships with neighbor and stranger alike. Godfrey had arrived in Europe already a practical and critical observer of life. His natural dispositions, intellectual gifts, and aesthetic sense now began to be refined, due in part to an increasing openness to culture in all its forms. Music, art, and architecture, an inherent curiosity about people, a beginning interest in affairs of Church and world, the learning of more languages—all exerted an influence on him that promoted personal growth.

By the end of his first year in Rome, Godfrey had entered a wider world, reached his majority, and pledged himself a son of Benedict forever. He had become something of his own person, had started to develop an adult relationship with Abbot Alcuin, and had tempered his romanticism about prayer and the holy life. He was ready for the more arduous apprenticeship in the intellectual and spiritual life that would be demanded of him over the next nine years, first apprenticing with professors and books, and then, once back at St. John's, apprenticing under the tutelage of his own students in the classroom and under the tutelage of Dom Virgil Michel as Michel's assistant in the production of *Orate Fratres* magazine.

Perhaps it was a premonition of the arduous work ahead that led him, at the end of his first year abroad, to muse: "Climbing up hill. Gives effect of always leaving the valley (all earthly things) behind more and more, and rising to better things."[46]

NOTES TO CHAPTER 2

1. GLD, diary, June 19, 1928.
2. GLD, diary, October 1, 1928.
3. Ibid.
4. GLD, diary, October 2, 1928.
5. GLD, diary, October 2–5, 1928.
6. GLD, letter to Abbot Alcuin, November 8, 1928.
7. GLD, diary supplement, 1928:A. [Many diary entries are not dated. When no date is given, reference will be made to the year of the diary followed by the letter or number of the page.]
8. GLD, letter to Abbot Alcuin, November 8, 1928.
9. Taped recollections of Joseph Cunningham, February 1988.
10. GLD, diary supplement, 1928:C.
11. GLD, diary supplement, 1928:B–D.
12. GLD, letter to Abbot Alcuin, November 8, 1928.
13. Ibid.
14. Ibid.
15. Ibid.
16. GLD, letter to Abbot Alcuin, December 5, 1928.
17. GLD, letter to Abbot Alcuin, November 8, 1928.
18. GLD, letter to Abbot Alcuin, December 5, 1928.
19. Ibid.
20. GLD, letter to Abbot Alcuin, Octave of Corpus Christi, 1929.
21. GLD, letter to Abbot Alcuin, July 6, 1929. The highest grade one could achieve at Sant' Anselmo when Godfrey was a student was *eminenter,* the second highest was *summa cum laude,* the third was *magna cum laude*—hence Godfrey's apology for what seems to be a very respectable grade. It was the lowest he received during his studies.
22. Abbot Alcuin Deutsch, letter to "Carissimi figli miei" [Godfrey and Paschal], August 18, 1929.
23. GLD, letter to Abbot Alcuin, December 5, 1928.
24. The 1928 diary, particularly the supplement, contains numerous descriptions of sightseeing in and around Rome.

25. GLD, letter to Abbot Alcuin, February 17, 1929.
26. Ibid.
27. GLD, diary supplement, 1928:L.
28. GLD, letter to Abbot Alcuin, July 6, 1929.
29. GLD, letter to Abbot Alcuin, February 17, 1929.
30. GLD, diary supplement, 1928:U.
31. GLD, taped interview, November 1987.
32. Taped interview with Paul and Doris Diekmann, December 1987.
33. GLD, letter to "Dearest Folks," Holy Week, 1929.
34. Ibid.
35. GLD, letter to Abbot Alcuin, December 5, 1928.
36. GLD, letter to Abbot Alcuin, February 17, 1929.
37. Abbot Alcuin Deutsch, letter to GLD, May 31, 1929.
38. GLD, letter to Abbot Alcuin, April 7, 1929.
39. Ibid.
40. GLD, letter to Clara Diekmann, March 15, 1929.
41. Ibid.
42. Abbot Alcuin Deutsch, letter to GLD, May 31, 1929.
43. GLD, letter to Abbot Alcuin, July 6, 1929.
44. GLD, letter to "Dearest Everybody at Home," July 30, 1929.
45. GLD, letter to Abbot Alcuin, August 29, 1929.
46. GLD, diary supplement, 1928:A5.

CHAPTER 3

A SPARK MUST FLY!" is one metaphor Godfrey has used to talk about the teaching of theology. "Contagion" is another: theology is a subject that "is contagious—or it ought to be."[1]

In Godfrey's theological development, a number of persons were "particularly contagious": Dom Anselm Stolz, O.S.B., that "whiz" of a systematics teacher at Sant' Anselmo who introduced Godfrey to patristic sources and guided his doctoral work to completion; Karl Adam, whose lectures in Munich Godfrey found captivating, leading him to read more of Adam and to reevaluate his own high Christology; Abbot Ildefons Herwegen, Dom Odo Casel, and other lecturers at Maria Laach, where Godfrey enjoyed a summer vacation and, later, several months of residency just as the now famous Liturgical Institute was getting off the ground. His experience at Maria Laach proved decisive in broadening and deepening his understanding of the Mystical Body and the role of the Spirit.

Stolz, Adam, and the men of Maria Laach, in turn, contributed to Godfrey's theological synthesis. Less directly, in the "spark" Godfrey received from each of these theologians, we can also detect the hint of themes that will become central to the liturgical movement in North America.

Godfrey may have been attracted to Dom Anselm Stolz partially because of the similarity of their backgrounds. Stolz's roots were in Westphalia, Germany; his father was a schoolteacher; he entered the Benedictine abbey of Saint Joseph of Gerleve at the age of seventeen, having been preceded into the monastery by an older brother. After studying philosophy at Maria Laach, Stolz pursued a doctorate in

51

theology at Sant' Anselmo from 1921 to 1925 and spent two years in post-doctoral work, first at the Gregorian University in Rome and then at the University of Münster. He became professor of dogma at Sant' Anselmo the year Godfrey arrived there to study. Stolz was only twenty-eight at the time.[2]

Godfrey's first classes with Anselm Stolz were difficult for him. Those were the days of neo-scholasticism. The main textbook used in daily morning and evening dogma classes was the *Summa Theologica.* "I wasn't able to get on top of it," he still recalls with frustration in his voice. "I was flooded with details—an interminable heaping up of questions. I couldn't put things together; I couldn't synthesize." But then, as an afterthought, "Needless to say, I've changed my mind about the *Summa* since then. One does tend to grow up!"[3]

At the end of that first year, Dom Anselm told his students to read two books over the summer months: Augustine's commentary on the Gospel of John and Matthias Scheeben's *Die Mysterien des Christentums* [*The Mysteries of Christianity*]. Both assignments were invaluable for Godfrey. His love of the Fathers can be traced to the reading of Augustine that first summer in Europe. Reading Augustine also taught him the complications and pitfalls of translation: "Augustine plays with words, and it is difficult and twice as long in translation and you still don't get the exact sense of the wordplay."[4]

Reading Scheeben was even more important:

> Scheeben was difficult to read, like Karl Rahner, but I was so enthusiastic. Reading Scheeben saved my sanity, I'm quite sure, and he provided a synthesis that I've never lost. Scheeben brought Platonic and Aristotelian philosophy together. He synthesized the major streams of our theological tradition. Above all, as the title *The Mysteries of Christianity* suggests, Scheeben insisted on the need of prayerful wonder in the search for God. He communicated a sense of mystery— God cannot be known; we must approach God with a sense of awe and trembling, with a spirit of prayer and a great sense of reverence.[5]

Apparently Anselm Stolz had been similarly moved by Scheeben. Anselm's approach to teaching theology was governed by *theologia cordis,* the "theology of the heart." Theology was not only, or even primarily, mental speculation. Above all, it was a loving approach to God with open mind and heart. "You never know whether to do theology sitting down or to get on your knees" is a favorite expression with which Godfrey summed up the theological pedagogy he learned from Anselm. "Theology of the heart" became characteristic of Godfrey's own teaching when he returned to St. John's.

In Godfrey's second year he again found himself in dogma class with Dom Anselm, this time impressed with Anselm's presentation of the sacramental life:

> On the basis of the Fathers, Anselm demonstrated that the mystical life is not a special kind of spirituality but is the organic development of the sacramental life. That is the sort of lesson that stays with you— the unity of all theology and the spiritual life.[6]

Godfrey remembers his relationship with Anselm as one of great affection. "He was very open, very friendly, very helpful. He took special interest in helping me. We became close friends."[7] That Anselm regarded Godfrey as a bright and promising student and, in fact, delighted in his young apprentice was evident in Anselm's selection of Godfrey as *defendens* in the annual *disputatio* in the spring of 1932. About this "honor" Godfrey wrote to Abbot Alcuin:

> Today, a big "hunch" took possession of me, and it is not a pleasant one. P. Anselm, our morning dogma prof. smiled at me so sweetly several times of late, and there was at the same time such a cold calculation lurking in his eyes, that I am afraid he has picked on me as the "defendens" in the coming public disputation in dogma. The Lord grant I may be mistaken, but I think not, since he told me today he had something to speak to me about.[8]

Godfrey's intuition was correct. He explained the disputation process to his mother and sister:

> I have just been nominated to compose a thesis and defend it for the annual theological disputation. It will take place on February 29. That again means work enough to kill a horse, for I will have to defend it publicly, before the Abbot Primate and the whole College, and, naturally, in Latin. Oh well, I can't do worse than make an ass of myself, and that would be good for humility.[9]

On the contrary, the evening was a triumph, as Godfrey dramatically narrated to Abbot Alcuin:

> The evening of the same day on which I sent you my last letter, the threatened blow fell. P. Anselm chose me as *defendens* in the *disputatio*

menstrua. No amount of wiggling and squirming on my part succeeded in freeing me from the burden. I knew it would be a good experience, but at the same time it meant sacrificing an entire month of time which could be only too well employed in studying for the doctorate exam. After examining the thesis for a week, I came to the conclusion that I could not possibly hold the theory of the professor (that St. Anselm's argument in *Proslogion* c. 2 & 3 was not ontological, but strictly theological) so I went to him and proposed my difficulties. The upshot of the matter was that I became *oppugnans,* and it was to be a dispute in real earnest. It took place on Feb. 29. It was earnest, all right. Fur flew on both sides, and one or other of the professors was aghast at the idea of an alumnus giving back-talk to the arguments of his teacher, but P. Anselm himself enjoyed the disputation immensely. Lack of time saved the *defendens* from a K.O. (He claims the same thing, but with inversed personnel). At all events "a fine time was reported by all" and I think the month spent in preparation not wasted, although I shall have to devote myself to those blessed doctorate theses with renewed energy now.[10]

Given his attraction to Anselm as teacher and friend, it is not surprising that Godfrey chose to write his dissertation under Anselm's direction. During a seminar with Anselm on Tertullian, Godfrey had settled on a thesis topic:

It will be about *De imagine Dei in homine secundum doctrinam Tertulliani* [On the Image of God in the Human Person According to Tertullian]. The subject is of no great consequence in itself; it will be no brilliant contribution to theological studies or anything of the kind, but, since it entails much research work into the sources of his doctrine, it will serve as an excellent introduction into the Fathers. Furthermore, since Tertullian is really the father of theological terminology as we have it today, it ought to be very useful to me. I am going to work on it a bit here at Engelberg, as they have a very good monumental library, which will allow me to study Tertullian's influence on the part of the mystery cults and Gnosticism of his day.[11]

Godfrey would waver briefly on his choice of a specific topic in the next year or so, but not on his more fundamental decision to explore the writings of Tertullian, a man who had intrigued him from the beginning of their acquaintance. Godfrey characterized Tertullian thus:

He was the violent defender of the faith of his time in the West, intent on crushing rather than enlightening his opponents, of whom there were many. One gets addicted to Tertullian as one gets addicted to highly spiced food. After Tertullian, every other writer seems bland. He was the Leon Bloy of his time. [Leon Bloy had opened his novel *The Woman Who Was Poor* with the words, "This place stinks of God."]

Poor Tertullian! He did so much for us. He was a great pioneer, too, in writing in the vernacular of his time and place, northern Africa. But he died a victim of his own zeal. So I determined back in 1933 that I'd try to pray for him every day of my life. Not that I've kept the resolution 100%—but I haven't done badly.[12]

Not badly at all! In fact, Godfrey has urged generations of students to join him in prayer for Tertullian. A summer-school class at the University of San Francisco gave Godfrey a T-shirt with the legend "Pray for Tertullian—he needs it." Godfrey wore the shirt proudly to the Golden Gate park the next day and was stopped by a jogger who, while continuing to jog in place, inquired, "Who is this Tertullian?" When Godfrey began to explain that Tertullian was a third-century Montanist from North Africa, "the man started to back up and then sped away, probably chalking me up as one more California aberration."[13]

Godfrey displays his Tertullian T-shirt at the University of San Francisco; Fr. Augustine Tashiro on right (1987)

Anselm Stolz had been a pupil of Lambert Beauduin's. The following excerpt from Stolz's writings, bearing the traces of Beauduin's vision of integral Christianity, suggests the "spark" Stolz ignited in Godfrey—an understanding of the unity of liturgy and life that Godfrey would promote the rest of his days:

> True mysticism [to which *every* Christian is invited] is always sacramental and thus is built on the liturgical life. By any other but the sacramental route it is not possible to be seized by the divine Spirit, incorporated into the body of Christ, and conducted to the Father out of one's own being, which has fallen away to sin and to the world. . . . The mere repetition of the sacrament of the Eucharist is not sufficient for anyone to become a mystic and to experience special relationships to the divine Persons. In the mystic, sacramental grace comes into consciousness: it must, in the sense explained, pass over into experience. The entire life of the mystic, the intellectual life included, must be penetrated as fully as possible by the sacramental, Eucharistic event, and transformed by it. It must receive its determination from the incorporation in Christ and from the deliverance out of its own sinful corporality. When [the mystic] has succeeded in maintaining in his [or her] whole life the connection with the Eucharist, in standing in Christ before the Father, in gaining an experience of this life, then is the Christian mystic perfect. Then, too, [the mystic] walks in the presence of God. For walking in the presence of God does not imply in the first instance a mere thinking about God, but is to be understood primarily in an ontological sense, that is, as being permanently in Christ before the Father. It can be psychologically helpful to guard the thought of God's presence. But *what is essential is to preserve inner, sacramental union with God, and to carry this into effect in every action.*[14] [Emphasis added.]

Karl Adam was a second theologian who had a contagious effect on Godfrey, and for Adam's influence Godfrey thanks Father Paschal Botz. Paschal and Godfrey had begun work at Sant' Anselmo together, but Paschal's health was too fragile for the climate of Rome. After "being chewed up by the Sahara winds" for many months, it was apparent that Paschal needed another climate. He transferred to Tübingen and began working under the direction of Karl Adam.

It was while visiting Paschal at Tübingen that Godfrey first heard Karl Adam speak. There was no classroom large enough to accommodate the crowds, so Adam used a large hall in the town. The day Godfrey visited, Adam was lecturing on the meaning of grace in St.

Theologian Karl Adam

Paul. The hall was filled. He didn't raise his voice. At first the lecture seemed abstract, but students were sitting on the edge of their chairs, drinking it all in. Godfrey remembers the lecture as if it were yesterday:

> Christian life does not consist of being baptized and then, as it were, through laborious effort, climbing the ladder until at last with tremendous effort and by the skin of your teeth you finally get your fingers up there. No. The great wonder about Christianity is that you start from the top. And that phrase "you start from the top" has been with me all my life. You start from the top; you start from the top.
>
> My class in Patristics has been nothing else than guided by that thought: the great message of Christianity is the fact of deification—that we are a new people with new life and new knowledge. We are divine, God's children. All the rest is nothing.[15]

The marvel is that we start from the top. These words, for Godfrey, functioned like an apothegm, the word offered by a desert father or mother in response to a disciple's request, "Dic mihi verbum"—"Speak to me a word of life." This was "the word" for Godfrey. He began to live on this word of life.

After hearing Karl Adam lecture, Godfrey was drawn to his writings. "*The Spirit of Catholicism* was a foundation book, the standard book of the new wave of theology which would culminate in Vatican II. Catholicism was at a standstill in Germany, and Adam's book came along like the angel of Bethsaida, stirring the waters."[16] Adam was forbidden to put out a second edition unless he agreed to change the text, but upon inquiry of Rome he was unable to discover what it was he was supposed to change. Godfrey was highly edified when Adam handed the book over to a disciple to change it for him!

Another book by Adam, *Christ Our Brother,* challenged Godfrey's notion of Christology. Adam taught that we are saved by the humanity of Christ. "To me, this was a strange doctrine at first. I wrestled with it. I had been raised on a high Christology, and that brought me right down to earth."[17]

Godfrey regarded Karl Adam as an exceptional teacher and was saddened to discover that he had fallen under the influence of Nazism, revealed in a pro-Nazi talk he delivered. Adam was hounded out of the classroom by students who shuffled their feet to make it impossible for him to teach. That cloud hung over him to the end of his life.

In 1952 Godfrey visited Karl Adam, then an old man in retirement. Adam's sight was failing and he was hard of hearing. He put his arm around Godfrey's neck and pulled him close so that Adam could read his lips. "He looked into my face and read my lips, this gentle, jovial genius, and smiled and smiled. It was lovely."[18] That was the last visit of the disciple to the wisdom figure, the last opportunity to receive an apothegm from the lips of Karl Adam.

Adam, of course, was not the only German theologian with Nazi sympathies. Godfrey passed on the rumors about another theologian to Abbot Alcuin:

> Have you heard that Prof. A. Baumstark has come out in vehement public utterances for Nazis, razzing Bishops for their disapproval of that party and saying we must obey God before men (bishops) and that only a General Council could decide against Nazis. He personally would "verzichten auf" [renounce] a church burial rather than not follow his conscience. Such utterances, preceded by ex-Abbot Schachleiter's denouncement of the Bishop of Linz's condemnation of Nazis has caused bad blood. Am afraid Baumstark's faux pas will

hurt Liturgical Movement's spread in Germany. Well, enough scandal.[19]

More theological "sparks" flew for Godfrey at the Benedictine abbey of Maria Laach, and this during two separate but prolonged visits. His first sojourn at Maria Laach was during the summer vacation of 1931. He wrote with great enthusiasm:

> Summer vacation is more than half over. Up to now, I have spent it, according to my own perhaps too generous estimation, well. I have succeeded in getting a lot of reading accomplished, for which so little time is left over at S. Anselmo, and which, nonetheless, is so necessary, lest all that one has learned remain a mere juxtaposition of bare-ribbed facts. Thus, e.g., I have read over twice and digested Karl Adam's *Das Wesen des Katholizismus* [*The Spirit of Catholicism*], have ploughed through Scheeben's *Mysterien des Christentums* [*The Mysteries of Christianity*], Vetters' *Augustin* and *Das Geheimnis des Leibes Christi* [books on Augustine and on the Body of Christ], E. Bishop's *Liturgica Historica*, Fortescue's *Mass*, Casel's works, etc, besides brushing up on Butler's *Monasticism* and reading many pamphlets and articles relating to liturgy. Father Prior has been so kind, moreover, to give us a number of lectures on things liturgical. All in all, I am extremely glad for the opportunity of spending vacation at Maria Laach. The very atmosphere seems to be full of "Mysterienfrömmigkeit" [piety based on Casel's Mystery presence], "pneuma" [spirit] and all the rest.[20]

And again, after he returned to Rome in the fall, he looked back on his summer's experience and reflected on "what we have to learn from Laach":

> My several months stay at Maria Laach was both pleasant and instructive. [words about how awful the weather was] But—why complain? In spite of all, I passed a very pleasant vacation at Maria Laach. The *Akademischer Geist* [the academic spirit] seems to hover over the abbey and *omnes qui habitant in ea* [and all who dwell in it]. And yet, the individual Fathers are what we would call in America "good scouts."

> You know, perhaps, that there is quite a little fun poked at Maria Laach, both by the rest of the Beuronese abbeys, and also by many of the clergy in general. They are considered to be slightly *überschnappt* [daft, crazy]; drive the *Mysterien-frömmigkeit* too far until it has become a mania with them etc.

Truthfully spoken, I do believe the accusations come from jealousy more than anything else. There might be some ground for fear that the monks become *überschnappt,* were it not for the Abbot [Ildefons Herwegen] and Prior [Albert Hammenstede]. They are both absolute jewels. I couldn't think of better men for their respective positions. Especially the prior, pious, yet eminently sane and human, as he is, would be enough to keep the whole community in the correct balance.

But why repeat all this tittle-tattle to you? Suffice it to say that in my honest opinion, we have more than one thing to learn from Laach. Consequently, I am very glad that you gave P. Oliver prospects of attending their academy when he gets finished at S. Anselmo.[21]

Once Godfrey had finished his course work at Sant' Anselmo, he was sent to Maria Laach for his final academic year in Europe, there—at least so Abbot Alcuin thought—to put the finishing touches on his thesis and to participate in the newly established Liturgical Institute:

I think it will be best to forego the seminars at the University of Munich, interesting as they might be, in favor of a full year at the Academy of Maria Laach. This because I would like to give the pleasure to the Abbot of Maria Laach [Abbot Ildefons Herwegen happened to be a personal friend of Abbot Alcuin from their days of study together in Rome] and mostly, because I would like to have you get the benefit of the courses, and I trust you will try to get the utmost out of them. Therefore get your thesis as far advanced as possible before you go there.[22]

In the fall of 1932 Godfrey began to take courses at Maria Laach and to do the collateral reading. He started to compare the methods of instruction at Sant' Anselmo and Maria Laach and became highly critical of the Sant' Anselmo system of education, which he referred to as "the Roman way":

During my four years at S. Anselmo I have been passive. Perhaps I was to blame also, but fundamentally it is the system that is at fault. . . . Since the only thing laid stress on was to pass the final exams, and since each professor demanded only that, and precisely all of that which he had given to us in the course of the year, the natural result was that everybody strove to get down, preferably by heart, that which we received in class. And to do *just* that, absorbed almost all our time. Thus all incentive to do reading on the subject, to get other thoughts on it, etc., was *ipso facto* taken away even if there had been time for such a thing at all. Everybody was intent on absorbing the prof's ideas, and giving them back to him again in the end. Passivity was the result. Many of the students, especially the more intelligent and wide awake, complained of being rocked to sleep intellectually, but, if they wanted to pass, they had to settle down to the system, and that was that.

Naturally, since most of our professors were really of high calibre, we learnt very much that way, and the many facts we did learn will stick, I suppose. But the mental attitude engendered is what I am complaining of. I usually received passably high notes, but they did not satisfy. I felt my brain being slowly but surely atrophied, petrified. I always comforted myself by saying that at all events, I am learning a lot of facts, and that as soon as I get away from S. Anselmo, I shall again be able to do creative work, to really *actively* do something. But four years is a long time, and a lot of damage can be done by the end of such a period. Hence, when I came to Laach, I threw myself into the work whole heartedly, have tried to awake the sluggish brain cells, and have given the memory a bit of a rest. I like the work and think I am really profiting. I work together with the professors, am taking two seminars, etc.[23]

Abbot Alcuin was of another mind on the subject and responded almost immediately:

I am rather inclined to favor the older [teaching system]—the S. Anselmo system. They had no books for collateral reading in the Middle Ages; they listened to the Master and tried to remember as much as they could, trying, of course, to thoroughly understand and develop his doctrine. Yet they produced thinkers. I do not wish to condemn collateral reading nor the seminar. But this method may be overdone. . . . You say you have become intellectually torpid; you think you were active while still at home. You were active—yes, at least in moving about and browsing here and there. Had you been thoroughly active, you would not have become torpid on account of the method used over there. But I do not believe you have been so sluggish intellectually as you think. You have not studied merely like an automaton; you have been alert and have absorbed. I am glad you had to memorize; no solid progress without it. That is our trouble over here— no memory. If you did not profit more at S. Anselmo, blame your training here—and our "active" ways.[24]

Godfrey became absorbed in his classes at Maria Laach and found little time to complete work on his dissertation. He wrote to Alcuin, bargaining for more time:

> If you really want me to get a solid background of liturgical training, I would propose that you allow me to stay another year. Then I could finish up my thesis during the 3 ½ summer months and defend it first thing next fall or around Xmas time. I could go up to St. Joseph in Westphalia to work with P. Anselm, the professor under whom I am doing the thesis, and thus be certain of finishing it before the fall term.
>
> If you want me to finish the thesis now, I would have to practically drop my liturgical work and give all my attention to the thesis for the next 3–3 ½ months. In this latter case, you will have to notify me *quam primum,* else it will be too late, since April is about the extreme limit for handing in a thesis.[25]

Abbot Alcuin didn't budge, notifying Godfrey in no uncertain terms to consider his thesis his first priority in order to be finished by the end of the year.

But who could blame Godfrey for trying to eke out another year at Maria Laach? The abbey was both an intellectual center for Catholics and a place where the pastoral liturgical movement found a home. The collection of *Ecclesia Orans* was the work of the abbey, with its famous first volume by Romano Guardini, *The Spirit of the Liturgy.* Odo Casel's work in *Mysteriengegenwart* [Mystery presence] was attracting numerous followers. *Old Sources of New Power* and *The Praying Church* were other volumes produced by the abbey at that time.[26]

Odo Casel was chaplain at a convent nearby and came occasionally to lecture at Maria Laach. Godfrey was enthralled and proceeded to read almost all of his books and major articles, having been won over by Casel's *Mysteriengegenwart:* "All my sacramental thinking in the years to come was a gradual unfolding of the deeper implications of Casel's theory that Christ's saving acts are present here and now so we can become part of them, and die and rise with Christ here and now." One couldn't help but be affected by *Mysteriengegenwart* at Maria Laach. "It was taken for granted. It was in the air we breathed."[27]

On another occasion, while acknowledging the familial spirit of the community, Godfrey poked gentle fun at the pervasive influence of "THE PRESENCE" at Maria Laach:

We were family there. There were good profs and very small classes. It was quite wonderful and we flourished. At Maria Laach they were always talking about "the presence." There was a wonderful joke. A visitor came and a brother showed him around. The visitor admired a certain painting of a fish and bread and said, "Look at that fish." The brother said, "That's not a fish; that's an *ichthus.*" They had the presence![28]

Godfrey's sacramental thinking was further influenced by the celebration of the liturgy at the abbey. One day, while musing about events that sparked the liturgical movement in Europe, he described the influence of the *missa recitata,* which had been celebrated in the crypt of Maria Laach since about 1926:

> Rome for several decades was very hesitant about [the *missa recitata*] and very reluctantly they gave permission in the course of time. But the idea and practice spread like wildfire and the Church has never been the same since. When people gather around an altar and celebrate, then something comes alive. The Church is no longer just an abstraction—we discover that we are Church. Where two or three are gathered, I am there. We are the Body of Christ; we are Christ; Christ is present in us. And two ideas are driven home: the idea of the Mystical Body and the idea of the local Church. The liturgy is not something that the priest does and we simply say "Amen." THIS IS OUR WORK in which he leads us, and as members of Christ this is our task. This is Church. All of us are co-offerers; all of us are co-responsible; all of us are co-sharers in this thing. And that led to a discovery of the basic responsibility of baptism. All gathered around the altar are equal, and all are doing the most important work the Church can do.[29]

It was during his days at Maria Laach that Godfrey received another apothegm. Abbot Ildefons Herwegen, a brilliant lecturer in sacramental theology, once said in a talk Godfrey attended, "The whole of the Christian life can be summarized in the one word 'transfiguration.' Remember that."[30] When Godfrey later asked Herwegen to elaborate, he said:

> The whole of Christian life is the celebration of one word—transfiguration. . . . The difference between the East and the West is that the East speaks of light, and the West speaks of basic created reality. But light transfigures, like a piece of iron in the fire. So we

are transfigured: we are in the light, we share the light, the life of God. That's what life means. And that's why life in the East has such a mystery. It is transfiguration.[31]

Godfrey stored away Herwegen's words about "transfiguration" to be treasured and pondered along with Adam's "You start from the top."

Godfrey's time at Maria Laach was an opportunity for him to integrate all that he had learned at St. John's and Sant' Anselmo. He treasures the synthesis that Maria Laach fostered for him:

> For me that was a time when I understood both Mystical Body and Presence. I knew that we were the Body, living members as vine and branches. But then I understood yet more. It can be summed up in a word: sacraments are not things; they are *acts*. They are acts of Christ. Christ is present, and his death and resurrection become saving acts in the present so that we can take part in them. They are sacramentally present. Vonier said the same thing: Christ is present sacramentally *non tam loco sed sacramentaliter non in tempore sed sacramentaliter* [not confined by space or by time, but present in sacrament]. Not only the presence of Christ, but the actions of Christ. That idea is staggering. The presence and action of Christ are present in the sacraments. That I learned at Maria Laach, never to be forgotten, and I have clung to it. It has meant very, very much to me. I have discovered that ultimately it means the same thing as the word "sacrament" properly understood—the saving act, activated here and now, in the present.[32]

Life at Maria Laach was not unalloyed delight. Godfrey's year there left him with the bitter taste of life under Hitler. Conditions were extremely trying, as he remembers them. For one thing, at Laach there simply was not enough food. The same had been true earlier in the summer when he was a guest at St. Boniface Abbey in Munich:

> I was a young monk and sat at the end of the table. By the time the platter got to me, there was never enough left. But there was plenty of black bread and beer—Andechs beer. I survived on bread and beer, and I gained forty pounds! Those forty pounds were nobly gained— I've been fighting them the rest of my life.

> The same was true at Maria Laach. Paschal visited me once, during Lent I think, and for supper we had two prunes and a sort of cake, and he didn't care for that and waited for the next course, but the abbot rang the bell and that had been supper.[33]

But food shortages were the least of their problems. Hitler had come into power in the fall of 1932. Godfrey discovered that the monks at Maria Laach were at first favorably disposed toward the Nazi regime. In fact, even outside the monastery, every friend and acquaintance of Godfrey's was pro-Hitler. They took seriously the things Hitler said. The situation of their country could hardly get worse, economically, morally. Hitler raised so many hopes. The power of the man was diabolical. One day Godfrey attended a rally and saw this power unleashed:

> He had a rally in Nuremberg, his capital, a beautiful city. I was warned not to go to this rally for youth, but I knew better. I was young; I was blond; I spoke perfect German—I don't know about the grammar, but certainly there was no accent. No one would mistake me for a foreigner.
>
> That rally was one of the most powerful events of my life. Imagine the most exciting football game you have ever attended. Imagine going without any bias one way or the other, but pretty soon you are swept away by the emotion of things and start shouting your head off. Multiply that by a hundred and it will give you some faint notion of what his organized rallies could be—people waving flags, shouting "Heil, Hitler!" and the like. On the radio you could dismiss him as a madman, but not so when he appeared and started speaking. He had a demogogic power to influence people. Within two minutes the entire crowd was ready to give their life for him. Of course, I was caught up in it, in spite of myself, and leaving the stadium I had to shake myself to get rid of the evil miasma. He had a terrible, terrible gift.[34]

A naive Godfrey and two confreres had previously tangled with the Nazis. During the summer of 1932 one of their outings was to a nearby Marian shrine, an important place of pilgrimage at a Franciscan monastery. After their visit to the shrine, they walked down the hill to a railway station and met a convoy of Nazi troops, perhaps fifty trucks in all, filled with Nazi youth. As Godfrey remembers:

> They were singing away, and we in cassock thought it would be a nice thing to raise our three fingers in greeting—the Catholic sign, the sign of the Trinity. They saw that and started cursing and yelling and asking the trucks to stop. We thought it was great fun. Next day there were huge headlines in all the Munich papers: NAZI YOUTHS IN-

SULT CATHOLIC PRIESTS. We almost precipitated an international incident.[35]

Perhaps a game, but only at first. Godfrey displayed a kind of innocent fascination with what was happening in Germany when he wrote to Abbot Alcuin:

> I think Munich may become interesting yet before many more months are past. I have ambled past the "Brown House" of Herr Hitler several times. Always there are several fascisti in uniform parading up and down and saluting each other like so many black shirts of the *Il Duce*.[36]

Innocent fascination yielded to horror. Within the year Godfrey and his confreres at Maria Laach had their eyes opened. At first the Nazis dealt well with the nobility, a group regularly attracted to the institutes and days of recollection that the abbey sponsored for Catholic intellectuals. Franz von Papen, a member of the lower nobility, was a frequent participant in Laach retreats and other gatherings. "Trust me," he urged the monks, "and things will be all right." They did trust him, Godfrey recalls, until the Nazi blood purge of 1933, when Von Papen, the evil angel, was seen in his true colors. Von Papen, friend and confidant of the monks at Maria Laach, was tried at Nuremberg in 1947, found guilty of war atrocities, and sentenced to eight years in prison.

Godfrey may well have been sensitized to the drastic events in progress in Germany because he had seen another dictator at work in Italy, though his assessment of Mussolini in his letters home was generally more detached and somewhat skeptical.

In one letter to Abbot Alcuin from Rome, Godfrey described participating in the royal nuptials of Umberto and his new bride. He narrated the circus atmosphere of the city, the parades, the crowds beyond numbering, including two women next to him who fainted " . . . and they had to do it standing up! Not an inch of leeway on any side in which they could perhaps have gracefully swayed before losing consciousness." And there followed a political commentary about the situation in Italy:

> One thing was unmistakable during those days: the love and enthusiasm of the people for the *principe* Umberto. . . . their handsome, adored crown prince.

I wonder how the Duce felt about the heartiness of the demonstration for the next king, especially since he knows that Umberto has a good strong will of his own, and doesn't love the black shirts any too well. Evidently, there's trouble stirring. There's bound to be something doing, and it's brewing very strongly at present.

I've heard from the Italian clerics, even from those that used to be ardent Fascists, that there is a very strong, general discontent all over Italy. It only needs organization to sweep out old Johnson and his whole crew, in one overwhelming swish. At present, of course, Johnson, with his well organized Fascisti army, has control of affairs pretty well. But the people are chafing. Up in Northern Italy, the peasants massacred two Fascisti soldiers. There is an ill-disguised feeling of bitter jealousy on the part of the regular, royal army, against the Fascisti militia. Who knows when the lid of the kettle will pop off?

Especially bitter is the resentment over the absolute censorship of the press and the mails. All letters, to or from anybody suspected of dislike of the regime, are opened, and usually confiscated. A cleric told me this, and he knows from experience.

Then there are the two or three kinds of secret police, one group set to watch the other, and the whole bunch set to watch everybody else. It is really a state of hysterical suspicion of everybody and everything, and the tension can't last forever.[37]

It is fascinating to watch Godfrey's developing consciousness of world events. The year he left the United States to begin his studies, Alfred Smith, the first Roman Catholic candidate, was running for the presidency of the United States. Not a word is mentioned in Godfrey's diary or his letters during the fall of that year about the American elections. His political sense appeared to be dormant throughout his first year in Europe, perhaps because of so much personal adjustment. It was inevitable, however, with Europe tottering on the brink of war, that Godfrey would be inexorably drawn into analysis and critique of the situations in which he lived.

Shortly before he returned to Sant' Anselmo in the spring of 1933, Godfrey described the election in Germany to his abbot:

Today is election day in Germany. During my six months stay in this country, three elections have been held. It's a disgraceful waste of money and energy: each time "die Gemüter werden mehr erregt" [the heart becomes more stirred up]. The list of daily political murders and squabbles is a blotch on the name of a country of culture. Especially heated is today's fight. It's a struggle for existence on the part of the communists. . . .

All manner of the wildest rumors are floating around about "discovered" plans of the communists. Maria Laach was officially warned by police that the Reds have evil intentions, and that a thorough nightly guard must be kept. Accordingly, every night a patrol of four or more men keep watch: the "fire-department" has had drills, and large electric lights are strung all about the premises, so that the entire surroundings can be flooded with light, should any nightly emergency arise. Everybody is all excited: the abbot gave a conference on the proximate end of the world last Wednesday.[38]

Living in Italy and Germany was perilous in the early thirties. Traveling between these countries posed additional hazards, both minor and major. When Godfrey left Maria Laach to return to Sant' Anselmo in 1933, Abbot Herwegen called him to his office. "You know the accusations that are being made against Catholic priests," Herwegen said, "that they are homosexual and that they endanger the economy by smuggling monies out of the country." Godfrey knew well about such accusations. He had actually participated in the smuggling not of money but of cigarettes into Belgium the previous Christmas; if he had been caught at the border, he would have received a fine of five thousand dollars and a two-year jail sentence. Even as he was being searched at the border during this cigarette-smuggling incident, he was thinking of the telegram he would have to compose to inform Abbot Alcuin. Those hours of uncertainty passed before his mind as Abbot Herwegen continued:

We owe a large sum ($20,000) to a monastery in Brazil. We owe that in justice, and now we have enough to be able to pay. And we should pay. Would you be willing to carry that money across the border when you return to Rome?

Foolishly, I said yes. I stripped and pasted the large brown envelope to my body and put my habit back on. Then I took the train. Going across the border, I was asked if I had anything to declare. I pretended not to know German. They began to search the baggage and everything else, then looked at me. I should have known from my experience with the cigarettes. They began to feel all over. I was absolutely certain that a guard felt the bulge and knew something was there. Then he looked at me for a long moment and finally said: "You may pass." I stopped in Zurich and, with great relief, I mailed the envelope.[39]

Godfrey's immediate world was being shaped by study and travel. But "learning the wisdom of the elders" was not confined to these experiences. The death of his father provided its own kind of wisdom.

It was during Godfrey's second year abroad that his "growing up" was hastened by the death of his father. From the beginning of his time in Rome, Godfrey's letters to his family had always contained some reference to his father's poor health, which apparently the family attributed to the flu:

> Dearest Dad, I'm just sorry that you are not entirely well yet. I had hoped everything would be spic and span after Easter, but, somehow or other, it doesn't seem to have been God's will that you be cured entirely right away . . . prayer is so necessary. You may be sure also that this prayer is not lacking on my part. Every morning, in the Holy Sacrifice and at Holy Communion, I remember you and all of you most earnestly, recommending you all to God's holy care.[40]

Conrad Diekmann's health did not improve. Early in January 1930, Paul took his father to a clinic in St Cloud. When Mr. Diekmann came out of the clinic, he was very quiet. Paul pumped him, for he knew something was wrong; then finally he asked him in German, "What is it?"

"I have cancer—bad," he replied.

"How long do you have?" Paul asked.

"Possibly a month or two. [Pause] Now I know. Now I can die." He died four weeks later.[41]

When Godfrey got word of his father's death, he was almost in shock, Father Paschal Botz recalls. Asking to be left alone that day, he stayed in his room to come to terms with God's will. The next day he wrote to Abbot Alcuin:

> Received the cablegram from P. Conrad yesterday. God's holy Will be done. I only hope he gives the folks at home abundant courage and confidence in His Providence, to bear it well. I took the liberty of having five Masses said for the repose of his soul. I will serve them then, starting tomorrow.

There is no need for me to ask you for a memento in your Holy Mass
for my father. I know you will kindly do so, and have done so. Thanking you, I remain, Always your loving son in St.Benedict.[42]

Godfrey received the loving sympathy of Abbot Alcuin with gratitude, but he was even more grateful and relieved to hear from Alcuin that the family's financial situation was secure: his sister Clara
had taken over her father's position as postmaster and station master
of Collegeville, a work Mr. Diekmann had assumed after thirty-five
years of teaching.

What appears to be quite genuine is Godfrey's acceptance of his
father's death with what he called "cheerful resignation to the will
of God," not a vocabulary particularly congenial to the late twentieth century but language Godfrey does not hesitate to use even today. It captures for him the reality of grace, which throughout his
life would always leave him, after a time of grappling with God's ways
in solitude, serene in the most difficult circumstances.

Those few lines he penned to his abbot immediately after his
father's death provide a rare glimpse of the faith that has sustained
Godfrey. His spirituality, to the extent that he has revealed it, appears to be solid, unshakable, utterly simple, and refreshingly un-
sophisticated. Occasionally, for example, he bargained with God:

> I never was so scared of exams before in my life. The matter was dif-
> ficult and there was very much of it. I had promised to make the seven
> churches and a number of other things if all went well, so the day after
> the last exam, when I found out that all had gone well, I tramped the
> 25 or more kilometers necessary in thanksgiving. As Paschal said:
> "Considering all you promised, the Lord could hardly afford to let
> you flunk."[43]

Occasionally Godfrey counted on his angel's intervention:

> Providence was with me. . . . I had decided not to take the Hebrew II
> exam, but to defer it to next Fall, since I couldn't get ready for it any
> more. The professor was agreed, but when P. Rector found out about
> it the evening before the exam was scheduled, he insisted that I take
> it. He excused me from choir that I might study, and I stayed up all
> that night almost, cramming. However, I couldn't hope to prepare
> all the selections assigned, so I merely studied the first verses of each,
> trusting to luck. Next morning, exams of Hebrew II started. Those
> that were in ahead of me came out saying that the professor began

any old place in the chapter, never at the beginning. I got more and more nervous. My hour struck, and I entered the room, convinced I was tempting Providence. You may imagine my relief when the Professor said "Domne Godefride, incipias cum capite V libri Isaiae." Nevertheless, I had only prepared the first 10 verses. Would that be enough? I began reading, slowly, always more slowly, hoping he would say "enough." Eight verses I had read. I then faked a long cough: no use. One more verse, no word from the professor. In despair I started verse 10, finished it, and was just going to begin spelling out verse 11 (I hadn't even prepared the reading of it) when sweetest of words "sufficit, nunc vertas" struck my dizzy brain. I translated and explained per longum and latum (for I did know those 10 verses well) till time was up. A "Summa cum laude" was the result. I hate to even think what the result might have been, had not my guardian angel made a conspiracy with the guardian angel of the professor. Thank God it's over. And thank God also that P. Rector insisted, else I would have to perspire over the stuff next year and would not have received my licentiate this year. I feel not the slightest interest in Hebrew. What do I care whether the Pothagh furtivum is not used in certain cases or whether the Shuagh is immobile or skips all over the page?[44]

Occasionally Godfrey hoped for his angel's forbearance:

Another year has passed—another year has been added to my guardian angel's score book. Many a time I have had the wish to be able to get a glimpse of the account: how many unused opportunities, how many neglected graces are chalked up against me. But perhaps it is better to be left in ignorance on that point, lest discouragement result. I can only look ahead to the coming year and resolve to do better; and that *de facto* was my New Year's resolution. 1932! I wonder where January 1933 will find me?[45]

Always he delighted in the *mirabilia Dei:*

The trip from Milan to Lucerne was wonderful. At Fluelen we changed to the ship which took us to Lucerne. I should think that any, even partially open-minded atheist, would simply be forced to admit his error, on seeing such a manifestation of God's goodness that seemed to almost shriek forth its message from every newly opened vista of glorious scenery. After all, how "flat" are all, even the best of pictures of Raphael, or any of the rest, compared to such beauty of nature. I hardly can blame the pantheists; what they say is nearly entirely correct, only they forget the other side, namely, God's transcendence.[46]

Always he seemed receptive:

> Christmas has come and gone as usual. I celebrated my three masses
> immediately after midnight ceremonies so that I was in church and
> praying from 10:30–4:00 A.M. Then I rolled into bed, thoroughly tired
> but just as thoroughly happy. For how can one help being happy on
> Christmas Day, when the Sweet Divine Babe is born for all mankind
> in Bethlehem, and is born again, so to speak, in each of our hearts,
> if we are but prepared to receive him.[47]

Godfrey also experienced a missionary call, and his exchange with
his abbot on this topic suggests yet more of his interior world. After
an opening paragraph about the sacrifices of St. John's to staff a mission in the Bahamas, Godfrey continued:

> All of which brings me to broach a subject which I have been meditat-
> ing on for some months now. I have weighed the pros and cons as
> well as I have been able to, and have definitely come to the decision
> to volunteer for the Chinese University. I hesitate even now to men-
> tion it, because I realize perfectly well that I owe everything to St.
> John's. Only with the community's generous help was it possible for
> my father to keep on sending me to school; and since I have entered
> the novitiate, I have always been receiving, receiving, receiving, both
> spiritually and materially, and I have never in any way been able to
> give anything in return. Two years ago, you privileged me by giving
> me the opportunity of coming to Rome, to take up the major course
> in Theology, thus putting me in still greater debt to you. I have made
> solemn vows for St. John's, and, after completion of my studies, should
> devote all my life and effort for St. John's, to fulfill the trust you have
> placed in me by sending me over here, to repay St. John's for what
> I have received at its hands, and lastly, to live up to my vow of stabil-
> ity, to be a member of the St. John's family, and as such to do all
> that lies in my power for that family.[48]

Godfrey attempted to make his case to be sent to the missions
chiefly by establishing that the Chinese University had a mission to
carry out the Benedictine work of evangelization. The same mission
that Boniface, Augustine, Ansgar, and others had accomplished in
the West was, in the East, also a particularly urgent mission ''when
it becomes daily more evident that the Occident is disintegrating, that
the Orient of the future will have a big role to play in the story of
civilization.''[49] Moreover, others were also studying, and Godfrey

believed he could be spared. He concluded with a statement that whatever the abbot decided, he would accept it as God's holy will, cheer-
fully giving up all further designs to go to China.

Abbot Alcuin responded:

> You want to go to China. You really do, do you? Well, I won't say
> yes, but neither will I say you nay; but I will say God bless and keep
> and increase in you the spirit of zeal and sacrifice. Which means to
> say that I am pleased that God has put this spirit into your heart and
> that if such be His will in your regard, I shall not deny you to Him,
> but like Abraham I shall be willing to sacrifice my son in whom I have
> placed hopes that he would some day be a useful member of this our
> monastic family. That is the extent to which I commit myself at pres-
> ent. I would not hesitate to give a definite promise, but I must first
> have some indication that such is God's will. Your mere desire to de-
> vote yourself to the work in China is not a sufficient guarantee; you
> may change your mind when you get back here. There may have arisen
> by that time a combination of circumstances which might make it
> morally impossible to let you go. I might have resigned or died by
> the time you have finished your studies and I do not wish to bind my
> successor, if I can indeed do so, by a promise given to you now to
> let you go to China. If Peking remains with us and you are wanted
> out there, I will be as game as circumstances justify and tell you to
> go. There now you will be satisfied with this for the present and nour-
> ish in yourself the spirit of obedience and forgetfulness of self, which
> is the priestly spirit of Christ. You write beautifully about your unpre-
> paredness for the sacerdotal dignity that will shortly be conferred upon
> you. I wish that sentiment would get so deeply in your soul that true
> humility would sprout therefrom with all its fruits. Alas! many a dea-
> con has given the expression to the same sentiment, but after ordina-
> tion it vanished and he never tried to make himself less unworthy of
> the priesthood's dignity. Quod absit a te! [Far be it from you!][50]

To which Godfrey, probably expecting the answer that Alcuin gave,
did need to make one rejoinder: "As far as changing my mind is concerned, I doubt whether there's much danger of that, for after all,
I'm not of the feminine gender, nor am I so hopelessly young any
more that my decision should change with the temperature."[51] Discussion of going to China disappeared from their correspondence as
Godfrey took up Alcuin's advice about preparing for his ordination.

What it meant for Godfrey to be ordained to the priesthood is apparent in the letters he wrote to his family and his abbot in the months before his ordination. Embedded in discussion of his preparations—the purchase of a chalice, the Mass practices he and Paschal walked through with each other—his devotion to his family and his wonder at his own priestly vocation are gradually articulated. To his family he wrote:

> I received permission from Father Abbot to get myself a chalice. Have already ordered it so that I may have it in time for my first Holy Mass. The design is very fine, simple yet beautiful lines. It will be of solid, hand-hammered silver, with the inside of the cup and the paten gold plated. Am sure you will also like it once you have seen it. The price is about $105. Including duty and the luxury tax, the sum will mount to perhaps $115. Where are you getting the money from? Are you paying it yourselves or is Uncle George chipping in?[52]

And then, in a postscript to Marie, he continued:

> Might add that in the inside, lower part of the chalice, I am having an inscription engraved, somewhat to the following effect: "Patris, matris, sororis Clarae, aliorumque omnium qui sacrificiis suis quottidianis accessum ad altare mihi panderunt, aeterno sacrificio quottidie sim memor."

> Paul, get busy and figure it out. Or you, Marie, you've had some years of Latin I think. Anyway, the text isn't final, but the idea I want to express is there, for it means this: "May I daily be mindful in the eternal Sacrifice, of my father, mother, and sister Clara, and of all others who, at the cost of daily sacrifices opened for me/made possible for me the accession to the altar." For God alone will ever be able to repay you mother, and dear Dad, for all the trouble I cost you, and for all the sacrifices you made so that I might be able to continue in the road to my chosen vocation. And you also, Clara. You have done far far more for me than sisterly charity itself could ever have demanded of you, just so that I could keep on in my studies for the priesthood. And even now, after Dad died, you have generously taken all the weight of the responsibility of keeping up the home, upon your own shoulders. God forgive me if I ever could be unfeeling enough not to be heartily grateful and appreciative of what it all cost you. And it really should be self-understood that, once I have attained my goal, I remember you all in the one and only way I could hope to be able

to repay even a small part of my debt to you. But I am having this
inscription put on, nevertheless, as a palpable, physical evidence that
you, mother, Clara, and dear Dad and all of you will daily have part
in the august Sacrifice of the Mass which it will be my unspeakable
privilege to offer up.

Just think! Only 6 more months! The time is simply flying.[53]

A few weeks later Godfrey wrote home about practicing to "say
Mass," for which more training was offered in the United States than
in Rome. Godfrey and Paschal worked together along with the master of ceremonies, helping each other, practicing, checking, critiquing:

Pretty soon now, Paschal and I will be taking the exams of the Vicari-
ate, prescribed before ordinations. Am practicing to celebrate Mass
now already. Although I had thought it would be easy, since I had
been serving Mass for so many years, and thus had such good opportunities of observing how things are done. Nevertheless, I find that
there are all kinds of fine points which I never dreamed of as being
in the rubrics. Everything is surely prescribed down to the most minute
details.[54]

Finally ordination day arrived—June 28, 1931. The ordination
took place in the Dominican Church of S. Maria sopra Minerva. The
vicar of Rome, Francesco Cardinal Marchetti Salveggiani, was the
ordaining bishop in a ceremony in which sixteen priests, thirty-three
deacons, twenty-six subdeacons, and a large number of candidates
for minor orders were ordained. Cardinal Pacelli, then secretary of
state, had originally planned to ordain the five men from Sant' Anselmo, but was otherwise occupied with trouble between the Vatican
and the Italian government. The ceremony lasted more than four
hours, after which Godfrey returned to Sant' Anselmo to write home,
pouring out his heart in a rare display of tenderness for his mother
and family and an equally uncommon revelation of his inner life:

Dearest Mamma,
The good God has today granted me the greatest possible of His
Graces. He has called me and raised me to the Order of Holy Priesthood. Dearest Mamma, your son Leo is now a priest of God forever,
a priest of the Most High according to the order of Melchisedech. To
think of it! I am now an *alter Christus,* "an other Christ." I have been
incorporated in His mystic Body in a most special way; I have been

made a shepherd of his flock; the power to change bread and wine into the Most Holy Body and Blood of our Lord has been conferred on me; the power to offer up the Holy Sacrifice of the Mass; the power to forgive sins; the power to confer yet other Sacraments. These truly Divine powers have been given to me, this morning, by the imposition of the bishop's hands. Divine powers have been given a weak human creature! Only a miracle of Divine Grace could accomplish that.

Dearest mother and all, join me in thanking the good God for His infinite bounty; and join me in asking Him for the Grace of perseverance, that I may always be true to my calling; that I will always be a good and zealous priest; that my whole life and all my efforts will always be solely and entirely for His greater honor and glory, and for the salvation of souls.

A priest! I simply cannot realize it yet. It all seems like a beautiful dream. But I know it is no dream: it is reality. And tomorrow I shall offer up my First Holy Mass alone. For already today, as you know, I have offered up the Sacrifice in conjunction with the consecrating bishop and the other newly ordained priests. My intention was: "For all who have helped me to God's Holy Altar, especially my parents, brothers and sisters, Father Abbot and Father Master." Then, of course, I made a memento for all relatives and friends, for all confreres, for all who recommended themselves to my prayers and for whom I am obliged to pray.

Tomorrow, my own First Holy Mass, I shall offer up for you, my dearest mother, and for my brothers and sisters. Then, the day after, I shall say the Mass for Dad and Julia.

Today, after the ceremony, I went aside from the others, and gave my first priestly blessing to you, Mamma. Although we are so far separated in space, it means little: space is as nothing to the Almighty God. And he surely will have heard the prayers of His newly-anointed one for his dear mother in America. Mamma dearest: The blessing of God Almighty, the Father, the Son, and the Holy Ghost, descend upon you and remain forever.

After thus giving you, who have given me life, love, and next to God, most of everything in this world, the first-fruits of my priestly life, I also blessed all other dear ones of the family, Clara, to whom I owe so much, Coonie, Bony, Bert, Marie, Paul.[55]

Godfrey, Paschal, and classmates on day of ordination to the priesthood, June 28, 1931

Godfrey (second row, fourth from right) visits with relatives on his father's side at Dinklage, Germany (1931)

It was the custom for the newly ordained in Rome to head to a favorite church for their first Mass. Godfrey celebrated his Mass of thanksgiving the following day in the Basilica of St. Paul Outside the Walls, a church of which he had written to his abbot after his first visit: ''the grand, open sweeps of St. Paul's fairly took my breath away.''[56] He described the experience of celebrating Mass to his mother:

> Today at 9 o'clock, I offered up my First Holy Mass, at the tomb of the Apostle Paul. It is all over now, but it still seems so strange. The goal towards which I have been striving all these years has been reached, and now I will daily celebrate Holy Mass. It is really impossible to realize it all as yet; I suppose the full force of it all will only strike me as the time goes on. After all, the Holy Mass is the biggest thing on this earth, and to think that I am now privileged daily to offer it up. God help me to offer it always with the greatest possible devotion and reverence, that this unthinkable grace bestowed on me be unto my own salvation and to the salvation of others.[57]

Paschal Botz and Godfrey had been side by side throughout the ordination. They went together to St. Paul's the following day, and Paschal recalls that Godfrey went first into the crypt to offer Mass as Paschal watched from the marble railing above. The bottom of Godfrey's alb had purple cloth under the lace. A passerby asked Paschal the name of the cardinal offering Mass.[58]

Some weeks later Godfrey wrote about all these events to Abbot Alcuin. A note of wonder pervades his sentiments:

> I take great pleasure in writing this, my first letter as a monkpriest, to my Father Abbot. . . . It all seems so strange as yet. The full realization of what has happened has not penetrated my consciousness, it seems. Every morning as I prepare for Holy Mass, I have the feeling of preparing for a new, great feast: every morning is a new celebration. It is all so beautiful, and at the same time so awe-inspiring: that I should have been elected among thousands to this great dignity and honor, I, who have only too many humiliating faults and imperfections; it seems improbable, and yet I know it is true. Only He who has deigned to elevate me to this high state can help me, so that I cooperate to the best of my ability to make myself less unworthy. I ask you also, Father Abbot, to remember me once in a while in your Holy Mass that God grant me this grace. In return, I might assure you, if you need assurance, that you, Father Master, and the whole community share daily in the fruits of my Mass.[59]

To which Abbot Alcuin responded:

> You wrote very beautifully about your soul's experience when the
> priesthood came to you. Ah that you might feel that way every day
> until the end of your life. But the first fervor passes away and some-
> times never comes back and sometimes only when old age is creeping
> upon us, as it is creeping on me. But, thanks be to God, He has not
> forsaken me and the holy sacrifice is a joy to me as in the days of my
> youth. This particularly since I became abbot. I suppose because I
> am making more sacrifices than formerly. *Hoc enim sentite in vobis quod
> et in Christo Jesu, etc.* [Let this mind be in you which was in Christ Jesus,
> etc.]. There is the secret: Christ sacrifices Himself by our hands; we
> must enter into the same spirit of self-sacrifice and be as forgetful of
> self as He, and all will be well. May this spirit increase in you.[60]

This exchange was typical of the warm relationship that had gradually developed in the correspondence between Godfrey and Abbot Alcuin. Godfrey almost invariably found in Alcuin's letters "quite a
bit of news and fatherly encouragement pervaded with affectionate
'pointers,' which spur one onward *currere viam Domini quae est via obe-
dientiae*" [to run in the path of the Lord, which is obedience].[61]

Despite the fact that an ocean separated them, Abbot Alcuin's
influence in Godfrey's tutoring was pronounced. Alcuin, for example,
was keen to correct when he thought it necessary. Godfrey dated a
letter "The Octave of Corpus Christi," which, Alcuin gently chided,
was "evidently a slip, since we are only now in the second day of
the Octave."[62]

When Godfrey used a word in his correspondence that he was
not sure how to spell, he used the excuse that a dictionary was not
close at hand, but Alcuin didn't let the opportunity pass:

> No dictionary was your amusing plea! Hence *hemorraghes* (should be
> _____rhages, as your Greek and the English rule of pronunciation
> should have told you—what?). Then Reinhart, not Rheinhart. . . .
> I go out of my way to mention these trifles just to tickle you a bit into
> sitting up and helping yourself when no dictionary is at hand.[63]

Godfrey complained long and loud that the professor of moral theology used the *Summa* and just gave his students *De virtutibus* but nothing on vice. Having gone to the professor to tell him what he thought
of the class, Godfrey communicated his disgruntlement to Alcuin. The
abbot replied:

I am not sure that you may not have wronged your professor of Moral Theology. From the brief description you give of his work I can readily understand that you and the rest of his pupils may consider him wandering in the clouds and not practical enough. Maybe he is not practical enough; I can not judge. But I would rather have you get a thorough grasp of moral principles than merely practical work (casuistry) without a grasp of the principles. If your mind is trained to deep and careful thinking by getting the method of St. Thomas, practical case work will be child's play for you. I mention this because I know professors are sometimes unfairly criticized by their students as not practical enough. Some one starts the criticism and the rest chime in. [64]

In the same letter Abbot Alcuin continued to develop Godfrey's powers of observation, evaluation, and articulation by urging, "I should like to have a sort of diary of your vacation." [65] Godfrey, the observer and storyteller, responded to this request with a wonderfully detailed record of his travels.

Regarding the use of money, Alcuin urged:

You will be careful not to spend money unnecessarily, and it will not harm you to deny yourself a little side-trip for some sight that you would like to see. Many of your brethren here will not have the opportunity to see Europe at all. The economic situation in the U.S. has not improved and we do not know how we will fare next year. If you can save a little here and there by denying yourself what you legitimately presume I would allow, in order to have something to give to the poor, you will be real monks and pleasing to God. [66]

On the question of the use of money, Godfrey was apologetic when he sent in his *conto* at the end of the academic year 1932, because, while his total expenditures were not as large as the previous year, the amount he spent on "smokes" had gone up. Perhaps, he mused, he should take up his pipe. That gave Alcuin a chance to comment on the use of time:

I note what you say about the price of German cigarettes and the remark that you must revert to the pipe habit again. I would prefer that you do this, not only because I am trying to keep down the use of cigarettes in the monastery, but because I think that, if you want to smoke at all to any extent, you will find the pipe more satisfactory and more compatible with work and study. I am smoking my pipe as I write this letter and many is the pipe I smoke while doing my

correspondence and while reading in the evening. One filling lasts
about ¾ of an hour. It would be a loss of time to roll cigarettes or
even to light as many as I could smoke in that length of time.[67]

Finally, Abbot Alcuin demonstrated a remarkable ability to read
the signs of the times and to plan for the future. In one letter he urged
Godfrey to meet significant Catholic leaders in Europe before returning
to the States:

> I wrote to Father Ernest yesterday that I want him to cultivate an in-
> terest in Political Economy during the summer vacation. This is bound
> to be a most important subject in the epochal changes which are com-
> ing over the politico-economic life of the nations. There is consider-
> able work being done by Catholic men in Europe on this subject—along
> lines that seem almost radical in comparison with the position held
> by many in the last century, but that in reality are based on sound
> Catholic principles that have been pushed into the background by the
> liberalism of the past century. There are few Catholics in this country
> that have been doing anything worthwhile in economics. I have there-
> fore given Father Ernest instructions as to what I want him to do dur-
> ing the summer. Among other things I told him to attend the
> Salzburger "Hochschulwochen," which were held last year and which
> I understand will be held also this year. Since you are going to Munich,
> I want you also to arrange to attend, so as to get acquainted with con-
> temporary Catholic leaders and their thought. This should not inter-
> fere with your getting to work on your thesis. The socio-politico-
> economic doctrine of the Church should not be foreign stuff to the
> Catholic theologian, since Catholic theology should have a bearing
> on Catholic life in its widest sense.[68]

On this note, it appears that Godfrey's European experience has
come full circle, his learning has been rounded out. He has sat at
the feet of several eminent European theologians and developed the
core of his own theological synthesis. "Sparks" flew from Dom Anselm, Karl Adam, and the community at Maria Laach. Godfrey was
tutored outside the classroom as well, through vacation travel, in the
midst of shattering world events, in facing his father's death, in his
preparations for priesthood. The hand of Abbot Alcuin rested lightly
but relentlessly on him during those years, a hand shaping one more
protégé. The work of Alcuin continued once Godfrey's studies were
complete. And other monks, notably Dom Virgil Michel, will now
become part of the tutorial process.

Godfrey completed his doctorate in sacred theology at Sant' Anselmo early in the summer of 1933, defending his thesis *De imagine Dei in homine secundum Tertulliani Scripta* on June 17. After six weeks of travel, he sailed on the *Champlain* on July 26, bidding Europe farewell, at least for the time being, though being irrevocably changed because of his years there.

NOTES TO CHAPTER 3

1. GLD, taped interview, November 1987.

2. A short biography of Anselm Stolz, O.S.B., is included in his book *Théologie de la Mystique* (Chevetogne: Editions des Bénédictins D'Amay, 1947) v–xi.

3. GLD, taped interview, November 1987.

4. Ibid.

5. Ibid.

6. Ibid.

7. Ibid.

8. Letter to Abbot Alcuin from GLD, Rome, Sunday in the Octave of the Epiphany, 1932.

9. Letter to "Dear Mother and Clara" from GLD, Rome, January 30, 1932.

10. Letter to Abbot Alcuin from GLD, Rome, March 6, 1932.

11. Letter to Abbot Alcuin from GLD, Engelberg, July 12, 1930.

12. GLD, taped interview, November 1987.

13. GLD, conversation, November 1987.

14. Anselm Stolz, *The Doctrine of Spiritual Perfection*, trans. Aidan Williams (St. Louis: B. Herder Book Co., 1938) 230–231.

15. GLD, taped interview, November 1987.

16. Ibid.

17. Ibid.

18. Ibid.

19. Letter to Abbot Alcuin from GLD, Maria Laach, Quadragesima Sunday, 1933.

20. Letter to Abbot Alcuin from GLD, Maria Laach, September 8, 1931.

21. Letter to Abbot Alcuin from GLD, Rome, Feast of Godfrey, 1931.

22. Letter from Abbot Alcuin to GLD, August 22, 1932.

23. Letter to Abbot Alcuin from GLD, Maria Laach, December 4, 1932.

24. Letter from Abbot Alcuin to GLD, December 16, 1932.

25. Letter to Abbot Alcuin from GLD, Maria Laach, December 4, 1932.

26. Letter to KH from Dom Burkhard Neunheuser, O.S.B., Maria Laach, October 15, 1987. Father Neunheuser's letter prompts some interesting con-

jecture about Abbot Alcuin's role in the founding of *Orate Fratres* and the Popular Liturgical Library of the Liturgical Press.

Father Neunheuser pointed out to me the great friendship that existed between Abbot Alcuin Deutsch, Abbot Ildefons Herwegen, and Prior Albert Hammenstede, the latter two from Maria Laach. Alcuin knew these men from their student days together at Sant' Anselmo. He would have known firsthand from them of the founding by Maria Laach of *Ecclesia Orans* and the publication of numerous works, both scholarly and popular, on the liturgy. Neunheuser's letter concluded: "He [Alcuin] had the idea to do similar work also in USA, together with Father Virgil Michel, in the foundation of the *Orate Fratres.*"

While *Orate Fratres* and the Liturgical Press are generally acknowledged as Virgil Michel's inspirations, Father Neunheuser offers a more balanced view of the role of Abbot Alcuin and the influence of Maria Laach in their inception. Others contributed to the development of the review. Martin Hellriegel, Gerald Ellard, and William Busch participated in discussions about its content, audience, etc. See Noel Hackmann Barrett, *Martin B. Hellriegel: Pastoral Liturgist* (St. Louis: The Catholic Union, 1990).

27. GLD, taped interview, November 1987.
28. Ibid.
29. Ibid.
30. Ibid.
31. Ibid.
32. Ibid.
33. Ibid.
34. GLD, taped interview, April 1987.
35. Ibid.
36. Letter to Abbot Alcuin from GLD, Munich, July 20, 1932.
37. Letter to Abbot Alcuin from GLD, Rome, February 1, 1930.
38. Letter to Abbot Alcuin from GLD, Maria Laach, Quadragesima Sunday, 1933.
39. GLD, taped interview, April 1987.
40. Letter to "Dearest Folks," Rome, July 5, 1929.
41. Paul Diekmann, taped interview, December 5, 1987.
42. Letter to Abbot Alcuin from GLD, Rome, February 12, 1930.
43. Letter to Abbot Alcuin from GLD, Engelberg, July 12, 1930.
44. Letter to Abbot Alcuin from GLD, Engelberg, July 7, 1931.
45. Letter to Abbot Alcuin from GLD, Rome, Sunday within the Octave of the Epiphany, 1932.
46. Letter to Abbot Alcuin from GLD, Engelberg, July 12, 1930.
47. Letter to Abbot Alcuin from GLD, Rome, Sunday within the Octave of the Epiphany, 1932.
48. Letter to Abbot Alcuin from GLD, Rome, February 19, 1931.
49. Ibid.
50. Letter to GLD from Abbot Alcuin, March 15, 1931.
51. Letter to Abbot Alcuin from GLD, Rome, Holy Saturday, 1931.

52. Letter to "Dearest Folks" from GLD, Rome, Feast of the Holy Innocents, 1930.

53. Ibid., in a postscript to Marie dated January 6, 1931.

54. Letter to "Dearest Mother, Clara, and all" from GLD, Rome, January 30, 1931.

55. Letter to "Dearest Mamma" from GLD, Rome, June 28, 1931.

56. Letter to Abbot Alcuin from GLD, Rome, February 17, 1929.

57. Letter to "Dearest Mamma" from GLD, Rome, June 29, 1931 [continuation of a letter begun on June 28, 1931].

58. Father Paschal Botz, taped interview, October 19, 1987.

59. Letter to Abbot Alcuin from GLD, Engelberg, July 7, 1931.

60. Letter to GLD from Abbot Alcuin, September 14, 1931.

61. Letter to Abbot Alcuin from GLD, Maria Laach, Quadragesima Sunday, 1933.

62. Letter to GLD from Abbot Alcuin, May 31, 1929.

63. Letter to GLD from Abbot Alcuin, May 22, 1930.

64. Ibid.

65. Ibid.

66. Letter to GLD from Abbot Alcuin, June 18, 1932.

67. Letter to GLD from Abbot Alcuin, August 22, 1932. It is interesting to speculate here about whether Virgil Michel's obsession with the use of time had been influenced and perhaps even encouraged by Alcuin Deutsch, as the abbot is clearly trying to influence Godfrey.

68. Letter to GLD from Abbot Alcuin, May 2, 1932.

CHAPTER *4*

GODFREY'S TRANSITION to life at St. John's was not particularly remarkable, although his appearance on arrival was certainly worthy of note! His sister Marie was among family and friends who welcomed him in mid-August 1933 upon his return. Godfrey arrived in an outfit quite unlike anything she had ever seen before—a habit and a pair of bloomers designed by the tailor at Maria Laach, new additions to his wardrobe, perhaps owing chiefly to his additional girth. Marie was mortified![1]

Godfrey found life virtually unchanged at home. The Great Depression had devastated millions of people, but his family, always frugal, continued to live adequately because of Clara's civil service job as postmistress. Similarly, the standard of living at St. John's differed little from the ascetical pattern he remembered.

Godfrey didn't have time to spare for the luxury of a "difficult adjustment." In his first years back home, Abbot Alcuin assigned him to teach in the high school and the college, to participate in the formation of the clerics, to give retreats to priests and religious, and to assist Virgil Michel in St. John's still young liturgical apostolate. Godfrey's flexibility, versatility, and enormous energy are evident in the way he learned to juggle these simultaneous responsibilities. Rather than being an occasion for conflict, his work in each area informed the work of the other areas, especially in the way his teaching and retreat preaching began to be shaped by his work in liturgy. He was least successful in formation work within the community, according to his own estimate—a judgment that led him to devise a creative escape. Each of these "careers"—teaching, formation, retreat work, and apprenticeship with Virgil Michel—deserves comment.

First, teaching. A number of assignments combined to launch Godfrey on what can only be called an astonishingly successful career as an educator in the areas of systematics, patristics, and Church history. His earliest experience in teaching, however, was a bit rocky.

Godfrey believes he was assigned to teach high school religion when he got back from Europe "as a kind of trial"—so he wouldn't get proud. "The most traumatic of my whole life" was the way he described those five years he slogged through the teaching of religion on the high school level—classes largely devoted to apologetics of the most simplistic variety:

> I felt miserable, I felt desperate. I felt I wasn't accomplishing anything. It wasn't that the kids weren't good. They were. It was partially the texts. We had two texts. One was Sullivan's *Externals of the Catholic Church*. It contained things like the description of an abbess. What difference does that make to a senior in high school? And the other half of the semester we used Conway's *Question Box*. . . .

As Godfrey recounted this, he let out an exclamation of disbelief at the ignorance of his listener:

> —you never heard of that either? Oh, you blessed child!

and then a brief exposition:

> Conway's *Question Box* was the epitome, the highest exemplification, of what a religion textbook should *not* be! In one book it adds up all the defective arguments ever brought against the Catholic Church, and arguments that conceivably *could* be brought against the Church, and in no case does it use more than ten lines to refute anything. I remember the argument that took care of Lutheranism—an important question for all of us because Minnesota is a Lutheran state. The basic argument against Lutheranism was that Luther was an ex-priest who married Katherine Bora, an ex-nun—and that settled the matter!
>
> I tried to have the texts changed, but I was not able to do so. Imagine trying to work with texts like that for a whole semester! I was sure that at the end of the semester the faith of those kids was weaker than at the beginning, no matter how hard I tried, because they must have sensed that with all that smoke there was some fire. It was a miserable experience![2]

Fortunately, both for Godfrey and for scores of his grateful students of later years, the trauma of teaching a high school religion class was relieved the following year by the assignment to teach a class in German literature, also in the high school. This appointment Godfrey found far more congenial:

> I spoke German fluently; I'd been to Germany. My father had come from there with a good classical library. My sister tells me now that when my brothers were called to work in the garden, I used to hide in the barnyard, up in the hayloft, reading German classical literature. (I don't think it's quite true, but perhaps it's symptomatic of something. . . .) Anyway, by the time I was eleven or twelve I had read all of Schiller, Goethe, Lessing, and all. I got an eternal love of Mary, Queen of Scots, from Lessing. I knew the classics quite well.[3]

Godfrey thoroughly enjoyed teaching German literature. His classes were both small and friendly. Undeterred when he could not find a suitable text, he decided to prepare his own mimeographed edition of those authors he wanted his students to read. In this German literature class Godfrey began to experiment with teaching styles and to develop some of his less conventional teaching methods:

> We sang songs, and once in a while we had a meal and enjoyed the fare. I never dared bring in beer, but sometimes some bratwurst, some summer sausage. It was a very pleasant thing, passing on a part of German *Kultur*. That was the only class I ever taught that was not religion, not theology.[4]

Religion and German literature in the high school were Godfrey's rather modest beginnings as a teacher at St. John's. Then, the second year after his return from Europe, he was asked to add college theology to his high school responsibilities, and later the same year, for the students in St. John's Seminary, he added a class in patrology. Soon patrology became his first love:

> It was by accident, really, that I got into patristics. There was no one else to teach it. I had not specialized in patristics in Europe. It's true my doctoral thesis used the material of Tertullian, but I used him as a source to develop concepts of systematic theology. In those days there was no place in the world where you could specialize in patristics. Now, of course, there is the Antonianum, but when I was a student, you

could prepare only by reading and studying under a scholar. Most scholars in the field were self-made.[5]

So, too, was Godfrey. He described his beginnings in patrology as somewhat tentative: "I tested the waters with my toes before going deeper." What he discovered in the waters was a love for the Fathers of the Church—Tertullian of course, fiery Tertullian, but also Ignatius, Clement, Augustine, Chrysostom, Irenaeus. "They started to grow on me."

Godfrey once again encountered what he regarded as inadequate class material and so began to translate selected writings of the Fathers and to mimeograph these papers for his students. His approach to patristics, as it had been to literature, was to put his students in direct contact with primary sources. He would ask students to read the original text, discover the principal objectives of the writer, organize the writer's thought, and be prepared to discuss the chief points in class.

Contact with the author and the world of the author was always primary, and Godfrey urged students to approach the text with simplicity and reverence, as one would approach the Scriptures. It was his conviction that these writers communicated tradition as it crystalized in the first, third, sixth centuries, and that one needed to approach them with a spirit of faith and an open and humble mind, for these are "Fathers of the bread of truth and life."[6]

Godfrey's classes have often been regarded by his students as much a retreat as an intellectual exercise. "Retreat" would be language compatible with Godfrey's understanding of what teaching theology is all about. After all, he had apprenticed in Europe with those who taught the "theology of the knees," who understood the doing of theology primarily as loving approach to the God of mystery with open mind and heart.

Godfrey has contrasted the teaching of theology with other disciplines:

> It is radically different from anything else. Of course, it requires a good grasp and interest in the subject and the ability to share that knowledge and interest with students. But it also involves the contagious nature of theology. I can understand the teaching task only as my obligation to share not only my knowledge and interest but also

my love of Christ, my enthusiasm for God. Unless students, by contagion, catch your enthusiasm for God, I think you have been a failure.

A spark must fly. What is given must not be just knowledge but wisdom, not moralizing but a life view that comprehends the totality of existence, the why and wherefore of existence, a sense that life is meaningful only when dedicated to God who is worth all dedication.

I discovered this in teaching the Fathers: Ignatius insisted on the fact that faith and love are inseparable—we cannot have true faith in the sense of commitment unless we have love also. Augustine would say: "One understands to the extent that one loves." That is true—one gains insight by loving.

My teaching is also profoundly influenced by the fact that I am a monk. I find that Benedictine spirituality is the *medula patrum,* the "marrow of the Fathers." Its core is walking in the presence of God and being aware of God. Teaching is not teaching *about* God, not communicating *truths* about God, but teaching *God,* which presupposes being aware of God, of Christ, of seeing Christ in others. Teaching God—I have made this the goal of my teaching.[7]

To a friend who was concerned about teaching a particular class on the sacraments, Godfrey offered the following advice:

Do not fear tackling the job. In teaching about God and the things of God, His *mirabilia,* His action through sacraments, it is of course not unimportant that you present facts correctly; but it is even more important that the students are infected by your appreciation of these facts, and develop a similar love and gratitude and humility. And in this, the Holy Spirit, the Author of the gifts of understanding and knowledge and wisdom, will be your chief helper. So prayer, and more prayer, plus the necessary work.[8]

There it is again—the metaphor of contagion. And for scores of Godfrey's students, his teaching can only be described as "infectious theology." The single word used repeatedly by an overwhelming number of Godfrey's students to describe his teaching is "enthusiastic." "Like a little boy," said one, "he is so animated in the classroom, and full of a sense of wonder as he shares his love for patristics, the Church, God, Christ." "Unfailingly vivacious," "convincing," "stimulating," "well informed," "deeply religious," "intense, exuberant and rock-solid," "passionate," even "entertaining" are adjectives used to communicate an experience in the classroom with Godfrey, an experience that one admirer declared "an explosive intellectual adventure."[9]

Nearly every student who has ever had contact with Godfrey is able to remember the content of one or other class in detail. He communicates perennial truths in a new way. His teaching over the years has been sprinkled with a collection of his own apothegms, which have stayed with his students: "What good is it if the bread is changed and we are not?" and "All is gift" are typical of the life-sayings with which Godfrey's students capture his "word of life."

"He wanted you not only to be informed about the subject but to *feel* it."[10] That would account for Godfrey's extraordinary expenditure of energy in the teaching process. A former student called him a performer, theatrical, a great showman, who would do almost anything—bang his head against the blackboard, for example—to capture students' attention. "His whole body was involved in teaching. He would shout, sigh, whimper, or *whatever* he needed to do to get his point across. It was a 'show' with real character and content!"[11] More than one student has wondered whether Godfrey might not drop dead in the classroom, so taxing is his performance. For Godfrey, that would be the best way to go—but of course with some word of Tertullian on his lips!

There are certain drawbacks to classroom exuberance. His very animation sometimes proved to be a distraction:

> The Patrology class, as I recall, was held in a basement room in the College of St. Benedict, with Father Godfrey standing on a raised platform at one end of the large room. In his excitement, words tumbled out of his mouth at great speed, while he seemed to be on the verge of falling off the platform. We waited for the day when he would actually fall off; however, he never did, during that class at least.[12]

A recurrent criticism of Godfrey's style of teaching prompts the question: Does Godfrey teach patristics or does he rather teach Godfrey? Every inspiring and enthusiastic teacher must constantly question personal motivation and be careful that the medium is subordinate to the message. Cult of personality is always a danger for someone with presence, powerful mind, charismatic style, and scholarly content, which comprise the teaching gift. Godfrey's is a phenomenal

Godfrey
describing
Doris Caesar's
bronze sculpture
of Mary
to a guest

Godfrey, wearing his Coptic cross, teaching Patristics at the University of San Francisco
(1981)

92

personality, a personality unabashedly as influential as whatever subject he teaches:

> From a perspective of forty years of acquaintance, I now say that we as students were as much influenced by the presence of the man in the classroom as by the theological knowledge we acquired. But how can knowledge be separated from either the teacher or the learner? Father Godfrey, a large, robust person with a powerful resonant voice rhythmically rising and falling as he professed theology and projected, transferred or revealed his own love of God and God's message. In the classroom, one did not struggle to hear; the voice was there loud, clear and confident. The size of the room made little difference. The person and voice always filled it. He possesses a mind that seemed to surround his topic of lecture, filling in detail and related information as a weaver deals with a fabric. . . . He was a man filled to overflowing with the Spirit and he was in love with God. He inspired us and led us to new heights of understanding because we felt the presence that dominated him. Here was a teacher who was in the Spirit of Jesus. Father Godfrey had such an awareness of the presence of God that the student, at least I felt, was encompassed by that presence. Here was a person who was dynamic and vibrant and filled with zeal to help others know the nature of the God and [hu]man relationship. He was always ready to answer our questions and seemed to do it with such ease that one felt he had prepared a whole lecture before coming to class just to answer that one question.[13]

Perhaps Godfrey has had extraordinary success as a teacher because he enables students to make connections. They report that his classes "opened whole new dimensions of life"; "made a person see the core of things"; "helped me to think about religion, even to this day."

In the classroom Godfrey attempts to demonstrate the relevance of theology in light of present-day issues. For example, the meaning of fasting in the *Didache,* a late first-century Church Order, quickly explodes into a contemporary "theology of the 'enough,'" a recognition of the relationship between fasting and stewardship of the things of the earth, an awareness that fasting is a type of exorcism or struggle with the kingdom of this world. The *Didache* is placed in dialogue with other early texts—*The Shepherd of Hermas,* Aristides, the Hebrew Scriptures—and examined in light of the issues of the day, ancient and modern. Students who participate in such a class are able to apply the "theology of the 'enough' " to something as current as an Oxfam fast or to Ethiopian relief efforts, experiencing as they do so a profound connectedness with Christian women and men of earlier ages. Godfrey helps to forge such links.[14]

Making connections is, for Godfrey, a way of life inside and outside the classroom. Whatever the topic, he analyzes its ramifications in light of whatever theological issues it suggests. In a recent conversation, when the subject of child abuse came up, Godfrey became lost in wonder at the pricelessness of a child, relating this to the Christ Child and our appreciation, or lack of it, of this aspect of the mystery of redemption.[15]

Godfrey participated in two innovations in the development of the theological curriculum at St. John's that are worthy of note. The first radical shift in theological education in the college was to offer a serious program of theology rather than religion classes for non-seminarians. This began shortly after the end of the Second World War, when some returning "Johnnies" demanded that as mature men they deserved something more substantial than the usual religion classes, disdained as fatuous by some. Up to that point "theology" was jealously guarded and reserved exclusively for divinity students. But no longer.

These students got more than they bargained for. Godfrey offered a one-semester course in the Church Fathers and a two-semester course in dogmatic theology. For the latter the text he selected was Scheeben's *Mysteries of Christianity:* "We struggled with it. Oh how we struggled! But pride on their part and mine refused to give it up. At least they were now convinced that theology is academically demanding and intellectually substantive."[16] Godfrey delighted in the impression that the use of this text made on Professor Josef Pieper, famous German theologian who visited St. John's during this educational experiment. Pieper, according to Godfrey, had contempt for America, "yet in *America!*, in a Catholic undergraduate school in *America!*, they are using Matthias Scheeben's *Mysterien!*"[17]

Godfrey's other innovation concerned the seminary curriculum. The seminary, its curriculum, and its teachers have always been a matter of deep concern for Godfrey. The education of the clergy at St. John's and elsewhere is a preoccupation and a passion for him. In the course of his semester of work at Tantur, Jerusalem, in 1971, he conceived of a plan to have every seminary student at St. John's spend a full semester in the Holy Land. Some of his reasoning is contained in a letter to Abbot Jerome Theisen, then chairperson of the theology department:

> This morning I sent a letter to Alfred [Deutsch], as dean of the divinity school, outlining and urging a plan for our sems (and perhaps some younger priests) to spend a semester of regular classwork here in Jerusalem and the Holy Land. [In addition to those considerations I outlined to Al] . . . it would be an unbeatable opportunity to get a really catholic ecumenical outlook and sympathy. Not only because sems of various churches would live together for a semester, but because no place can beat or even approximate Jerusalem for getting a feel of variety and complexity of Christian divisions. . . . Rome is Western and Latin, with exceptions so minute they hardly count. . . . Here in Jerusalem, the Western, and specifically the Latin Church, is in the distinct minority. The rich variety of the Eastern Churches clearly predominates. And they're all here, including the Ethiopians, Armenians (strong), Chaldeans and what have you. Jerusalem is a mare's nest of religions, cultures, customs, garbs, hatreds and everything else. And not to be forgotten: it is the place in the world to become aware of and acquainted with the Jewish tradition (including the fanatically orthodox ones, who are just now posing a national problem because they are taking violent action against autopsies). Perhaps it's not the prime place to discover the Moslem world, but it is good,—and has the advantage of presenting in ominous form the Moslem-Jewish conflict. Such a semester, at probably lesser cost than if spent at home, would give biblical depth plus broad ecumenical background, and could easily prove the best in the entire course of theological training. *Dixi.* [18]

A spring meeting of the School of Divinity faculty endorsed Godfrey's suggestion, and a semester in Israel became a required element in the seminary curriculum. Godfrey himself has frequently accompanied the students for their semester of course work in Israel, acting as both teacher and tour guide in this place of holy ground.

What may be most exceptional about Godfrey's reputation as a teacher is that teaching has always been a part-time affair for him, constantly vying for his attention and energy with numerous other duties inside and outside the monastery, even from those first years after he returned from Europe.

Another responsibility he assumed was master of clerics, work Godfrey was never particularly happy to perform. The master of clerics was the immediate superior of those monks in philosophy and theology prior to their ordination. The duties of this office, which Godfrey filled from 1934 to 1938, were to give a weekly conference after the manifestation of faults [the monastic custom of self-accusation generally concerning minor infractions of the monastic rule], to correct obvious faults, to commend when possible, and to give a report at the end of each year to the abbot and professed community at the time of request for solemn vows. The master of clerics was something of a disciplinarian, a chore Godfrey detested, particularly because he was younger than some in the group, and some of his charges "were a bit wild." During his stint there were between fifty and sixty clerics, some of them from other monasteries.

Godfrey dreaded the weekly conferences. Having just returned from graduate studies, he sometimes got carried away with his own eloquence and knowledge, according to one of his clerics, and some did not take him seriously. Others simply didn't want to be bothered with all that stuff! Godfrey was crushed. He wanted to share what he had learned but

> they were not up to it! It was difficult to deal with those things I was most interested in. For example, I thought the Divine Office was worth every effort, even heroic effort, but they made fun of that—"here's this guy from Rome and he's trying to impose his ideas on us"—and I found that depressing. I became shy in their presence. . . .
>
> I was too young to be a leader, and I was convinced I didn't have the charism for leadership, in the sense of leading them on to a higher ideal. This troubled me very much. I think a priest is essentially a leader—*presbyteros* means "leader"—and I began to wonder what I was doing as a priest if I had no charism for leadership. It bothered me.[19]

Was this ever resolved?

> In a way, yes. I tried to exert leadership in ways I could, and meanwhile I just lived with failure as I experienced it. I was not permanently depressed, but during those years I had a very bad inferiority complex.[20]

In order to get out from under, Godfrey devised an ingenious plan. Just before leaving for Catholic University to teach in the summer school of 1938, he approached some of the clerics whom he regarded as part of the ''loyal opposition'':

> I told them that while I was in Washington, they should see the abbot and ask for my removal. I heard nothing at all while I was gone. When I returned, it was late at night, so I went to my room and found my bed occupied—by my successor! That's the way it happened. I never discussed it with the abbot. I was without a job when I returned.[21]

A slight exaggeration. Actually, during his absence Godfrey had been relieved of only *one* of his many responsibilities. Another of his ministries that began to flourish about this time, his work as itinerant retreat master, would occupy him for nearly fifty years. This, like teaching, was an area in which Godfrey met with exceptional success, both among priests and women religious. From the beginning he had Abbot Alcuin's confidence and encouragement. When asked by a religious superior if Godfrey could give a short course in liturgy and some retreat conferences to a group of women religious, the abbot endorsed him without reservation. He wrote:

> He is young in years, being only 28 and ordained only five years ago; but he is an able young man with the doctorate in Theology from the Collegio San Anselmo in Rome. He had considerable travel in Europe, and while his contact with Sisters has not been much up to the present, I feel that he will not only be able to conduct properly the course in Liturgy, but will also be helpful to the Sisters in the conferences which he has been asked to give. He is a good priest and a good religious, and I do not hesitate to recommend him.[22]

Thus, Godfrey's retreat ministry was launched.

The style of retreat for which, eventually, he was in demand as a retreat director was a ''liturgical retreat.'' In broad strokes, a liturgical retreat looked something like this:

> Had *Missa Recitata* daily, daily homily after the Gospel, reading on feast or saint of the day, lectures with liturgical twist etc. On Sunday, both times, we had an ''offertory procession.'' At the High Mass (at which retreatants sang responses), after Offertory verse, I paused, and retreatants in procession brought to silver platter on Communion railing a little envelope in which they had a slip containing their retreat resolution. Server brought plate to a small table placed on side of altar. They liked it very much. Had explained to them, of course, all

about the meaning of Offertory, and how they should offer themselves, their labors and troubles and resolutions. And the older the women, the more excited about it they were.[23]

This may sound tame to late-twentieth-century ears, but Godfrey was promoting this liturgical retreat in 1937!

Not everyone was ready for such novelty. An old Eudist priest, chaplain at the convent where a liturgical retreat had been preached, took Godfrey aside one day and gently chided him for introducing such innovations in Mass. How could these innovations be justified, since, in the priest's judgment, they broke up the Mass action? The following morning Godfrey attended the Mass this chaplain celebrated for the sisters, "and here the good Father gave those Sisters an excellent homily—but immediately after Communion! *O Tempora. O Mores.*"[24]

Many priests and women religious delighted in the new world opened up to them through Godfrey's conferences. A note to Abbot Alcuin from Bishop Winkelmann of Wichita spoke of the gratitude of all the priests who were privileged to make a retreat under Godfrey's direction: "We all agree it was the retreat of our lives because it was a liturgical retreat. I am sure that any diffidence or misconception of the liturgical movement has been banished once and for all as a result of the masterful conferences of good Father Godfrey."[25] The letter delighted Abbot Alcuin, who responded to the bishop that he would pass along Winkelmann's commendation to Godfrey. Typically, Alcuin hoped Godfrey would not rest on his laurels: "It ought to serve him as an inspiration to do even better work along this line."[26]

Word spread. The early success of Godfrey's retreat approach occasioned numerous invitations. Over the next few decades Godfrey honed his "liturgical retreat" like a polished jewel, adding material, changing his examples, inserting new theological concerns and emphases, but always speaking from what he called "scrambled jottings that I have on a few slips of paper." Fortunately, a request from Father Eugene Walsh, who "wanted to get off on a good start" in giving his first retreat for priests, was the occasion for Godfrey to become self-conscious and articulate about his retreat content and method:

> I am delighted to hear that you are going on the retreat circuit. It has been my experience that very much good in the way of apostolic indoctrination can be accomplished during a retreat, so long as one

doesn't too obviously *promote* a cause. It has happened repeatedly that after the retreat priests have expressed surprise that I didn't talk more about the liturgy. They didn't realize that every single lecture, actually, was about the liturgy insofar as everything revolved around the holy Sacrifice of the Mass. I suppose that in the course of time they will have stumbled to the facts of the case.

So far as an outline of my retreat is concerned, I really have nothing on hand. But I think I can briefly sketch what I usually do. After the preliminary opening talk which compares the retreat to Lent and draws the conclusion that the characteristics of Lent should therefore also apply to the retreat: namely, a certain amount of self-denial, that is silence in this case, and a few other things if you wish; reading (and here I especially stress the reading of Holy Scripture of the New Testament); prayer; and of course the daily Sacrifice of the Mass. Then in the first major talk I make clear that the entire retreat will be based on what they and I have in common, namely, the daily Sacrifice of the Mass as the center of our life and particularly as the *fons* of all sanctity. All the following conferences develop this point. And it is really quite remarkable how all the major items that usually come up in a retreat can be approached from this angle.

Thus I give one or two lectures on prayer, deriving the basic lessons of prayer from the spirit of sacrifice. Another lecture on baptism as the great vocation and our obligation as priests to make our people aware of the fact that God lives in them and that we share in the divine life. Usually also I have a lecture on confirmation, with emphasis on the Spirit that has been given to us in our own ordination, and our own obligation to be men of the spirit and help our laity to become mature and adult Christians. Other lectures are on Holy Scripture—usually I have two lectures on this subject, again drawing lessons from the manner in which the Church herself presents Holy Scripture to us in the Mass and in the liturgy. Of course the breviary prayer comes in here also as an extension of the Mass of the Catechumens, so to speak. Another lecture on self-denial and the spirit of sacrifice. Perhaps another one on the spirit of ministry that every priest must renew in his daily Mass.

One of the most effective talks, judging by comments, is on faith and how faith is not merely a private act of an individual, but it is something that fills the church and is expressed most effectively and most importantly in the offering of the Holy Sacrifice; I try to bring out that faith is not merely intellectual assent but involves commitment and dedication and then recall how the Creed was used in baptism and why it is given to us in the Mass, precisely to renew that spirit of commitment. Other lectures are on chastity in the sense of dedication; again something which every Mass must renew.

Usually there is a holy hour closing the retreat and I devote that to the notion of charity; how the eucharist is by definition the sacrament and sacrifice of charity, and how the spirit of community and fraternal charity must be activated among our people by an intelligent sharing in Christ's own great act of charity.

That's about it. I have never written out my talks. I just use some notes which I change occasionally and keep adding new ideas and new material to the basic outline of the Mass as the source of all sanctity.[27]

Several years later Godfrey received a similar SOS from Monsignor George Higgins of the National Catholic Welfare Conference. Higgins had agreed, in a moment of weakness, to give a priests' retreat, and subsequently decided he ought to have his head examined, since he had never given a retreat of any kind. To Higgins's request Godfrey was not nearly so generous as he had been to Walsh, but this brief reply suggests something of the passion of his approach to retreat ministry:

Quite frankly, I can't seem to whip up much anguish over your predicament. If you haven't given any retreats, it's about time you took a plunge. And I can't imagine you at a loss for words when facing your fellow priests, and telling them about the needs of the Church today. Forget about St. Ignatius' method, and tell them about your own thoughts on what a modern priest should be interested in. They'll be forever grateful to you for breaking away from the usual pattern about warnings concerning dealings with housekeepers, and the mutual obligations of pastor and assistant. Share with them some of the excitement of the new opened windows at the first session of the Council. And there you have your retreat.[28]

Godfrey's approach to giving retreats was very much like his approach to teaching. Often his students found his classes "like a retreat." In both the classroom and the chapel he had the opportunity to set hearts afire, and he seized it. He placed his listeners in touch with primary sources. It is interesting to note that retreat work was emphatically *not* a distraction from his work in the liturgical apostolate but was a subtle—and sometimes not so subtle—opportunity to promote the ideals of the liturgical movement, which had, by the time of Godfrey's return from Europe, become a "family affair" at St. John's.

Shortly after his return from studies, Godfrey assumed some of his "family responsibilities" by becoming an assistant to Fr. Virgil Michel in the publication of *Orate Fratres*. This appointment would surely not have been a surprise to him, since as early as January 1932 the abbot had written: "If you were available now, I might be tempted to call you home, as I am in somewhat of a pinch, since I have to excuse Father Virgil again on account of his eyes."[29]

The selection of Godfrey to work with Virgil Michel when he returned from Europe could have been predicted. His correspondence revealed his developing liturgical interests at Maria Laach. He made numerous references in his letters to the liturgical movement on both sides of the Atlantic and to interesting liturgical practices he witnessed as he traveled. In particular, Godfrey showed his continuing interest in the liturgical contribution that St. John's was making at home and abroad. In his letters home he applauded the success of Liturgical Days at St. John's, promoted books that he thought the Liturgical Press should translate, and suggested potential authors for *Orate Fratres*.

Occasionally his letters contained expressions of concern or advice for the abbot regarding St. John's role and responsibility in the liturgical apostolate of the United States. The following, written at the conclusion of Virgil Michel's three-year recuperation from a nervous breakdown, is typical of Godfrey's involvement in the monastery's liturgical apostolate. This twenty-two-year-old's enthusiasm for the liturgical work of St. John's was undiminished by an ocean's separation:

> P. Virgil is back! That is good news indeed. I hope he will have recovered sufficiently to take over the editorship of the *Orate Fratres*. For I think it beyond dispute that the magazine suffered to a quite pronounced extent since his relinquishment of the helm. Excepting the Liturgical Day number last year which was excellent, the other issues seemed to lack a program, an orderliness and vision in the selection of articles, nor was the Apostolate, the "With Our Readers" especially, as pertinent and inspiring as P. Virgil's crisp and invigorating comments. Even the literary standard (not to speak of the flagrant spell-

ing and composition mistakes in several of the numbers) was not as
high. I hope you don't think it impertinent of me to mention all this.
It's easy to criticize, I know. But then, since the *Orate Fratres* has made
such an enviable name for itself in the past, it hurts so much to notice
that it didn't keep its high level, unavoidable though that may have
been in some respects. Honestly, Father Abbot, St. John's has such
a good reputation, even among the Americans at S. Anselmo, just
because of the *Orate Fratres* and the Liturgical Movement it is foster-
ing, that one gets very jealous and touchy about its keeping the high
standard it has set. After all, it seems clear that the work St. John's
is doing for the deepening of the true religious life in America, is its
most important mission at present. So one cannot help but be anxious that P. Virgil, who has contributed all that was in him to make
it a success, be again entrusted with the editorship of the *Orate Fratres,*
if he is at all capable physically to assume the burden.

By the way, the *Small Catechism of the Mass* by Bussard is just the thing.
Then too, its external form is so neat and trim. Fr. Joachim is doing
excellent work also on the *Orate Fratres*. His cover designs have evoked
a lot of favorable comment over here. He has ideas and talent for such
work, it seems. I hope he gets a chance to develop it.[30]

    Godfrey's burgeoning liturgical interests were not lost on Abbot
Alcuin, who seized the opportunity to offer more advice:

I note with pleasure what you say about *Orate Fratres*. Whether Father
Virgil will go back to it, I can not say at present. But I am glad to
gather from your letter that you have done some solid reading during
your stay at Laach, which together with your observations there, ought
to be useful some day for *Orate Fratres*. Keep up along that line and
put it to practical use also for your own spiritual development. You
still write with neo-sacerdotal fervor of the holy Sacrifice. Unless
you confirm yourself in the "Mysterien frömmigkeit" [a spirituality
grounded in the liturgy] your fervor will wear away before another
year passes.[31]

    In the same year that Father Virgil returned to St. John's and
resumed the editorship of *Orate Fratres,* Godfrey became his assistant.
It was the fall of 1933. They worked together until Virgil's death
five years later. Virgil had been summoned home—some think
prematurely—from his recuperation among the Chippewa of Cass
Lake to be the dean of St. John's University and lead its effort for

accreditation. Godfrey's assistance freed Virgil for other work, such as writing, teaching, translating, editing, and lecturing, as well as beginning some new liturgical projects and lending his support to others.

Probably to Godfrey's great relief (lest he ever have to teach high school religion again!), one of Virgil Michel's major projects in which Godfrey participated was the preparation of a religion textbook series for grade school through college in collaboration with the Dominicans of Marywood, Michigan. The aim of these texts, later to be called the *Christ-Life Series,* was

> to form a generation of liturgically trained and apostolic Catholics who, from the first day in grammar school to the last day in college, would be exposed to, and eventually penetrated by, the ideology and ideals of the liturgical apostolate. So trained, such Catholics would make the Mass the source of their piety, know and experience the vital role of the sacraments and sacramentals in daily living, have some knowledge and appreciation of the Church's prayer life, and gain a familiarity with the missal so as to follow the liturgical year as a spiritual guidebook by which to walk continually with Christ.[32]

That statement, while meant to express the aim of a series of religion texts, also sums up the hopes of those who were promoting "active participation" in the liturgy. Active participation was predicated on education, a lesson Godfrey would not forget, and one that he would promote in a slightly different guise once he had the reins.

Virgil Michel also was overseer of the Liturgical Press, which, from its founding, was vigorous in advocating active participation in the liturgy. Among the publications of the Press in those years was the *Parish Kyriale,* which promoted congregational singing by supplying music for the more common chant Masses. Another project that Father Virgil had hoped the Press might accomplish was the publication of an English breviary for women religious and the laity in order to make available the treasures of the Roman Breviary, the psalms, Scripture readings, and liturgical prayers. His successors picked up this project.

It was also the work of the Press to provide translations of the more significant European publications. Godfrey recalls one such opportunity shortly after he returned from Rome:

A book came from Salzburg, and it was by a man by the name of Josef A. Jungmann, a Jesuit. We had never heard of him. It was 1933 and Jungmann was young then. The book was *Die Frohbotschaft und Unsere Glaubensverkündigung* [The Good News and Our Proclamation of the Faith], his catechetical work. It must be remembered that Jungmann's first interest was catechesis. Father Virgil was excited about it and asked me to read it. I was also excited and wrote immediately to Salzburg, asking permission to translate it and publish it at the Press.

We received an answer that the book had been withdrawn from circulation with no further explanation. Later we discovered it was the Jesuits who had withdrawn it because the book implicitly criticized Peter Canisius and the catechetical method. Jungmann had attempted to move us back to teaching the person of Christ rather than truths about Christ. Jungmann submitted to his superiors.[33]

Jungmann's approach, namely, the proclamation of God's saving word, which he described as the indispensable kerygmatic dimension of catechesis, became standard catechetical theory. But by the time his catechetical writing was vindicated, he had earned worldwide fame for his liturgical work, particularly the classic *Missarum Sollemnia* [*The Mass of the Roman Rite*].

Virgil Michel's numerous projects invited, actually required, the collaboration—full, conscious, and active—of the monastic community. Members of the community were called upon to translate. There was frequent community discussion of the role of liturgy in the life of the Church and the individual Christian. Those monks who staffed parishes in the vicinity were encouraged to work with their communities. Novices and clerics were initiated into the study of liturgy.

Collaboration extended beyond the walls of St. John's. When Virgil was unable to accept a speaking invitation, he would sometimes ask another monk to stand in for him. His multiple interests beyond liturgy also had an effect on the monastery. He talked about Jane Addams and Hull House; he acquainted the community with the Catholic Worker, Peter Maurin, and Dorothy Day; he invited Catherine de Hueck Doherty, foundress and director general of Friendship House, to St. John's and, at her prompting, began the integration of the college by enrolling four black students from Harlem.

In many of these endeavors Godfrey had a privileged relationship with Virgil Michel, begun because of their collaboration and deepened by Virgil's need on occasion to unburden himself. Godfrey recalls long talks with Virgil during the last years of Virgil's life. He was a driven man, yet a man who sometimes shared his problems with his assistant.

As Godfrey remembers it, Virgil would sometimes come to his room. Initially the conversation would be about business—book reviews or manuscripts or to ask advice. One such conversation that stands out in Godfrey's memory concerned two books by Monsignor Fulton J. Sheen that Virgil was reviewing for *Orate Fratres: The Mystical Body of Christ* and *The Fullness of Christ*. Virgil was particularly appalled by the book on the Mystical Body, since he had hoped it would be the popular and inspirational book for which the liturgical apostolate had need. He talked over with Godfrey the numerous theological imprecisions, the inaccuracies of diction and spelling, and, most troubling of all, his conviction that Sheen had plagiarized parts of the text. A scathing review by Virgil was subsequently published in *Orate Fratres*.[34]

After such "professional" conversations Virgil would sometimes stay on and the conversation would shift to more personal topics, often to the subject of Virgil's relationship with the abbot:

> Virgil talked to me about his problems with the abbot, frequently and with anguish. He wanted to be a good monk—he was a good monk! His relationship with the abbot was perhaps a greater cross than his inability to relate to others.
>
> In the early stages [when Virgil was a young monk] he and Abbot Alcuin were good friends. . . . Alcuin liked to sponsor people and then take credit for what they were doing, boasting of it—"Look what I've done; my boy is doing this!"
>
> Abbot Alcuin kept in touch with the abbot of Beuron and knew about the liturgical movement in a general way. When Virgil became acquainted with it, the abbot was delighted—until Virgil began to take credit for some of these things. Virgil was going his own way. He saw some insights which he did not share with the abbot and vice versa. Virgil no longer a novice. There was a clashing of wills. Abbot Alcuin was perhaps a little miffed that he was not getting the credit he thought was his due. Alcuin thought things should move in a certain way. He thought Virgil was getting too much credit. I am quite sure that is what led to Virgil Michel's breakdown.[35]

Following this recollection, Godfrey was quick to add that whatever clashes occurred between Virgil and the abbot were between them. He never witnessed a clash, only a very dejected Virgil Michel after such conversations.

Gradually Godfrey was given more responsibilities for *Orate Fratres*. At first Virgil helped Godfrey edit papers, but after several years of collaboration it became customary for Virgil to bring a whole batch of manuscripts that he had accepted and leave them with Godfrey:

> I would do all the editing; I had no readers at that time. I put out the whole magazine really. Virgil accepted the papers, sometimes consulting me, but usually not, and then I would get everything published.

> Then he would come with the published paper and criticize it—but this in a very supportive way. He was encouraging. He never really put me down in the sense of making me feel badly. He would say: "You might have done this a little better"—that sort of thing. I don't think I was ever depressed by anything he said.[36]

In those talks and through all their collaborative ventures, Virgil was gradually handing things over to Godfrey and actually preparing him for his next rite of passage, namely, assuming the role of editor of *Orate Fratres*.

On November 26, 1938, Dom Virgil Michel died after a short bout with pneumonia and a streptococcus infection. His death was announced simply:

> Dom Virgil Michel, O.S.B.

> Founder and editor of ORATE FRATRES, philosopher, educator, selfless apostle of Christian social reconstruction, above all faithful monk and priest, minister of the mysteries of God, on the vigil of this new liturgical year entered into eternal life:

> Introivit ad altare Dei sublime.[37]

Godfrey recalls his shock and confusion when Virgil died:

> Virgil Michel died when he was forty-seven years of age. It was a tragedy. Days before he had been vigorous. His illness was so brief; no one was prepared for the shock.

> The day he died I was desperate. I couldn't imagine myself taking on his task. By no means was I the giant that he was—and I knew it. So I walked the chapel the night when he hovered near death, praying God to take my life and to spare Virgil's.

Virgil was able to integrate everything into a whole; I was not the universal man he was. He could carry it through. But then I stood in his shoes, and the community supported me. One begins to realize that it's the community's work. What the community can do is more than the sum total of the individuals. I shared his views, to be sure, but if his work had not become a community affair, I probably would have become an elementary school principal in a Nebraska school.[38]

In Godfrey's first editorial for *Orate Fratres,* he summarized the achievement of Dom Virgil and the vacuum his death had created at St. John's:

Father Virgil's death has meant a severe loss to numerous fields of Catholic thought and endeavor in America. Above all, however, the liturgical movement will feel his departure most keenly: for to it he devoted the greatest amount of those gifts and that apostolic zeal with which God had so liberally endowed him. He was interested and active in almost every movement that aimed at Catholic restoration. He threw himself with all his astounding energy into every work that seemed to him necessary for advancing Christ's kingdom. And in all he became to a remarkable extent a leader, a sure guide. American neo-scholasticism, the cause of Catholic education, the crusade for a Christian social order, the Catholic Rural Life movement, the Christian approach to the racial question, the Catholic Press, the retreat and mission apostolate, the movement for Christian reunion—all are the richer for his having contributed his zeal and vision.

His most striking trait, in fact, was his many-sidedness, or rather, his rounded-out, integral Christian being and thought. For all these movements in which he played a part were to him but so many facets of the central reality: the restoration of all things in Christ, the Christ-life to be lived by [all people]. Hence his constant insistence on the liturgical revival as the *unum necessarium,* the one thing necessary, without which all else is but as beating of the air, or as sounding brass. For the liturgical movement, to him, meant a conscious living and growth in Christ which must also necessarily manifest itself outwardly in every phase of [human] activity.

He died on the last day of the Church year, on the vigil of the new. Many have remarked on this coincidence. Systematic and logical in all he undertook, he was so to the last. For, liturgically speaking, he could not have chosen a more appropriate day to meet his Savior in the parousia. And he went forth to meet Him with humble but confident trust.

His death means a particularly grievous loss to the editorial staff of
ORATE FRATRES.[39]

Literally overnight Godfrey Diekmann became the editor of *Orate Fratres*. It was a work that was familiar and congenial. But "the editor of *Orate Fratres*" was also a position of symbolic importance. Virgil Michel, in that role, had been the leader of the liturgical movement in the United States. At the age of thirty, Godfrey donned a mantle of leadership that would settle comfortably on his shoulders in the course of the next few years. A second threshold had been crossed. It was time to put the "wisdom of the elders" to the test.

NOTES TO CHAPTER 4

1. Marie Diekmann, taped interview, October 11, 1987.
2. GLD, taped interview, April 1987.
3. Ibid.
4. Ibid.
5. Ibid.
6. Sister Mary Anthony Wagner, O.S.B., taped interview, October 14, 1987.
7. GLD, taped interview, November 1987.
8. Letter to Sister Mary Anthony from GLD, January 21, St. Agnes [no year given].
9. These impressions have been offered by men and women who were students of Godfrey's over the last five decades.
10. Letter to KH from Sister M. Paula Thompson, November 15, 1987.
11. Ibid.
12. Letter to KH from Sister Maureen Truland, November 4, 1987.
13. Letter to KH from Professor William Cofell, December 3, 1987.
14. Class notes, GLD, St. John's University, Patristics, Fall 1987.
15. Monsignor Vincent A. Yzermans, taped interview, October 23, 1987.
16. GLD, taped interview, October 1987.
17. Ibid.
18. Letter to Jerome Theisen, O.S.B., from GLD, Tantur, November 30, 1971.
19. GLD, taped interview, July 1988.
20. Ibid.
21. Ibid.
22. Letter to Reverend F. R. Cotton, chancellor of the diocese of Louisville, Kentucky [and later bishop of Owensboro], from Abbot Alcuin Deutsch, May 12, 1936.
23. Letter to Dom Christopher Hagen, O.S.B., from GLD, First Sunday of Lent, 1937.
24. Ibid.
25. Letter to Abbot Alcuin Deutsch from Bishop Christian Winkelmann of Wichita, June 15, 1944.

26. Letter to Bishop Christian Winkelmann from Abbot Alcuin Deutsch, June 17, 1944.

27. Letter to Fr. Eugene Walsh from GLD, St. Blase, February 3, 1959.

28. Letter to Msgr. George G. Higgins from GLD, February 5, 1963.

29. Letter to GLD from Abbot Alcuin, January 25, 1932.

30. Letter to Abbot Alcuin from GLD, Maria Laach, Feast of the Nativity of B.V.M., 1931.

31. Letter to GLD from Abbot Alcuin, September 23, 1931.

32. Paul Marx, *Virgil Michel and the Liturgical Movement* (Collegeville, Minn.: The Liturgical Press, 1957) 220.

33. GLD, taped interview, April 1987.

34. *Orate Fratres* 10 (1936) 281–285.

35. GLD, taped interview, July 1988.

36. Ibid.

37. Frontispiece of *Orate Fratres* 13:2 (December 25, 1938).

38. GLD, taped interviews, April and October 1987.

39. "With Our Readers," *Orate Fratres* 13 (1938) 82–83.

CHAPTER *5*

During the five years that I had been privileged to work with Virgil Michel I had learned to know the many-sidedness of his genius. His interests were catholic, and in the sacramental principle of "recapitulating all things in Christ" he had found the integrating center. He was an inspiring example of a man with wholeness of vision. The social problems of the day in particular claimed his passionate interest. More than anyone before or contemporary to him, he brought the lessons of the liturgy to bear upon their solving. This constituted perhaps his greatest single contribution. In America the liturgical movement has, as a consequence, never been just a sacristy affair. After his death, who was there to carry on where Father Virgil had pioneered?[1]

A goodly portion of the "carrying on" fell to Godfrey, who found the challenge of Virgil's work less daunting than the intangible legacy of the man's wholehearted commitment. "The most important lesson Virgil taught me was a sense of absolute dedication. If something had to be done, it *had* to be done! Dorothy Day once said of Virgil Michel that he would give as much of himself in talking to three as to three hundred. This I learned from Virgil—total dedication."[2]

Not without energy and dedication himself, Godfrey set to work. For the next twenty-five years he devoted himself to popularizing the liturgical movement in the United States as it gradually developed a distinctly American agenda and continued to attract a cast of American proponents. Translating the movement's vision into reality was no easy task, particularly when one considers the state of the immigrant Church in the United States at that time. The American Church posed special difficulties that the European liturgical movement did not have to contend with. One commentator summed up the situation in the United States as follows:

The very size of our country is a reason why something like the liturgical movement has had such a hard time in getting a foothold and in bearing fruit. How can a Catholic in Oregon know what has been done in Vermont or Massachusetts? To this we must add the different "national" backgrounds and traditions of the faithful in this country. The Germans and Slavs have a tradition of singing in their churches, while the Celts follow the Mass with silent reverence in order to let the "hedge priest" escape from his pursuers as fast as he can. The Romance-language peoples act differently again, which becomes nowhere as evident as in the "Italian Mission" at Brompton Oratory, where the liturgy is embalmed by the will of the priests who run the church according to Father Faber's infatuation with post-baroque Rome. These differences are easily multiplied and the poverty and far separation of Catholics from each other add yet other reasons for the slower development and thus the uniform growth of the Catholic parish and religious life in this country. In view of these facts, the general remedy for all cases in doubt has been to stay as close to Trent as possible. It was safe and prudent. No sooner had the Catholic put foot on American shore than he [or she] took refuge under the umbrella of Trent, and the United States became the most Tridentine country on earth. What was apparently settled by the Council of Trent was with great fidelity observed. The great trees in the Church were Trent and Canon Law and the underbrush covering the space between these trees was the growth of the "Old Country" tradition.[3]

In retrospect, it is difficult to imagine the uphill struggles that faced Godfrey and other liturgical reformers during the forties and fifties. "Interest had to be aroused, apathy to be overcome, and there was misunderstanding and no small amount of opposition"[4] that faced anyone who developed an interest in the liturgical movement. In the early, heroic days of the movement, the very word "liturgist" was used for name-calling: "A person who was just [odd] or 'arty' or somehow different in his views was given the stamp: he is a liturgist. You could hardly say anything worse under the law of Christian charity. Being liturgical smacked not only of heresy, stubbornness and a hankering for novelty; it was almost a moral blemish."[5]

Godfrey's first great achievement after he stepped into Virgil Michel's shoes was to get the help of H. A. Reinhold, a priest and pastor from the state of Washington, as a regular contributor to *Orate Fratres*. The collaboration of Hans Anscar Reinhold, known universally as H.A.R., had been suggested by Godfrey's confrere, Father Emeric Lawrence, who had met the man at Harvard. Reinhold, a Jew who fled his German homeland in 1935, was as vigorous in his protests of anti-Semitism as in his expression of concern for every dimension of social justice as a means to peace, and these and other topics had already brought him to the public's attention in the pages of *Commonweal*.

In his column, called "Timely Tracts," H.A.R. was bright, sometimes acerbic, always radical, in the true sense of that word. Favorite targets included priests who raced through Mass; pseudo-intellectuals who disdained parish, church, liturgy, ceremony, and even ordinary courtesy; all forms of ritualism; anything false or inauthentic ["bread—a cross between plaster of Paris and a rubber sponge!"]; clearly outdated traditions; and saccharine spirituality. H.A.R. deplored, for example, the picture of the priesthood and religious life offered by Bing Crosby and Ingrid Bergman in *The Bells of St. Mary's* as "a Charlie McCarthy version of the consecrated life."[6] He detested dishonesty, escapism, and make-believe in whatever form. At the same time he promoted a genuine intellectual understanding of liturgy, doctrine, and Scripture, and often urged the reform of the Church's worship. The vernacular, the altar facing the people, communion from the cup, full participation of the laity in all the sung parts of the celebration, the reform of Holy Week, and the restoration of Epiphany "to the splendor and power that is its own" were among his "desiderata to be prayed for," some of them as early as 1940.[7]

H.A.R., who sometimes referred to himself as "the Timely Tractor," said what was on his mind. He said what had to be said. His words could reprove and sting:

> What about those whom Christ called blessed because they "hunger and thirst after justice"? Can we deny that Marx, Lenin, their fellow rebels, and many a "Red" in our own country are possessed by this thirst and hunger for justice, while most of us parrot Christ's words and the papal encyclicals—and go on leading a more or less quiet and comfortable life in families, convents, rectories and other institutions which offer some amount of temporary or lasting security.[8]

"Timely Tracts" might have disturbed, but they were never ignored. One grateful reader, after ten years of H.A.R.'s columns, sent the following tribute:

> A toast to the one H.A.R.
> Our brilliant liturgical star!
> Every month in *O. Fratres*
> The blood in our art'ries
> He quickens and thrills—with a jar.

The limerick's author continued: "That's really how his Tracts affect me. After reading them, in spite of my 80 years, I want to go out and do something for the Kingdom of God."[9]

Another subscriber found H.A.R. to be the proverbial pickerel in a pond of carp. In European monasteries in the Middle Ages, carp were kept in a pond to be served to visiting nobility. Before they were to be cooked, the carp were taken from the dirty pond water and put into clean water to cleanse their system. But since they were very lazy fish, a pickerel was put in to chase the carp around and get them ready for the table. The subscriber did not specify whether the carp referred to the editors, the rest of the contributors, or all the readers.[10]

Godfrey claims that it was an *episcopal* carp pond which H.A.R. stirred up, and not just because of his pointed writings. In fact, H.A.R. had an irreconcilable misunderstanding with his own bishop in Yakima, Washington, and was eventually befriended by Bishop John Wright of Pittsburgh and incardinated there until his death. Reinhold was a brilliant man, the author of six books, the founder of the Vernacular Society, the goal of which (worship in one's own tongue) came to be known simply as "The Cause" and earned its advocates a new term of opprobrium—"vernacularists"!

For fifteen years H.A.R. wrote "Timely Tracts," clearly the cutting edge of the American liturgical movement. No adequate replacement was ever found for him, though Andrew Greeley's "Timely Tracts" in the late fifties came very close. Godfrey recalls his colleague H.A.R. with great fondness:

> I don't remember H.A.R. as in the same category as the rest of us. People admired him so, youth admired him. He was sort of a radical who loved to go off to have lunch with a group of bright people and talk and talk. He was a genius. He had a unique style, and I didn't want to destroy that. He was witty, too. But he would begin to write,

and maybe a whole page would be only two sentences. For H.A.R., one thing led to another in a stream of consciousness. I had to break this up into sentences without destroying its bite.

His chief contribution was in carrying on the relationship of liturgy and the social question. In some areas H.A.R. was more conversant than Michel. He could read something and then was great at finding related matters in various fields. Every "Timely Tract" that came was a surprise. It was a pleasure to work with him.[11]

H.A.R.'s willingness to write for *Orate Fratres* filled an immediate and pressing need after Virgil Michel's death. Once H.A.R. had been discovered, Godfrey could attend to broader questions of editorial policy. Under the direction of Virgil Michel and his editorial board,[12] *Orate Fratres* had acquired a distinctive thrust. "We are not aiming at a cold, scholastic interest in the liturgy of the church," Michel had written, "but an interest that is more thoroughly intimate, that seizes upon the entire person . . . affects the individual spiritual life of the Catholic and the corporate life of the natural social units of the church, the parishes, so properly called the cells of the corporate organism which is the entire living church, the mystic body of Christ."[13]

An analysis of the content of *Orate Fratres* in its earliest years suggests that its initial editorial preoccupation was the restoration of the active participation of the assembly in the liturgy of the Church through sound catechesis, particularly in its attention to lay piety; the doctrine embedded in the texts of the community's prayer; the meaning of symbols, gestures, and postures; the unfolding of the life of Christ and the saints in the liturgical calendar; a return to Scripture and patristic writings as sources of intelligent participation; and the encouragement of chants and hymns.[14]

Gradually Virgil Michel had developed a reform agenda as well. To articles and editorials about the history and present pastoral practices of the community's life of prayer he added quite concrete suggestions for the reform of its patterns of worship, advocating, among other things, vernacular celebrations; evening Masses; Masses facing the people; architectural changes, especially in the size and placement of the altar; and lay participation in the Divine Office.[15]

Godfrey disclaims making any changes in the editorial policies of his predecessor, though, he says, "unconsciously more of my own interests found their way into the journal. I encouraged more theological articles and an emphasis on sacramental theology and on history. I had a section devoted to European developments and often included some articles in translation. A great achievement was to get Karl Adam to write for me, not just in translation.''[16]

Godfrey always kept one eye on the European liturgical scene, both for interesting new developments and in order to discover potential collaborators. During his stint as editor he recruited such international scholars as Josef Jungmann, S.J., of Austria; Clifford Howell, S.J., of England; Vincent Kennedy, C.S.B., of Toronto; and Albert Hammenstede, O.S.B., of Maria Laach, Germany, for the editorial board. In addition, the list of authors in *Orate Fratres* during Godfrey's twenty-five years as editor reads like a Who's Who of the best international scholars and pastors, among them: Pius Parsch; Karl Adam; Lambert Beauduin, O.S.B.; Odo Casel, O.S.B.; Gerald Vann, O.P.; Eugene Boylan, O.C.S.O.; Augustine Bea, S.J.; C. C. Martindale, S.J.; Giacomo Cardinal Lercaro; Johannes Hofinger, S.J.; Annibale Bugnini, C.M.; Louis Bouyer, C.Orat.; Yves Congar, O.P.; Jean Daniélou, S.J.; A.-M. Roguet, O.P.; Balthasar Fischer; Pierre-Marie Gy, O.P.; Bede Griffiths, O.S.B.; Josef Pieper; Theodor Klauser; Caryll Houselander; Hubert Van Zeller, O.S.B.; David Stanley, S.J.; Bernard Häring, C.SS.R.; Jerome Hamer, O.P.; and Josef Ratzinger.

Under Godfrey's tutelage the number of subscribers increased. In 1941 he recorded some interesting statistics:

> Within the past two years, subscriptions to O.F. have increased twenty per cent. . . . Once an interest is aroused and a real understanding, it is usually lasting: as witness the fact that nearly 90 percent of O.F. subscribers renew subscriptions annually. Subscribers: about 45 per cent clergy; 35 per cent religious; and 20 per cent laity. We have subscribers in every State, and in 32 foreign lands. . . . Particularly gratifying is the growing interest in seminaries throughout the country.[17]

In some seminaries, perhaps, there was growing interest in matters liturgical, but sometimes that interest had to be clandestine. One student of that era recalled:

> When I was a seminarian at St. John's Seminary in Boston from 1938–43, we were not allowed to have any newspapers, magazines, or other journals—not even the *Sacred Heart Messenger*. However, each

week my family would mail my laundry to me in a large laundry box. Tucked away between the shirts and shorts each month was a copy of *Orate Fratres*. This magazine was an oasis of inspiration and insight in the midst of the conservative studies of that day.[18]

As editor of *Orate Fratres*, Godfrey was in a highly visible position. Many readers had looked to Virgil Michel for liturgical leadership in all matters, great and small. Now Godfrey was designated putative liturgical expert in virtue of assuming the position of editor of *Orate Fratres*. He became the arbiter of liturgical practices, the Solomon responding to every possible kind of query: What color should be chosen for the antependium when the Blessed Sacrament is to be exposed at the end of a funeral Mass? What is the exact number of canonized saints? May a sister sacristan handle the sacred vessels? Where should one purchase vestments? What happens when the priest has gone and a particle of host is discovered? When should one pause in reciting the Our Father, the Hail Mary, and the Creed? What are the best rules of Latin pronunciation? What advice might be offered on the translation of Greek Odes and similar hymns? How does one use the *Shorter Breviary?*[19]

Godfrey received letters from teachers of liturgy, members of altar guilds, lay women and men interested in liturgy, pastors looking for warrants for certain practices, people with manuscripts both good and bad. If Godfrey liked a manuscript, he accepted it enthusiastically; when he could not accept a manuscript, he wrote a lovely letter regretting the decision of his editorial board. To correspondents Godfrey was unfailingly courteous and thorough in his responses, in the end often urging that a spirit of prayer and common sense prevail: "Do not worry about the niceties about which there is so much controversy."[20]

But not infrequently Godfrey fell behind in his correspondence, "due to the same streak in me which is responsible for the late issue of the most recent number of O.F. . . . It is hard for me to keep a schedule—not to speak of regularity in correspondence." Over the years Godfrey's apologies for tardiness became a highly developed art form. Sometimes they were brisk and cheery: "I owe you half a dozen apologies. Please give me a plenary indulgence." Sometimes they were self-deprecating: "Your letter haunts me. But I've got a pretty tough conscience. So I was able to hold out until this afternoon, when an unclaimed hour clamors to be used the way it should. So my lazier self has capitulated to my better self, and the letter to friend Paul is in the making." Sometimes they bordered on the abject: "Being a Christian, I shall not remind you that patience is a virtue, even if expended on one who does not deserve that it be expended on him. In other words, I'm sorry."[21]

Creative apologies generally prefaced correspondence with his friends as well. To Martin Hellriegel, who affectionately addressed Godfrey as "Father Pax Dei," a play on his name, Godfrey responded:

> I blush to write to you at this late date. In monastic language, "What culpa can I make for my remissness?" Father Abbot has more than once chided me about my failure to keep up with correspondence. Briefly, I am ashamed of myself, and wish I could make some atonement. But I know that you know that my failure to write is not due to unconcern for a revered and beloved elder brother.[22]

It may well have been the mounting letters, often filled with liturgical queries, that first planted the idea of enlisting the services of Fred McManus for a regular column in *Orate Fratres*. Godfrey certainly recognized the need for a more life-giving interpretation of liturgical legislation. Too many people, in Godfrey's view, saw liturgy merely as rubrics. Canon law was in the driver's seat.

In 1958 Godfrey introduced his readers to Father Frederick R. McManus, a young Boston canon lawyer. "Fred had a great ability to stretch the laws insofar as required by the demands of life. No other magazine offered anything like his monthly 'Responses.' I was so proud of them."[23] The publication of McManus's *Rites of Holy Week* had already demonstrated that rubrics are meant to serve a more profound pastoral-liturgical end. Nevertheless, Godfrey decided to guarantee Fred's orthodoxy to his readers: "The fact that he teaches canon law in the Boston major seminary should help to reassure any who incline to suspect 'liturgical reformers' of trying to get around the law or of twisting it to suit their own purposes. His column will be both canonically safe and pastorally sound."[24]

Now liturgical conundrums (e.g., "May religious women in the light of the new Instruction read the Epistle and Gospel for Masses in their own chapels used exclusively for themselves, their novices, etc.?"[25]) could be referred to a canonical expert. Thus began a deep and lasting friendship between Godfrey and Fred, marked from the beginning by mutual respect and deference.

While Godfrey may not have changed the editorial thrust appreciably, he did become involved in changing the name of *Orate Fratres* when, in its twenty-fifth year, it was so obviously incongruous that a magazine with a Latin name was in the forefront of promoting vernacular worship. The name *Worship* was selected from among more than eight hundred suggestions that came from places as distant as Pakistan, Wales, and South Africa.

The shift from *Orate Fratres* to *Worship* was the occasion for a certain amount of misunderstanding—and a few canceled subscriptions, partially because "worship" was thought to be a Protestant term, partially because the whole question of the vernacular could make normally mild-mannered people fanatical in their support of it or violent in their opposition. One reader even suspected a feminist plot:

> To the Editor: Don't change the name. That's not the trouble—make your articles factual and realistic instead of dreamy and wishy washy. Emphasize the Latin—leave the women and the vernacular alone— they are not and should not be in the picture.

To which Godfrey responded, tongue in cheek:

> We include this communication, not because it is necessarily representative of the many letters we have received on the subject (about evenly pro and con), but because its forthright advice somehow recalls the similarly outspoken advice which John Cassian of old gave his monks: Diligently avoid all women and bishops, because women try to seduce you, and bishops try to lay hands on you![26]

In Godfrey's twenty-five years as editor, he had a knack for anticipating new movements and new needs. In 1955 Mother Kathryn Sullivan, R.S.C.J., a brilliant, self-taught Scripture scholar was invited to provide a series of commentaries on the Hebrew Scriptures. As rationale for this innovation, Godfrey wrote: "The Church's liturgy consists largely of Scripture; and it is in the liturgy, above all, that the Church presents the Scripture as the life-giving word of God to all her children, and tells us how she understands it."[27] Kathryn Sullivan's articles were so well received that two years later a Scripture section became a regular feature of *Worship,* first prepared by

Frederick R. McManus

Gerard S. Sloyan

Barnabas M. Ahern

Mother Kathryn Sullivan

120

Kilian McDonnell, O.S.B., and later by Barnabas Ahern, C.P. This section was discontinued after the birth of *The Bible Today,* for which Godfrey claims at least partial midwifery.

In place of Scripture a new feature was begun, a section devoted to catechetics and liturgy under the direction of Gerard Sloyan, then director of the program in Religious Education at the Catholic University of America. Though reluctant to accept yet another commitment, Sloyan agreed after receiving a particularly impassioned letter from Godfrey, which concluded that "there was vigorous and unanimous agreement that the one man in the country who could direct such a section is yourself . . . please forgive me for dogging your holy heels but I really see no other solution that would be satisfactory."[28] Catechetics was less an addition to *Worship* than a highlighting of that which had been of perennial concern: the necessity of a firm catechetical foundation for genuine liturgical renewal. This need was addressed explicitly in the pages of *Worship* until the appearance of a new publication, *The Living Light,* obviated the need for this regular *Worship* feature.

A lasting legacy of Godfrey's editorial decision-making was the selection in 1950 of Frank Kacmarcik as the designer of covers, typography, and graphics for the magazine. Kacmarcik vividly remembers his first cover design for *Orate Fratres,* a depiction of Isaiah that was "both daring and extremely controversial at that time. The shape of the foot, for example, was a point of highly emotional discussion, as were the length of the fingers, the shape of the head and the nose, and other critical matters. It was all under the rubric of a notion of symbolism that had us all in its throes at the time."[29]

The relationship between Godfrey and his cover artist was rarely smooth. Godfrey did go to bat for Kacmarcik when the latter was relieved of his teaching duties at St. John's in 1954. Together with a number of other influential monks, Godfrey wrote a letter to Abbot Baldwin Dworschak opposing the decision to terminate the professor of art. On the other hand, some of Kacmarcik's early designs were controversial, and Godfrey took much of the heat. Sometimes Godfrey opposed Kacmarcik's work, according to the artist, because Godfrey wanted no dispute with bishops, lest his influence in the liturgical renewal be endangered. Between editor and artist there was an uneasy alliance at best.[30]

Toward the end of his tenure as editor, Godfrey anticipated the future direction of *Worship*. Writing to Abbot Baldwin in 1957, he stated:

> Research and popular liturgical writing are not incompatible. It is precisely the great scholars, such as Bernard Botte, Capelle, Bouyer, etc., who write the most effective articles of a "practical" nature. . . . A good "shot in the arm" of articles of a somewhat more substantial content would be a godsend; or perhaps we could publish 2 issues a year devoted for the most part to more scholarly material. . . . It is high time such research take place, and that America begin to make its contribution *in depth* to the liturgical movement of our times should scarcely need proof.[31]

After the promulgation of Vatican II's Constitution on the Sacred Liturgy, *Worship,* once *the* house organ of the North American liturgical movement, was supplemented by columns in diocesan papers, pastorally oriented magazines, newsletters, and numerous books devoted to spelling out in detail the implications of the Constitution for pastoral practice. Aelred Tegels, O.S.B., its next editor, described the thinking behind *Worship's* transition at this juncture:

> How should the role of *Worship* be conceived in this new situation? Since it would be assumed that new periodicals would, for the most part, take a concretely pastoral approach to problems of liturgical renewal, we concluded that *Worship* could serve the cause most effectively by concentrating largely on a basically theoretic—yet pastorally very concerned—approach to the problems of renewal, thus becoming, in some measure, the more scholarly review that Dom Virgil had foreseen.[32]

Godfrey's editorial efforts from 1938 to 1963 are captured well in his own words:

> For 30 years *Worship* has been promoting the liturgical apostolate. The liturgical movement connotes various things to various people. But the editors of *Worship* and its international group of associate editors have consistently interpreted it to mean: the theology of the sacraments (the Eucharist above all) applied in practice to the spiritual life. We have stressed the essentials: praying and living with the Church, for the greater honor of God. And we haven't neglected the relevance of this to the whole field of social action.[33]

Thus Godfrey provides a summary of his work as editor of *Orate Fratres/Worship* and at the same time offers an amazingly succinct definition of the liturgical movement this journal served so well as "house organ."

During Godfrey's tenure as editor, the liturgical movement was rapidly coming to full term in the United States, but not without enormous effort, the contributions of many, and the tenacity of a vision that continued to capture imaginations and hearts. The movement prospered, in part, because it did not exist in a vacuum but acted as a kind of fulcrum, or a point of convergence, between two other great movements of the early twentieth century.[34] These *three* simultaneous movements in the Church—the biblical, the liturgical, and the social—were all the stronger for the presence of the others, each movement advancing because in dialogue with the others. The *biblical movement* developed and expounded the Pauline doctrine of the Mystical Body of Christ. The *liturgical movement* flowed out of this theological vision, and thus called for more active participation in the liturgy of the Mystical Body of Christ. The *social movement* urged participation in the apostolate of the Mystical Body of Christ. Perhaps more appropriately, these three movements might be regarded as three streams flowing from the same source.

The liturgical movement prospered because of the compelling simplicity of its mission—that the liturgy become the directing principle of our lives—and because of a series of gatherings that brought people of similar vision together to experience strength in numbers, to study and pray in common, and to celebrate a movement coming of age. The first such liturgical gatherings took place while Godfrey was still in Europe—one-day conventions held first at St. John's and then in St. Cloud. These were modest harbingers of the Liturgical Weeks that began in 1940 and were, for the next several years, under the aegis of the Benedictine Liturgical Conference.

Dom Damasus Winzen, O.S.B., Godfrey's former classmate and later expatriate German monk of Maria Laach, who taught at Immaculate Conception Seminary in New Jersey, was influential in stimulating interest among the American Benedictines for this sponsorship. In 1939 Winzen assembled about a dozen young Benedictine monks, Godfrey among them, mostly friends who had met one another during their studies at, or visits to, Maria Laach. The gathering, which took place at the Convent of the Sacred Heart in Grosse Pointe, Michigan, was simply a study group of like-minded spirits, reviving among themselves the camaraderie of those who possess the "Laacher pneuma." A second meeting, held in Cincinnati in tandem with the Confraternity of Christian Doctrine conference, gave some clarity and direction to Winzen's dream, namely, to establish Benedictine Liturgical Weeks modeled on the well-known and highly popular *Semaines Liturgiques* held annually at Louvain, Belgium, under the auspices of the famous Abbey of Mont César. "Who better than the Benedictines," he asked, "to start a parallel conference in the United States?"[35] Thus was born the Benedictine Liturgical Conference as the Liturgical Week's national sponsoring body.

The purpose of the first Liturgical Week, as spelled out by Winzen and his friends, and later refined in a planning session in Chicago, was twofold:

> a) To provide a common forum which the various liturgical leaders throughout the country may attend, and at which they may discuss their various problems for the purpose of achieving coordination of effort and refinement of method towards the accomplishment of their goal.

> b) To focus the interest of liturgical leaders, of priests and religious generally, and of as many of the local clergy and laity as possible, upon one fundamental liturgical theme, viz., "The Living Parish: active and intelligent participation of the laity in the liturgy as members of a parish." Thus limited, the discussions at the Liturgical Week can not, it is admitted, touch directly upon all liturgical problems of current interest. . . . However, if the present national gathering proves successful, steps could easily be taken to make it an annual affair, at which other important problems could be successively taken up.[36]

The meeting was more than "successful." It was a watershed event for those who assembled in Holy Name Cathedral, Chicago, October 21–25, 1940. Samuel A. Stritch, then archbishop of Chicago, was delighted to serve as patron for a week of serious liturgical study and worthwhile liturgical functions. He also welcomed the opportunity "to correct the faults of many who are confusing the Liturgical Movement with Liturgical Archeology."[37]

The Liturgical Week enabled people from all over the States to come together for the first time, to pray in common, to probe issues

Cincinnati Liturgical Week, 1958

Beginning of the Benedictine Liturgical Conference

Preparing for a Liturgical Week in Martin Hellriegel's rectory: Hillenbrand, O'Connell, Busch, Laukemper, Carroll, Hellriegel (standing), Sheehan, Schmidt, Sause, Diekmann, Stack (back to camera)

125

of mutual concern, to view and learn from the demonstration of various rites, to meet firsthand those whose articles and columns they had read, to reminisce about Virgil Michel, who had died only two years earlier, and to start to form deep and lasting friendships with like-minded "liturgists" and "vernacularists"!

During the Chicago Liturgical Week, Godfrey was one of the featured speakers; his topic was "Initiation into Christian Life and Worship Through Baptism." The famous Godfrey speaking style was already evident in this address: a vision of sacramental life solidly grounded in patristic sources, always oriented to the Church's pastoral life and always delivered with such dynamism and conviction that his hearers became captivated by his point of view.

In this address on baptism, Godfrey developed its essentially social significance, citing St. Paul, Justin, Tertullian, Cyril, Thomas Aquinas, and others to bolster his position, examining the etymology of terms such as "christening" to uncover deeper meanings in the familiar, situating his subject in the history of liturgical practices, and then advocating concrete parochial steps toward liturgical renewal.

In that speech fifty years ago, Godfrey urged the renewal of baptismal promises on Easter, the recovery of the baptismal significance of the sprinkling rite, parochial celebrations of baptism on Sundays, rediscovery of the baptismal significance of the Creed and the Our Father, and a focus on the baptistry throughout Eastertide to arouse a baptismal consciousness especially during that season. Except, perhaps, for the suggestion that the young ladies of the parish might decorate the baptistry, this address is thoroughly contemporary.[38]

Twelve hundred sixty persons attended that first Liturgical Week in Chicago, among them most of the pioneers of the American liturgical movement. H.A.R. was there, of course, and later wrote about the event:

> I am firmly convinced that the Liturgical Week in Chicago was the beginning of a new era in American Catholicism. Not many know about it and only a few appreciate its significance. But the very fact that from all over the country layfolk and priests, secular and religious came together, not to show off, not to dine and wine, not to talk big words and pass thundering resolutions, not to impress by numbers, but to find themselves laden with responsibility, rich with spiritual wealth, filled with the spirit of Christ's victory, concerned with the

true things of God, this very fact is significant. We have finally returned to the means with which twelve apostles and a martyred Church conquered the world.[39]

When asked who were the most influential in those early days of the Liturgical Weeks throughout the forties, Godfrey singled out H.A.R., Martin Hellriegel, Reynold Hillenbrand, William Busch, Gerald Ellard, and Michael Mathis. Indeed, each of these men played a major role in the American liturgical movement.

Martin Hellriegel was the obvious person to address the Chicago week on the topic "The Meaning of the Parish in Practice," for he was not a theologian but a pastor, first for twenty-two years with the Precious Blood Sisters in O'Fallon, Missouri, and then for nearly forty years at Holy Cross Parish in St. Louis. Both places were models of pastoral liturgical practice. Hellriegel was the American counterpart of the Austrian Pius Parsch. He was interested in popular piety, in parish and family piety, in devotional piety—perhaps occasionally to excess! It was said of him that almost every day he had a new devotion, a new saint, a new practice—and he loved ceremony![40]

Hellriegel was a towering and impressive figure, a man of faith and enthusiasm, a genial host who attracted people to himself; he was a very warm friend and noted for his hospitality. A good number of the early Liturgical Weeks, in fact, were planned in his living room, though he never became president of the Liturgical Conference because he did not have the requisite practical gifts. He wrote over a hundred articles for *Orate Fratres,* and he had a wonderful way of playing with words; yet he was less known for his writings than for his pastoral sense and his integrity. People made pilgrimages to St. Louis just to be part of the Sunday Eucharist in Hellriegel's parish, known across the nation as a place where people prayed well.

Reynold Hillenbrand, a priest of Chicago, taught at the preparatory seminary and later became rector of Mundelein Seminary. He was a man immersed in Catholic social action. Hillenbrand was not a theologian, nor was he willing to call himself an academic, yet he *was* an expert on papal encyclicals—interesting when one considers that the most outstanding encyclicals of modern times have been the social encyclicals, together with *Mystici Corporis* and *Mediator Dei.* It has been said that "all activist Catholics invoked the social encyclicals as a kind of talisman, often without understanding them, but the

H. A. Reinhold

Martin Hellriegel

Reynold Hillenbrand

William Busch

Gerald Ellard

Michael Mathis

scholarly rector at St. Mary of the Lake actually read, studied, and patterned his social goals on the popes' letters."[41]

It was by these encyclicals above all that Hillenbrand was inspired, and he had an uncanny way of inspiring others. At the seminary he introduced Theology for Catholic Action under the guise of instruction in the liturgy. He was convinced that Christians would gain strength for Catholic Action by participating in the liturgy. Hillenbrand had the wonderful twin gifts of charm and humility. He was considered a prize by his colleagues and was much loved by the scores of priests he taught. At the first Liturgy Week, Hillenbrand played the role of genial host as well as keynote speaker. In his opening address, he suggested one more reason why the liturgical movement was taking root in 1940:

> We might not be as far as we are except for the last sobering decade—with its disillusionment; with its struggle, its suffering; with its revelation of hard realities, too easily overlooked; with its mounting feeling of the necessity of reconstructing this poor, sorry world—of the necessity of a profound renewal of the Christian spirit—of the necessity of a deep appreciation and intensification of our Christian heritage, which is the God-life in us; with its sense of futility in the old trumpetings; with its disclosure of the ineffectiveness of the old emphases.[42]

Hillenbrand, Hellriegel, Reinhold, Diekmann—is it any wonder that some people thought the liturgical movement was a German invasion? And actually there was another German-American of note at that first Week—William Busch, called "Billy" by his friends, a priest who taught at the St. Paul Seminary. Busch was called the elder statesman among these figures, having been an advisor to Virgil Michel. Busch's role in the liturgical movement was that of "translator," not only as an educator but primarily because he put the works of theologians such as Parsch, Pinsk, Klauser, Kramp, and Herwegen into English, making some of the best of European scholarship available on this side of the Atlantic. It was appropriate that besides delivering an address in Chicago, Busch was asked to set up the only display allowed by the organizers, an exhibition of books and pamphlets.

Though Busch's classes in Church history tended to be dry, students would get him off onto the topic of liturgy, where he was absolutely inspiring. Outside the classroom he had a wry sense of humor, a real wit. Once, for example, he declared that the preposition is the most difficult part of speech in our language: "Our rector," he said, "thinks that we're all *behind* him. Actually, we're all *after* him." Billy Busch was an early leader who became a bit disoriented when the liturgical movement started to move too fast for him.

While not a German, Gerald Ellard was another historian by trade whose specialty was historical liturgy. Sometimes called "Liturgerry" by his students, Ellard was enormously respected by his peers, who were, as Godfrey recalls, "very proud of him because he was the one real scholar in our midst."[43] Ellard was an associate editor of, and steady contributor to, *Orate Fratres,* and the author of pamphlets for the Popular Liturgical Library of the Liturgical Press. He was also a frequent speaker at National Liturgical Weeks, valued from the very beginning for the solid historical framework he contributed to each "theme." At his death *Worship* magazine called him a kind and gentle human being marked by mildness and meekness, and it gave him the highest accolade, stating that "to many Ellard was a symbol, a symbol of liturgical life and growth."[44]

Another of the pioneers was Michael Mathis, a man of enormous charm, a Holy Cross priest at Notre Dame, late on the liturgical scene, since his early training was in biblical studies and in missiology. But it was Mathis who, in 1947, established the Notre Dame summer sessions in liturgy, which grew into the premier graduate program in liturgy in this country. What he contributed by establishing this program was the scientific and academic underpinning of the liturgical movement in the United States. Besides, he was a genuinely fine man, dedicated to God, completely generous with people. A lovely phrase was used of him by Godfrey, namely, that he was committed to "hospitable pastoral care." By all assessments people delighted to call Mathis their friend.

There were, of course, other figures who were part of the Liturgical Weeks and the growing circle of friends drawn together by their common interest in the liturgy: Ermin Vitry, a displaced monk, eccentric as could be, who would get up and play the piano at 2 A.M. but wrote wonderful pieces on music and liturgy for *Orate Fratres* and was the author of a book implausibly titled *Being at Ease with the Liber Usualis;* Monsignor Joseph Stedman, author of a missal that sold over fifteen million copies; Thomas Carroll, Bill Leonard, and Shawn Shee-han, all priests from Boston who played significant roles in the Liturgical Weeks of the forties and fifties, and who were committed to expanding the scope of the movement beyond its monastic origins and early predilections; Joseph P. Morrison, rector at Holy Name Cathedral in Chicago, site of the first Liturgical Week, a powerhouse, a practical man, a genius at public relations; Bernard Laukemper, another Chicago priest, in whose rectory basement the Liturgical Conference was born; and, of course, bishops such as Edwin O'Hara, Vincent Waters, Paul Hallinan, Karl Alter, Victor Reed, Leo Dwor-schak, and Charles Buswell—all of them champions of the liturgical apostolate.

But what of the women and the laity in general? Did they have a role in the liturgical movement and the Liturgical Weeks that it spawned? It is interesting to note that Virgil Michel had been sensitive to this question. The first editorial board that Michel assembled for *Orate Fratres* included two laypersons: Donald Attwater of Great Britain, an expert on Eastern Churches and liturgies, and Justine Ward, founder and benefactor of the Pius X School of Liturgical Music at Manhattanville College of the Sacred Heart.[45]

But the liturgical movement after Virgil Michel was sometimes inbred, often clerical, and, for a number of years, solidly monastic. There were scarcely any laypersons in evidence, though we can identify a few. Ade Bethune, for example, East Coast artist most famous for her stylized woodcuts, stumbled into liturgy through her contact with Dorothy Day. Ade was at the Catholic Worker in New York when Father Daniel Lord offered Dorothy Day one scholarship for his Summer School of Catholic Action. Dorothy sent Ade, who there met and studied under Gerald Ellard and became captivated by the liturgy. Maurice Lavanoux was a layman who launched the Liturgical Arts Society and worked with architects, artists, and pastors, teaching them that in producing churches "the material fabric must always subserve that 'Church which is His Body' gathered here to worship corporately within its walls.''[46] There were Dr. and Mrs. Alfred Berger of Cincinnati, who anticipated *N.C.R.* cassettes by several decades, recording liturgical conferences and spreading the "liturgical word" far and wide through their Tape-of-the-Month Club. Therese Mueller, a lesser-known pioneer, wrote *Family Life in Christ* and *Our Children's*

Year of Grace. Gertrud Mueller Nelson, a frequent national speaker today, learned well from her mother about the relationship between worship and family prayer. Then there was Mary Perkins Ryan, a member of the planning committee and a speaker for many Liturgical Weeks, as well as an author of *Speaking of How to Pray,* which was a fine synthesis of doctrine.

Perhaps Mary Perkins Ryan's intervention at the Liturgical Week of 1940 suggests some of the hesitation behind lay participation in the liturgical movement:

> I was once on a train and thought it was a nice day to read the breviary, so I pulled out my little black book and went to work. I didn't mind the conductor collecting the ticket. I know he didn't know what I was doing. And I didn't mind a couple of people who came and sat next to me. But then in the door came a priest and, with one reflex action, I found I was sitting on the breviary and reading a copy of the *Saturday Evening Post.* I wondered for some time why I had done that; now I realize that it was because I was afraid the good Father would think I was pious. . . . There is nothing we are more afraid of.[47]

By 1943 the Benedictines withdrew from sponsorship of the Liturgical Weeks, although not without an internal struggle. Abbot Alcuin Deutsch of St. John's and Abbot Columban Thuis of St. Joseph's Abbey in St. Benedict, Louisiana, had served as president and vice-president respectively, acting in the names of the American Cassinese Congregation of Benedictines [Abbot Alcuin] and the Swiss-American Congregation of Benedictines [Abbot Columban]. After three years Abbot Alcuin insisted that the arrangement of rotating Benedictine presidents be stopped and the organization be given to the larger Church, where he believed it belonged; but Alcuin had a hard time convincing Columban that this should no longer be a Benedictine organization. Columban was a dear friend of the secretary of the Benedictine Liturgical Conference, Father Michael Ducey, O.S.B. Ducey was aloof, sometimes scheming, a man obsessed with the monastic nature of the liturgical movement and disgruntled at the thought of lay incursions into a monastic preserve.

Michael Ducey, in fact, decided to make a new Benedictine foundation devoted exclusively to God's praises through the liturgy and the work of the liturgical apostolate. He was an uninspiring sort of man, yet possessed with "founding fever," unhappy unless he could become a superior. In October 1948 Ducey wrote to prospective members who, in his judgment, had assured him of their interest.[48] Godfrey, to his utter amazement, was a recipient of one of Ducey's letters. He responded:

> Thanks for your flattering invitation. But I shall be brutally frank at the very outset and state that I have not now, nor ever did have, the slightest intention of leaving St. John's and joining your prospective monastery. And I am certain that never, in any of our correspondence or conversations, did I give you any reason to believe that I entertained any such intention, certainly not consciously. If you received a contrary impression, I am sorry; but I can truthfully say that I don't believe I was responsible for any such impression given. *Quidquid recipitur.* . . . If I discussed your plans with you on occasion in a friendly manner, that is *toto caelo* different from manifesting any intention of identifying oneself personally with them.
>
> There: I have said it as strongly and clearly as I could, lest there be any further misunderstanding. I admire your idealism, and wish you well with your project,—although I am not optimistic about its fulfilment, if for no other than canonical reasons: transference from one Congregation to another, etc. But that is in God's hands—and in those of the Sacred Congregation of Religious.
>
> Father Paschal [Botz] came to my room a short while ago, and he was equally astonished at having received such a communication from you. I trust your hopes about other "prospective members" are not based on equally unsubstantial grounds.[49]

Not enough "prospective members" came to light, and Ducey's dream fizzled.

Meanwhile, the Benedictine Liturgical Conference was quietly superseded by the Liturgical Conference in 1943. According to its new constitution and by-laws, the primary objective of the Liturgical Conference was "to continue to organize an annual nationally representative Liturgical Week, and to promote other means of liturgical action in the United States."[50] Godfrey was elected to a three-year term on the executive committee and remained an active board member and participant in the planning of the Weeks until the mid-sixties. Always more prized than his board work, however, were his talks. According to Shawn Sheehan,

Every local conference wanted Godfrey as a speaker. His enthusiasm came across. During the Liturgical Weeks, the organizers would often sit out some of the talks and gather for their own discussions and consultations. Billy Busch would always say, when it was time for Godfrey's presentation, "Let's go hear Godfrey." Godfrey was dynamic and usually had a fresh approach to things. He represented the essence of what the liturgical renewal was—which people by and large still don't understand. Godfrey brought together theology and spirituality and real, personal religion, and showed how all that is expressed when liturgy is properly appreciated.[51]

The Benedictines had provided generous financial support for the conference. After their sponsorship was withdrawn, annual dues from active members were the only means of subsidizing this shoestring operation over the next several decades. For years the office of the Liturgical Conference coincided with the location of the secretary's office supplies; rectory living rooms generally accommodated its board meetings; speakers waived gratuities—minor inconveniences at best, since those who gathered for the planning of the Liturgical Weeks and for the events themselves thought of one another less as professional colleagues than as personal friends. They enjoyed one another's company, looked after one another in moments of need, kept in touch by letters, visited one another in times of sickness, and preached at one another's anniversaries.

Stories abound to illustrate their close personal ties:

Shawn Sheehan and Tom Carroll were best of friends. A few months after Tom Carroll died, Godfrey sent a note saying he knew that Shawn must be very sad and lonely. Shawn was very touched and thought the note typical of Godfrey. He adds that it was also typical of Godfrey to forget that he had done this and a month or so later to write a similar note.[52]

When Reynold Hillenbrand was hospitalized, Godfrey wrote to his abbot asking permission to accompany H.A.R. and Donald Attwater, who were driving across country, as far as Tulsa to visit "Reynie":

> You may recall that he was in a serious auto accident in February, near Tulsa. He is now in his third complete cast, and not showing improvement. Can only move his head. I think it would be an act of charity that would be deeply appreciated by him (we have been quite intimate friends for a number of years).[53]

Friendship was extended in good times and bad. When H.A.R. ran afoul of his bishop in Yakima, Washington, a misunderstanding that threatened Reinhold's canonical status, St. Cloud bishop Peter Bartholome pressured Abbot Dworschak to drop him as an associate editor of *Worship* and to take H.A.R.'s name off the masthead. Bartholome suggested rather menacingly that continuing to accept articles and to list H.A.R. on the masthead "is actually causing harm to the liturgical movement since it becomes suspect in the eyes of the Bishops of the country."[54] After enlisting Fred McManus in the discussion, and securing a favorable canonical opinion from him about H.A.R.'s situation, Godfrey responded to his abbot:

> As I see the matter now, it would seem a serious injustice to Father Reinhold (if he is in fact canonically justified in his present position) to drop him as an Associate Editor or to refuse printing his articles. It would certainly create an international sensation. And why should *Worship*, which Father Reinhold has helped so much, be expected to throw the first stone?[55]

Godfrey's solution: no longer to list *any* of the associate editors! Several years later, when H.A.R.'s situation was finally straightened out, he sent a telegram to Godfrey: "Put us all back on the masthead."[56]

There were also lighter moments. Shawn Sheehan, for example, likes to tell the story of a meeting in the late forties when Godfrey was rooming with Tom Carroll, then president of the Liturgical Conference. Tom was a great snorer, so early one morning Godfrey arose, placed a tape recorder near Tom's bed, turned it on, and quietly said, "The next voice you hear will be that of the president of the Liturgical Conference." Later in the day, during the middle of an executive board meeting, Godfrey played what he had recorded to great roars of laughter.[57]

The number of liturgical pioneers was relatively small. It is not surprising that the same names regularly crop up as speakers, at summer schools, on boards, and in print as new initiatives were undertaken by one or other of their friends.

An interesting enterprise in the waning days of the thirties was *Liturgy and Sociology,* a magazine that never got off the ground, despite first-rate authors and an interesting concept, because of the unworldly ways of its editors, Dorothy and Tom Coddington. Its doom might have been predicted from the beginning. The Coddingtons had hosted a ten-day institute on liturgy and sociology in the Berkshires but had neglected to arrange for beds, bathing facilities, or even food for any of the participants—Godfrey among them. More successful were other journals that joined *Orate Fratres* [1926] in providing broad liturgical education: *Liturgical Arts* [1931], *Altar and Home* [1934], *Catholic Art Quarterly* [1937], and *Living Parish* [1940].

A variety of educational programs and summer courses also played a significant role in developing liturgical consciousness. The forerunner, of course, was the Pius X School of Liturgical Music at Manhattanville College of the Sacred Heart, co-founded by Mother Georgia Stevens, R.S.C.J., and Mrs. Justine Ward in 1916. The Pius X School was a place where organists, choir directors, and other musicians participated in the restoration of sung prayer in the liturgy under the delightful direction of Mother Stevens, a woman whose very presence could produce a "mirthquake."

In 1941 Reynold Hillenbrand organized a liturgical summer school for priests at St. Mary of the Lake, Chicago. His staff included his friends Busch, Ellard, Diekmann, Hellriegel, and Reinhold. In 1942 the Catholic Choirmasters' Correspondence Course (the name was later changed to the Gregorian Institute) was begun by a layman, Clifford Bennett. The CCCC offered correspondence courses, records, degrees, and certificates. Godfrey spent that summer in Washington teaching courses in Eucharist and sacraments for the first time at the Catholic University of America, making "a splendid impression"[58] and beginning an association that continued into the eighties.

While Godfrey was at the Catholic University, Abbot Alcuin took the opportunity to send him some advice about teaching:

> I am happy that your classes have been progressing well during the first two weeks of the course, and I am confident that you will not muff the chance of inspiring both your large [fifty] and your small [ten] class with a deep and abiding love for your holy religion. For it is not necessary that you make any effort to inspire them—your own love and appreciation of the liturgy and our religion will naturally flow over onto the students without any particular effort on your part. In fact, an effort to be inspiring sometimes has the opposite effect.[59]

In 1945 Sister Mary Madeleva, C.S.C., began her School of Sacred Theology for women at St. Mary's, Notre Dame, the first school of its kind in the country. The Ladies of the Grail also fostered a variety of courses during the forties, and Godfrey was a frequent lecturer at Loveland, Ohio, and other sites, though he sometimes found the pace exhausting:

> The end of the first day at Grailville. They're nice people, surely; but they do expect a person to produce, i.e., to shake "inspiration" out of one's sleeve at a moment's notice, at least six times a day, besides the regularly scheduled conferences.[60]

The Ladies of the Grail were very active in promoting a lay spirituality rooted in the liturgy, particularly in the Mass and the Divine Office. They also published a variety of liturgical materials, perhaps the most widely acclaimed of which was their book *Restoring the Sunday.*

In a way, each of these enterprises paved the way for Michael Mathis's dream of a full-blown Liturgical Summer School, which was finally realized in the summer of 1947. Mathis invited Godfrey to participate in that first Notre Dame program with a typically gracious letter: "By reason of your contribution to the liturgical movement, quite apart from my own personal high esteem of you, I feel sure that you are not only qualified to teach on this program, but that you will add grace to our professorial staff."[61]

Godfrey took his place alongside Reinhold, Hillenbrand, Laukemper, Winzen, and Ellard during that first Notre Dame summer. His topic was "The Christian Way of Life—The Sacramental Way." Students were offered an exceptional array of courses: History of Liturgy in the Latin Rite, Theory and Practice of Chant, Liturgical Places, Liturgy and Catholic Action, Stational Churches and Lenten Masses, The Ecclesiastical Year, Scripture Background for the Ecclesiastical Year, Aims and Objects of the Liturgical Movement, and A Layman Looks at Liturgy. This latter course may appear prophetic. Yet there was a certain ferment in the forties for a genuine lay theology, an issue that John Courtney Murray had addressed in the pages of *Theological Studies* in 1944.

Tuition at Notre Dame was ten dollars per semester hour. Faculty received twenty dollars per day for lecturing, plus train fare, room and board—modest remuneration, but as Mathis pointed out, "It is impossible fully to pay for things of the spirit by mere money."[62]

The summer school at Notre Dame combined theory and practice—that was the genius of Michael Mathis, who designed a program not only for learning but also for liturgical living. According

to a press release: "The practical side of the program will be woven
into the order of the day by liturgical functions and their explanations in the light of the liturgical lesson of the day."[64] Indeed it was,
with gusto!

5:30 A.M.	Lauds sung, preceded by five minutes instruction by the liturgy lecturer of the week.
6:00 A.M.	Missa Cantata with a homily by the lecturer of the week.
8:45 A.M.	Terce in lecture room, preceded by ten minutes of instruction for Terce and Sext by lecturer of the week.
9:10 to 10:10 A.M.	Lecture on the History of the Sacred Liturgy.
10:20 to 11:20 A.M.	Lecture on some Important Feature of Liturgy other than History or Rubrics.
11:30 to 12:15 P.M.	Plain Chant.
12:15 to 12:30 P.M.	Sext in lecture room.
4:30 to 5:00 P.M.	None and Vespers, preceded by five minutes instruction by Father Mathis, C.S.C.
5:00 to 5:50 P.M.	Preparation for Matins for the following day by Father Mathis, if such is not already published.
5:00 to 5:50 P.M.	Informal discussion on liturgy once a week, on Wednesdays.
6:30 P.M.	Compline in chapel.[64]

From fairly modest beginnings, the Notre Dame summer sessions
grew rapidly. The rigors of the program were actually attractive; the
lecturers were excellent. Godfrey returned in 1948 and several summers thereafter, delighted and flattered to be associated in the same
program and on the same campus with men like Josef Jungmann,
Jean Daniélou, Boniface Luykx, Johannes Hofinger, Donald Attwater,
Clifford Howell, and Louis Bouyer. In the summer of 1949 he decided
to sit in on Jungmann's classes and later gave this assessment:

> Fr. Jungmann's course is splendid. He is not only one of the greatest
> scholars in the field, but he has the genius of integrating a wealth of
> details into meaningful patterns, and above all, of showing the rele-
> vance of the spiritual life. He is handicapped by poor knowledge of
> English: all he does is read his translated lectures. And that can be
> trying at times. But he is such an attractive personality. He radiates
> such humility and simplicity that most people in class are quite will-
> ing to make allowances.[65]

Godfrey's assessments of his colleagues were characteristically generous: Donald Attwater's classes were among the most popular on campus. Clifford Howell did a "bang-up job!" Louis Bouyer reminded Godfrey of his friend Tertullian—a powerful orator who could move and persuade, though his listeners were never quite sure which side of an issue he would take, and always needed to know against whom he was arguing.[66] During those summers Godfrey developed friendships with scholars he would meet again at international liturgical meetings during the fifties. Meanwhile, on the East Coast, another summer program was launched the same year the Notre Dame program began. Boston College was the site of a Social Worship School, which featured many of the same topics as did Notre Dame and occasionally the same lecturers, although Godfrey never participated in the Boston College sessions.

There were yet other educative enterprises in those days. At the time of his death, Virgil Michel, in collaboration with Sister Jane Marie and the Marywood Dominicans of Grand Rapids, had been in the midst of preparing catechetical materials for grade school children. The *Christ-Life Series* was incomparably superior to previous grade-school religion primers, providing a solid liturgical foundation for teaching the mysteries of the faith. Godfrey continued in a somewhat haphazard fashion as a consultant to this project during the forties, stopping off in Grand Rapids in the midst of other travel as Sister Jane Marie and her Dominican collaborators developed the *Christian Religion Series* for the high school years. At the same time college students were offered a grounding in liturgy through Gerald Ellard's series of texts: *Christian Life and Worship* [1933], *Men at Work at Worship* [1940], and *The Dialog Mass* [1942], all of which went through several editions.

Across the country a deeper sensitivity to liturgy was further promoted by the publication of Monsignor Joseph Stedman's *My Sunday Missal* [1932], sometimes known as the "Stedman (You-Can't-Get-Lost) Missal," which was an instant success and went through numerous reprintings. By 1940 the *Leaflet Missal* was also being sold in great quantities, with the happy result that "there were missals, missals everywhere—and also people who knew how to handle them."[67]

The liturgical pioneers were involved in other associations of a more political nature, the Vernacular Society chief among them. The

Vernacular Society was founded by H.A.R. in 1946. Its president for a good number of years was Monsignor Joseph Morrison of Chicago; its secretary was Colonel John K. Ross-Duggan, who came to be called "Mr. Vernacular" because of his total identification with his work. Ross-Duggan, a layman, retired from business to devote his energies to "the Cause." He founded and edited *Amen,* a magazine that promoted the vernacular, and he himself traveled the world over for the same purpose. Rarely diplomatic, the Colonel sometimes used strong-arm tactics and made himself a nuisance. He was an indefatigable lobbyist for an English liturgy, as were the Vernacular Society's more than ten thousand members he had gradually marshaled to "the Cause."

In many ways the vernacular became the liturgical movement's symbol for full, conscious, and active participation. The hope of the pioneers was modest at first: readings in English seemed reasonable, then some of the prayers said in common. But almost no one believed, even on the eve of Vatican II, that within the decade the Church's entire library of liturgical texts would be in the process of translation, a work to which Godfrey, former member of the Vernacular Society, devoted himself with great enthusiasm.

But that is to rush ahead of the story.

The forties were a time of incredible liturgical initiative and creativity, of education, of popularizing. During these days Abbot Alcuin acted as Godfrey's booking agent, sending him off to direct retreats, to give lectures, to teach at the Ursuline College in Louisville, Mount St. Scholastica in Atchison, and the Pius X School of Liturgical Music in Manhattan, besides regular stints at the Catholic University and Notre Dame. In a letter to his abbot we get an insight into what kept Godfrey going at such a breakneck pace: "Every time I have given one of these courses, I have been more impressed by the tragedy of all these good souls having been deprived for so many years of the basic understanding of what the Mass should be and mean in their spiritual lives."[68]

In 1946 Abbot Alcuin was asked by the National Center of the Confraternity of Christian Doctrine to appoint one of his priests to work toward the beatification and eventual canonization of Pope Pius X. The previous year Godfrey had prepared a paper on Pius X for a symposium;[69] who better, in Alcuin's view, to further the cause of

Pius X among the Benedictines? Godfrey happily took the challenge. It was Pius X, after all, who had rescued liturgists from the accusation of modernism and rescued liturgy from its identification with outward ceremonial. Promoting Pius X's cause was a way to repay the debt that all liturgists felt toward that Pope.

Years later, Godfrey reminisced about Pius X's influence:

> The chief obstacle to wider interest [in the liturgical movement] was the general conviction, learned in "liturgy" textbooks in the seminary, that liturgy meant rubrics. And why get excited about more, even if conceivably better, ceremonial? Such concerns could safely be left to monks. Worst of all, that understanding of liturgy was evidently shared by the hierarchy, not excluding those in the highest positions. We could cite no papal encouragement for the view that liturgy is "the life of the Church," the normal "school of Christian piety," apart from St. Pius X's declaration that "the first and indispensable source of the true Christian spirit is active and intelligent participation in the public worship of the Church" (Motu Proprio on Sacred Music). And how we clung to that statement, cited it times without number, and tried to "exploit" it in terms of its pastoral implications![70]

Pius X was beatified within five years and canonized in 1954.

One further assignment in the forties should be mentioned. For several years Godfrey served as a chaplain for prisoners of war, first for Italians and later for German soldiers. Italians captured in North Africa had been incarcerated in camps near Princeton, Minnesota. Every Sunday Godfrey celebrated Mass for them and delighted to converse with them in Italian. A large number, as he recalls, had relatives in the United States, but they were only vaguely aware of their whereabouts—"New York," for example, but whether city or state they did not know. Godfrey became a "one man Red Cross," writing scores of letters to Italian parishes around the country, helping to identify and contact relatives. A good number of grateful Italian soldiers stayed in touch with him when the war was over.

A less rewarding assignment was that of chaplain to the German prisoners of war held in four different camps in northern Minnesota. Each weekend Godfrey would take a bus as far as Ball Club, where an old Chevy was available for his use. Godfrey was a notoriously bad driver who had almost killed Abbot Alcuin and himself in a snowstorm and has subsequently driven only under duress. In this instance

Italian prisoners
of war
to whom
Godfrey
ministered
in 1944

duty called. From Ball Club he drove great distances on back roads and logging trails, getting stuck, praying to St. Anthony, moving on, trying to make it to at least three of the four camps each Sunday.

The laws of the Eucharistic fast were very strict in those days. It was after 4 P.M. on Sunday before he was able to break his fast. As an auxiliary military chaplain, he wrote to the Military Ordinariate requesting permission to drink water during the long Sunday fast—which permission was refused! Looking back, Godfrey muses, "And like a damn fool I complied!" Sunday after Sunday he had a fierce, constant headache until he could get some food.

Unlike the Italians, who flocked to Mass, the young Germans had been completely indoctrinated and remained Nazis to their fingertips. They were forbidden by their officers to have anything to do with outsiders. When Godfrey arrived at a camp, one of the higher officers would attach himself to Godfrey so that there would be no chance for anyone to go to confession. In two years' time only five or six men were able to sneak to confession, and twelve to fifteen men assembled for Mass on any Sunday. Once Godfrey asked a lieutenant how it was possible for these young men to remain so staunchly loyal to Hitler. He was informed, "They have to believe in someone."

142

These trips were hard, the work discouraging. Late Sunday night a bus deposited Godfrey about a mile and a half from the monastery, and he would hike back to St. John's between one and two in the morning, having covered about five hundred miles in the course of the weekend.[71]

Chaplain, teacher, speaker, organizer, editor—all these commitments filled Godfrey's days. And to each he gave himself with absolute dedication, that virtue he had most admired in Virgil Michel.

NOTES TO CHAPTER 5

1. Godfrey Diekmann, "Ten Years of H. A. R.," *Orate Fratres* 23 (1949) 275.

2. GLD, taped interview, July 1988.

3. H. A. Reinhold, "Gift for Father Godfrey Diekmann on His Jubilee as Editor of *Worship,*" in *The Revival of Liturgy,* ed. Frederick R. McManus (New York: Herder and Herder, 1963) 10-11.

4. William Busch, "Past, Present and Future," *Orate Fratres* 25 (1951) 482.

5. H. A. Reinhold, "More or Less Liturgical," *Orate Fratres* 13 (1939) 152.

6. H. A. Reinhold, "How to Defeat the Critic," *Orate Fratres* 20 (1946) 133.

7. See, for example, "My Dream Mass," *Orate Fratres* 14 (1940) 265-270; "Parable of the Liturgical Priest—And of What Came After," *Orate Fratres* 16 (1942) 557-561; "Desiderata to Be Prayed For," *Orate Fratres* 20 (1946) 230-235; "The Dexterity of Missing the Point," *Worship* 26 (1952) 129-134.

8. H. A. Reinhold, "The Apocalyptic Present" *Orate Fratres* 14 (1940) 365.

9. Sara B. O'Neill, *Orate Fratres* 23 (1949) 326.

10. Anon., *Orate Fratres* 23 (1949) 276.

11. GLD, taped interview, July 1988.

12. Editorial policy had been shaped by Virgil Michel and his first board, a remarkably diverse group of men and women: Mr. Donald Attwater, a lay convert to the Roman Church and specialist in Eastern liturgies, who was by his own assessment the only person in England, lay or cleric, concerned with popular liturgical writing; Father William Busch, professor at the St. Paul Seminary, called the proto-evangelist of the liturgical apostolate in the United States because of his writing and speaking on liturgy while Virgil was still apprenticing in Europe; Father Patrick Cummins, a Benedictine from Conception, Missouri, who had been the rector of Sant' Anselmo and was trained in Scripture and theology; Father Gerald Ellard, S.J., professor at St. Mary's Seminary, Kansas, who in 1925, in *America* magazine, urged that the liturgy be "opened up to the laity"; Mother Mary Ellerker, O.S.D., of Duluth, who had come from England to the United States to found a community of nuns for social work and who wrote liturgical books for children; Father Martin Hellriegel, chaplain at O'Fallon, Missouri, where he had introduced the dialog Mass in 1922; Father Leo Miller, professor at the Josephinum in Ohio and a translator of sig-

144

nificant European sacramental and liturgical works; Father James O'Mahoney, an Irish Capuchin classmate of Virgil Michel's at Louvain, who became one of Ireland's best-loved writers and preachers; Father Richard Power of Springfield, Massachusetts, a capable theologian and writer whose pamphlets on sacraments published by the Liturgical Press were very popular; and Mrs. Justine Ward, of the Pius X School of Liturgical Music at Manhattanville College of the Sacred Heart, New York. For further information on these men and women, see Paul Marx, *Virgil Michel and the Liturgical Movement* (Collegeville: The Liturgical Press, 1957) 106–136.

Of these, Hellriegel and Ellard had been with Michel on Christmas Eve, 1925, when the idea of the journal crystallized and it was christened *Orate Fratres*. Years later Hellriegel wrote of "that Holy Night of Christmas, 1925, when at 11 P.M. Virgil Michel, Fr. Ellard (then still a student) and I decided that the Review should be called *Orate Fratres* for whose success I then offered the Midnight High Mass at the O'Fallon, Missouri convent of the Sisters of the Precious Blood" (from a postcard from Martin Hellriegel to Godfrey Diekmann, undated but probably in the year 1962).

13. *Orate Fratres* 1 (1926) 1–4.

14. This analysis has been proposed by R. William Franklin and Robert L. Spaeth in *Virgil Michel: American Catholic* (Collegeville, Minn.: The Liturgical Press, 1988) 73–78.

15. Ibid., 83–85.

16. GLD, taped interview, July 1988.

17. Letter to Mr. Edward Skillin from GLD, April 4, 1941.

18. Letter to KH from Msgr. John J. McEneaney, June 28, 1989.

19. Taken from correspondence in the monastic archives at St. John's Abbey.

20. Ibid.

21. Ibid.

22. Letter to Martin Hellriegel from GLD, June 23, 1942.

23. GLD, phone conversation, September 1989.

24. "Liturgical Briefs," *Worship* 32 (1957) 44.

25. Letter to Father Fred McManus from GLD (quoting a letter from Sister Anne Catherine, C.S.J.), December 16, 1959.

26. "Communications," *Orate Fratres* 25 (1951) 474.

27. Letter to subscribers from GLD, Easter, 1957.

28. Letter to Gerard Sloyan from GLD, July 15, 1962.

29. Frank Kacmarcik, "We Are Formed or Deformed by Our Environments and Arts," *Worship* 55 (1981) 365.

30. Frank Kacmarcik, taped interview, October 30, 1987.

31. GLD, memorandum to Father Abbot, July 1957.

32. "Fifty Years of *Worship*," *Worship* 50 (1976) 470.

33. Letter to subscribers from GLD, Easter, 1957.

34. William Busch, in an article published on the twenty-fifth anniversary of *Orate Fratres*, credits Father John P. Monaghan of Staten Island as the first to suggest three simultaneous movements in the Church in a presentation dur-

ing the 1944 New York Liturgical Week. Monaghan named these movements the theological, the liturgical, and the pastoral. From our vantage point, it is possible to recognize that it was the biblical movement rather than the theological, strictly speaking, that gave expression to the Pauline doctrine of the Mystical Body of Christ. See "Past, Present and Future," *Orate Fratres* 25 (1951) 485.

35. GLD, taped interview, summer, 1988.

36. Michael Ducey, "Secretary's Report," The Benedictine Liturgical Conference (April 18, 1940) 3.

37. Samuel A. Stritch, letter to Monsignor Joseph P. Morrison, rector of the cathedral and chairman of the local planning committee, April 23, 1940.

38. Godfrey Diekmann, "Christian Life and Worship Through Baptism," in *National Liturgical Week, 1940* (Newark: Benedictine Liturgical Conference, 1941) 54-63.

39. H. A. Reinhold, "Dosed Religion," *Orate Fratres* 15 (1940) 30-31.

40. I was told by a priest from St. Louis that there were those who actually took their children out of Monsignor Hellriegel's parish school because they thought the children spent an inordinate amount of time rehearsing for the liturgy.

41. Edward R. Kantowicz, *Corporation Sole: Cardinal Mundelein and Chicago Catholicism* (Notre Dame: University of Notre Dame Press, 1983) 198.

42. Reynold Hillenbrand, "Introductory," in *National Liturgical Week, 1940* (Newark: Benedictine Liturgical Conference, 1941) 5.

43. GLD, taped interview, July 1988.

44. Thomas Carroll, "Gerald Ellard, R.I.P.," *Worship* 37 (1963) 330.

45. By the time of Virgil Michel's death, Justine Ward had retired from the board. New members who had been added between 1926 and 1938 included: Father Paul Bussard, student of William Busch, founder and editor of the *Leaflet Missal;* Father Vincent Kennedy, professor in the Institute of Medieval Studies in Toronto, who had worked under Andrieu and Mohlberg in Europe; Father Ermin Vitry, Benedictine editor of *Caecilia* and a musician, teacher, and director of Gregorian chant; and Father Damasus Winzen, a Benedictine scholar from Maria Laach who fled Germany and eventually founded Mount Saviour Monastery in New York.

46. Gerald Ellard, "The American Scene, 1926-51," *Orate Fratres* 25 (1951) 506.

47. Mary Perkins Ryan, "Minutes of the Question Period," *National Liturgical Week, 1940* (Newark: Benedictine Liturgical Conference, 1941) 153.

48. Michael Ducey, letter to GLD, Feast of St. Teresa, 1948.

49. GLD, letter to Michael Ducey, October 19, 1948.

50. *The Liturgical Week Bulletin* 16 (1944).

51. Shawn Sheehan and William Leonard, S.J., taped interview, December 12, 1987.

52. Ibid.

53. GLD, letter to Abbot Alcuin, August 13, 1949.

54. Quoted by Abbot Baldwin Dworschak in a letter to GLD, December 19, 1957.

55. GLD, letter to Abbot Baldwin Dworschak, January 29, 1958.

56. H. A. Reinhold to GLD, n.d.

57. Shawn Sheehan and William Leonard, S.J., taped interview, December 4, 1987.

58. Reverend W. H. Russell, letter to Abbot Alcuin Deutsch, August 19, 1943.

59. Abbot Alcuin Deutsch, letter to GLD, July 15, 1942.

60. GLD, letter to Abbot Alcuin Deutsch, August 13, 1949.

61. Michael Mathis, letter to GLD, February 17, 1947.

62. Ibid.

63. Press release, University of Notre Dame, March 17, 1947.

64. Michael Mathis, letter enclosure to GLD, February 17, 1947.

65. GLD, letter to Abbot Alcuin Deutsch, July 19, 1949.

66. GLD, taped interview, November 1987.

67. Gerald Ellard, "The American Scene, 1926-51," *Orate Fratres* 25 (1951) 506. I have relied on Ellard for the chronology of events from 1926 to 1951, departing from his record only as other evidence suggested discrepancies in the dates he assigned to events.

68. GLD, letter to Abbot Alcuin Deutsch, August 10, 1939.

69. See Godfrey Diekmann, "Lay Participation in the Liturgy of the Church," in *A Symposium on the Life of Pope Pius X* (Washington: Confraternity of Christian Doctrine, 1946) 137-158.

70. Martin Hellriegel and Godfrey Diekmann, "Perspectives on American Liturgical Renewal," *Aids in Ministry* [AIM] (1979) 4-9.

71. GLD, taped interviews, fall 1987 and summer 1988.

CHAPTER *6*

I N THE SUMMER OF 1952, Godfrey had the great joy of returning to Europe for the first time since his student days. In many ways this trip marked the beginning of a new chapter in his life. He left for Europe with the intention of meeting liturgical leaders on the continent and making contacts for *Worship* magazine and the Liturgical Press. These goals he accomplished. His travels also gave him an international visibility that led inevitably to invitations in subsequent years to become part of liturgical consultations in Europe.

For three and a half months Godfrey (accompanied for six weeks by his sister Marie) toured Ireland, England, France, Spain, Belgium, Holland, Germany, Austria, and Italy. He visited liturgical centers, met European scholars, studied liturgical experimentation when and where he discovered it so as to report back to his monastery and to his readership. Everywhere he was received graciously, often because his hosts were familiar with *Worship* or because they had known Virgil Michel:

> One of the surprises of my trip is that I've met at least a dozen people who have vivid recollections of Fr. Virgil Michel. Several people at Mont César, e.g., including Abbot Capelle, spoke in terms of veneration concerning him. And here at Chevetogne, Dom Lambert Beauduin (the old champion! who has now been allowed to return to the monastery he founded, to die in peace) and Dom Olivier Rousseau had words of high praise for him.[1]

In the same letter Godfrey delighted in his success to that point: "I've had very good luck so far meeting most of the men I'd hoped to see. I'm quite sure the contacts made will result in a number of top-notch articles for *Worship*. The magazine is regarded with favor: it is considered to be 'high grade popularization'."[2] And in his diary there is the note: "Père Gy says *Worship* is the one American magazine he regularly reads with pleasure. It is always alive!" Godfrey added: "Gy a great guy! Keep close to him."[3] Frequently, favorable opinions of *Worship* are mentioned in his diary; only once does he record criticism. At Chevetogne, during the Fathers' recreation, some asked about the cover designs of *Worship:* "Seems all knew them. Most did not like them."[4]

One after another, his interviews concluded with the promise of a contribution for *Worship:* from A.-G. Martimort, an article on sacraments as acts of Christ and the Church; from Sebastian Moore, something on Eucharist in Irenaeus; from A.-M. Roguet, editor of *La Maison-Dieu,* permission to condense and reprint articles from that journal; from Augustin Mayer, a piece on the theology of sacramentals; from Bruce Marshall, an article on the need for consciousness of the social nature of sin in order to shed a more contemporary light on devotional confession.

Godfrey was intent on meeting other editors—of *Questions Liturgiques, La Vie Spirituelle, Liturgie et Paroisse, La Maison-Dieu, Liturgy, Irenikon, Rivista Liturgica, Revue des Sciences Philosophiques et Théologiques, Life of the Spirit, Blackfriars, etc.,* in order to compare notes about content and circulation. He discovered, for example, that *La Maison-Dieu* had three thousand subscribers to begin with but that the numbers didn't increase; people dropped their subscriptions when they found out what kind of liturgy was being propagated. He learned that *Liturgie et Paroisse* reached one out of four priests in France and Belgium, an enviable statistic to one so keen on clergy education.

Godfrey visited liturgical centers and inquired about the work of the staff, always interested in continuing education, the development of short courses, popular publication, and the reception these endeavors received from the populace at large and from the hierarchy. Repeatedly he investigated the teaching of liturgy and sacraments, and often discovered that liturgy professors were putting together their own textbooks, since sacramental theology courses were judged deficient in laying necessary foundations. He enjoyed a visit to the Liturgical Institute at Trier; he seemed saddened to hear that Maria Laach had no intention of reopening its doors to students.

Godfrey made contact with a number of men whom he invited to publish with the Liturgical Press. He visited Herbert Finberg in London and secured a promise of work on a revision of the Easter Vigil commentary, as well as a Holy Week book and a family ritual. To Godfrey's relief, Finberg was "willing to put up with the Confraternity psalms and the 'you' form, and was not out for money!"[5]

C. C. Martindale, "old, scrawny, full of spirit," agreed to edit a book of collects for the Press. Godfrey described Martindale's room at Farm Street as "plastered with faded photographs. He loves people and understands their problems." As they parted, Godfrey asked for a blessing from this man he described as an old patriarch, an uncle of the liturgical movement.[6]

One piece of business Godfrey dreaded, namely,

> . . . the prospect of meeting Fr. Parsch and explaining the long delays in the appearance of the English *Jahr des Heiles* [*The Church's Year of Grace*]. A lot of other people over here have also asked when, tandem aliquando, the translation will appear. It's such a standard "guide" that everyone takes for granted that it should be available in all languages. One sign, on a church door, even speaks of it as "iron rations" of a modern Christian.[7]

More than all these business ventures, Godfrey devoted pages of his diary to the most minute details of liturgical celebrations as he observed them. Use of the vernacular, celebrants facing their congregations, interesting forms of congregational participation, choir and congregational singing, social awareness on the part of congregations which collected food for the poor or sponsored a shelter for the homeless—all of these are recorded faithfully. He noticed people standing for communion, the canon recited aloud, the sound of running water in a baptistry, the widespread use of hand missals. He heard of baptism by immersion and saw a Book of the Gospels carried up the aisle. He watched people write their intentions in a book placed by the door of the church and heard these intentions read aloud at the offertory. He noticed that popular devotions and official cult seemed to coexist peacefully. He constantly made comparisons: "The English have an innate sense for the dignity of worship; the Irish for the warmth of worship. Hence a clash: Irish priests and bishops predominate in English scene."[8] He heard that the *missa recitata* was normal in many places and discovered much experimentation with the singing of psalms, rewritten and paraphrased if necessary to fit hymn tunes.

In one place he observed "ceremonial concelebration"—the practice of having priests, vested in alb and stole, seated in the front pews, all receiving communion from the celebrant—and heard that it was the normal form of celebration for priests' meetings, retreats, and diocesan synods. In another place he discovered the practice of synchronized Masses—many celebrations taking place at the same time under the same roof in unison—though at the latter place, when he probed the custom, he was assured that all Beuronese monasteries were in favor of *true* concelebration, neither ceremonial nor synchronized!

Everywhere there was evidence that education was paying off, that major changes were taking place. In Orléans, for example, they were "seriously considering all priests' communicating at the conventual Mass after a retreat by Père Bouyer."[9] In Paris, Godfrey witnessed catechesis in process:

> This Sunday the pastor introduced a new practice (after explaining, and reading a passage from Ambrose's *De Sacramentis). Amen* means not only "so be it," but is an expression of *credo,* I believe. Hence at Communion, priest holds aloft Host, saying simply, *Corpus Domini,* —recipient answers *Amen* and then receives. Crowded Church. Almost all received.[10]

And, all the while, Godfrey evaluated what he saw according to the one criterion that continued to animate both the European and American liturgical movements: Were people praying?

> Yesterday I attended several of the "revolutionary" Mass experiments in Paris. Whatever else may be said of them, they do pass the pragmatic test. It was a religious experience of a high order: the church crowded and an intensity of participation that must be seen and heard to be believed.[11]

About this same celebration, he noted in his diary: "Everybody seemed literally on toes, watching, joining in. Such willing interiority!"[12]

Occasionally Godfrey rebelled when local liturgies did not please him. At Engelberg, for example, he attended a polyphonic Mass dominated by the choir in the organ loft, condemning the rest of the community to silence—but not Godfrey. "I quietly sang the responses."

Wherever he went he traded stories with those he met. It was rumored, for example, that the Sacred Congregation of Rites had never received a single liturgical magazine and that most of its effort went into beatification and canonization processes. He was told that the bishops of Switzerland were determined to put a brake on liturgists, that the Dutch bishops met every quarter for the purpose of repression, that the French bishops were all favorable to the liturgical renewal, although only about ten did anything concrete to support it. He even learned of one less than successful professor who gave a year-long course in liturgy and spent the first semester on the biretta![13]

From mid-July to September 1, Marie Diekmann traveled with her brother, visiting museums, cathedrals, monasteries, and shrines of all sorts. And there was plenty of time for side trips: to the Oxford pulpit where Newman preached; to a baptistry in Poitiers dating from the time of Hilary; to Lourdes, a commercial nightmare on first sight, yet a place of deep faith. At Lourdes they were deeply moved by those who had come: an old priest bathing his eyes, a woman her ears, a mother presenting her crippled child. "They didn't cry; I did," Godfrey recorded, and he mentioned, too, the difficulty of shaking off the profound emotions stirred in him there.

They approached Mont St. Michel by car and imagined the enthusiasm of ancient pilgrims catching first sight of their goal. Godfrey regarded Mont St. Michel as a miracle of grace, art, and faith. He found other spots less aesthetically pleasing. He mentioned in his diary the difficulty encountered when Romanesque churches are done over into Gothic without enough money to redo the whole, "so they build a gothic sanctuary on a Roman nave, usually considerably higher. Many churches are like a dress with a big bustle."[14]

Marie rarely crops up in Godfrey's travel diary, although he does mention the indignity she suffered at St. Peter's—banned for indecent exposure of her arms!

Perhaps most touching in his jottings are the references to the war and its aftermath:

> War: tragic, almost catastrophic loss of young manhood—one cousin had three sons: one died in Italy, another in France, and the third missing at the Russian front since 1943—only in early 1952 did they receive word he had died in a hospital in '43 as a result of wounds. The agony of uncertainty and waiting against all hope.[15]

Godfrey recorded a visit to a cemetery where 4,400 Americans were buried, but the reality of the war was driven home for him even more poignantly by the walking wounded. Everywhere there seemed to be "one-legged men wobbling along on crutches, hundreds of soldiers for whom the government had not furnished artificial limbs." Godfrey talked personally with people who had refused to send their children to Hitler youth camps, who had sheltered Jews, who seven years after the end of the war were still experiencing rationing of food and essential supplies or were being charged such exorbitant prices that the average working-class family continued to suffer deprivation. These firsthand experiences had a sobering effect.

The trip was, all in all, a time of coming home. Godfrey returned to places like Monte Cassino and experienced that instinctive familiarity of knowing the number of steps in a dark passageway. Such was true for the whole of the journey: seeing Paschal Botz's photograph in Karl Adam's room; stopping again at Sant' Anselmo and Maria Laach and meeting former mentors as colleagues; visiting with relatives in Germany; making conversation with strangers on the trains by language and sign; sampling every imaginable cuisine; delighting in the arts, and this time making a purchase—a Rouault for 60,000 francs.

At the same time, this was a serious study trip, and Godfrey was not the young student on holiday but now the editor of a prestigious journal establishing his credentials across the seas. From this time forward he became a regular participant in the international study weeks which had begun the previous year and which would prove to be decisive in shaping the agenda for liturgical reform adopted by the Second Vatican Council.

The First International Congress of Liturgical Studies, a rather modest meeting despite its title, had been convoked at Maria Laach in 1951 at the initiative of the German Liturgical Institute at Trier. About forty-five scholars, chiefly from Germany, France, and Belgium, attended the study sessions and discussed two topics: the Easter Vigil and the Mass. Discussion of the Easter Vigil included evaluation of the modest revisions permitted *ad experimentum* the previous Easter but authorized by Pope Pius XII with little forewarning. In discussions on the Mass, participants specified twelve reform desiderata and identified a series of questions for further discussion.[16]

Godfrey and his sister Marie at Salzburg (1952)   *Godfrey and Marie in the Alps (1952)*

Marie and Godfrey with Swiss guards after a papal audience (1952)

154

The following year a second congress was convoked jointly by the German Liturgical Institute and the French Center of Pastoral Liturgy. Nine nations were represented at this congress, held at Ste. Odile near Strasbourg. The participants took up those issues that had been set aside for study the previous year, questions chiefly concerning the conclusion of the Eucharistic Prayer and the communion rite. At this congress, as at the first, they sought to eliminate repetitions, to simplify, to restore rites that had been lost, and to arrange the sequence of prayers and ceremonies in a more harmonious whole.[17]

Godfrey was aware of these two meetings and, in fact, commented on them in a letter to Abbot Baldwin during his travels: "The 'big' meeting (the continuation of that which took place in Maria Laach last July) which was to have convened in Paris in the latter part of July, has been postponed and transferred to Strasbourg—middle of October."[18] By that time Godfrey would be home, alas, even if he could have wangled an invitation. But his trip did produce that dividend the following year.

In May 1953 Godfrey received a letter from Johannes Wagner, director of the Liturgical Institute at Trier, with an invitation to attend the Third International Congress of Liturgical Studies to be held at Lugano, Switzerland, in September. Wagner indicated that seven other Americans were invited: Ellard, Hillenbrand, Hellriegel, Mathis, Morrison, Reinhold, and Ross-Duggan—the latter because of Cardinal Ottaviani's express wish that a few of the laity participate.[19]

What to do! Godfrey thought it over and decided not to ask his abbey to finance a second trip to Europe in as many years. He let the matter drop. Not so H.A.R., who sent a note to Abbot Baldwin urging Godfrey's participation: "I am going and I think with the rather 'wild' J. K. Ross-Duggan as a 'delegate' the U.S. would look strangely and incongruously represented. Fr. Godfrey would save face for us."[20]

"Did I get my ears pinned back!" was H.A.R.'s assessment of Abbot Baldwin's response. Godfrey quickly wrote to the abbot to clear up the matter: No, he had not prompted H.A.R.; yes, he had received an official invitation, but "I felt it would be less than reasonable to ask the Abbey to pay for another trip—no matter how important the meeting, or that it would entail at most 6 or 7 days (and about $700).[21] The matter seemed settled.

Then Abbot Baldwin received another letter in a decidedly different style—this time from Martin Hellriegel:

Did I ever have the pleasure of meeting you? My sincerest greetings to you and thanks for the great encouragement you are giving the Liturgical Apostolate. You may have heard that I received an invitation to speak at the International Liturgical Congress at Lugano. My schedule this year has been, and is, so filled that I had to turn down this so appealing opportunity.

During the Executive session [of the Liturgical Conference] at Grand Rapids last week the members decided that your able Father Godfrey should be present at Lugano, all the more since "the greatest things are expected of this Congress," as Bishop Dr. Stohr of Mainz informed me. In his position as editor of *Worship,* as a member of one of the largest, if not THE largest, Benedictine Monastery, and in virtue of his deep theological knowledge, not to forget his knowledge of German and Italian, Father Godfrey is most qualified to take a very active part in the deliberations at Lugano. The Bishop of Mainz further informed me that, when the Holy Father heard of the main speech being given by Cardinal Lercaro of Bologna, he decided to send Cardinal Ottaviani to Lugano. Never before did it happen that a Cardinal, even two, took part in such a liturgical gathering.

We realize that Father Godfrey had been in Europe last year, we also know that an Abbot in his very responsible position may not even permit a semblance of preference, still we are convinced that hardly anyone else would be able to represent this country so well as Father Godfrey.

We are also fully aware of the financial side. It will take about $700.00, which is no small item for a Monastery with its endless financial responsibilities. During the meeting I suggested to the members that, whoever can, pitch in towards Father Godfrey's trip, provided you, dear Father Abbot, will give your consent.[22]

Across the top of the letter is the abbot's notation: "Told him that Fr. Godfrey had been given permission to attend the Congress."[23] In fact, perhaps because Monsignor Hellriegel had made it sound so appealing, Abbot Baldwin was also among the five Americans to attend!

Significant in the preparations for this meeting, collaboratively organized by the national liturgical organizations of Germany, France, Italy, and Switzerland, was the decision to combine several days of scholarly study, as at Maria Laach and Ste. Odile, with an open conference, which drew nearly one hundred fifty persons, among them three cardinals, fourteen bishops, and representatives of the Holy Office and the Sacred Congregation of Rites. Such evidence of official ecclesiastical interest in the liturgy prompted Godfrey to surmise:

> By asking that this third Congress be held nearer to Rome, to allow officials of the Roman Congregations to attend more readily, the Holy See clearly indicated its approving interest that even the most weighty questions of liturgical reform be frankly and openly discussed by competent experts, and gave reason to hope that such reforms are in fact being seriously contemplated.[24]

The conclusions of the Lugano Congress, published in *Worship* together with select addresses, included (1) an endorsement of the principle of active participation [not praying at Mass but praying the Mass] as a most fruitful source of the Christ-life; (2) a request that the mother tongue be used for the proclamation of the Scriptures; (3) a request that communities might also pray and sing in their mother tongue; and (4) a request that the entirety of Holy Week be submitted to a reform similar to the restoration of the Easter Vigil.[25]

Godfrey's jottings during the meeting added color to the official communiqués: "Lercaro, in speech, ends up as great request: hope that lessons of Mass may be in vernacular. P. Robyns thinks the decision has already been made in Rome and all this is diplomatic window dressing. . . . Landersdorfer [bishop of Passau, Germany] says liturgical movement monkeyed around with peripheral things long enough. Now, with Easter Vigil, we're getting down to essentials. . . . As a priest, being almost shocked when receiving thin little hosts. A sign so slight is an unnecessary tax on faith. . . . Representative of *Herder-Korrespondenz,* disturbed by Cardinal Ottaviani's speech, asked what to do and was told by a *Bishop* of the Holy Office that O's speech was a private utterance, and that if he wished, he could criticize it openly."[26]

By all accounts, Lugano demonstrated widespread support for reform based on the best norms of the tradition and conducted in an atmosphere of freedom. Openness, dialogue, appreciation for the liturgical movement against the outright attacks of the past, even a kind of euphoria seem to have pervaded those days in Switzerland. H.A.R. summarized this turning point first by describing the presence and "active participation" of the hierarchy, no longer adversaries of the liturgical movement but enthusiastic participants in its realization.

Then he characterized the spirit of the Lugano dialogue:

> No one was silenced, and no one "pulled his rank." All were inspired by the one thought: where it is in fact impossible to bring the people to the liturgy, the liturgy must be brought to the people. (If this is not clear, read the guiding rubrics of the new Easter Vigil!) The most radical demands came from those who now live in parts of the world where the liturgy of the Church has for all practical purposes become the only and last means of pastoral work, and from the mission countries. If some of our local "worry warts" whose eyebrow raising and clucking have been the backdrop and musical score of our own liturgical movement had been present at this gathering, I fear their armor of rubrical literalness would have been rent like the temple's curtain. The only suspicion ever cast on anyone was that of pastoral over-solicitude. And since, from Cardinal down to small town pastor and curate all of us were more or less "guilty" of this ailment, with symptoms varying according to national, geographic and "conditional" temper, none was looked at askance and the fraternal spirit was not for a minute absent. There was a remarkable international sense of humor.[27]

After the Lugano meeting of 1953, which Godfrey judged to be a watershed event, the modest study week held the following year at Mont César might have proved a disappointment. On the contrary, while the Mont César congress was less newsworthy, Godfrey declared that sparks flew—of the academic kind.[28] The fourth international study week, held at the Abbey of Mont César in Louvain, had two items on its agenda: the advisability of a several-year cycle of readings in the Lectionary and a discussion of Eucharistic concelebration. The Holy Father's message, through Monsignor Montini, that "these two actual and important themes are being studied from historical, theological, and pastoral points of view,"[29] was received with gratitude and delight.

Indeed, their airing was thorough. Because the issue of a several-year cycle of readings had surfaced at earlier international study weeks, there was unanimity that "since the Scriptures are not primarily for private meditation and edification but are committed to the Church to fulfil her task of teaching the truths of salvation to the people of God, a greater number and variety of scriptural lessons in her official eucharistic worship seem called for."[30] The debate centered on appropriate principles for the development of an expanded cycle of

At the Lugano meeting: (standing) John Ross-Duggan, Michael Mathis, Godfrey; (front) H. A. Reinhold

readings: Should Old Testament readings be included in greater numbers, and if so, would this unduly prolong the Sunday celebration? What traditional themes must be addressed during the seasons of the Church year? Should there be alternate texts for the major feasts? How might a Lectionary better serve catechetical ends in mission churches where a priest is often absent and the community experiences the need for a more copious presentation of God's word? What texts must be included because of the weight of tradition? Would a three- or four-year cycle of readings mean hand missals would become too bulky?[31] To this latter conundrum Godfrey anticipated a solution:

> Why not print our New Testaments with an easy-to-use index, indicating which parts are used for the respective Sundays in Years II, III and IV? And in the text itself, the pericopes could be printed in bold-face, with marginal references to their liturgical use; thus even in a private reading of Scripture by our people, there would result a desirable closer tie-up in their minds between Scripture and the liturgy.[32]

The subject of concelebration was treated in much the same way: presentations of the history of concelebration were followed by theological debate and pastoral discussion. Karl Rahner's presence assured that his thesis in *Die vielen Messen und das eine Opfer* [English

159

translation: *The Celebration of the Eucharist*] that the frequency of celebration should be governed by the question of greater *devotio* would be a central issue. Privately, Godfrey expressed disappointment with the discussion:

> Except for the "practical, liturgical" aspects of the problem, it was not much more than an expansion, with further corroboratory details, of the articles by Dom Botte and P. Raes, in *Maison-Dieu,* No. 35, and a restatement by P. Rahner of his theological investigations contained in his book. . . . On the other hand, this goes to show that the line of historical research is already quite clear in its results—which would of course bring us that much closer to an ultimate theological answer.[33]

Decisive in moving the discussion were the pastoral issues that were raised: the difficulty in monasteries of priests participating in the conventual Mass and then celebrating privately; the scandal at places of pilgrimage when so many priests want access to the same altar that celebrations are hasty and without reverence; the chaos at large gatherings of priests when attempting to make accommodations for numerous individual celebrations; and the utter incongruity of synchronized Masses. Participants were eager for a restoration of true concelebration; they discussed adaptation of the rite, vesture, placement of concelebrants, and other details of an issue which, in their minds, was resolved.[34]

On the way to this international gathering at Louvain, Godfrey had stopped at Versailles to attend a national liturgical conference, very much like the Liturgical Weeks in the United States but arranged in separate segments for the clergy and for the laity, with virtually the same speakers addressing the same topics in each group. For three days he mingled with the 750 French priests in attendance, interested, of course, in addresses by Martimort, Doncoeur, Chavasse, Gelineau, Bouyer, Deshayes, and others, but also fascinated by his presbyteral confreres: more than half simply attended Mass and went to communion; they walked up and down in pairs praying the Breviary together; they talked about pastoral liturgical problems during meals and between conferences; they pondered the presence of Christ in the worshiping assembly; they sang Gelineau psalms, which Godfrey pronounced "slightly reminiscent of Negro spirituals." According to Godfrey's journal, they were altogether a solid, balanced lot, full of hope and initiative even in the face of the dechristianization of the culture around them. [The theme of their study week was "The Role of the Renewed Liturgy in the Work of Re-Christianization."] "French malaise!!!" Godfrey concluded: "There is no evidence of it." The lifestyle of the French clergy was also a matter of great interest to him: about ten percent of the participants wore street clothes; most arrived on bikes and motor scooters; some used cigarette holders![35]

Godfrey was the only American among the forty-three participants at the Louvain study congress, and one of two at Versailles. That fact may account for the more copious and detailed notes in his travel journal, a booklet filled as well with *Worship* contacts. He jotted down who promised to write, who should receive a complimentary copy, how the magazine was being received, and even the idea, gleaned at St. André, that the Liturgical Press might be housed in the new library St. John's had on the drawing boards. The journal also provides a typically thorough record of expenditures for his travels: the sum of $98.09, exclusive of airfare, for sixteen days in Europe!

The year 1955 was a fallow one for international liturgical gatherings, perhaps in anticipation of the Assisi Congress of 1956, a conference being planned as a tribute to Pope Pius XII during his eightieth year. Pius XII was recognized as the pope under whose leadership

> the liturgical movement [became] a *pastoral*-liturgical apostolate that is the pulse-beat of the Church's work for the salvation of souls. And it was primarily in order to give liturgical and pastoral leaders of the world an opportunity to express their gratitude to His Holiness that the Assisi congress was organized.[36]

The Assisi Congress was coordinated by the national liturgical offices of Italy, France, Germany, and Switzerland, assisted by subcommittees in other countries. Each country was allowed a certain number of delegates because the facilities at Assisi were limited. Godfrey and Michael Mathis, C.S.C., of Notre Dame, were given the task of selecting the hundred members of the delegation from the United States.

When Godfrey got wind of the rumor that Cardinal Spellman was to be appointed by the apostolic delegate as head of the American delegation to Assisi, he made a special trip to Washington to argue against the appointment of "someone who knew nothing about liturgy." To Godfrey's great relief, Archbishop Edwin O'Hara was named.

O'Hara was a giant of a man, founder of the National Catholic Rural Life Conference and instrumental in the organization of the Confraternity of Christian Doctrine. Earlier in the year, he had been elected president of the Liturgical Conference.

> [O'Hara] left an indelible impression on the liturgy of the Church in the United States through his leadership in preparing a new version of the Sacred Scriptures and in editing the *Collectio Rituum*. The range of his interests was truly amazing. His vision was unbounded. His energy and zeal were truly apostolic.[37]

For all of these reasons, Archbishop O'Hara was greatly mourned when he died in Milan on his way to Assisi just one week before the opening of the congress.

Godfrey's "way to Assisi" was not without incident. After teaching summer school at Catholic University, he had arranged to spend two weeks in the Holy Land before arriving in Assisi for the preliminary "study congress"—in this instance a meeting to be devoted to the reform of the Breviary. Once in Israel, Godfrey joined three American seminarians and a Scripture professor from the Franciscan Biblical House of Studies in Jerusalem, touring and crisscrossing all of Jordanian Palestine. Then,

> Saturday we were arrested twice. Once we were accused of having taken pictures of military installations; and the second time, because we got too close to the Israel border (we were, in fact, unwittingly in no-man's land) we were accused of being Jewish spies. That could have gone badly. At first they refused to believe our passport identification. But finally, after several hours of grilling, they let us go.[38]

To this day Godfrey tends to thrive on such adventures. Over the years they have added to his wealth of stories and delighted countless audiences!

Godfrey arrived in Assisi in time for the fifth international study congress, attended by about thirty scholars. Simultaneously, the first international gathering of missionaries to discuss the problem of liturgy in the missions had attracted twice that number. According to the press release that Godfrey prepared, Breviary reform aroused special interest because of its bearing on the spiritual life of the priest.

"Each heard him speaking in his own tongue!"—The Assisi Congress, 1956

Godfrey at the head of the table at a dinner during the Assisi Congress (1956)

163

The discussion was none too soon: "Requests for a breviary that would be more suitable to the daily life and working conditions of priests in active ministry have been voiced frequently and by responsible ecclesiastics for well over five centuries"![39] Among specific elements that were in need of reform, there appeared to be a consensus:

> Obvious and universally desired improvements include: a careful revision of the historical lessons, that is of the lives of the saints; a better choice of patristic lessons, which would, for instance, eliminate some of the allegorical toying with numbers that may have edified the congregations of Augustine's and Gregory's day, but seems far-fetched and artificial to modern audiences; broadening the choice of patristic readings to include more of our Eastern Christian heritage; revision of the Scripture lessons, especially by eliminating the introductions, for example, that Sophonias was the son of Chusi, the son of Godolias, and so forth, and getting to the heart of the respective book instead.

> There is quite general agreement, too, that the Office should be shortened somewhat, but a great variety of opinion about how this could best be accomplished. Most seem to favor a distribution of the psalter over two or more weeks instead of the present one week.

> And yet all these revisions, important as they are, do not really touch the heart of the problem: how to make the breviary come alive as the daily prayer of the priest and of the Church. The fact is that the hours of the Divine Office have in practice to a large extent lost their basic purpose of sanctifying successive parts of the day and have become a formalistic anachronism—a sum total of prayer formulas to be "gotten in" somehow in the course of 24 hours.[40]

The solution, according to Cardinal Lercaro, was to recover the ancient distinction between the diocesan clergy's public prayer and the monastic Office.[41]

Godfrey was somewhat distracted during these preliminary study days by word that he was to arrange for simultaneous translation into English during the major Assisi meeting. Fifteen hundred were expected, representing all the major European languages. Shawn Sheehan remembers arriving in Assisi and being roped into service as a translator together with all Godfrey's other friends!

For Shawn, one particular moment stood out. Organizers had let it be known that the question of the vernacular was *not* to surface for public discussion during those days. One day Shawn and Godfrey were together in the translation booth during Jungmann's address, "The Pastoral Idea in the History of the Liturgy," in which he spoke of the shift from Greek to Latin in Rome and in the Western Church *for pastoral reasons*. Applause broke out in the crowd. Jungmann looked up, amazed. Godfrey and Shawn were in a room about the size of a telephone booth, and Godfrey began jumping up and down saying, "It's a revolt! It's a revolt!"[42]

Godfrey adds to the story: "Thereafter one of the Vatican representatives summarily returned to Rome. There was a certain amount of anxiety about this until it was discovered that the delegate left not because of Jungmann's allusion to the vernacular but because the man's bed was infested with fleas—and this in the episcopal palace of Assisi!"[43]

The real highlight of the Assisi meeting, according to Godfrey, was the talk entitled "The Liturgical Revival in the Service of the Missions" by Bishop Wilhelm van Bekkum, a member of the Society of the Divine Word. He addressed the need of adapting the liturgy to the customs and cultures of peoples, a very bold initiative in the fifties. The bishop himself was aware that he was going out on a limb and, to the dismay of the translators, he kept changing his speech until the very moment of delivery. The speech caused a sensation. Godfrey is convinced that speeches like Bishop Van Bekkum's paved the way for numerous reforms, liturgical and otherwise, during the Council. Official Roman interest in the missions proved to be of great benefit to the universal Church.[44]

The climax of the congress was an audience with Pope Pius XII, an extraordinary conclusion to an extraordinary meeting. The Pope referred to the liturgical movement as a sign of God's providential care and spoke of the work of the Spirit to draw all people more closely to faith and the treasures of grace through active participation in the Church's liturgical life.[45]

The warmth of the Pope's endorsement of the liturgical movement did not satisfy everyone in attendance. Colonel John K. Ross-Duggan, that indefatigable and single-minded promoter of the vernacular, had hoped against hope that the Pope would make some concession in the use of the mother tongue during his speech. Such was not forthcoming, and as Pius XII was leaving, Ross-Duggan called out, "Take him away! Take him away!" Bill Leonard, who was standing next to him, tried to silence him, but Ross-Duggan would not be pacified. "He'll never do us any good," he said. "Take him away!"[46]

Prior to the Assisi Congress, the board of directors of the Liturgical Conference in the United States had approved a series of resolutions which they asked Archbishop O'Hara to communicate to the Holy See. The preface to the resolutions included the rationale for their preparation:

> It is because we know that the pastoral purpose of the reforms makes the Holy See eager to hear from the liturgical apostolates in various parts of the world that we record these resolutions which express the desires of this group for the continuation of the liturgical reform. We believe that they fit in with the pattern already established and that they would have special value for the Church of our region.[47]

There followed eighteen specific proposals for reform of the Eucharistic celebration and two proposals regarding the Breviary. On the way to Assisi, Martin Hellriegel and Al Wilmes, then secretary of the Liturgical Conference, were in Germany when they heard of Archbishop O'Hara's death. They decided to duplicate the resolutions of the Liturgical Conference and make them available to everyone in attendance at Assisi. This move angered some bishops; they felt that the Liturgical Conference had no right to usurp the bishops' role with Rome. Unofficial groups had no right to speak for the whole country—or for its bishops![48]

Because of excellent publicity prior to the Assisi meeting and the professional press coverage it received throughout, and because of the Pope's obvious endorsement of the directions of the conference, the liturgical movement, overnight, received a great deal of publicity. Suddenly, Godfrey lamented, it was fashionable to be in favor of this new and revolutionary movement. On the contrary, as Godfrey assessed the significance of Assisi:

> As a matter of sober fact, the talks at Assisi were not "revolutionary" in any honest interpretation of that word. I heard nothing said there by any of the eminent speakers which I had not previously and repeatedly seen expressed in writing, by responsible liturgical leaders, either in books or articles. What was new at Assisi was that these ideas were now voiced over an international loud speaker with the approval of

the highest Church authorities. . . . Assisi was a happy interlude, a stimulating experience of shared ideals and hopes. But now we must knuckle down again to the daily hard work of the apostolate and to the mountainous tasks yet to be accomplished.[49]

Another international congress deserves attention as a harbinger of the changes to come. In 1958 the Abbey of Montserrat was host to the sixth annual international study congress, which dealt with the topic of Christian initiation. Once again, and much to his delight, Godfrey received an invitation to participate from Johannes Wagner of Trier. But he also experienced a certain doubt that Abbot Baldwin would support his participation. In a letter to Wagner he mused about his prospects:

> [Abbot Baldwin] is superior of a large monastery, the big majority of whom quietly stay at home year after year, and relatively few of whom have had occasion or opportunity to visit Europe. I know for certainty that my several past trips to Europe have not caused any unfavorable comment or envy. My confreres were generous enough not to begrudge me and to take for granted that attendance at these meetings was important for my work as Editor and for the contact it afforded with European thought for the American liturgical apostolate generally. Nor has my health been good for the past two years. Father Abbot has generously allowed me to stay in Nassau [where St. John's had made a foundation] for nearly four months and I do feel much restored in health.[50]

Godfrey's solution: that Wagner write directly to the abbot indicating why it would be desirable for Godfrey to attend! Wagner's intercession apparently did the trick.

"Are you back from Spain yet?" asked Gerald Ellard, in a letter pressing Godfrey for newsy details of the meeting at Montserrat. "What 'top secret' information would you have to pour out, if I were there in Collegeville for the next quarter hour? Did you meet at Montserrat? How many were there? What was the theme; what general results? What general news of LM [the liturgical movement] did you pick up?"[51] To which Godfrey responded conversationally:

> The meeting itself at Montserrat treated of baptism and confirmation. Thirty people were present including the usual stalwarts. Among them Bishop Stohr, Abbot Capelle, Antonelli, Lucas Brinkhoff, OFM (Holland), Chavasse, Fischer, Gy, Jungmann, Martimort, Raes, Roguet,

Schnitzler, Aloysius Stenzel, Wagner, plus several men from Montserrat itself and a contingent of five other Spaniards, including Auxiliary Bishop Miranda of Toledo, President of the official Pastoral Liturgical Commission of Spain. Besides Antonelli, of the S.C.R. [Sacred Congregation of Rites], two officials of the Holy Office were present: Msgr. Garofalo (who proved to be the life of the party, full of quips, but who gave a splendid analysis of the idea of baptism in the New Testament), and Msgr. Agustoni, secretary to Cardinal Ottaviani, and brother of Father Agustoni of Lugano. Much of the discussion turned on the catechumenate and ways and means of restoring it to significance in the changed conditions of our own time. There were also present several men from the mission fields, including Father Brunner, S.J., of Manila, and a superior of the White Fathers. There was considerable opposition voiced to the present wording of the exorcisms which derive from a time when baptism was administered to converts from paganism. On the other hand, the need of an awareness of sin and the power of Satan must not be lost sight of, nor the great drama and conflict between the kingdom of Satan and the kingdom of God, even after the historical redemption. No resolutions were passed. It was generally agreed that the editio typica must be carefully worked out to preserve the traditional drama of conflict while national rituals would have to take cognizance of local conditions in the wording of the exorcisms.[52]

Godfrey added some observations of a more general nature about appropriate strategies of liturgical reform:

Another strong impression I received was that the responsible members of the Paris Centre de P.L. [Pastorale Liturgique] are really much more conservative than the Germans, or than a lot of younger priests of France and Belgium. In fact, it came to an open showdown several times, although always in an atmosphere of fraternal friendliness and understanding. The men of C.P.L. are afraid that the Germans, as well as most of the Belgians, are too willing to determine basic questions on the basis primarily of pastoral needs—on spiritual utilitarian grounds—without sufficiently keeping account of liturgical theology and history. Considerable annoyance was expressed at the editor of *Paroisse et Liturgie* (Saint André) by several people at Montserrat. They feel that he spoils things by agitating for immediate action in various fields of liturgical reform, and thus harms the careful build-up, theologically, historically, liturgically, that *Maison-Dieu,* for instance, had been accomplishing. They feel particularly disturbed because the magazine has such a large following now in the younger priests, both in France and Belgium. On the other side of the spectrum is *Questions [Liturgiques]* (Mont César) whose editor is overly cautious.[53]

Finally, because Ellard was an associate editor of *Worship,* Godfrey concluded his letter to his collaborator with a word of business:

> Sorry that the crowded program at Cincinnati allowed so little time for personal visiting. I would have liked to discuss with you the general contents and development of *Worship.* We received criticism recently that we were departing from pastoral subjects and going into general academic fields too much, and I believe there is justice to the criticism. But how change? . . . Please help with advice.[54]

One last significant liturgical congress took place in Munich in 1960. "I'd be highly flattered to be taking your place,"[55] wrote Fred McManus when a conflict in Godfrey's schedule prevented his participation. The Munich week included further conversation on the topic of concelebration, this time conducted by Canon Martimort, as well as discussion of the theology of the communion prayer in the Orient led by Alphonse Raes, and Johannes Wagner's lively presentation on church architecture and the interior arrangement of a church.

Meanwhile, back at St. John's Abbey, church architecture had preoccupied Godfrey's community for most of the fifties as plans for a new abbey church gradually took shape. The plans represented a stunning departure from certain "inherited prejudices" about what a church *should* look like. It was risky business breaking ground in 1958:

> Building the church is a major act of faith on the part of the monastic family. We felt that if we did not courageously tackle the problem now, it would very likely mean indefinite postponement. This would have repercussions beyond our own monastic circle. The proposed abbey church has received such wide publicity, even internationally, that not to go ahead with it now would be a serious blow to very many who look upon it as one of the most important ventures in contemporary church architecture. . . . Especially in view of the fact that some members of the hierarchy—several of them not too far removed from Collegeville—have been quite vocal in expressing their disturbance at this "ecclesiastical garage" that St. John's is proposing to build, postponement at the present time might very likely be interpreted as retreat on our part, and would therefore have serious repercussions

among those who sympathize with what we are trying to do. So, in God's name, we start.[56]

The abbey church at St. John's is remarkable in many respects. Planned in the decade before the Second Vatican Council was announced, and dedicated before the convocation of the first session, the church in nearly all respects anticipated the liturgical reform that it would soon house. And add to the flux of the liturgy itself the potential dissension such an undertaking could arouse in a large and vocal monastic community! "Unless the Lord Build the House," an article by Virgil Michel some twenty years earlier, had spelled out the dangers: "Budget, rubrics, professional honor, taste, *vox populi,* human respect for wealthy donors—what a mess it can all produce at times. Where can a basis for unity and harmony be found in such a welter of chaotic individualism?"[57]

Godfrey attributes much of the success of the planning process to Abbot Baldwin, sometimes called "Baldwin the Builder," who had the courage to break with the past and allow the abbey church to take the lead in contemporary architectural development. Abbot Baldwin, in turn, acknowledges that the church is the product of the whole community. For six or seven years, most intensely from 1955 to 1958, the monks engaged in a rigorous planning process in collaboration with Marcel L. Breuer, Hungarian-born architect whose most significant work to that point was the design of the UNESCO building in Paris. The community abstracted from any consensus of what a church ought to look like and started with the more basic inquiry of what would take place within. Their success in wedding form and function was captured by the editor of *Blackfriars,* Illtud Evans:

> No building is more free from the megalomania of mere display. The heroic dimensions of the structure are all ordered to a single end— and that is within.

> And here it can be said without hesitation that the church is a triumph of intelligence and humility. Of humility most of all, because the imaginative genius of Marcel Breuer which has so often, in such buildings as the Paris UNESCO, moulded the concrete forms with masterly authority, has here submitted itself with fidelity to the sacred purpose of the place.

> At every stage of the building the monks of St. John's provided a detailed theological justification of what the forms of worship demand.

It was the architect's business to implement them, and a great architect will respect these restrictions—if such they seem to be—for they provide, as it were, the verb that he is to conjugate. And that verb is "to worship": not any worship, but the sacramental worship of the Mass, which gathers the people of God about an altar to offer a sacrifice which their baptism has entitled them to share. But their share is not a mere presence: it is a work to be done, and there is a hierarchy of order to be preserved.[58]

Subprior John Eidenschink, chairman of the building committee, and Abbot Baldwin Dworschak discuss the plans of the abbey church with Hamilton Smith (standing) and Marcel Breuer.

Godfrey's correspondence yields a fine example of the kind of rigorous theological discussion that shaped the final plans for the church. This letter is to Père Gy of the Liturgical Institute in Paris:

> We have definitely planned to eliminate the communion rail. We figure that it has come to denote in people's minds not merely the distinction between sanctuary and nave, that is between priest and people, but actually separation. And we feel this is most undesirable, particularly because Communion itself is the sacrament of union, and for it to be distributed at a symbol of separation seems most inappropriate.

We know that it could be of a very slight and unobtrusive character, but de facto it has come to mean separation from the sanctuary and the altar in the minds of the people. We therefore propose to indicate the distinction by three steps, basing ourselves on the paragraph in the Holy Father's allocution after Assisi in which he says that the Head and the body are not to be considered as two separate entities, but form one unit which together is operative in worship. Instead of the customary communion rail, we plan to have four small "tables," only about a foot wide and about four feet long, and about three feet high. The celebrant will be standing on one step higher than the people who will receive, and the latter will receive standing. There are several such tables in a neighboring diocese and my own experience with them has been very satisfactory. . . . Our plan is to have only one single altar in the entire church. We feel that the significance of the single altar is important. Hence we plan to sink the tabernacle into the altar, but have it extend above the altar about four or five inches. When Mass is not being celebrated attention will be called to the tabernacle by placing over it a larger tent or "tabernaculum."

May I ask for your opinion on these two points?[59]

The design of the abbey church at St. John's, the product of years of discussion within and beyond the community, the architectural jewel of the early sixties which anticipated so many of the liturgical reforms of Vatican II, clearly benefited from Godfrey's European travels, his keen eye for architectural details, and his access to experts for these various "unofficial" inquiries. While he was in Europe, for example, he scouted around for a low tabernacle that might be sunk into the main altar, locating one possibility in Paris. He inquired about, and sketched pictures of, altar tables flanked by free-standing candles. He questioned the possibility of running water for the baptistry and was assured: "There is nothing against this—and no need to ask Rome." In the midst of the congress at Montserrat he sent an SOS to Abbot Baldwin: *"Very important:* There's serious conflict of opinion whether Gospel lectern should be on side we've planned it in our church. . . . if at all possible, or if not already too late, can decisive laying of conduits for electricity be postponed until we get a ruling?"[60] And a second letter, after his visit to the Sacred Congregation of Rites, confirmed that the location of the lectern had to be shifted in the St. John's plans.

Much was shifting—or would be once the Council was convened. Andrew Greeley remembers visiting St. John's in the late fifties when

*Godfrey
in front of
the new
abbey church
(1965)*

the new monastery church existed only in a model. According to Greeley, Godfrey proudly displayed the model and praised all the features of the new church, almost as if he were the architect. Greeley asked the perhaps not too innocent question: "But Godfrey, what if it is not the architectural wave of the future?" Godfrey stopped dead in his tracks, frowned as though this thought had never occurred to him, and then waved his hand: "Impossible!"[61]

Ah, the best laid plans! At one point Godfrey made a special trip to Rome to inquire whether there was any hope of securing permission for concelebration. He was given a categorical "NO"; the discipline would certainly not change in his lifetime. On the basis of that pronouncement, the crypt of the church was lined with chapels—about three dozen of them—each dedicated to a different saint and each furnished with lovely contemporary art pieces. Two years after the church was dedicated, Eucharistic concelebration was approved at Vatican II. Ironically, St. John's was one of the places designated for experimentation with the rite of concelebration in 1964.

The plans also called for a separate St. Benedict chapel, commonly referred to as the Brothers' chapel, a place where lay brothers could pray the *Short Breviary* in English apart from the choir monks. Permission for vernacular recitation of the Divine Office was granted shortly after the Council ended.

The baptistry, too, reflects the unsettled times in which it was designed. Godfrey had argued vigorously for its placement at the entrance to the church, an ample, open space with running water as a lively reminder of baptism as entrance into the life of grace and faith leading to the table. How odd, then, to place a traditional font in the middle of this larger pool, a duplication of symbols for which no one now seems willing to take the credit.

But perhaps of all the artistic decisions that were made, the choice of window design and artist remains the most neuralgic. Nearly thirty years after the dedication of the abbey church, the community remains divided about the selection of Bruno Bak's design, "the splendor of the liturgical year," for the façade window, rather than Joseph Albers' "large cross," a design reportedly favored by architect Breuer. Godfrey argued against Albers' design, which he claimed was "docetic," a guaranteed conversation-stopper then as now. His confreres have speculated that Godfrey supported Bak because he felt sorry for the man, who was struggling to support his family. They were, incidentally, living in the old Diekmann home in Collegeville. Apparently a verbal contract with Bak also influenced the community's vote to retain him. Evans of *Blackfriars* suggests the problem:

> It is only in the glazing of the immense window, with its hundreds of uniform hexagons, that a note of uncertainty emerges. This could have been the greatest statement in stained glass of our time. It is true that the problem for the artist was a formidable one, but here the architect should surely have worked with a commissioned artist from the start. To fill so closely articulated a pattern must make enormous demands on the designer, and one cannot pretend that the hesitant abstractions have really succeeded.[62]

The church was dedicated in August 1961. The following year Godfrey's Christmas letter speaks of its significance: "1962 for all of us at St. John's meant also the first full year of worship in the new Abbey church. It is beyond doubt a palpable grace, daily more appreciated, and an object of ever-deepening wonder. 'How awe-inspiring is this place!' Monastic life centers so satisfyingly now in the daily current of public prayer.''[63]

It is possible to see in the development of plans for the abbey church and in its construction a metaphor for the creative ferment abroad in those years before Vatican II. Several initiatives at St. John's and beyond were remarkable harbingers of things to come.

During the fifties St. John's had begun its Mental Health Institutes for priests, ministers, and rabbis, a highly successful forerunner to the adoption of pastoral counseling in the seminary curriculum generally, and the endorsement of clinical pastoral education by Roman Catholics. Besides learning more about mental health, participants in this institute had, in some cases, their first opportunity to discuss theology in an informal and friendly ecumenical atmosphere.

Indeed, St. John's became known as a congenial site for ecumenical exchange. In the late fifties some of the St. John's seminarians took the initiative of beginning a seminar with one of the Lutheran theological seminaries in the Twin Cities. About a dozen students from each school agreed on a subject, exchanged bibliography, read each other's authors, and then had a three-day conversation. Some professors trailed along in the second year to see what was firing up their students. One of the participants from the early days of this dialogue, Jack Eichhorst, eventually became the director of St. John's Institute for Ecumenical and Cultural Research, founded in 1967 and perhaps in some measure an offspring of these early ecumenical stirrings.

In 1960 St. John's launched a Scripture Institute, a summer program combining liturgy, Scripture, and the place of the laity in the Church. These components belonged together, according to Godfrey and others who conceived the plans, because one cannot be understood without the others. Again, participants represented a variety of Christian denominations. A number of rabbis were also included. On its faculty at the beginning, Godfrey vividly remembers the ecumenical prayer that took place without fanfare, and years later he spoke of its significance:

> Praying together is no longer an exceptional phenomenon. It is no longer news. And yet, in another, deeper sense, it is always new. Every

time we meet, we are laying another stone, not for the wall that has so tragically divided us, but for the up-building of the earthly Jerusalem, the counterpart of the heavenly City—for the construction of the Church which, Jesus told Peter, shall be built, and of which only God really knows the blueprints.[64]

The first of its kind in the United States, the Scripture Institute had over thirty imitators when St. John's bowed out of the field in 1968.

St. John's also sponsored a series of ecumenical colloquies beginning in December 1960. Godfrey was among the invited participants of this first ecumenical dialogue in North America to receive the official approbation of the Holy Office. Five Protestants and five Catholics gathered for three days to discuss "what divides us" and "what unifies us." According to Godfrey, the Spirit was constantly present during those days, an important precondition for reunion:

We must have the realization that this work for unity is not primarily our work. Sometimes we are inclined to feel that way about it. We must pray, we must establish relations with non-Catholic brethren. Unless we have the conviction that this is first of all God's work, we can hardly expect any results. Let's put it this way: reunion is something in the distant future. I don't think we should fool ourselves. But unity is not something of the future. Unity is something which already exists, because God has established unity. . . . For years we concentrated on the word "separated," but now we must shift and see ourselves as brethren, brothers and sisters, and realize its implications.[65]

Neither ecumenical interest nor theological ferment was confined to St. John's, of course. The Pittsburgh Liturgical Week in 1960, for example, had "The Liturgy and Unity in Christ" as its theme. With both Protestants and Orthodox in attendance, the conference board had to shape a genuinely ecumenical program and to struggle with appropriate forms of worship. Although the Liturgical Week received the blessing of the newly elected John XXIII, not everyone was sold on ecumenism. Fred McManus, then president of the Liturgical Conference, lamented to Godfrey: "The view has been expressed locally [marginal note: 'confidentially, by the apostolic delegate'] that all Protestant-Catholic dialogue should be confined to occasions when a minister comes to the rectory for instruction."[66]

During 1960 the Liturgical Conference, for twenty years a peripatetic organization operating on a shoestring budget out of the secretary's and the treasurer's basements, established a secretariat in Washington. As a member of the board, Godfrey expressed his concern about increasing expenses: "As to the suggestion about raising registration from $3. to $4., my first reaction is strongly negative. Three dollars does not sound like an excessive amount to the average person, but as soon as you deal with four dollars, this is so close to five that it begins to look expensive."[67]

How the Liturgical Conference made ends meet remains a mystery, but the role of Liturgical Weeks in preparing for the Council is undisputed. Throughout the fifties and early sixties the Weeks held in various parts of the country continued to attract and to nourish a growing number of participants. Because it was the policy of the board to select sites where the local Ordinary was willing to welcome the gathering, the Week often ended up in the Midwest, though as Reynold Hillenbrand of Chicago remarked to Godfrey, "We ought to get out of the Midwest. It is closer to redemption than other parts of the country."[68] The Conference board more and more performed a tightrope act in trying to meet the sometimes conflicting expectations revealed in the evaluations: "It appears that 50% of the participants at Notre Dame (1959) think the Conference is rash, imprudent, and radical; 50% think it is staid, reactionary, pussy-footing."[69]

As its president, Fred McManus was tireless in working on behalf of the Liturgical Conference, attempting to anticipate needs, prepare materials, supply catechesis, and forge the links that would strengthen the liturgical apostolate. In all of this, Godfrey was his close collaborator and strategizer. In 1960, two years after the Bishops' Committee on the Liturgical Apostolate [later to be named the Bishops' Committee on the Liturgy] was formed, Fred protested to Godfrey that the bishops had shown not the least interest in the opinions of the Conference nor asked its help. Some bishops obviously felt that all initiative for liturgical renewal should remain in the hands of the hierarchy. Godfrey responded:

> If every initiative for liturgical reform must emanate from the hierarchy, I am afraid that we would have to be very careful indeed. However, a number of national organizations draft resolutions. This is a harmless enough procedure and yet something that usually gets very good publicity. Such resolutions in our case embody the general trends

of papal reforms in recent years and could, certainly by implication, put us on record for a continuation of such reforms in definite areas. Even Archbishop Brady [of St. Paul, Minnesota] could hardly object to that, and I do see some virtue in it. We will not attract interest in the Conference, among priests especially, unless we make it clear that we are intensely interested in such reforms. . . . The groundswell of opinion will by-pass us unless we speak out within the limits that the Episcopal Committee allows—but stretching those limits as far as possible.[70]

Shades of things to come when Godfrey and Fred teamed up at Vatican II!

One last "movement" in the United States that prepared for the Council is worthy of mention. One evening in the early fifties Jack Egan, Joe Gremillion, and Louis Putz were dining together. Conversation turned to the Catholic Left, and the three decided it would be a good idea to bring this group together. On the spot they began to draw up a list of "experts" in various fields whom they wanted to invite to a first meeting of the group, christened "Friends of Friends." There were people on the list from the liturgical movement, family life, labor, journalism, social action, and Scripture. Since Jack Egan was friendly with Bishop Wright, then the bishop of Worcester, the Trappist monastery at Spencer, Massachusetts, was chosen as the site for the first meeting site in 1955, in tandem with the Worcester Liturgical Week. About fifty attended, Godfrey among them, though perhaps he went with some slight misgivings. Prior to the meeting he confided to Reynold Hillenbrand that he was working mightily to secure the presence of H.A.R., "lest they all drown in sociological and organizational emphases."[71]

A second "think tank" devoted to exploring the signs of the times was convened in 1957 in Illinois. Several bishops were added to the guest list, including Bishop Wright, known by some—then— as "the darling of the liberals." In 1959 the group met again at a retreat house on the northern side of Lake Erie. In each instance the gatherings provided the solitude for three full days of serious discussion, the opportunity to keep abreast of developments in various fields, and some planning for the future.[72]

In hindsight, it is clear that all the movements represented in Friends of Friends; all the academic enterprises in the areas of Scripture, psychology, and ecumenism; all the international study weeks and congresses on liturgy, as well as the relentless catechesis of associations such as the Liturgical Conference and magazines such as *Worship;* all the occasions to pray together across denominations and the opportunities to dialogue together across ideological barriers— all these initiatives converged at Vatican Council II.

1. GLD, letter to Abbot Baldwin Dworschak, July 13, 1952.
2. Ibid.
3. GLD, diary entry, July 5, 1952.
4. Ibid., July 13-15, 1952.
5. Ibid., June 14, 1952.
6. Ibid.
7. GLD, letter to Abbot Baldwin, August 18, 1952.
8. GLD, diary entry, June 15, 1952.
9. Ibid., June 23, 1952.
10. Ibid., June 22, 1952.
11. GLD, postcard to Abbot Baldwin, June 23, 1952.
12. GLD, diary entry, June 22, 1952.
13. Ibid., passim.
14. Ibid., June 23, 1952.
15. Ibid., September 4, 1952.
16. Cf. "Conclusions of the First Congress, Maria Laach, 1951," *Worship* 28 (1954) 157-160.
17. Cf. "Conclusions of the Second Congress, Ste. Odile, 1952," *Worship* 28 (1954) 160-161.
18. GLD, letter to Abbot Baldwin, July 13, 1952.
19. Johannes Wagner, letter to GLD, May 15, 1953.
20. H.A.R., letter to Abbot Baldwin, no date, but probably July 1953.
21. GLD, letter to Abbot Baldwin, July 26, 1953.
22. Martin B. Hellriegel, letter to Abbot Baldwin, August 26, 1953.
23. Ibid.
24. "The Lugano Conference," *Worship* 28 (1954) 116.
25. "Conclusion of the Third Congress, Lugano, 1953," *Worship* 28 (1954) 162-167.
26. GLD, diary entries, passim.
27. H.A.R., "A Turning Point: Lugano," *Worship* 27 (1954) 559-560.
28. "Louvain and Versailles," *Worship* 28 (1954) 537-545.
29. GLD, 1954 travel journal, 19.
30. "Louvain and Versailles," 538-539.

31. GLD, 1954 travel journal, passim.

32. "Louvain and Versailles," 540. The presumption of Louvain participants appears to be that the Lectionary in possession would become Year I, possibly with the exception of some obscure epistles.

33. Excerpt from a confidential report Godfrey mailed to about twenty colleagues after the meeting.

34. GLD, 1954 travel journal, passim. Interestingly, identical pastoral reasons were advanced at Vatican II for the restoration of concelebration.

35. Ibid.

36. Godfrey Diekmann, "Preface," *The Assisi Papers* (Collegeville, Minn.: The Liturgical Press, 1957) vi.

37. Ibid., xiv.

38. GLD, postcard to Abbot Baldwin, September 3, 1956.

39. Godfrey Diekmann, written for NCWC News Service, "Breviary Reform, Topic of Special Importance at Assisi Liturgical Conference, Being Made by Holy See." Press release dated November 5, 1956.

40. Ibid.

41. Giacomo Cardinal Lercaro, "The Simplification of the Rubrics and the Breviary Reform," in *The Assisi Papers,* 203–219.

42. Shawn Sheehan, taped interview, December 4, 1987.

43. GLD, taped interview, fall 1987.

44. GLD, taped interview, spring 1987.

45. Pope Pius XII, "Allocution," *The Assisi Papers,* 223–236.

46. Story told by William Leonard, S.J., of Boston College during a colloquium he organized at Boston College, June 19–23, 1983. Leonard gathered a group of liturgical pioneers whose reminiscences of the early liturgical movement were recorded on video tape during the course of those days.

47. Resolutions of the board of the Liturgical Conference, August 20–23, 1956. In point of fact, every resolution was subsequently adopted by Vatican II.

48. Story pieced together from: Al Wilmes, letter to KH, February 16, 1988; Shawn Sheehan and William Leonard, S.J., taped interview, December 1987.

49. Godfrey Diekmann, "Assisi in Retrospect," *Worship* 31 (1957) 49–50, 52.

50. GLD, letter to Johannes Wagner, March 21, 1958.

51. Gerald Ellard, letter to GLD, September 8, 1958. Ellard concludes this letter on a personal note suggesting the friendships that were fostered and sustained through annual contact at the national Weeks: "It was nice seeing you at Cincy, but the Week is now so large it almost excludes the former visiting along the edges of the program. John Ryan suggested having a five day Week with nothing but visiting scheduled for the third day!" Ellard signs his letter: "Gerald Ellard, S.J. (sometimes called "liturgerry" here)."

52. GLD, letter to Gerald Ellard, September 30, 1958.

53. Ibid.

54. Ibid.

55. Frederick R. McManus [FRM] to GLD, June 21, 1960.

56. GLD to Mrs. Helen Cotting, May 1, 1958.

57. Cited in Maurice Lavanoux, "The Reality of a Dream," *Liturgical Arts* 31 (1962) 5. This article provides a summary of the planning process as well as an excellent appraisal of the completed church. See also Colman Barry, *Worship and Work* (Collegeville: The Liturgical Press, 1980) 336ff.

58. Illtud Evans, "St. John's Abbey Church: An Appraisal," *Worship* 36 (1961) 517.

59. GLD to Pierre-Marie Gy, no date [between 1956 and 1958].

60. GLD to Abbot Baldwin, September 14, 1958.

61. Andrew Greeley, taped interview, November 24, 1987.

62. Evans, "St. John's Abbey Church," 518–519.

63. GLD, Christmas letter, 1962.

64. GLD, from a sermon preached on Reformation Sunday, November 1, 1981.

65. GLD, talk at a Minnesota stand-up, March 3, 1960. The proceedings of this first colloquy were published under the title *Christians in Conversation* (Westminster, Md.: Newman Press, 1962). Godfrey's presentation gives the Catholic perspective on the theme "Factors That Unite Us."

66. FRM, letter to GLD, March 4, 1960.

67. GLD, letter to FRM, October 23, 1961.

68. Reynold Hillenbrand, letter to GLD, March 24, 1954. Notable exceptions: Boston, Worcester, and Pittsburgh all had the strong support of the Ordinary.

69. FRM, letter to GLD, no date, but likely written in the fall of 1959.

70. GLD, letter to FRM, September 9, 1960.

71. GLD, letter to "Dear Reynie" [Hillenbrand], August 11, 1955.

72. I have pieced together the details of these summit meetings from interviews with Shawn Sheehan and William Leonard, December 4, 1987, and with Monsignor Jack Egan, November 17, 1987. Godfrey also writes about them to Abbot Baldwin during the Council when there is some question of holding a post-conciliar Friends of Friends at St. John's. GLD to Abbot Baldwin, November 16, 1963.

CHAPTER *7*

On January 25, 1959, Pope John XXIII announced his plans to convoke an ecumenical council. It would be, he hoped, a new Pentecost, a time to examine and renew the doctrine, discipline, and organizational structures of the Church, and to work toward the unity of all Christians. An antepreparatory commission was organized to consult widely about what subjects should be treated at the Council and what structures should be put in place. Then on Pentecost Sunday of the following year the preparatory commissions were established, among them a commission on the sacred liturgy. Cardinal Gaetano Cicognani was named its president, and Father Annibale Bugnini was appointed secretary.

When Godfrey was invited to become a consultor to the liturgy commission, he could hardly contain his excitement. He wrote to Fred McManus, who had also been named to the commission:

> Two days ago I got word from a confrere in Rome that I had been appointed as a consultant for the liturgical commission preparing the agenda for the General Council; and yesterday I received a clipping of the August 26 *Osservatore Romano* listing all the members—including your own good self. The list looks wonderful. I was able to spot only one or two obstructionists among the 46 names mentioned. And a lot of them have been outstanding in their efforts for pastoral liturgy. Some good guardian angel must have been on the job. I was particularly happy to see the name of Bishop Malula of Leopoldville, as well as a number of other mission bishops.[1]

A few days later Godfrey's official appointment came through, much to his relief. "I had almost begun to get nervous, with all sorts of

183

harebrained imaginings about someone blocking the actual official appointment."[2]

Some commission appointments seemed a bit idiosyncratic. God-frey points, for example, to the case of "Bishop Adsum." When the preparatory commissions were being established, earlier responses to the antepreparatory commission's invitation to bishops to send *vota* or recommendations on any topic were taken into account. Only one bishop from Ireland had returned any suggestions concerning the liturgy—a Bishop Joseph Walsh of Tuam—so he became an invited, though not very active, member of the liturgical commission. God-frey always suspected that the bishop did not understand all that was going on, but he was a most agreeable type who knew and used the word "placet," and who, when called upon, said, "Adsum, adsum," so that became his nickname.

However quirky the membership of other commissions, "Adsum" appears to have been an exception on the liturgy commission. Many of those appointed to the liturgy commission as members or consul-tors had been active in the international liturgical study weeks and congresses of the fifties. These people were not simply theoreticians but were leaders of the liturgical renewal of various countries and were well aware of the questions that had to be treated. They included edi-tors of liturgical magazines, bishops active in the liturgical movement, theologians writing in the field, and pastoral liturgists. Because of their previous collaboration, they knew one another's thinking and had agreed on a certain number of issues in previous settings. So there was, from the outset, a remarkable consensus about the major issues and a very hopeful spirit. Godfrey could hardly wait to get started:

> I wonder what it all entails. Will this mean that the Commission sifts the liturgical *vota* presented by the world's hierarchy, and presents defi-nite plans to the Council for the thorough reform of missal and brevi-ary? It is all quite exciting—and no doubt will entail a lot of work. But it is exhilarating to know that so many men prominent in the litur-gical apostolate through the years will have at least some chance to put in their oar.[3]

Godfrey wasted no time getting his own oar into the water. He drafted a questionnaire concerning vernacular in the Breviary to be circulated among clergy in the United States. In this initiative he was heartily supported by Fred McManus, who urged him to include some questions on the vernacular in the Mass as well. It seemed clear that the needs of the laity had to be stressed if vernacular proposals were to have any chance at all. The big obstacle to the vernacular, some believed, was a Roman willingness to sacrifice the needs of the laity so that the clergy would not lose their Latin. The questionnaire revealed an overwhelming consensus that the time was ripe for the vernacular as well as for simplifications, reduction in the number of Hours recited, and a Breviary adapted for private use rather than one based on choir recitation. Some suggestions about the implementation of the vernacular were ingenious, for example, a proposal to recite the Office in alternate years in Latin and English, and another request that individuals might freely choose one day a week for the vernacular.[4] Godfrey tallied the results, knowing he would have an opportunity to address this issue in the commission.

The first meeting of the liturgical commission was scheduled for the middle of November 1960. Godfrey and Fred arranged to meet a few other consultors in Rome a day or so ahead of time to plan their strategy. Godfrey wrote about this to Johannes Wagner: "All of us feel that a concerted front will be necessary in order that such major problems as the vernacular and concelebration will be honestly faced."[5] These and subsequent "strategy sessions" won over new collaborators, among them, J. B. O'Connell, the Englishman. Godfrey described his propagandizing of O'Connell to H.A.R.:

> I suspect his interests still lie predominantly on the height of mitres; but he is willing to listen, and Fred and I both feel that we were able to pump a lot of ideas and resolutions into his head during the week or so we were together. He is a member, whereas Fred and I are only consultors; and the members are the big-shots; we are merely lay sisters.[6]

The "big-shots" and the "lay sisters" met together for the first time on November 15, 1960, in order to formulate their work and to divide up the duties of the various subcommissions that were established. Godfrey was appointed secretary to the subcommission dealing with "Linguistic Adaptation to the Traditions and Ethos of Peoples," the subcommittee that eventually drafted articles 37–40 of the Constitution on the Sacred Liturgy. Johannes Quasten, a member, chaired the committee; consultors included Bishop Joseph Malula of Leopoldville, Bishop Francis Muthappa of India, Father

Cipriano Vagaggini of Italy, Father Johannes Hofinger of Austria, and Father Boniface Luykx of Belgium. During that first meeting of the preparatory commission in Rome, this group examined all the relevant *vota* and formulated a draft of the general principles that would support the cultural adaptation of the liturgy, including the role of bishops' conferences in determining appropriate adaptations for their respective regions.

Godfrey's contribution to the subcommission's work included drafting formulation of the following memorandum, an excellent summary of contemporary issues that impinge upon the celebration of liturgy and demonstrate the necessity of serious cultural adaptation:

Need of liturgical reform and adaptation so keenly felt today because:

1) For 400 years the principle of uniformity of Latin Liturgy so rigidly understood and imposed.

2) Contemporary development of anthropological, ethnological, sociological and psychological sciences, which have brought about a universal and more conscious awareness of legitimate cultural and racial diversities. De facto, far greater diversity today, even between countries in West, than existed when Eastern and Western rites first developed—for in those days there was still a unifying Hellenistic culture more or less shared by all.

3) Excessive, pro dolor, rise of nationalism, which resents imposition of religious forms embodying a different specific cultural heritage (Greco-Roman), more especially since identified historically with colonizing traditions.

4) Technological age today; whereas the liturgy derives from a totally different cultural background, and hence its sign can only with difficulty be understood by modern man—and even if understood, will seem to some extent irrelevant or alien. Moreover, different living conditions, tempo of life, etc., today demands corresponding adjustment in framework of daily prayer life (cf. esp. divine office).

5) Ritual in many of its blessings and ceremonies presupposes a Christian milieu (e.g. processions). Few Christian countries today.

6) Even apart from all above considerations, not a few rites and ceremonies, instead of clarifying the meaning of the actus liturg. [liturgical act], can be understood only after complicated historical explanations (because these rites arose as a result of specific historical situations

of adaptation), and even experts are not always in agreement about their correct explanation. Instead of clarifying and arousing faith, they tend to obscure the *finis* [end] of the rite. In other words, we now have to explain the ''explanation.''

7) Modern age characterized by highly developed science of means of communication (propaganda: advertising). These means (radio, TV, press, movies) are used very effectively by enemies of the Church—communism, secularists—to put across their message. Modern Christian bombarded from all sides by these means of propaganda—all in a highly effective vernacular, intelligible by the masses. What better way to counteract than by employing Church's chief means of teaching, i.e., the liturgy, in an equally effective and intelligible fashion.[7]

Godfrey remembers the subsequent meetings of this subcommission and how bold the members thought their formulations were. Now he recognizes that the work of his subcommission, while broad in its implications, was only a modest beginning of essential inculturation in a world Church.

Godfrey's correspondence provides a number of glimpses of the first meeting of the preparatory commission. In his Christmas letter of 1960 he expressed his delight in meeting Pope John: ''November 10–16 I was privileged to attend the first meeting in Rome of the Pontifical Liturgical Commission preparing for the coming Vatican Council II. Good Pope John's speech was a heart-warming inspiration. (One feels like hugging him. He's the perfect embodiment of one's ideal of a favorite uncle: jolly, and thoroughly good.)''[8]

To H.A.R. he was a bit more candid:

Actually there isn't much to tell, even if there were not the solemn oath of secrecy. (Did I tell you earlier that I had to take two oaths: one to observe secrecy; and two, not to take a bribe!) The meeting itself started out rather poorly, but by the time it was finished most of us felt that an honest effort was made to allow not only for free speech but actual honest facing of facts. However, even if all the various subcommittees that were appointed for various aspects of the problem do their work well, all of this material has to pass through the screen of the great Central Committee before it reaches the Council. And the Central Committee has people like Spellman and McIntyre on it. It has others also, such as Archbishop Alter. But there will be the real decisive point.[9]

Meeting of the preparatory commission on the liturgy prior to Vatican II (1960). Godfrey is the tallest person on the right.

Godfrey kisses the ring of Cardinal Gaetano Cicognani at a meeting of the preparatory commission on the liturgy (1960). Far left: Annibale Bugnini; far right, Boniface Luykx.

It is understandable that in the first sessions members were taking one another's measure. Officials of the Sacred Congregation of Rites, men like Joseph Loew and Ferdinand Antonelli, who had been present at some of the international congresses, had been passed over when the commissions were announced. Pope John XXIII did not appoint any curial officials to commissions except for the prefects like Gaetano Cicognani who served as presidents. Godfrey remarked on their absence and couldn't quite make up his mind about those who had been placed in charge of the commission:

> As you know, Bugnini is the secretary of the Commission. Cardinal Cicognani is an old man and is aware that his knowledge of the field is inadequate, so Bugnini's role will be critically important. I am still not sure in my own mind about him. He has gone on record in writing on the side of the angels repeatedly. . . . And yet, he is a diplomatic Roman. Perhaps this simply means that he knows the situation and how much the traffic will bear.[10]

Cardinal Cicognani did make his views clear on one topic. A very stout man, he regularly dozed through most of the discussions, but when the vernacular came up he miraculously woke up, sprang to his feet, and started denouncing anything like an effort against Latin, "the bond of unity of the universal Church," forgetting in the process that the sessions were conducted in Latin and drifting into Spanish.

Godfrey likes to take some credit for the eventual triumph of the vernacularists. When their fortunes seemed most bleak because the question of Latin was dropped from the agenda, Godfrey and Joseph Pascher, a member of the preparatory commission from Germany, wrote an urgent letter to Pope John, asking for a full discussion of vernacular. Whether the Pope ever directly intervened on the basis of this note is not clear, but the question of the vernacular came up for discussion in the preparatory commission during its second meeting, April 12-21, 1961.

The subcommission on the use of Latin, under Monsignor Pietro Borella, was to make its report. Bugnini has described the unfolding of the vernacular drama as follows:

> As the plenary meeting of April 12-24, 1961, drew near, the secretariat thought it more opportune to remove the question of Latin from the agenda and leave it to be dealt with under particular headings. Two factors suggested this decision: the rising tide of disagreement, which

could have a negative effect on the entire work of the commission, and the rather muddled text that was being presented to the commission for its examination. Some of the *periti* and members were dissatisfied with this decision; they wanted a public debate of a general kind. Some of them appealed to the president against the secretariat, which they accused of favoring the vernacular. Cardinal Cicognani decided that the question should be discussed at the meeting and prepared a personal statement on it.

For more than two hours on the appointed day, the *periti,* one from each country, pleaded—some of them in sorrowful tones, including Father Godfrey Diekmann, an American Benedictine, and Professor Frederick McManus of the Catholic University in Washington, D.C.—that the door be opened to the mother tongues. It was an evening of deep emotion; all were shaken, being deeply moved by what had been said and heard. Finally, the Cardinal spoke. He had collected from the Book of Leviticus all the passages describing the Ark, the temple, and the liturgical services, in order to bring out the beauty of the liturgy and the need of being faithful to tradition. His exposition was itself given in a rather unusual mixture of Latin, Italian, and Spanish, and was thus the most eloquent possible proof of the position taken by the commission that the vernaculars should be used.[11]

Parenthetically, Balthasar Fischer helped Godfrey translate his "sorrowful pleading" into good Latin so that he could make his presentation.

Spirits rose and fell as the work of preparation pressed on. Sometimes, despite the strength of the membership on the liturgical preparatory commission, there was a certain hesitancy about the support that might be expected for the various topics being drafted. On one occasion, after the work of the day, a small group was taking stock of the world's bishops. It was a low moment, Godfrey recalls, when the group asked themselves: How many bishops do we know who are really concerned about the liturgy and think it is of the highest importance in spiritual life and pastoral work? "I think we discovered slightly less than thirty bishops who we felt would be active in promoting the liturgy on the floor of the Council. And when we had such uncertainty about the fate of our work there was the temptation not to go all out as we had planned."[12]

And then a speech turned all the participants around and gave them great courage for the work ahead. Bishop Otto Spülbeck from

Meissen, Germany, spoke one day and pleaded with the commission to be as radical as possible. He spoke off the record, saying it would be very difficult for him back in East Germany if his words got back there. He described the conditions in East Germany, where all the external supports of the Church had been swept away. All that was left was the Sunday Eucharist. And for these people, in the midst of an alien political situation, Sunday Mass was the one thing that could keep them close to the Church, would give them renewed strength, would give them an energy to remain loyal, would be their weekly inspiration to remain Catholic. Spülbeck said, "Unless Sunday Eucharist becomes a true religious experience for them, unless they really are able to know what is happening, unless every Sunday the liturgy—without explanation—becomes a recommitment for them, then the Council will have done its work in vain." And he concluded with a challenge: "Be bold as you can, so that the liturgy becomes an experience of faith and of unity for those who attend."[13]

Godfrey remembers the speech and how it galvanized the commission from that point on:

> This was a TREMENDOUS appeal for us. We could see the situation, and we felt that in some way it was true in the world at large because we are *all* in a world of secular values. The liturgy must have the sense of being a commitment, of being understood as that, of involving people, not just being a Sunday obligation to be performed. . . . That speech gave us courage to be as radical as we possibly dared to be. It moved us from caution to boldness.[14]

One other event in the preparatory phase stands out for Godfrey. It was the day Pope John came to their session. The Pope had wanted to meet with each commission at least once. On the day he appointed for a visit to the liturgical commission, Godfrey's group was discussing the Liturgy of the Hours. The Pope was delayed, so they began their work. When he arrived he signaled for the group to continue and listened for about ten minutes to the discussion before asking to speak.

He began in Latin but "stumbled all over the landscape." The group loved him and tried telepathy, but in vain. Finally, Pope John excused himself and switched to Italian. He talked a full hour about prayer—spontaneously, since he did not know the topic ahead of time, and he talked specifically about prayer in the life of a priest. The talk was wonderful. It was obvious that he was a man of prayer. To the question of Lauds and Vespers being the hinge Hours of the day, Pope John said, "Perhaps, but I say the entire Office, including Compline, before 8 A.M. and then I'm finished with it!" The group of liturgists didn't know quite what to say and so remained silent. Although the Pope was late for his next appointment, it did not keep him from having a personal word with each one: "Where are you from?" "Are your folks still living?" It was an unforgettable experience.[15]

In August 1961 a draft of the Constitution on the Liturgy was circulated among members of the liturgy commission for their observations. Godfrey's response is exceptionally thorough—a five-page document with comment on each of 121 articles. In a cover letter to Father Bugnini he summarized his reaction to the schema:

> In general: please accept my sincere and hearty congratulations for a job magnificently done. It is a splendid synthesis—and now all that remains is to polish or edit some details. My own comments are minor. Only in one case do I vigorously dissent: concerning the singing of the whole office when performed in choir or in common. Ideally, yes. Practically, a romantic dream, absolutely impossible of fulfilment, except perhaps in the rare case when the community has nothing else to do except chant the office. We would make ourselves ridiculous by proposing something that can never be realized in practice.[16]

The third meeting of the liturgical commission was scheduled for January 1962. Godfrey was unable to attend because of a previous commitment to address the annual meeting of Protestant pastors in the Upper Midwest, the first time the group had invited a Catholic priest to speak to them. According to Godfrey's report to Fred McManus, it was another ecumenical triumph:

> The talk to the Protestant ministers was very cordially received. In fact, so cordially, that I began to examine my conscience whether perhaps I hadn't made myself clear! About 600 of them, all shades. Only one unfriendly question in the discussion period; about Mary, of course. But one could sense that the great majority of those present were embarrassed by the pugnacious tone of the objection, and they rooted for me, even though they couldn't accept my answer. It was a very worthwhile experience, and one I think will open up a lot of further "dialogues."[17]

In Godfrey's absence, Fred kept him apprised of the goings on in Rome—in and out of the liturgical commission—some of which Godfrey found quite alarming. How was one to read the signs of the times? First, the Pope addressed the Pontifical Institute of Music on the beauties of Gregorian chant. Then a N.C. press release suggested that the Pope was promoting the use of Latin in seminaries. Next, *L'Osservatore Romano* reported that Amleto Cicognani, prefect of the Congregation for the Eastern Church [now Churches], who had forbidden the vernacular two years earlier, now not only approved the use of vernacular in Oriental liturgies but spoke of widening its use. Godfrey's hopes were "bucked up" one minute, "dashed down" the next: "I suppose all these contradictory things are so many eddies, preparatory to the stream flowing smoothly in one direction in the Council itself. If only one knew which direction!"[18] There appeared to be reason for alarm. Fred summarized the Roman political scene for Godfrey:

> The forces of reaction are extremely strong and are convinced that irreparable harm is being done to the Church by those deviating from the Italian line. The chief points:
>   1. Language—they wish to withdraw the concessions made thus far!
>   2. They are opposed not only to centralization of the Curia in its practice but also to any de-Italianization, since only with the Italians is there any hope for the Church.
>   3. They are totally opposed to any definition or declaration concerning episcopal power, lest this increase.[19]

Fred's informant, Boniface Luykx, also claimed that some matters which had been voted on by the central commission had been dropped by Tromp, the secretary to the commission, who allegedly admitted that while this might *seem* improper, nevertheless it was necessary "for the good of the Church!"

Meanwhile, Bugnini, the secretary to the liturgical commission, seemed to be wavering, overtaken by all sorts of doubts and fears about the schema on the liturgy, stating quite frankly that the text had to be palatable to "Eminenza" [a reference to Cardinal Gaetano Cicognani] before Cicognani would present it to the central commission. Eminenza, apparently, had two objections to the draft of the constitution: the position on vernacular and the prospect that the Divine

Office might be shortened unduly. "On other points he is a lamb, although his appearance belies the comparison."[20]

Cardinal Cicognani died on February 5, 1962, and the presidency of the liturgical commission was assumed by Cardinal Arcadio Larraona, who was, at the time, also prefect of the Congregation of Rites. Cicognani had signed the schema approved by the preparatory commission only a few days before he died. This put Larraona in the position of having to accept and present to the central preparatory commission a schema with which he was hardly in sympathy.

Larraona's appointment was further cause for alarm. From the scuttlebutt around Rome, Fred was not sanguine about the appointment: "I'm afraid I credit him with all the woes of the Congregation of Religious [his previous appointment]. This would include all the arch-centralization, the opposition to the short breviaries, the under-the-counter condemnation of the biblical introduction a few years back, etc." Fred also noted wryly that there were many people in the Congregation of Religious who were delighted that Larraona had been promoted to higher things![21]

In the spring of 1962 Godfrey and Fred McManus launched their counteroffensive. Keeping the schema intact was worth fighting for. Josef Jungmann, doyen of the liturgical movement, had said of it to Godfrey: "Well, if the Council is willing to accept this document, then I shall say my Nunc Dimittis." Since the full draft of the schema on the liturgy was about to be released, it seemed wise to pay a visit to two American members of the central preparatory committee, Cardinal Meyer and Archbishop Alter, before the March meeting of their committee, to give them some idea of what prompted the actions of the liturgical commission, explain some of the positions taken, indicate the relationship of some points to problems peculiarly American, and even clarify any obscurities in the Constitution itself.[22]

Once the central preparatory commission had met, Godfrey was eager for news from Archbishop Alter and subsequently passed it on to Fred:

> The overall picture is good. He stated that there was a very obvious opposition on the part of quite a number of the more elderly gentlemen, who were fearful of all this talk about the need of adaptation. However, he did not recall a single instance of outright "non placet" in regard to any of the items on our agenda. There were a number

of approvals "iuxta modum"; but he thought that in many instances this criticism was motivated, not by the carefully worded texts of our suggestions, but rather by some of the explanatory material. He himself thought that our Commission had done an excellent work.

The problem of the vernacular, of course, loomed large in the discussion of the Central Committee. He told me an amusing story of a cardinal expressing his alarm at the encroachments of the vernacularists, and giving quite a harangue about the sacredness of Latin as the language of the Church. When another cardinal pointed out to him that the first eight Councils of the Church were in Greek, and not in Latin, this more or less took the wind out of his sails. He seemed to have been quite unaware of this fact.

Archbishop Alter thinks that the solution of this and other problems will very largely be committed to a much larger extent than heretofore to national councils of bishops. This would of course be entirely in accord with our hopes. At all events it seems certain that the problem of language has not been sidetracked by the recent Apostolic Constitution.[23]

The deliberations of the central preparatory commission in April 1962 seemed to crystallize not simply the topics and the shape of the agenda for the Council but also the political maneuvering, the jockeying for positions of influence, the alignments of kindred spirits with kindred persuasions. A few months later, on the eve of the Council, Godfrey made this summary:

To the extreme right there is a strong minority, centering in the Roman curia. On the other end of the spectrum, there is another minority of great personalities, such as the Cardinal Archbishops of Montreal, Vienna, Munich, Utrecht, and some of the bishops of Germany and France. And in between there is the large majority of uncommitted bishops with whom, because of their number, the decisions of the Council will rest. The main hope therefore seems to be to reach this large uncommitted center. It seems providential, that after the initial meeting, October to December, they will return home and have some time to think over the matters with which they were confronted in Rome, perhaps for the first time. Hence it is of the utmost importance, that everything be done to reach these bishops, with suitable "propaganda."[24]

However interesting the political climate in Rome, 1962 was also the year when Godfrey was embroiled in some nasty political dealing on the home front, and this in two separate incidents at the Catholic University of America. Since the early 1940s Godfrey had been on a rotation for teaching at C.U.A. every third summer. In the fall of 1961, Gerard Sloyan, then head of the Department of Religious Education, wrote to Abbot Baldwin to confirm Godfrey's appointment for the following summer:

> It seems barely credible but three years will soon have passed since Father Godfrey taught in the summer session here. I therefore come, hat in hand, to ask if he may return to us, in the rhythm of the three-year cycle that you and Abbot Alcuin and he have so generously adhered to since 1944 (1941?). He has classes of greater size and enthusiasm than any lecturer we have ever had. If his physical strength holds, his power for good seems unending.[25]

Abbot Baldwin confirmed the appointment: "It has been taken for granted that Father Godfrey would teach at the Catholic University, provided he was wanted."[26] In February 1962 Sloyan had to retract the invitation, much to his dismay. The rector of the university, Monsignor William J. McDonald, conveyed to Sloyan through a third party that Godfrey "should be good enough not to join us this summer." Sloyan continued: "There is absolutely no word of who your un-friend is. . . . I wish you'd give me a little assurance in a quick note that you're not disturbed over this setback. It's a kind of tribute. You are unquestionably this country's leading pastoral figure, and this kind of thing is the price."[27]

Needless to say, Godfrey was disturbed! Sloyan's letter came as a severe shock: "The most disturbing feature about the whole thing is that one doesn't know where the opposition, and the accusations, arise from. If only the thing were above board, that it could be fought with normally fair means."[28] Godfrey told Sloyan that Abbot Baldwin had written the rector of Catholic University demanding a written explanation, since "no greater injury can be done to a teacher of theology than to impugn his orthodoxy." Furthermore, dropping Godfrey would stir up a lot of speculation and rumors. Finally, Godfrey offered a word of support for Sloyan, his colleague and friend:

> Your position there is of capital importance to Catholic life and teaching in the United States. Whatever happens in my case should in no way compromise your highly important work. Please don't worry about me. I have recovered my peace of mind and am personally resigned

to whatever will happen. The demand for an explanation from the Rector is not merely for my own gratification, but is something which the community of St. John's has a right to. At present I am much more upset about your predicament than my own.[29]

In a few days Sloyan had pieced together some of the story. He believed that McDonald "listened in to an anti-Godfrey tirade somewhere in his travels," a tirade perhaps originating at 3400 Massachusetts Ave. N.W. [residence of the apostolic delegate]. The onset of the rector's disapproval coincided with the annual meeting of the National Conference of Catholic Bishops in Washington, another event at which a tirade may have been delivered. After tracing developments, Sloyan surmised: "Your offense, it now appears, is favoring in print, many months before the fact, what the Holy See is now dead set against in *Veterum Sapientia.*"[30]

Sloyan's speculations were confirmed by the rector in a letter of March 6, 1962, to Abbot Baldwin:

> Inasmuch as you have sought whatever information I might have I feel, also, that I should tell you that some members of our University administration received complaints with regard to certain views propounded by Father Godfrey in his classes. Since this is a Pontifical University I, as Rector, am responsible to the Holy See and to the hierarchy for such matters. Even since your letter arrived the issuance of the Apostolic Constitution *Veterum Sapientia* has shown clearly the mind of our Holy Father on questions that might have been heretofore debatable. [*Veterum Sapientia* was interpreted by some to contain a stern prohibition against discussing the whole matter of the vernacular any further.] It is unnecessary to press this point because I know that you are keenly conscious of its importance.[31]

Godfrey was not yet satisfied and asked Sloyan whether he should make a trip to Washington to press for more substantial answers, but Sloyan counseled against such a move:

> Avoid a confrontation with our William. His ignorance of fact is massive, and his use for what passes as data with him alarming. First, it is neither your orthodoxy nor good name that is in question. It is simply that he has heard someone speak strongly against you. His list of scholars who have been represented to him as *non gratae* is as long as your arm—anyone who has done anything pastorally or theologically productive in other words.[32]

Godfrey's deepest concerns are revealed in a response to a "note of sympathy" he received from John Tracy Ellis:

> What I am really worried about is that distorted rumors of the whole matter will gain currency and might very probably militate against my being invited to Rome during the Council. Our preparatory Commission has been under the impression that the Commission itself would be disbanded as soon as we had finished our work. However, we were recently informed that we should keep ourselves in readiness for the Council—whatever that may mean. We suspect that it means that the various commissions will be called to Rome for the Council to act as consulting bodies for the Fathers of the Council. So if my name is tainted, and more particularly if the Apostolic delegate is associated with the whole matter, the heads of our Commission may want to play it safe and not include me in the general invitation. This is something which I would certainly like to avoid. For the prospect of being present at the Council, in any capacity whatever, is an exciting one. And since there seems to be no way of fighting the decision that has been arrived at in Washington, by the Rector of the University, I personally hope the whole matter will be promptly forgotten.[33]

And so it was, being handled privately with no press coverage. But a year later a similar incident became front page news.

A public controversy developed when it was disclosed that the administration of Catholic University had removed the names of four prominent theologians from a list of candidates for a Lenten lecture series sponsored by the university's graduate-student council. The speakers in question were two eminent Jesuits from Woodstock College, Father John Courtney Murray and Father Gustave Weigel, Father Hans Küng, a member of the University of Tübingen faculty, and Godfrey. The university's official press release gave the gist of it:

> *Religious News Service* Monday, February 18, 1963. Msgr. Joseph McAllister, vice rector of the Catholic University, explained that the action implied no personal criticism of the priests or their views on issues arising out of the Vatican Council. "But they represent a very definite point of view, a very definite attitude, in regard to certain ecclesiastical matters now being debated," he said. "The university did not want to put itself in the position of championing this view or that," he explained. "A number of matters quite controversial ecclesiastically came up at the Ecumenical Council and there are strong views on both sides."[34]

Dinner and interview by Vincent Yzermans (center) during Vatican II with the four who were banned from the Catholic University of America: (left to right) Gustave Weigel, Godfrey Diekmann, John Courtney Murray, Hans Küng.

Indeed! The press release exposed the university to a great deal of ridicule on both sides of the Atlantic: " . . . it is hard to conceive of anyone concerned with the Church who does not have some 'very definite point of view.' " "[The Catholic University of America] has saddened and somewhat humiliated us all." "The fault of these theologians lies not in having wrong ideas but in having ideas, period." "It seems incredible to have to say it, but a university with any intellectual pretensions really ought to be open to some views besides the narrowly orthodox." "Strange, isn't it, that the same university allows one of its official publications, the *American Ecclesiastical Review,* to defend with vigor the conservative point of view held by a minority of the bishops of the Council?" "It is sad, and unhappily significant, that it should be the Catholic University that stands as the symbol of the wrong kind of silence." More than twenty Catholic papers protested the action, calling it beyond all comprehension, a retreat to the Middle Ages, a test of liberty, a failure of the ecumenical spirit. One claimed that the arguments were simply silly. Cardinal Joseph Ritter, archbishop of St. Louis, a member of the university's board of trustees, made his displeasure clear in a letter to the rector:

199

As you know quite well, I feel very strongly about the importance of the Catholic University and its continued well-being and development. For this reason, I thought it best to let you know my views on the current furor raised by the University's refusal to permit certain specific speakers to be invited to address the students. As a member of the Board of Trustees for the Catholic University, I was greatly displeased to learn of the University's decision to bar four Priests, prominent in their fields of theological endeavor, from addressing the students.

As a member of the American Hierarchy, responsible for the University, I deeply regret the deleterious effect such a short-sighted decision will have on our Catholic University's reputation. Personally, I am indignant that such an incident could take place in any Catholic institution of higher learning in our country.

I note that in his public explanation for this denial of permission to issue invitations, Monsignor McAllister said that the Administration felt that, by inviting them "at this time," the University would seem to be "put in the position of taking sides on these issues which are still being debated in the Ecumenical Council."

Since the "definite points of view" espoused by these theologians are pertinent to the Council and are still being debated, it would seem that the cause of truth and of learning would be benefited by admitting any one of these theologians to speak at the University. Since the "point of view" of such Faculty members as Monsignor Joseph Fenton are all too well known, the University can hardly lay claim to assuming a neutral position.

The Catholic University should be a ferment of intellectual activity and discussion of conciliar topics should be carried on and encouraged In this, as in other subjects of genuine interest, it would be hard to imagine a presentation by a speaker who did not have a "definite point of view" as anything but insipid.

I am profoundly dismayed that the officials of a citadel of learning could fail to realize the slur on the reputations of these four eminent and orthodox Priests by ruling them unacceptable "at this time."

Finally, I believe that the very spirit of the Second Vatican Council has been compromised by this decision. It is tragic that at the very time Pope John has led the Church into an ecumenical dialogue, the Catholic University has shown unmistakable signs of fear over an exchange of views among Catholics.[36]

Cardinal Ritter reflected the attitude of many bishops. Godfrey's invitations to give priests' retreats and to conduct Clergy Days tripled almost immediately after the announcement of the ban. Gus Weigel reported the same popularity. Another unexpected sequel to the university's action was that books of theologians who "had ideas" suddenly showed a decided upswing in sales. Godfrey's book, *Come, Let Us Worship,* a collection of his Liturgical Week addresses over the years, promptly sold out and went into a second printing.

At the end of the first episode at Catholic University, Godfrey feared for his reputation. By the time the press finished with the second episode, it was laughable; Catholic University had become the target, not the four theologians. Godfrey began to delight in the distinction he had gained by association. Several years later a limerick commemorating the whole affair circulated at Vatican II:

> Of Murray, Weigel, Diekmann and Küng
> The praises were everywhere süng.
> > The delegate then
> > Seemed out-of-date when
> He gave orders to have them all hüng.

Had the first of these episodes hurt Godfrey's chances to be invited to the Council as a *peritus?* It's difficult to trace cause and effect, but when the Council opened in the fall of 1962, Godfrey had not been summoned. As a consultor to the liturgical preparatory commission, he had high hopes of going to Rome for the Council itself. He had suggested as much in a letter to J. B. O'Connell: "Father Bugnini stated that the Commission is nequaquam [by no means] dissolved after its 'final' meeting in January. I wonder what this signifies and whether we will be invited to be present at Rome during the Council."[37] Often in correspondence with Fred McManus, Godfrey speculated about their prospects, whether he should cancel classes, how soon a decision would be made.

In the end, one was taken and one was left: Fred McManus received an appointment and Godfrey did not—perhaps the greatest disappointment of his life. "How I wish I could accompany you," he wrote to Fred, and then graciously invited Fred to become an official correspondent for *Worship,* "perhaps an advantage in getting information or gaining access to some sessions."[38] The rumors of Godfrey's appointment continued; his name had been mentioned in a syndicated column from Rome as among the "experts." Godfrey described the agony to Fred:

> For a day or so I was living in high hopes. And just yesterday when coming out of class, I was told there was an urgent message for me at the Porter's office; a cablegram from Europe! I violated all monastic modesty in rushing to the Porter's office, only to discover that the cable was from London, reminding me of an article that was overdue for *The Way*. If you have your ups and downs, I had my big up and down yesterday. And this morning (October 23rd) your letter of October 18th arrived, with no mention of my having been appointed. So that has driven the last nail into the coffin. I'm offering up my disappointment for the Council, and more particularly for your own important work. May it prosper.[39]

Godfrey followed the opening of the Council and all the news emanating from Rome avidly. He was dying to know what was going on and said as much to Fred: "I would, of course, forever be grateful to you if you would keep me informed of what is happening, so far as your vow of secrecy allows. (Or am I still included in that as one who belonged to the Preparatory Commission?")[40]

Fred obliged with delightfully newsy letters, giving Godfrey a glimpse of the Council (the opening ceremonies were like a nineteenth-century pageant; the Pope's talk was wonderful, condemning only negative approaches; the bishops were already interested in going home because of the incredibly poor arrangements). Fred also sent detailed information about the fate of the schema on the liturgy:

> Wagner quotes the Germans as saying that the liturgical constitution is the only schema worthy of an ecumenical council. Liturgically: nothing but rumors. Evidently Antonelli is to be secretary of the commission. He admits our constitution is good in itself but fears that it is too specific and too advanced for the bishops—who took to Thursday's baroque Mass with delight. I fear he will not be helpful, since he was not on the preparatory commission. He hesitates over vernacular in the Mass and he wants to go slowly. . . . Ottaviani attacked our constitution bitterly, saying all liturgists are iconoclasts. Lienart responded that the bishops are the liturgists and the constitution was supported by the German and French. . . . Even [Amleto] Cicognani told Bugnini that Ottaviani's attack was unworthy. Nevertheless Bugnini is accused of having contravened the will of the commission (!) and of being a vernacularist (!). Frightful issues. I am not at the mo-

ment sure whether it is good to be here. One day up, one day down. Tomorrow the 2nd general congregation. Pray and hope.[41]

Three days later Fred wrote again:

Having spent a ridiculous day of the usual ups and downs, I write to unburden my soul. The people here are more confused than ever. . . . Hallinan is an excellent man and may well turn out to be a real hero, in spite of his devotion to Krol, Dearden, and Vagnozzi. Vagnozzi told me yesterday with great glee that the liturgy constitution will have "rough sailing."

The Germans are afraid that liturgy coming first may be fussed over too minutely even apart from die-hard opposition. But the decision to put it ahead of theology was evidently forced on the body of presidents by those who are utterly contemptuous of the theological schema. K. Rahner, Congar and De Lubac are supposedly doing new schema as substitute.

. . . I am not sure whether I had seen Bugnini and Antonelli when I wrote last. Bugnini has learned from his provincial that the Holy Office has nothing against him and his fall from grace is due to Larraona and Antonelli. One fantastic story is that Antonelli has prepared an entirely new constitution on the liturgy and will circularize it among the Fathers. This seems absurd since Larraona did in fact present ours which was *de facto* accepted by the central commission.

. . . People like Wagner, Jungmann, Quasten, Häring (a fine man whom I met for the first time) have been inquiring for you. I wish you were here—not in the sense of the postcard from the vacationer, but because you can deal so well with the German and the French. Our best hope in that regard is to set up a strong contact through [Bishop Leo] Dworschak or someone like him who would then report to Hallinan. I can carry messages all right but I don't think Hallinan truly accepts the position of Wagner and Martimort in relation to their respective episcopal bodies.[42]

Godfrey delighted in the news and followed every detail:

Your report on the demotion of Bugnini at the hands of Larraona and Antonelli sounds ominous. The latter was of course bitterly disappointed that neither he nor Loew, or anyone else of the SCR, had a role in the Preparatory Commission. I suspect that he resented Bugnini as a climber, who disregarded all the preliminary work on the missal and breviary that had been done in the SCR, in order to start da capo. One can only hope that his resentment of Bugnini will not carry over too drastically to include all of Bugnini's work on the Preparatory Commission.[43]

Godfrey relished each bit of news, filtered it through his own insights and preoccupations, and sent it on to encourage others who were following the Council from a distance. To Thomas Merton he wrote:

> The Holy Father's opening speech was most encouraging. Even our own Bishop of St. Cloud, who is really quite conservative, in a letter to the Abbot and community, stated that Ottaviani, standing to the right of the Holy Father, looked a bit uncomfortable. Hence the joke now making the rounds in Rome. Where are Cardinals Ottaviani and Ruffini these days? Oh, haven't you heard? They are on their way to the Council of Trent.

> Today the Fathers tackle the Constitution on the Liturgy. We had, as a matter of course, expected that Bugnini, who was the secretary of our Preparatory Commission, and who steered our constitution through the Central Committee, would also be the secretary of the Liturgy Commission for the Council itself. But a letter from Rome brings the rather disturbing news that he was eliminated, and that Father Antonelli O.F.M., will be appointed secretary of the Liturgy Commission. The latter is a sound man, but he is afraid of the vernacular, and is always urging that we go slowly. Ottaviani is very unhappy about the liturgy constitution. He has recently stated that all liturgists are iconoclasts. And very likely it was his influence that removed Bugnini. The news that Archbishop Hallinan was elected to the Episcopal Liturgical Commission is, however, heartening. I have a theory that all good Newman chaplains make good bishops. Hallinan is my prize exhibit for the theory. I hope you get your novices to do some extra praying and fasting during these critical days of the shaping of the liturgy.[44]

Besides not being at the Council, Godfrey was also able to "offer up" something else quite concretely by way of prayer and penance, as Pope John had requested for the success of the Council: an operation for a double hernia and subsequent pulmonary embolism with complications in his circulatory system. In letters to friends he minimized the severity of his illness so that some, like Clifford Howell, seemed quite shocked:

I am appalled to learn of all that you have been through, had no idea it was so bad, and thank God with all my heart that you have pulled through. I had thought it was just a case of hernia which involves a slash or two with a scalpel, a stitch or two, and a week or two in bed doing nothing. But you've been wallowing in blood clots, pneumonia, pleurisy and Sacraments of the Sick with all the trimmings![45]

Although Godfrey was removed from the action, that didn't prevent him from taking his part during the first session. Senator Eugene McCarthy, onetime novice and frequent visitor to St. John's, was scheduled to attend a NATO meeting in Europe. Godfrey suggested that he might have a visit with the Holy Father while in Europe "to push the liturgy agenda," and to this end wrote to Fred to make the necessary arrangements: "I feel this would be as weighty as similar recommendations from a half-dozen members of the hierarchy. And Gene does make a wonderful impression. I am sure he and the Holy Father would get along famously."[46]

In November Fred mentioned that a good number of the original liturgical commission members were either in Rome or were coming on their own to help out and he urged Godfrey to do the same, perhaps whetting his appetite by sending more news:

Fundamentally the problem is procedural. The bishops will discuss the entire text—and are only in the middle of chapter 2 now. This, however repetitious, is not a tragedy—it preserves the freedom of discussion which may be vital later on—but there will be no *vote* whatsoever until the Liturgical Commission prepares and offers its views on the amendments now being offered by the Fathers. The plan is that when we have amendments on chapter I ready, we interrupt the discussion for a vote on each point—placet or non placet. Next we insert the amendments in the schema and prepare it for a placet, non placet, placet iuxta modum vote. If the ⅔ placet vote includes some iuxta modum, the modi have to be considered. This can go on indefinitely. I think our great achievement in the Commission so far—thanks to Martimort and Bonet (a Rotal Auditor and a fine man)—is to insist that nothing goes from our Commission to the Fathers and nothing is said in the name of our Commission without a ⅔ vote within the Commission. Braga and an OFM (who studied in Paris and is vouched for absolutely by Gy and Martimort) are assistant secretaries to Antonelli (who is now known as homo ambiguous) and will make any real procrastination because of mechanical, typing problems impossible.

The [U.S.] bishops are extremely timid among themselves and I should like to get a little sociological and psychological study done on them. One real problem is Bishop Waters who is just a little to the right of Robert Taft ["Mr. Republican," conservative senator from Ohio—*not* the Jesuit] and has been named chairman of the U.S. Bishops committee on liturgy *at the council.* . . . Hallinan is very good indeed; I only wish it were not a case of getting him a Berlitz-type education in the liturgy while we operate. Buswell is a saint, besides being very sane.

The Delegate has spread the story that Bugnini refused to make changes ordered by the Central Commission. Not only is this calumnious, but it appears that the shoe is on the other foot: that someone did make changes when the text was in proof; Martimort says it was Ottaviani, Pizzardo, and Marella. The viciousness of Roman curial interplay is frightening; Vagnozzi is quoted as telling a meeting of papal diplomats that they must fight to *strengthen* the Curia.

Generally speaking (and humanly speaking) I am hopeful so far as the Patres conciliares are concerned. My fears are mostly in our Liturgical Commission where the will of the pastoral bishops could be frustrated or delayed—and of course in the Curia, which would never implement the liturgical constitution. There seems to be a great hope that many of the bishops are having their eyes opened and that the passage of time is much on the side of acceptance of the liturgy constitution.[47]

Godfrey's Christmas letter in 1962 captures his great disappointment at being sidelined during those heady days as well as his generous assessment of the progress that was made in the first session—as far as he can piece it together:

Some of you (to judge from your letters) are still under the impression that I was in Rome for this first session of the Council. Unfortunately, I did not have that privilege. Several NCWC news reports did state that I had been summoned as one of the "experts"—and so of course my own hopes ran high, until it became clear that the report was false. I'm still in the dark as to how it originated. But the keen disappointment was something concrete that I could "offer up" for the success of the Council.

The news from the Council—both official and what filtered through leaks, particularly in the Italian press—has from the outset surpassed the most optimistic forecast. The overwhelming approval by the Council Fathers of the first chapter of the Liturgy schema, containing the general principles of liturgical renewal and reform, means that the main battle in the matter of liturgy has been won: for the principles that have been approved sanction all the chief objectives for which the liturgical movement has been striving these many decades. The remaining chapters still to be voted on spell out their application in greater detail. The contents of this Chapter One have not been made public: and Pope John, after the final vote on December 7, told the assembled Fathers that it would not be promulgated until the close of the Council. However, *Osservatore Romano* a few days later carried a lengthy article of comment by Fr. Cyprian Vagaggini, in which he summarizes all the chief points, and in fact quotes entire sections, including that on the vernacular, verbatim! Among other things, he states that the all-important principle of "distribution of roles" has been approved: i.e., that all who take part in the Mass, priest, minister, choir, people, do all those things, and *only* those things, which pertain to their respective office. In other words, no more duplication of any kind! This principle alone entails a far-reaching liturgical restoration, and calls for Hosannas of grateful joy. I am at present busily engaged in translating the *Osservatore* article for the January issue of *Worship*. Read it—and rejoice![48]

No sooner had the Council disbanded than the more conservative faction among the Curia began to pick away at the work accomplished in the first session, despite the overwhelming approval of the Council Fathers for the first chapter of the schema on the liturgy. In the spring of 1963, as Fred prepared to depart for a meeting of the liturgical commission, he wrote a note to Godfrey: "More than ever I wish you were along. It looks like a rough one. Larraona apparently hasn't given up hope he can junk chapter I—and Antonelli will be his evil genius I fear. Pray that we get somewhere."[49]

Godfrey was outraged: "Your fears that Cardinal Larraona together with our friend Antonelli are actually trying to have the approved Chapter I reconsidered came as an incredible shock. My first reaction was: they wouldn't dare!"[50]

At the same time Godfrey was once again preoccupied by the possibility that he might receive an appointment:

How I wish I were with you to experience the actual struggle. . . . I have heard from Father Yzermans that Bishop [Leo] Dworschak,

Paul J. Hallinan,
Archbishop of Atlanta

writing in his own name and that of Bishop Bartholome, suggested to Archbishop Hallinan (as the American member of the original liturgy committee) to have me declared a peritus for the second session of the Council. This was about four weeks ago. So my hopes, though fading, are not entirely extinguished.[51]

From Rome Fred confirmed the rumor:

Most confidentially, Hallinan has sent your name to Cicognani (just this week) and (at my suggestion) has put it to Larraona that, if you are appointed a conciliar peritus, he (L) should designate you to our Commission. He (L) is boxed I think because he made a great to-do at our opening session last fall to the effect that of course anyone among the conciliar periti who had served on the preparatory commission would be assigned to our group. . . . Incidentally, if you do get appointed, there is a good chance that our commission will turn into a post-conciliar commission (even during the council) to do the actual work. For that reason I really pray that the thing goes through for you.[52]

A few days later Godfrey confided his hopes to J. B. O'Connell: "There is an outside chance that I may be attending the second session of the Council. This is based on a rumor that two bishops suggested my name for appointment as peritus. I can only hope that the rumor has some foundation. For I would dearly love to be present when such history is being made."[53]

AND THEN IT CAME!!!

Dear Father Godfrey:

At Bishop Dworschak's request, I spoke to His Eminence, Cardinal Cicognani, while I was in Rome for a Commission meeting, asking that you be named a *peritus* of the Council. The Cardinal readily acquiesced, and this morning I received the official notice that I herewith enclose.

Father McManus and I are delighted that you will be in this position when we meet in September. I spoke briefly with Abbot Dworschak, here in Atlanta Monday, and told him that with his and your approval I would write to Cardinal Larraona, and ask that you be named *peritus* to the Commission on the Sacred Liturgy.

Since I will not be taking any priest from our Archdiocese, I would prefer that in any announcement of your appointment, no mention of my part be made. Those of us on the Commission are just happy that we will have your presence and help on it.

I hope your health has improved, and that you will be able to interject a little rest and relaxation into the heavy schedule you already have. May God bless you always.

Sincerely yours in Christ,
✝ Paul J. Hallinan
Most Reverend Paul J. Hallinan
Archbishop of Atlanta[54]

Godfrey was away from the abbey conducting a retreat for Protestant clergymen when the letter arrived, hence a slight delay in the response:

I am profoundly grateful to you for having requested my appointment, and I can only express my determination and hope that I shall not prove a disappointment to you, but can in some small measure be useful. I would of course be delighted, further, to be included among the Commission on the Sacred Liturgy. Father Fred McManus and myself have been working in close collaboration these many years past, and it would be a great honor indeed to be able to continue working with him on this decisively important task.[55]

Who were these *periti*—these experts—whom Godfrey was now joining? They have been described as "scholars ordinarily removed from the power structure in the Church, who moved into new positions of prominence and effective leadership," winning the respect and admiration of bishops both for the intrinsic value of their contributions and for the evident quality of their own Christian lives.[56] They were called "a council within a council," a relative handful of men, some of them regarded as renegades of the Church. "Some of them had been sacked from their jobs. Others had their books suppressed, even put on the Index. Most of them had suffered in one way or another from the attentions of the Holy Office of the Roman Curia."[57] At the Council "they were hearing some of their theories, once condemned as dangerous or heretical, enshrined in documents that future ages will undoubtedly regard as the crowning achievement of the Second Vatican Council. . . . New ideas about what the Church is and who belongs to it, the priesthood of the laity, the collegiality of the bishops—all these and many more had been thought out, developed, and propagated by a comparative handful," a good number of whom were named as *periti*. "For the bishops and the rest of the Catholic Church, the new Council decrees might seem the beginning of a new era. For the men who pioneered them, it was the end of a long road."[58]

They were mostly European: the Germans were represented by Guardini and Rahner; the French, by Chenu, Congar, De Lubac, and Daniélou; Schillebeeckx was Flemish; Küng was Swiss. Many were appointed by cardinals as their personal theologians during the Council. They were ghostwriters for interventions, mediators and interpreters for a world press. They were invited to discussions among bishops and sometimes to give formal addresses. Their views were sought by many on all aspects of the Council. Their greatest contribution, of course, was service on the various commissions.

According to Monsignor Vincent Yzermans, many *periti* appointed before the Council were friends of the pre-Vatican II Roman Curia. American bishops went to Rome as "babes in the woods"; during the opening days of the Council they discovered that the Germans were bursting the Council wide open and getting their own *periti* named. Americans followed their example until the number of *periti* from the United States had gotten quite large and Amleto Cicognani called a halt to fairly wholesale appointments. Yzermans approached Hallinan and said, "We have to get Godfrey here." He then sent a letter to Bishop Leo Dworschak; it got misdirected to the bishop's nephew Abbot Baldwin Dworschak, but eventually Godfrey's appointment came through. It was a distinction to be chosen during the Council itself: John Courtney Murray was among those so named.[59]

Godfrey was thrilled to be heading for Rome. He wrote his thanks to his mentor, Bishop Leo Dworschak:

> Saturday morning I received a package from Archbishop Hallinan, containing the official documents from the Secretariat of State, appointing me as peritus for the Council. I had already known privately, through Father Yzermans, that you had suggested to Archbishop Hallinan in your own name and that of Bishop Bartholome that he request this appointment. But since the information was given to me confidentially, I did not feel it proper for me to express my thanks to you. Now, Archbishop Hallinan states in his letters, both to Father Abbot and myself, that he has made the request at your suggestion. I am most deeply grateful to you for having initiated the request, and to give me the opportunity of being witness in Rome of history in the making. It has been a wonderful experience to note the warm satisfaction of the confreres when told the news. For the appointment is indeed an honor to the entire abbey, and I have not been slow in communicating to the brethren privately your own role in the affair. I can only hope that I shall not prove a disappointment to your expectations, and that in some small measure at least I can prove useful in Rome.[60]

Bishop Dworschak also was delighted: "It had been a great disappointment to me that you were not designated as [a peritus] for the first session. . . . I don't know how much actual work remains on the liturgical schema beyond the voting. I understand that the commission has completed its work of reducing the multitude of suggestions and amendments to concrete propositions to be voted on by the council fathers. But I do hope that your designation as a peritus will insure your being retained as a consultor for the special commission which later will revise the liturgical books."[61]

Godfrey's appointment was none too soon as far as Fred was concerned. Now at least he would have his close ally in waging the war of attrition with the representatives of the Congregation and their allies who were trying their best to weaken the Constitution on the Liturgy. At every turn Fred felt outmaneuvered by Larraona and company. His frustration is apparent in a letter to Archbishop Hallinan:

> [The roadblocks] would include the use of secret ballots, the loading of the subcommissions, the device of the subcommission of presidents, the fact—when you come to think of it—that only about six or eight of the experts were in fact from outside Rome, the failure to take the vote of the experts before and distinct from the vote of the members, etc., etc.[62]

For Godfrey, a man who once confessed how much he loved Rome for all its "devious medieval plotting," these tidbits were delicious appetizers for the days ahead.

NOTES TO CHAPTER 7

1. GLD, letter to FRM, September 2, 1960.
2. GLD, letter to FRM, September 19, 1960.
3. GLD, letter to FRM, September 2, 1960.
4. GLD, summary from personal papers, no date.
5. GLD, letter to Johannes Wagner, November 7, 1960.
6. GLD, letter to H.A.R., December 21, 1960. Parenthetically, Godfrey and John O'Connell became fast friends during the preparatory meetings, as this letter to Canon O'Connell attests: "Until we met, I thought of you only as a formidable authority in matters rubrical, one to whom one mentally pays obeisance, and is secretly glad it can be done from a distance. But that mental image has been thoroughly changed. You are a warm and delightful personality and I am grateful that circumstances have allowed us to become friends,—as well as fellow warriors in the cause." [GLD, letter to J.B. O'Connell, December 20, 1961.]

7. GLD, personal papers from the preparatory commission, no date. The following is the document, sometimes in telegraphic style, which Godfrey, as secretary, drafted after the first discussion of cultural adaptation in the subcommission, and upon which subsequent work was based.

SCHEMA

I. *Principia generalia.*

1) Christus Ipse. He, the Founder of the sacraments, must be our Exemplar in the use of them through time. The Incarnational Principle. Christ adapted Himself, in His manner of teaching, in His way of action, to the capacity of intelligence and to the culture and traditions and religious inheritance of His audience. He used what was at hand, and built upon it.

2) The Primitive Church followed Christ's example. The Church became incarnate through the first centuries in the Hellenistic civilization of the Mediterranean world, by adapting, in so far as it was spiritually useful, the external expression of the essentials of salvation she had received from Christ to the normal power of receptivity and to the framework of cultural

and religious reference of these new peoples. The entire history of the early development of the sacramental rites is a history of such progressive adaptation; even pre-Christian, and sound pagan customs and practices were not scorned, but were occasionally embodied when judged useful, and remoto scandalo. And it was precisely the Western (Roman) Church which continued, longer and more generously than most of the Churches of the East, to practice flexibility in this matter of adaptation: e.g., change of language; influence of the Gallican liturgy on the final shaping of the Roman.

3) Sacramenta propter homines. True, Eucharist and other sacraments are worship of God: but they are also, and immediately, for the sanctification of man, basically enabling him to fulfil his essential task of worship. But "man" is not an abstraction: he is a concrete being, in concrete circumstances, with concrete powers and conditionings of receptivity and understanding.

a) Sacraments are "signs of faith." They not only presuppose faith in the recipient, but are expressions of faith: the faith of the Church *and* of the recipient. Text and rites are meant to stir up and deepen the recipient's faith, so that the redemptive opus Christi meets with the fullest possible opus operantis of the "faithful." Hence they should be reasonably *intelligible*. The Church in the historical development of the sacramental rites generously expanded the essential signification deriving from Christ: she wanted the "sign" to signify more clearly, convincingly, and attractively, in order that thereby the aroused faith of the recipient enable him to enter more fully into this saving "encounter" with the Redeemer. The ex opere operato of the sacraments in the concrete and normally achieves its divinely willed effect to the degree of the ex opere operantis (i.e., of the "faith") of the recipient. Hence the imperative importance of undertaking such changes or adaptations in the sacramental rites which will contribute to their most intelligible signification for the people of our time: i.e., which are most conducive to arousing and deepening their faith in this redemptive mystery.

To state this in another way: the Church added prayers and rites in "explanation" of the essential signification; in actual fact, because of language and strangeness of some of the symbolic rites, these additions would seem now to add rather to the obscurity of the sign. We now in many cases have "to explain the 'explanation'."

Aliis verbis: emphasis on "signification" of sacraments must again be brought into proper balance with the post-Scholastic one-sided emphasis on their causality.

b) The same conclusion of need of adaptation, will be arrived at from the principle that the liturgy is "the work of the people of God." It should be a rationabile obsequium: of the people of God of our time, with their concrete capacity of understanding as conditioned by the civilization in which they live as well as by inherited religious traditions and values. "Quidquid recipitur, ad modum recipientis recipitur," has application here too.

4) Equal value of all the Rites in the Church. The non-Roman Rites, not just museum pieces. All the Rites represent the historic process of "adaptation." They were bridges with contemporary cultures and religious sensibilities, embodying these into Christian worship. Because they are of equal status and dignity in the Church, eventual adaptation of sacramental rites should not be thought of in terms exclusively of adapting the "Roman Rite" to new conditions (e.g., in mission countries). Non-Western (non-Roman) traditions of Rite may be equally valuable, and in some cases, a more acceptable basis for adaptation.

II. *Applicationes.* (Essential concern: adaptation to make the sacramental signs more "significant" for the people of God living in these contemporary times.)

1) General. E.g., language, music (including instrumental), vestments, liturgical colors, calendar (feasts); ritual blessings for modern industrial age (present Ritual presupposes rural, pre-industrial era); restoring Scripture to more meaningful role; adapting rites of Sacraments to changed conditions and to modern needs (rite of Confirmation; greater and more joyous solemnization of marriage); restoration of some form of "public prayer service" (divine office) to the laity in a pastorally practicable format; etc., etc.

(Cf. Bishop Van Bekkum, in *The Assisi Papers,* and Fr. Hofinger, in *Liturgy and Missions.* Though treating chiefly of mission problems, much of what they suggest has more general validity and applicability.)

2) In Mission Countries. (A special sub-commission has been appointed in the Commission of Propaganda, to study questions of "Adaptation of the liturgy to mission countries." Should get in touch with them, to present as far as possible a "united front.")

3) In other Countries: Occidentales (i.e., non-mission, with a greater or lesser history of Christian life and tradition).
E.g., changes in Calendar—to fit Southern Hemisphere. Changes in "catechumenal" rites in baptism. Etc.

The need of liturgical adaptations for mission countries seems to be generally recognized and acknowledged. The need of similar adaptation for traditionally "Christian" countries meets with less acceptance. And yet, in some respects, our "Occidental" situation is worse than that of mission countries, and our need of help is greater. Primitive peoples still have the feeling for "sign," and the feeling for necessity of worship, which we in the West have largely lost; they are less "depersonalized" than we have tragically become; they have a stronger sense of tribal and community loyalty and responsibility, which aids them in implementing the ideal of community worship and mutual concern. To an appalling extent, the Western countries have become de-Christianized; and as it is often more difficult to bring back an apostate to the practice of his religion than to win over a non-Christian, so too the situation in the Western, traditionally Christian countries, calls perhaps for more drastic and generous measures of "adaptation" than are necessary in mission areas.

4) Peculiares coetus (familiae religiosorum).

E.g., some form of abbreviated Divine Office for those now not bound to the breviary; a more or less uniform rite of profession for religious women, more closely modeled on some of the basic features of the consecratio virginum; calendar reform (feasts of order restricted to order, and perhaps with exception of several founders of historically great orders, not to be imposed on universal Church); etc.

III. Vota

1) That in the official determination of "adaptations," the hierarchy of a nation, or perhaps preferably of an entire geographical or cultural "region," be given a large and weighty voice. At the present time, there are 41 national "Conferences of Bishops," who meet regularly to discuss the religious problems of their respective countries and plan common programs to advance the kingdom of God among their people. They are in closest touch with their flocks, and can best sense and interpret their needs. It was no doubt providential that the Council of Trent brought order and uniformity into the chaotic multiplicity of liturgical rites that prevailed at the time. But in reaction to the previous multiplicity, there resulted a rigidity which can be equally undesirable, and detrimental to the normal proper functioning of the sacraments as meaningful signs, inasmuch as it makes no allowance for cultural changes brought by time, and for the variety of existing religious temperament among different peoples.

The Holy See has repeatedly praised the Eastern Rites precisely because, preserving unity in essentials, they nevertheless in their variety express in manifold ways the beauty of Christ's Bride, the Church. There is no one who denies that the original development of the Eastern and Western families of Rites was a good thing, since they corresponded so admirably to the differences of religious sentiment and experience in Eastern and Western peoples. Sacramenta propter homines. And yet it may be questioned whether the then existing differences were as vast as those that now obtain between various peoples included in the category of "Western civilization." East and West, in the first centuries of Christianity, shared a common culture, and had common backgrounds of religious traditions, to a degree that cannot be taken for granted, e.g., in comparing Catholic life in Australia and Spain, or in the United States and in Italy, or in Portugal and Germany. A common pattern of culture and of values simply no longer, alas, exists even in the "Westernized" world. And most certainly not in the world at large: the Belgian Congo and Belgium are two different worlds! Unless that basic fact be honestly faced, and steps taken to adapt the Universal Church's way of worship to meet the fact in so far as such adaptation is found necessary and useful, it will mean a rejection in practice of the incarnational principle established by Christ Himself, and faithfully adopted by the Church in the springtime of her life. And the bishops of a country, or of a "region," precisely because of their loyalty to Peter and to the Universal Church, can best advise as to the specific conditions and needs of the people committed to their care. Nor would such adaptations according to the decisions of the local hierarchy be something new: even at the present, some variety in the Ritual according to countries is permitted; this would simply be an extension of that practice. Disciplined variety, carefully supervised by the respective competent hierarchy, is the oldest and best tradition of the Church.

2) That the present abuse of individual petitions to the Curia by specifically interested parties be curtailed. Pressure can now sometimes be brought to bear by small, well-organized and vocal groups, for specific liturgical changes, which it is difficult to withstand. Again, if the hierarchy of a country or region were given greater voice in determining what changes or adaptations would be useful, the influence of such pressure groups would eo ipso be voided.

*****

To the schema itself, Godfrey appended this memo, which gives some insight into the working procedures adopted by the subcommissions:

The above is the schema, slightly "fleshed out," which we agreed upon during the meetings of our sub-committee in Rome. Each member of the sub-committee is expected to develop the schema *fully,* and to prepare a complete statement (with full documentation of the first part: the General Principles), *as if his statement were the one to be presented to the General Council.* The schema itself is of course no more than a practical "work plan." You may wish to add or subtract, or to modify some of the divisions and subdivisions. Feel free to do so; but it would be desirable if the over-all schema be maintained. Too, you may feel yourself more especially competent, or interested, in one of the other points; e.g., Fr. Hofinger in the field of mission adaptation. By all means, expand that particular aspect more fully. Thus, if each contributes in greater detail his own special field of knowledge, the total synthesis will be more complete and satisfactory.

Unfortunately, time is desperately short. The Secretary of the Commission (Fr. Bugnini) demands that the *final copy* be in his hands in Rome not later than March 15. Accordingly, we agreed on the following:

By January 15, *your complete statement should be in the hands of Dr. Quasten, in Washington, D.C.* (It may be in Latin, English, French or German.) Dr. Quasten, the Relator, and Fr. Diekmann, the Secretary, will then come together to synthesize the various statements into one whole. This composite work will be in the hands of all members of the sub-committee by *February 5,* for your comments, revisions, and perhaps some additions. By February 25, these annotated copies should be in Dr. Quasten's hands, in Washington, D.C. Again Dr. Quasten and Fr. Diekmann will collaborate in producing the final copy in Latin (of which, of course, all collaborators will receive carbon copies).

You will notice that among the Proposita et Monita of the SCR, distributed to all who belong to the Pontifical Liturgical Commission, the section on "Adaptation of the Rites or of the Liturgy to the Traditions and Genius of the Various Peoples" is especially detailed, and called one of the most important matters of concern. Nor is there question of limiting adaptation to mission peoples! You may wish to make your own some of the SCR suggestions. The problem of language must be faced also by our sub-commission, even though a special sub-commission has been appointed to give its recommendations: for unless the various sub-commissions such as ours, or those on the Mass, or the sacraments, or the divine office, point out how relevant this question is for their own particular topic, the "Language Sub-commission" can accomplish little.

May the Spirit of Light and Strength aid us all!

8. GLD, Christmas letter, 1960.
9. GLD, letter to H.A.R., December 21, 1960.
10. Ibid.
11. Annibale Bugnini, *The Reform of the Liturgy—1948-1975* (Collegeville, Minn.: The Liturgical Press, 1990) 24. Eventually the matter was resolved by omitting a section on vernacular in the Constitution and scattering references to use of the mother tongue through other chapters as pertinent.
12. GLD, taped interview, fall 1987.
13. Ibid.
14. Ibid.
15. Ibid.
16. GLD, letter to Annibale Bugnini, September 17, 1961.
17. GLD, letter to FRM, January 27, 1962.
18. Ibid.
19. FRM, letter to GLD, no date [early in 1962].
20. FRM, letter to GLD, no date [spring 1962].
21. GLD, letter to FRM, February 20, 1962.
22. GLD, letter to FRM, January 27, 1962; FRM, letter to Cardinal Meyer, March 12, 1962.

23. GLD, letter to FRM, April 25, 1962.

24. GLD, letter to George Tavard reporting a conversation with Tom Stransky, August 2, 1962.

25. Gerard Sloyan, letter to Abbot Baldwin, October 20, 1961.

26. Abbot Baldwin, letter to Gerard Sloyan, October 24, 1961.

27. Gerard Sloyan, letter to GLD, February 15, 1962.

28. GLD, letter to Gerard Sloyan, February 23, 1962.

29. Ibid. About this time McDonald refused to reappoint Sloyan as "head" of his department, but appointed him "acting head" so as to keep his [McDonald's] options open.

30. Gerard Sloyan, letter to GLD, March 4, 1962.

31. William McDonald, letter to Abbot Baldwin, March 6, 1962.

32. Gerard Sloyan, letter to GLD, March 23, 1962.

33. GLD, letter to John Tracy Ellis, March 7, 1962.

34. Catholic University of America, official press release, Religious News Service, February 18, 1963, 22.

35. *Commonweal; America;* Kansas City *Reporter;* Davenport, Iowa *Catholic Messenger;* Indianapolis *Criterion;* the London *Tablet.*

36. Joseph Cardinal Ritter, letter to William McDonald, February 19, 1963.

37. GLD, letter to J. B. O'Connell, December 29, 1961.

38. GLD, letter to FRM, October 3, 1962.

39. GLD, letter to FRM, October 23, 1962. About his own appointment Fred McManus speculates: "I always thought Antonelli put me on the commission instead of Godfrey as 'the lesser of two evils.' I had known Antonelli since 1953 and he probably thought that, unlike Godfrey, I was harmless!"

40. Ibid.

41. FRM, letter to GLD, October 15, 1962.

42. FRM, letter to GLD, October 18, 1962. Dearden, in fact, turned out to be highly supportive, even if a bit cautious.

43. GLD, letter to FRM, October 23, 1962.

44. FRM, letter to GLD, November 1, 1962.

45. Clifford Howell, letter to GLD, February 14, 1963.

46. GLD, letter to FRM, November 2, 1962. McManus recalls visiting with Gene and Abigail McCarthy at the Excelsior Hotel. He believes that they may have brought a message for Pope John XXIII from President John Kennedy.

47. FRM, letter to GLD, November 1, 1962. McManus had misjudged the timing of the vote. As soon as the debate on the schema was concluded, Joachin Nabuco phoned Cardinal Tisserant and suggested that a straw vote be taken. Tisserant, without consulting Felici, the general secretary, proposed a vote to accept the schema as the basis of further amendments. The vote carried overwhelmingly, and a tremendous milestone was passed.

48. GLD, Christmas letter, 1962. It was said that Vagaggini fell under a heavy cloud after this summary was published because the article broke the superficial secrecy rule. Of course, the secrecy rule, such as it was, worked in favor of those who hoped that the Constitution on the Liturgy could be forestalled.

49. FRM, letter to GLD, April 9, 1963.

50. GLD, letter to FRM, April 30, 1963.

51. Ibid.

52. FRM, letter to GLD, May 6, 1963.

53. GLD, letter to J. B. O'Connell, May 10, 1963.

54. Archbishop Paul J. Hallinan, letter to GLD, May 14, 1963.

55. GLD, letter to Archbishop Hallinan, May 29, 1963.

56. James Shannon, "The 'Quiet Americans' Behind Vatican II," *Our Sunday Visitor,* November 21, 1965, 8.

57. Desmond Fisher, "The Men Behind the Council," *Sign,* September, 1965, 12.

58. Ibid.

59. Vincent Yzermans, taped interview, October 23, 1987.

60. GLD, letter to Bishop Leo Dworschak, May 20, 1963.

61. Bishop Leo Dworschak, letter to GLD, May 25, 1963.

62. FRM, letter to Archbishop Paul Hallinan, April 14, 1963.

CHAPTER *8*

THERE IS NO DOUBT that Godfrey had a sense of history in the making as he flew to Rome in September 1963 for the second session of the Council. As he was languishing at St. John's the previous year, he had written to Fred McManus urging him to keep a diary of the day-to-day events of Vatican II. Since much of what will follow in this chapter is based on Godfrey's jottings during the Council, his letter to Fred gives a good indication of what he hoped to capture in his own Council diary:

> Have you thought of keeping a diary? Even though it will cost you a lot of time, I hope you can be persuaded to jot down all the rumors and all the information that comes your way. Think of how valuable the letters of Ullathorne[1] were in giving the most reliable picture of the first Vatican Council that we possess. And if you don't do it, who are on the side of the angels, think of what the calamity would be if Joe Fenton or someone like him were to poison the wells of future understanding. It would almost seem to me that you have an obligation to this shaping of future historical understanding. History with a capital H is being made these days. The mosaic pieces that you would be able to furnish, including all the frustrations, will otherwise simply not be available.[2]

Godfrey's letters and diaries provide a splendid mosaic of the main events, the personalities, and the currents of Vatican II as he witnessed and interpreted them. He faithfully recorded everything he saw and heard—the speeches, amendments and votes in the aula (though sometimes these entries were abbreviated: "Bishop So and So—not much!"), conversations with observers, gossip overheard in the coffee bars, rumors of insurrection among this group or that, press conference exchanges, procedural frustrations, even ecclesiastical jokes: "Have you heard the story of the Franciscan, the Jesuit, and the Benedictine at the Christmas crib? The Franciscan asks: 'Is the child wrapped warmly?' The Jesuit inquires: 'Has he been enrolled in one of our schools?' And the Benedictine wonders: 'Does the crib face the people?' "[3]

Despite the fact that Godfrey wished for—but did not possess—opera glasses to follow the proceedings more closely, there was nothing that escaped his notice:

> There I am in St. Andrew's tribune, opposite the Protestant Observers: i.e., on what might be called the fifty-yard line, since we are very close to the 12 Presidents and the 4 Moderators who are the quarterbacks of the show. And it *is* interesting to watch Cardinal Meyer stifling a yawn, or Cardinal Spellman trying to smile bravely when a Council Father ringingly calls for smaller dioceses which will allow the Bishop to know all his priests and their problems personally. Or to watch Doepfner and Suenens put their heads together, and then lean over to Lercaro, who then leans over to Agagianian—and so one has advance notice that they are going to suggest calling a halt to the discussion on the current chapter. Or to watch Ruffini doing the hatchet job at the beginning of each discussion of a new chapter, and thereby unwittingly alerting the entire Council what the party line is.[4]

Godfrey's writings are filled with the human details that make "history with a capital H" come alive. In most instances he cannot resist adding his own inimitable commentary. He declared, for example, of the liturgy that opened the second session of the Council: "Entrance 'procession' lasted one hour and ten minutes! Bishops strolled in, more or less four abreast. Ridiculous. Procession is a symbol. After first five minutes, becomes boring and burdensome—defeats its purpose." And then, having divulged that the celebration had been prepared by Archbishop Dante and Vatican M.C.'s "who know nothing about liturgy," he became thoughtful about the procession he had just witnessed: "Overwhelming impact is still: this is a white church!"[5]

A particularly delightful glimpse of Godfrey's day-to-day activities is his somewhat staccato description of a "typical day" at the Council:

> Rise at about 5:45—Mass at 6:15 at "Holy Spirit in Sassia" about 50 meters away. So early because large numbers of bishops, residing

in neighboring hotels, come flocking in about 6:45, and so, unless I walk much further, to another church, I have to be finished before brass comes. ("In Sassia"—in the Church of Saxons, i.e. *English* Saxons. This was the early medieval English quarter of Rome, only several hundred meters from St. Peter's.) Pick up 2 cups of coffee and donuts or rolls at a coffee bar for about 15 cents. (At first, I was on "half-pension" at Hotel Alicorni—i.e. breakfast and one other meal. But I was too irregular—and the meals at the hotel, besides being quite expensive, were of very mediocre quality. Now I can pick up breakfast at a "bar" and have good talk with the old gent, who is a sort of depository of best gossip of journalists who all dropped in at the place some time during the day before. I can pick up cheaply at any one of several nice "trattorias" in neighborhood at much more reasonable price than at hotel.) (My favorite is Marcello's—which Fr. Luke recommended to me. Please give Luke warmest greetings of the padrone—and the little cook!)

Morning session at St. Peter's starts at 9:00. So the hour before, I usually try to get my Office prayed. Session always starts with Mass, often in different rite. But if in Latin, always Dialogue Mass, with rump section of Sistine choir adding some hymns (of course, at times strictly forbidden by the September Instruction of 1958: In Rome they only *make* the laws—but they are to be *observed* outside of Rome). Altar faces people. About a week ago, Archbishop McQuade of Dublin, who is the Cardinal McIntyre of Ireland— not yet having allowed participation—celebrated the Mass, and made a supremely bad job of it, as if he were mumbling a Mass behind a sacred Irish hedge.

I'm on a balcony, opposite the Protestant and Orthodox observers . . . watching Cardinals twiddling their thumbs when things get dull— which is often enough. A lot of Italian and Spanish bishops are talking "for the record" in order to immortalize themselves as having talked at the Council. When this happens, there is a general exodus towards the coffee bars (a real godsend, but so crowded that you're liable to be chewing a bishop's mozzetta instead of your bit of cake, unless you're careful). Best story of Council so far: At the johns, since Council Fathers couldn't understand Italian signs, green and red lights now flash "sede vacante" and "gloriose regnante." (For Marie etc.: these phrases, literally, "Vacant See" and "Gloriously Reigning," are used to describe Diocese either without or with resident occupant of See.) Session closes regularly at 12:15.

After session, unless I'm tied up with something, I sneak back to hotel (only 2 blocks from St. Peter's), take light lunch somewhere, and then a nap! Succeed in doing this ⅔ of time. At 3 p.m., briefing session for English-speaking journalists (including Paul Blanchard). This week, I've had to stand in for Fr. Fred McManus, to report on liturgical schema, and to prepare outlines of what has happened. (Fred's father died suddenly, and he flew home for the funeral. Is expected back by end of week. I hope he does return soon. He's invaluable, especially because of his expert knowledge not only of liturgy, but of canon law and the rubrics.) This briefing session usually until 4:30. Then, at 5, either a meeting of official liturgical commission (to which I was appointed a few days after arrival in Rome: i.e. the commission that is working at the schema on the liturgy, to work in the suggestions of Council Fathers), or I attend one of the many talks being given, to groups of bishops, or to journalists, by theologians like Rahner, Küng, Congar, etc., or by one of the bishops. Dinner about 7:30 or 8:00—almost always with a group of Council experts, Protestant observers, this or that bishop, etc. And such a gabfest hardly ever breaks up before 10:30. Am in bed usually by 11:00.

Such is order of typical day. Variations, of course. At present, am working on a talk on Mariology that I'm to give as part of a panel of theologians, to U.S. Bishops next Monday, and on another talk to West African bishops. (Have also accepted invitations to speak at North American College and at Graduate House for U.S. priests.) About 10 days ago I had the thrilling experience of hearing a talk which 3 of us had prepared, given verbatim on the Council floor by a French Archbishop, in the name of the whole French hierarchy.[6] And am working at several more such ghost-writing jobs. So I keep busy enough! But feel fine, do get about 8 hours of sleep, and try to keep off my legs as much as possible. The sore on right leg seems well healed. Am wearing elastic stockings.

Lot of people who were here for 1st session seem to think this second session not as exciting as first. Perhaps, because the *uncertainty* and excitement of 1st session, when it hung in balance whether Council would go "right" or "left," no longer prevails. Although there are differences of opinion, even violent, the general direction of the Council was assured in 1st session. Now, the net result seems quite assured. Yet for me, since it's first experience, it's all quite exciting. That is: total picture. The daily sessions—three solid hours—flatten one's tires quite effectively. Not so many good stories current as during 1st session. Recent one: Cardinal Bea prays: "Curia, eleison."[7]

Such is Godfrey's description of a "typical" day, yet it is difficult to imagine any of his days in Rome as typical in the sense of
either commonplace or routine. He was constantly in demand as
speaker, writer, interviewer, spokesperson, and confidant. One day
found him preparing a *relatio* on the diaconate for Archbishop Guilford Young and the bishops of Australia. On another day he ham-
mered out an essay on Breviary reform for the United States hierarchy.
He regularly made himself available to Archbishop Hallinan on all
questions having to do with the schema on the liturgy, judging emendations, preparing preliminary suggestions on an English-language
liturgy, briefing the archbishop prior to plenary meetings of the United
States hierarchy. Once, nearly missing a ghostwriting deadline for
Hallinan, he chided himself: "Don't postpone!"

Godfrey regularly entered into "a keen battle of wits" with members of the international press, a group who had "highly sensitive
noses in spooring out the news behind the releases." One day, for
example, Godfrey leapt into a debate to clarify for the press how religious life might be distinguished from the vocation to holiness of all
Christians. In his response, an enthusiastic presentation on the evangelical counsels, he could not, for the life of him, remember the vow
of obedience—"What would Freud make of that?"[8]

At another press conference Godfrey responded to a request from
several American journalists to clarify the meaning of celibacy in light
of the debate about a married diaconate. Godfrey acknowledged to
the press that celibacy was a discipline of the Church which could
be changed, a custom differing in East and West, a reality subject
to egregious failures in practice, yet, in his judgment, an ideal to be
retained. He developed for them a positive concept of celibacy, not
something greater than marriage but akin to and even a species of
marriage—a spiritual marriage, a fuller dedication of life and life-
energies to Christ and, therefore, to all people. If celibacy is merely
negative, he stated, if it is simply a giving up, it is male or female
"spinsterhood," the spinsterhood of the selfish, of pinched and warped
personalities. Then Godfrey gave celibacy an interesting twist:

> Celibacy is misnamed as a "single state," if by that is meant any-
> thing like taking advantage of freedom from the duties of married life
> in order to be more or less exclusively concerned with self. After all,
> it is axiomatic that charity, the love of God, is the highest command-

ment; love of neighbor is identical with it. Unless celibacy is distinguished by greater love and service of one's fellow(s), it is not Christian celibacy; it might be called unnatural.

> . . . it might be said that many married Catholics are resentful of the celibate clergy who insist on laws concerning married life. "You are easy talking," they say. Perhaps, if some of those who are in holy orders are married men, deacons, for example, then they could give an example of clerical married life. They would have the experience of marriage in their own lives, and would contribute to a better rapport and mutual understanding between clergy and laity.[9]

As one of the theologians most respected among the press, Godfrey enjoyed an admirable rapport with them and was highly sensitive to breaches of courtesy in their regard. He was appalled when "Krol, at press conference last Wednesday, talked down to journalists. Deeply resented. Told them they haven't got the Holy Spirit guiding them. Their answer: granted, but all we want is honest information about how the Spirit guided the Fathers."[10] This incident prompted Godfrey to muse: "Would be the best thing in the world if every bishop once a month would have to face a barrage of journalists, and his priests and people, who could ask him questions, ask him to give an account of his stewardship."[11]

Godfrey also spoke to various groups around the city. He gave a talk on liturgy and ecumenism and another on concelebration at the North American College—and having been told that his talks were better than any others so far, he noted that "the fellow who said this was an Irishman." As word got out, he was invited to repeat these presentations in other houses of formation. In addition, he agreed to interview American bishops on their liturgical concerns for Vatican radio. These tapes would then be made available to the networks in the United States. To this request he added a realistic postscript in his diary: "Yes. But when???"

From all reports Godfrey was ubiquitous, and despite his serious illness of the previous year, his energy seemed unbounded. He delighted in the company of bishops, journalists, seminarians, and other *periti*. With the latter, this latecomer on the scene was instrumental in strategizing more frequent meetings in order that they might function more effectively:

P.M. meeting of U.S. periti at U.S.O. in order to help ourselves to
grasp better the agenda of Council. To help U.S. bishops? It was felt
that latter aren't eager to call upon periti—and may be suspicious of
what we are doing. Hence we meet every Wednesday at 4:30 (my
suggestion—in order to allow hearing great theological talks every
Wednesday evening at 6). Introductory talk of 20 minutes, and then
discussion. Invite bishops who may wish to come.[12]

Of all the company he kept during the Council, Godfrey seemed
to gravitate most frequently to the Protestant observers, who constituted, as one bishop confided to him, "a group of dedicated men who
have a grasp of the significance of this Council that should humble
most of us bishops."[13] The observers, in turn, were perhaps attracted
to Godfrey because the Fathers of the Church served as common
ground. It was among the observers that Godfrey's charism as a
maître d' began to flourish:

Much of what spare time I have has been employed in establishing
friendly relations with the Protestant Observers. Have been something
like a headwaiter, in arranging meetings with them and members of
the hierarchy, usually dinner meetings in the evening, followed by
several hours of good talk. Some of them I had known earlier, others
had been at Montreal, and I've gotten to know still others here. A
group of highly intelligent and dedicated men. Last week the Paulists
sponsored a meeting between Observers and U.S. Bishops and periti
at Grand Hotel, at which Dr. Outler of Southern Methodist gave a
splendid talk: gist of it was, that the Observers expect of the Council
that the Catholic Church not compromise for sake of a false eireni-
cism, but to be more truly and fully Catholic, and thus give witness
to the whole world, including Protestants, of best traditional Christian values.[14]

"Godfrey was central to everything," said Martin Marty, who
remembers meeting Godfrey among the informal community of Protestant observers and the press. Marty was at the Council as a journalist but was curious to get into the sessions. He knew enough Latin
and wanted to get the flavor of the Council from inside, but as a member of the Missouri Synod, which was unecumenical, he was not
trusted by Roman Catholics. Godfrey interceded with Bishop Bartholome, playing on the fact that a former bishop of St. Cloud, a
Benedictine, was also named Martin Marty. Bartholome was charmed
and secured the necessary pass.

Returning home with American bishops aboard the Vulcania *after the 1964 session of the Second Vatican Council*

Subprior John Eidenschink, Abbot Baldwin Dworschak, Dr. James Kritzeck, Bishop Leo Dworschak, and Godfrey in front of St. Peter's Basilica

228

At dinner during Vatican II: Oliver Kapsner, Terence Murphy, Godfrey, John Cogley, Joseph Lichten, Vincent Yzermans

Dinner at a residence for Council participants: Godfrey second from left, Bishop George Speltz of St. Cloud fourth from right

229

Among the observers and the press Godfrey happily assumed the role of tutor during a stroll, a meeting, a chance encounter. Once Godfrey and Martin Marty were at dinner together with a group of Spanish bishops. The Marty family were high-church Lutherans and ate fish on Fridays. At this meal the Spanish bishops ate meat, even though it was a Friday. Godfrey explained to the puzzled observer the mind of the Spanish, who could be excused from the law if they did five hours of arduous work. They considered the use of Latin in the session to be arduous work and thus more than ample reason for a dispensation. While Marty had thought of Catholics as monolithic, Godfrey explained the differences between Spanish, Irish, German, and so on.[15]

Given his natural inclination to socialize with the observers, it is not surprising that Godfrey occasionally caucused with George Lindbeck, Albert Outler, Robert Cushman, Douglas Steere, or one of the other observers, offering his critique of the schema on ecumenism. According to his diary, his analysis of the draft on ecumenism—that it needed to take a more *incarnational* approach, stress universal redemption, examine the visible structures of the church—was subsequently presented by the observers to the Secretariat for Promoting Christian Unity.[16]

It was with particular gusto that Godfrey took up his primary work of participating in the liturgical commission. Immediately after he had arrived at the Council, and with the presumption that he would be appointed to their commission, Archbishop Paul Hallinan and Fred McManus acquainted him with some controversial, behind-the-scenes emendations that had changed the schema on the liturgy between the first and second sessions of the Council. After the revised text of the liturgy schema had been approved by the liturgical commission at its plenary meeting in April 1963, Cardinal Larraona, prefect of the Sacred Congregation of Rites and the commission's president, called a rump commission in July consisting of those members living in or near Rome—"mostly canonists who knew nothing of liturgy," Godfrey was told. Thus "stacked" in the cardinal's favor, the commission introduced changes into the liturgy schema, including the necessity of "approval" of decisions of episcopal conferences; restored older terminology such as "Extreme Unction," which had both theological and liturgical ramifications; and suppressed some articles of the text altogether, for example, some of the material on concelebration.

These were not insignificant revisions, and they did not sit well with the full commission. Archbishop Hallinan was thoroughly disgusted with Roman politics and chicanery. He recounted to Godfrey how he had lost his temper in the commission and, speaking in English, declared that he had *never in his life* met with such dishonesty. Backed by others, Hallinan insisted that the July meeting lacked all competence and demanded that the schema approved in full session be restored.[17]

Hallinan triumphed at the next meeting of the commission, the first meeting to welcome Godfrey among the participants. As Fred introduced Godfrey to one after another bishop, Bishop Bekkers of Holland remarked: "Ah, one of the big four banned from Catholic University." Godfrey noted approvingly that "this man was obviously fully informed." But little time was given over to introductions. Hallinan's report, "insisting on restoration of the original text . . . won out in essentials. Very lively and at times shouting debate. Wagner, Fred and Martimort carried the ball."[18]

Could this be the meeting to which Xavier Rynne referred in his commentary on the Council?

> After one of the liturgical Commission's rather heated meetings, the French liturgist Father Martimort gave biblical credit to six men who had insisted on the extensive reforms called for by the majority of the Council Fathers and rejected by the standpatters in the Commission, saying: "Three there are who give testimony in heaven: Bishops Hallinan, Jenny and Martin; and three there are who give testimony on earth: Fathers Wagner, McManus and Martimort." Thus neatly distinguishing between the bishops who did the voting and the experts who prepared the texts (cf. 1 John 5:7-8).[19]

"Devious medieval plotting" was nowhere more evident than in the procedures of the commissions. There were no parliamentary procedures, nothing to serve as a lever to exert pressure when commissions bogged down. There were no rules for the chairpersons, who were usually members of the Curia determined to preserve the status quo and who simply sat on business if they found it *non placet*. In the words of one frustrated bishop, Leo Dworschak of Fargo: "No bureaucracy in history ever functioned more efficiently to bog down in its own inefficiency.''[20] ''Bogging down'' was a technique used particularly effectively by the leadership of the liturgical commission:

> The big difficulty is that a majority of the Chairmen on the Commissions, who are the heads of the corresponding congregations, feel that they are the judges of what can go before the Council whereas their function is simply to implement the will of the Council Fathers as manifested in the debate on the floor and the voting that takes place there. Now they seem to feel in some of the commissions that it is up to them to decide what will and will not be put into the final decrees or constitutions. We had a very good example of that in some of the modi on the liturgy. In spite of the fact that very large numbers proposed exactly the same ''modus'' the commission refused to give us a chance to vote, while we did vote on some which had only a very few council fathers backing them.[21]

Members of the liturgical commission met frequently outside the sessions to exchange the latest rumors, to report on conversations, to plan strategy on current commission issues, and to anticipate future work. Godfrey's summary of one such session is fairly typical:

> Meeting of liturgists at Mater Dei. Martimort, Wagner, Fischer, Gy, Hänggi, Franquesa, Howell, Paul Gordon (Beuron), Bishop Van Bekkum, Bishop Jenny and about five more with an OSB bishop of Brazil. Agenda: Most important. Get post-conciliar commission appointed and keep it out of the hands of the Sacred Congregation of Rites. Bishop Jenny will approach Cardinal Lercaro, who is to see the Pope. Latter should appoint at same time as he promulgates approval of liturgy schema.

> Martimort: told of plot to force triple vote on schema—on vernacular, chalice, and concelebration. We decided that thereby the enemies will be digging ditch into which they themselves will fall. For if 1000 juxta modum votes, will appear formidable. But if 200 against chalice, 400 against concelebration, 300 against vernacular, will make less impression.

> I gave a brief report on Montreal, and urged contact with Protestants, especially in three year cycle of readings.

> Plotted how to get daily Mass to conform to liturgical rules. Salve Regina sung during Gospel procession!!! Hymns during Canon, no homily, no communion!!! Eucharistic meal—no one invited![22]

The daily liturgies of the Council were a continuing source of annoyance for Godfrey and his friends. Occasionally, however, liturgical mistakes played into their hands: "Pope celebrated Mass—anniversary of his predecessor's election. He *stumbled* on prayers at foot of altar. Consolation to many. Also will guarantee that these prayers will be dropped in the final revision!"[23]

The regular meetings of the liturgical commission were generally the occasion for enormous frustration. Godfrey recalled one session in which a whole hour was wasted trying to convince Cardinal Larraona that "placet juxta modum" meant "Yes, with *this* or *that* reservation." Larraona insisted that it meant "acceptance," not a qualified "non placet," and was simply inclined to disregard the suggested emendations.[24] Cardinal Larraona was not the only one who was bewildered by the voting. Some of the Council Fathers consistently voted "non placet" on every item put before them. This became obvious one day when the subject under consideration was an emendation to the liturgy constitution exhorting all bound to the recitation of the Breviary to do so with greater devotion and intelligence. Twelve voted "non placet" on that proposition. Some speculated that a simple proposition stating the doctrine of the Trinity would fare the same.[25]

Besides the question of cultural adaptation of the liturgy, two other issues, themselves interrelated, were dear to Godfrey's heart and the focus of his energies in the liturgical commission: adaptation of the Breviary and adoption of the vernacular. These issues had long preoccupied him; now he had the time and the platform to lobby intensely for their resolution. He described the evolution of his concern about the Breviary in these words:

> I had given scores of retreats in the United States and I realized that there was a crisis of prayer among priests. The breviary was considered to be their basic prayer but many didn't understand the Latin. At the same time they excused themselves from doing much other prayer because they were bound to the breviary. But they didn't know what they were saying, so there was little or no prayer life for many priests.[26]

After the Assisi Congress in 1956, Godfrey had stayed in Rome, knocked on doors of various congregations, and tried to speak of the gravity of the problem, but he met with incomprehension.

They were always friendly, I must say that about Roman policy. But they would ask questions: "Is that so?" "Well why don't they study Latin?" And I would have to admit that many had studied Latin for eight years. And they would say "Well?" They simply could not understand the problem why some couldn't get it after eight years. I could get nowhere.[27]

Godfrey loved the Office, especially the heart of this prayer, the psalms. He often repeated—and agreed with—the assessment of Pope John XXIII that the psalms invited "a rejoicing in truth, a daily teaching for life, consolation, and comfort in difficulties and trials." But teaching, consolation, and comfort seemed contingent upon understanding—and that, after so many years of priests' retreats, he was prepared to doubt in a great number of cases. Again and again, whenever and wherever Godfrey could find a hearing, he would argue that conferences of bishops be permitted to judge local conditions and, if the need became apparent, to give permission for the recitation of the Divine Office in the vernacular.[28]

Happily, the schema of the liturgy constitution gave to the local Ordinary the authority to grant the use of the vernacular in individual cases "to those clerics for whom the use of Latin constitutes a grave obstacle to their praying the office properly."[29] For this Godfrey takes at least partial credit in his diary: "Re: Divine Office in English. Agreed that allowing individual Ordinary to give dispensation may be best pastoral solution. (This had been my suggestion to Preparatory Commission!)"[30]

Early interpretations of the meaning of this vernacular concession seemed to suggest that it applied only to diocesan clergy and that religious, at least those living the monastic life, would retain the Latin language. This filled Godfrey with alarm:

Every religious with whom I have personally discussed the matter shares my conviction that unless we also will soon be granted full assurance of the permissibility of choir recitation in English, we are doomed to extinction. It is really as serious as all that. Within another six months, I have no doubt that about 90% of the younger generation of priests in the U.S. will be reciting the Breviary in English. And what young candidate for the priesthood would ever consider the monastic life if there is even the possibility of having to spend three hours a day praying or singing the Office in Latin.[31]

Why exempt the monastery from vernacular recitation of the Office? "The authorities in Rome seem to have no conception of American conditions. They think of a monastery as a place where the cultured elite of the country go to have their aesthetic sensibilities titillated."[32] But Godfrey argued that a monastery is a place where lay people come to pray and meditate, and there they sit, during the Divine Office, "bombarded with unintelligible sound. If the Divine Office is in fact the prayer of the entire Church, a monastery is an ideal place where lay people can come and be introduced to this prayer. This is impossible under present circumstances."[33]

Godfrey worked for a vernacular Breviary with one more concern, and this one was close to home: the daily separation of Offices for monks and brothers at St. John's:

> We have two chapels now, the church itself, in which the clerical monks recite and chant the Office in Latin, and a chapel in the crypt, in which the lay Brothers recite and chant the Office in English, except for Matins, for which they have substituted a daily Bible Vigil. We take for granted that they belong with us at the daily Conventual Mass. For this is a sign as well as a source for spiritual community. But the same should be said of the Divine Office. Why should members of the same community pray in separate chapels?[34]

Why, indeed! Godfrey continued his crusade on this issue well after the Council had adjourned. He became courier of a letter to the Roman authorities drafted by Abbot Baldwin and signed by other Benedictine abbots. Cardinal Cicognani, Secretary of State when Godfrey arrived in Rome, understood the reasons proposed by the Benedictines and said he would speak with the Holy Father. For weeks there was no word. Then, after two months, the cardinal said that he could not bring this issue before the Holy Father. It was necessary that the Benedictines carry on the tradition of chant, and for this they needed Latin. The Benedictines eventually got a letter through the subsecretary, Monsignor Angelo Dell'Acqua, a friend of the Abbey of Montserrat, and it was Paul VI who granted the permission. Godfrey refers to this incident as evidence that the Pope was a prisoner of the Vatican. Normal paths of communication with him were carefully monitored![35]

Godfrey's other crusade was for an extension of vernacular use in the celebration of Eucharist and the other sacraments. As a charter member of the Vernacular Society, he had been promoting the mother tongue for years in his speaking and publishing. Why did this issue assume such large proportions for him? The vernacular was a way of communicating other things, not an end in itself. The vernacular was Godfrey's cause, just as for H.A.R., for example, the cause was the altar facing the people. For Godfrey, vernacular was the prow of the ship, the cause with a capital "C," which would serve as the impetus for that full, conscious, and active participation in liturgy for which all the pioneers had labored.[36]

It may be difficult from this vantage point to comprehend what all the fuss was about. A letter from Gerard Sloyan to Godfrey in the late fifties captures the volatility of the liturgical language issue. Christine Mohrmann, a staunch advocate of liturgical Latin, had given a series of lectures at the Catholic University of America. Sloyan attended her lectures and provided this summary for Godfrey:

> I was properly impressed with her learning (had read her little Canon book with Bernard Botte [*L'Ordinaire de la messe*]), but came to conclude from the talks that the cause of pastoral liturgy has no warm friend in her. She is for the mystery of language for the sake of that mystery (a sacrament of awe, so to say); she thinks that vernacular departures from Greek in the East in the centuries after the 5th made heresies; she thinks that, having hammered out a Christian Latin for the necessary purpose of praying in it in the 3rd–5th centuries we have somehow done a perfect work. In a word, she has no conception of what the last Mass crowd is like in its total incomprehension and would, I think, be shocked to be told that Wyclifites and Lollards had a good measure of success because they shared the mystery rather than kept on mumbling Latin. I guess what I minded most was that, in a community of learned folk, she was not in any mood to be a learner. There were even a few bemused smiles at "liturgists."[37]

"Liturgists" were often equated with "vernacularists," and both terms conveyed a certain measure of opprobrium. On the other hand, vernacularists did not think of themselves as wild-eyed radicals. They simply posed the following questions:

1. Will we better understand what is going on if we have English?
2. Will we be able to offer the Sacrifice of the Mass with greater devotion? Might it better transform our daily lives if it were in English?

3. Would the Mass and Sacraments teach us our faith better if English were used? Remember that most Catholics in the world today do not own Missals, many cannot read, and few countries have Catholic schools like ours.

4. Do you think that we could more easily attract converts if we had English?

5. Might not the Orthodox Churches come closer to reunion with us again if we used the language of the people as most of them do?

6. Do you in essence then think that you could pray and worship better in the language in which you speak and think? Or, do you think that the present system of Latin is best?[38]

It was Colonel John Ross-Duggan who formulated these questions on the eve of the Council and appended them to a petition that he circulated in the United States and Canada, hoping for a groundswell of support for the vernacular among the laity. The gist of the petition: "that permission be granted to celebrate the liturgy in the English language so that all may understand what is being said and done, to the greater glory and honor of God and the good of souls."[39]

That permission, of course, would be forthcoming, but not without a great struggle. Godfrey records one particular meeting of the liturgical commission when there was disagreement even among "those on the side of the angels":

> Vernacular—on the presidential prayers in vernacular: Grimshaw, Hallinan, McManus and I are the only ones who fought. . . . Even Wagner spoke up for keeping the collect in Latin! "It would be beautiful to have this island of Latinity in the Foremass, as it would be to have an island of vernacular in the Canon." We argued violently. . . . I was so mad I could spit. Wagner, Martimort, not *honest*. There, priest whispers collect in Latin, and commentator reads it aloud in *German*.[40]

The day after this "battle," Bishop Van Bekkum apologized to Godfrey and Fred for not having supported them.

Meanwhile, vernacular was an issue in the Council hall itself. One day Godfrey bumped into Archbishop Gray of Edinburgh, who wanted badly to speak on ecumenism out of his experience of recent dialogue with Presbyterians. He wrote his speech in English and couldn't find anyone to translate it for him. Godfrey estimated that Gray understood only about half of the discussion. Another bishop confided to

Godfrey that though he was trained in Rome, that had been twenty years earlier. This second bishop estimated that with concentration he was able to grasp about eighty percent, "but often the twenty percent contains the crux, or the special nuances which are essential." For Godfrey this raised a theological question: how far did this state of affairs infringe on "freedom of speech" and hence on real ecumenicity?

The solution: simultaneous translation—and that had been the subject of a rumor which had swept the Council:

> BIG NEWS (OCTOBER 13) Cardinal Cushing convinced Pope Paul to install simultaneous translation system!! As soon as possible. (Perhaps now Cushing will stay?) What repercussions this will have on whole question of vernacular in liturgy!! Solid *façade* broken through! Fiction about Latin and *universalitas* finally acknowledged. Perhaps only when system introduced will Council become truly ecumenical, allowing bishops to *listen* and participate (i.e., speak). But it will be difficult to find competent translators.[41]

The rumor proved to be unfounded. The mechanics of simultaneous translation seemed to elude the secretariat, which had warned that there might be a five-day lapse between one speech and another that answered it. There was also some concern that simultaneous translation might be picked up outside. There would be no assistance for the many bishops who were in the same boat as Cushing and Gray.[42]

While the battle for vernacular speeches was lost, resistance to vernacular prayer was slowly changing to support. "GOSSIP: At meeting yesterday of U.S. bishops, unanimous vote for vernacular breviary and strong feelings expressed." About this rumor Godfrey mused that if the bishops insisted on the vernacular for their own prayer, they would be shamed into concessions for the laity in the Mass. His hunch appeared to be correct. The "latest gossip" a few days later included this piece: "McManus: *'Deepest secret:* U.S. Bishops, as a result of Hallinan's talk last Saturday, voted with only 6 negative votes, *to go all out* for vernacular, right down the line.' Hallinan: 'And now we're trying to find out who the 6 are—3 of them we are pretty sure of.' "[43]

Meanwhile, another issue of great import was being debated on the Council floor. Its outcome Godfrey regards as a personal triumph.

The issue was this: Should there be a separate schema *De Beata Maria Virgine, Mater Ecclesiae,* or should a chapter on Mary be incorporated into the schema on the Church? Debate was heated. Some said that without a special document devoted to Mary, the world would deduce that she had been neglected; others countered that she should not be treated in isolation, and, in fact, it would dishonor Mary to separate her from Christ and the Church. Tempers flared over this charged issue. From the perspective of the Protestant observers, a separate schema would be a disaster.

On the eve of the vote to resolve this issue, the bishops of the United States assembled a panel of experts to provide background for their deliberations. The panel included: Father Barnabas Ahern, C.P. (the background of the schema); Father Eugene Maly (the scriptural basis); Father Godfrey (the patristic background); and Father William Coyle, C.SS.R. (Mary in modern theology).

For his part, Godfrey quoted one patristic source after another to demonstrate that Mary was revered not because of her physical virginity but because she was most like Christ in faith and obedience, completely God-centered in her life, a perfect disciple. In his judgment, incorporation of Mary into the document on the Church would not downgrade devotion to Mary in the life of the Church but put it in its proper context, ensuring a more solid basis of devotion rooted in biblical and patristic theology. About 250 bishops were present, including some from Canada and Australia. Many complimented Godfrey afterwards, calling his presentation a great intellectual treat.

When the Council vote was called, Archbishop Felici, in his wording of the proposition, attempted to tilt the vote toward a separate schema. He proposed that the alternative before the bishops was having a separate schema on Mary or placing her *at the end* of the document on the Church—as if tacked on. "Ultimum caput" he stressed several times.

In the end, it was clear that the panel made the difference in an exceedingly close vote. Of 2,193 present, 1,114 voted to incorporate Mary into the schema on the Church; 1,074 voted for a separate schema; and there were five void votes. The majority was just a little over 51 percent.

Bishop Dworschak, a man who had found Godfrey's presentation brilliant, reflected on the significance of the vote:

One factor which saved the situation was the fact that a goodly number of Latin American bishops have become frightened that a great
many of their people have little religion left except a distorted form
of a cult of the Blessed Mother which in many cases is material if not
formal idolatry. They want to get the devotion to Our Lady into its
proper perspective; hence, they supported our point of view.

Another factor in the successful vote was the excellent job done by
the panel at the meeting of the U.S. Bishops yesterday afternoon. I
am convinced that a number of U.S. Bishops would have voted with
the conservatives if they had not had the benefit of the presentation
made by this panel on the subject of Mariology. A switch of only twenty
votes would have defeated the project; and I feel quite sure that at
least twenty votes of U.S. Bishops were switched as a result of that
meeting.

. . . I may be a bit prejudiced, but I feel that Father Godfrey did
the best job.[44]

One commentator on the Council described the aftermath of the
vote with these words: "Shock, pessimism, as well as relief, swept
many of the Fathers. There had not been an overwhelming vote at
all; the ecumenical movement had almost been torpedoed. Would the
Council henceforth be split down the center? Had there been a rever-
sion to earlier divisions?"[45] Others read the vote more optimistically:
This vote was an important turning point in the Council, since it was
clear that the progressives were able to muster an absolute majority
on a point with a large group in opposition. Surely, then, a two-thirds
vote on progressive ideas in the future might be possible.[46]

Votes such as these that brought the deep divisions of the Council to the light of day also fueled the rumor mills. Godfrey recorded
many of them: When Tromp (secretary of the theological commission), was asked whether the talk on the Council floor was influenc-
ing him and others in emending the schema *De Ecclesia,* he declared
"NO. Our job is to protect the purity of faith." Barnabas Ahern confided to Godfrey in strictest secrecy that the Pope had brought pressure upon Ottaviani, "but hesitated to unseat him lest Ottaviani
become a martyr to his followers." Archbishop Ligutti, quoting Joseph
Fenton, stated that the theological commission had been "appointed
by God to save the Church." Placid Jordan quoted Cardinal Spellman:
"When the secretary at the beginning of each day's Council session

announces 'Exeunt omnes,' I'm beginning to think the Holy Spirit leaves, too.'' Archbishop Vagnozzi railed against *periti*, ''who are responsible for all the trouble we're having with the Church.'' Hans Küng declared that the schema *De Ecclesia* avoided the really critical ecumenical question: *"Did* Christ restrict eucharist to those who have imposition of hands?'' No less than fourteen national episcopal conferences petitioned the Pope to ''reconstitute or at least shake up the theological commission in order to assure progress.'' Cardinal Tisserant, asked whether he really felt that passing out ''propaganda'' against the communications schema in front of St. Peter's was against the Council rules, replied: ''No, but I didn't approve of *what* was passed out.'' Cardinal Ottaviani said that the Holy Office had already undergone *aggiornamento.* When pressed whether, if Council Fathers decided on further steps, he would agree, Ottaviani replied, ''We'd give it serious thought.'' Boniface Luykx, who hoped for a new foundation in the Congo, was convinced that clerical celibacy was impossible: ''Most priests have at least one wife and some recently are taking up polygamy.'' ''An Italian bishop has requested that a College of the Laity be established in Rome—a seminary for the laity!!! As if we don't have enough trouble with our seminaries for priests, now he wants the laity isolated from the world in their training.'' *"Dicitur* that rest of Patriarchs would like to exclude Latin Patriarch of Jerusalem.'' ''Curia members have special 'privilege' from the Congregation of Rites to celebrate Mass privately in their chapels on Holy Thursday—and Dante has regularly made use of it.'' Cardinal McIntyre to one of the *periti* at a dinner: ''What is all this fuss about liturgy? Why all this agitation for change? I don't understand what it's all about. Tell me.''⁴⁷ And so they passed their days.

Mercifully, and perhaps because of papal pressure, the liturgical commission started to make some headway:

> For first time we made wonderful progress! (Wagner corroborated what Bugnini had hinted: that pressure has been exerted from *highest* source, to get on with the work. Liturgy schema *must* be finished before end of session.) Larraona rushed and prodded—so that in one session we finished entire chapter on De Sacramentis. Wagner, on question of vernacular, suggested compromise solution: Ritual all in vernacular; Pontifical in Latin. Vigorously opposed by McManus. Our ''modus'' solidly backed by U.S. bishops and others (601) to eliminate ''excep-

ta forma" will be presented to Council without comment. All our commission's work will have to be finished by *November 15th.* [48]

The liturgical commission completed its work according to schedule, thanks to the patience and persistence of the "side of the angels." The Constitution on the Sacred Liturgy was put to a final vote, chapter by chapter, on November 22, 1963.

Sometimes there is a convergence of events and circumstances that serves, in retrospect, like a vortex. November 22, 1963, was such a day. It would be difficult to underestimate the import of the vote that day, though the *Council Daybook* records the event somewhat dispassionately:

> In the council assembly, precisely at 12:05 p.m., the document providing for sweeping reform of the public worship of the Church was given complete approval by the council Fathers with only 19 dissenting votes out of a total of 2,178 votes cast. One vote was null.

> Announcement of the completion of the schema was greeted with warm and prolonged applause from the council Fathers. Eugene Cardinal Tisserant, dean of the Sacred College of Cardinals and ranking prelate of the 13 council presidents, expressed the thanks of the council to the Commission on Sacred Liturgy for its work, mentioning particularly the president of the commission, Arcadio Cardinal Larraona, and his predecessor, Gaetano Cardinal Cicognani, who died in February, 1962. [49]

Thanks were due, as well, to men like Godfrey Diekmann and Frederick McManus, who were indefatigable in their liturgical labors during the Council and for years preceding it. The following is typical of tributes paid to them:

> Diekmann and McManus—their names are invariably linked— contributed something specifically American to the Council. Popularizers rather than innovators, they translated the theory of liturgical reform into concrete concepts. They were the essential middlemen, almost the salesmen, of the new ideas. They explained, persuaded, enlightened. No one—bishop, priest, or journalist—with any openness of mind could come away from a conversation with Diekmann or McManus without having learned more, understood more, enthused more. Their pulpits were lecture rooms in Rome's seminaries, hotel reception rooms, sidewalk cafés, and mealtime trattorias.

By sheer force of personality, they beat down the barriers of prejudice and suspicion. If evangelization owes anything to human factors, McManus' patience and helpfulness to the press and Diekmann's sweeping enthusiasm come high among the factors explaining the success of the liturgical reform.[50]

No one, of course, was surprised by the nearly unanimous vote that day. Unanimity had been hard-won over the months of debate. Nevertheless, headlines like

APPROVAZIONE QUASI UNANIME
DELLO SCHEMA SULLA LITURGIA
VOTANTI 2178—PLACET 2159

in *L'Osservatore Romano* would have been unthinkable among even the most optimistic promoters of the liturgy a year before. Bishop Leo Dworschak's diary adds a bit of color and a note of historical significance to the event:

> We all expected that the vote would be practically unanimous and therefore were not surprised when [the results were announced]. But nevertheless there was a great cheer and the loudest round of applause heard so far in the council hall. Applause is really prohibited, and the cases where the rule was violated in the past, the applause usually came from the end of the hall where the younger bishops (usually called Boy Scouts) are sitting. But this time the applause was universal. Lercaro then paid a great tribute to the members of the Liturgical Commission, its chairman and members, for their hard labors during the many months since the Council opened in 1962. One could tell that he was as thrilled as we because his voice quavered as he talked.

> I thought of Father Virgil and the days back in 1925 and 1926 when Virgil started the Liturgical Movement in the U.S. and he was working feverishly getting some material into the hands of the few priests who were interested and I used to help him by doing a great deal of typing and proof-reading for him. (He fired me as a proof-reader because I missed more mistakes than I corrected!) I am sure that in his wildest dreams Father Virgil did not expect to see the changes in public worship of the Church which were made official in the action of the Council today. At the same time, I never expected to see even the small improvement which I visualized to become a reality during my own lifetime. The thrill with which I witnessed the proceedings today is something I will never forget.[51]

As Godfrey witnessed the voting from St. Andrew's tribune, his thoughts also turned to Virgil Michel:

> Twenty-five years after Virgil's death. One wishes he were here to see this! Virgil Michel anticipated the course of events. There is not one reform being implemented that he did not point to as a goal to be achieved. It is an accomplishment to be such a prophet. He saw aright and projected this development on the sound theological foundation of the Mystical Body. He drew conclusions from right principles.

> This document is not the introduction of a few new practices but a thorough reorientation of theological thinking with appropriate pastoral conclusions. The rethinking of our spiritual orientation cannot be done in a few years! There is no time in the history of the Church when such radical rethinking has taken place, not only in these past twenty-five years, but especially in the last five years.[52]

Godfrey's diary alludes to that other document, published sixty years earlier to the day, which launched the modern liturgical movement. On November 22, 1903, Pius X, scarcely three months in office, issued his *motu proprio* on the "Restoration of Sacred Music." Pius X's document had been a bolt out of the blue. A Church that for centuries had been drifting into an individualistic piety was summoned to "active participation in the most sacred mysteries and in the public and solemn prayer of the Church." Godfrey mused on the rightness of the vote taken on the anniversary of Pius X's landmark document. He also recorded wryly that Cardinal Spellman, never friendly to the liturgical reform, left the hall just before the vote was announced!

Who would have guessed a year earlier when the debate began that a document which contained such far-reaching reforms would only become *more* revolutionary in the discussion? All the hopes—and then some—of those involved in the liturgical movement had now been blessed. Euphoria reigned. A great celebration was in order.

About ten or twelve Americans and their friends gathered at the Hilton Hotel. An orchestra was playing, people were dancing. Godfrey and others interspersed toasts with reminiscences about this amendment and that speech, about the maneuverings in the aula and behind the scenes, about their own naiveté and the on-the-job education they had received in Vatican politics—"devious medieval plotting."

Then a woman leaned over from a neighboring table and asked: "You are Americans? Do you not know that today your president was shot?" Godfrey called a waiter and asked him to find out if the rumor was true. The waiter returned and confirmed the report: "Your president has been shot. He is dead."

That same stunned incredulity with which the news of President Kennedy's assassination was received all over the world seems, in this context, even more poignant. The news spread throughout the room; people stopped dancing; the orchestra quit playing; many people drifted out of the room, including Godfrey and his friends, leaving half-eaten dinners and all their victory toasts. The party was over. Godfrey recorded in his diary that he celebrated a Requiem Mass for John Fitzgerald Kennedy early the next morning through uncontrollable tears. The tears started again when he saw the American flag at half-mast over Castel Sant' Angelo as he walked back to the Vatican.[53]

It is no wonder that the rest of the second session of the Council was largely anticlimactic. There was a general feeling of "letdown." Not much more was expected. Argument on the Council floor was desultory. The liturgical commission turned its attention to sorting out what could and could not be done immediately upon publication of the schema. Godfrey had anticipated questions of implementation of the Constitution in an interview some days earlier:

> One needs to distinguish between two developments. One is a thorough revision of all the liturgical books: Missal, Ritual, Breviary, and so on. There is a post-conciliar commission which will be set up to deal with this and it will take perhaps five years. But meanwhile, there is no reason to wait! It is clear that faculties are being granted to national bishops' conferences. They can take some steps now: the approval of music, the prayers of the people, translations of the rites of the sacraments, etc.

> But even more important is the basic plan of instruction, *the sooner the better.* This is not just an introduction of *practices* but a far more difficult problem, that of restructuring our whole spiritual life on the basis of the liturgy, the Mass above all. The most important objective is to plan and effectuate systematic instruction of the people, of rethinking things in terms of Christ, the Church and our role in the Church. This is a life-long program and we can never instruct sufficiently.

This instruction must begin immediately or we'll have spiritual activism, or as Paul says, "tinkling symbols." If the liturgical movement
is not basically a spiritual movement, it is nothing, and that means
a constant instruction and learning by doing, but the two must go hand
in hand. Of the two, learning is more basic, not only for the laity but
for priests. Priests must be willing to read, to study, to find the un-
derlying motives for the reform. Unless they realize that these things
flow from the very nature of the Church, they will not be sufficiently
personally involved to make this matter one to which they devote themselves with all their heart.[54]

Godfrey experienced a great sense of urgency to begin at once,
to attend to liturgical catechesis, to bring new conceptions of Church
and of the role of the laity in the Body of Christ to public, visible
expression in the liturgy. It is no wonder he lost patience one day
with the deliberations of the liturgical commission. When the discussion turned to asking the Holy Father for the "privilege" of dropping Prime and choosing one of the three day Hours, Godfrey
intervened with a strong plea: "This is clericalism. We are concerned
only with benefits to the clergy. Why not also ask that we immediately adopt the principle of distribution of roles." Godfrey appreciated that Fred backed him up—but no one else. In exasperation,
Godfrey asked: "Where the h--- is Wagner and the others in fighting for these things?"[55]

There yet remained the official promulgation of the Constitution
on the Sacred Liturgy on December 4, 1963. Godfrey's diary provides a glimpse of the event and his assessment of its significance,
as well as another diatribe about a liturgical celebration so incongruous with the event it marked:

> December 4, 1963. Joined procession of observers—all decked out in
> formal doctoral or ecclesiastical robes for the great occasion. All quite
> excited. A number of them—Lindbeck, Skydsgaard, Outler—
> congratulated me on final proclamation of liturgical schema. Felt that
> if Council does nothing else—it will have been one of the great Coun-
> cils in the history of the Church. Outler: "Tell your Catholics this.
> Some of them we've met here are too impatient. There is the danger
> of spiritual schism."
>
> Pope carried in! Blessed bishops right and left; Recitata, thank God,
> but Sistine choir with motets; sang polyphonic Sanctus and Benedic-

tus after the Consecration (contrary to the Instruction—and impossible for people to take part) and Ubi Caritas after the Agnus Dei. No communions. And this on the day when the schema on the Liturgy is being promulgated! *Why* only a low Mass on this great occasion? Grandiose splendor—last time in history? What about Camara's hope, for simplicity and poverty—so often echoed on Council floor—poverty *in capite et in ducibus* [in head and in leaders].

After Mass: Obedience to the Holy Father: All Cardinals, bishops in copes, priests in chasubles, deacons in dalmatics. Genuflect, kiss ring (except Oriental Patriarch who didn't genuflect, only bowed). Gossips will be busy for long time speculating about "favor" in which each is, according to amount of time Pope spoke with him and smiled at him.

During "obedience"—all stand and sing Credo III. Glorious *experience*. Creed of Church at General Council. Loud "Orate"—Pope and all kneel; choir begins hymn to Holy Spirit. Veni Creator Spiritus intoned by Pope. Choir alternates with Gregorian chant by all—the first time audience has chance to open up in song—and tremendous, joyful volume, as if a dam released.

Felici reads parts of the schema on the Liturgy: "Paul the Sixth, servant of the servants of God, one with the Fathers of the Council. . . . " During the voting and tabulation, motets—showed again how limited our repertory: Salve Regina, Magnificat, Christus Vincit.

Felici brings results. Kneels before the Pope. The voting is announced (2147/4) and the date the Constitution on the Sacred Liturgy will take effect (February 16, the First Sunday of Lent). Then, following the voting on the schema on communications, "a third rate document by second rate bishops on a first rate topic, so they say," the Pope addressed the audience:

"The difficult, complex debates have had rich results. They have brought one topic to a conclusion, the sacred liturgy. Treated before all others, in a sense it has priority over all others for its intrinsic dignity and importance to the life of the Church and today we will solemnly promulgate the document on the liturgy. Our spirit, therefore, exults with true joy, for in the way things have gone we note respect for a right scale of values and duties. God must hold first place; prayer to God is our first duty. The liturgy is the first source of the divine communion in which God shares his own life with us. It is also the first school of the spiritual life. The liturgy is the first gift we must

make to the Christian people united to us by faith and the fervor of
their prayers. It is also a primary invitation to the human race, so
that all may lift their now mute voices in blessed and genuine prayer
and thus may experience that indescribable, regenerative power to be
found when they join us in proclaiming the praises of God and the
hopes of the human heart through Christ and the Holy Spirit. . . . ''

Godfrey's commentary on the close of the second session of Vatican II concludes: ''Outler may be correct. So much has happened
these last three years that it's almost a sin against the Holy Spirit to
be impatient!''[56]

NOTES TO CHAPTER 8

1. A reference to Bishop William Bernard Ullathorne (1806–1889), whose letters were used to construct a history of Vatican Council I. See, for example, *The Vatican Council (1869–1870) based on Bishop Ullathorne's Letters,* ed. Edward C. Butler (Westminster, Md.: Newman Press, 1962).

2. GLD, letter to FRM, October 23, 1962.

3. GLD, 1963:207. Diaries from 1963, 1964, and 1965 will be referred to by pagination rather than date, since not all entries are dated.

4. GLD, letter to Abbot Baldwin Dworschak, November 16, 1963. A later diary entry suggests that Godfrey's view was shared by others, namely, that Ruffini acted as a "barometer" of the minority:

> At Press Conference this P.M., Häring, who is a member of the theological commission, quite frankly stated that whenever Ruffini speaks, journalists may conclude that the exact *opposite* is the mind of the great majority of the theological commission. That there are several intransigents whose names you can guess, but that majority are of same mind as the obvious majority on the Council floor [1963:145].

5. GLD, 1963:6.

6. Archbishop Martin of Rouen used the text of a memorandum prepared by Gregory Baum, Fred McManus, and Godfrey in an intervention at the Council on October 3, 1963. The memorandum dealt with the discrepancy between the schema under consideration *(De Ecclesia)* and the first chapter of the schema on the liturgy, which had already been voted on and passed by the Council. The point at issue was contradictory conceptions of the nature of the Church. Godfrey did not mention whether these three were also responsible for ghostwriting Martin's introduction: "My speech will be short for the sake of brevity and charity." It drew a good laugh.

7. GLD, letter to "Dear Coonie and rest of 'Round Robins,' " October 14, 1963.

8. GLD, 1963:117.

9. Michael Novak, *The Open Church* (New York: Macmillan, 1964) 125–127.

10. GLD, 1963:143–144.

11. Ibid.

12. GLD, 1963:59.

13. GLD, 1963:115.

14. GLD, letter to Abbot Baldwin Dworschak, November 16, 1963.

15. Martin Marty, taped interview, November 30, 1987.

16. GLD, 1963:177.

17. GLD, 1963:3.

18. GLD, 1963:15. There are other diary entries that allude to the Catholic University affair. One evening, for example, there was a dinner in honor of John Courtney Murray and his victory in the theological commission. He had been successful in introducing a chapter on liberty of conscience. "The four horsemen of the C.U.A. affair were called upon for speeches" [1963:170]. Others remember that this dinner actually honored all four men.

19. Xavier Rynne, *The Second Session: The Debates and Decrees of Vatican Council II, September 29 to December 4, 1963* (New York: Farrar, Straus, 1964) 304–305.

20. Dworschak diary, October 22, 1963. Bishop Leo Dworschak of Fargo, uncle of Abbot Baldwin Dworschak, gave a copy of his diary of the Second Vatican Council to St. John's University. It is available in the Rare Book Collection of the university library.

21. Dworschak diary, November 23, 1963. Dworschak's frustration was compounded by an announcement that the size of the commission would be increased to thirty. His retort:

> We do not need bigger commission; we need some chairmen of the commissions who will allow them to function in a manner which will permit them to interpret the mind of the Council. What we need is that some of the members of the commission be fired, or at least that the commissions as a whole would be allowed to elect its own chairman and secretary. The device of permitting each commission, after it is increased to 30, to elect another vice chairman and secretary is very obviously a cover-up. It will accomplish exactly nothing, if the announced changes are all that will be done with the commissions [Dworschak diary, November 21, 1963].

22. GLD, 1963:64.

23. GLD, 1963:119.

24. GLD, 1963:117.

25. Dworschak diary, October 23, 1963.

26. GLD, taped interview, July 1988.

27. Ibid.

28. GLD, "Ad n. 23, in relatione De Officio Divino," a memorandum prepared on April 18, 1961, for submission to the preparatory commission, concluded with this request.

29. *Documents on the Liturgy 1963–1979: Conciliar, Papal, and Curial Texts* (Collegeville, Minn.: The Liturgical Press, 1982) 21.

30. GLD, 1963:4.

31. GLD, letter to J. B. O'Connell, March 3, 1964.

32. GLD, letter to Archbishop Paul Hallinan, February 21, 1966.

33. GLD, letter to Archbishop Paul Hallinan, June 9, 1964.

34. GLD, letter to J. B. O'Connell, March 3, 1964.

35. GLD, taped interview, October 1987.

36. Martin Marty, taped interview, November 30, 1987. Marty drew my attention to the way "vernacular" functioned for Godfrey; it was he who spoke of it as the "prow of the ship."

37. Gerard Sloyan, letter to GLD, May 15, 1957. Johannes Quasten is reported to have said of her, "Christine Mohrmann is extraordinarily erudite and brilliant in her writings—and always wrong!"

38. Colonel John K. Ross-Duggan, questionnaire prepared and circulated in the summer of 1962 in the name of the Vernacular Society of the United States and Canada.

39. Ibid.

40. GLD, 1963:168.

41. GLD, 1963:69.

42. GLD, 1963:202. Godfrey believes that Latin hastened the death of Gustave Weigel, S. J., who served as translator to the observers. The speeches were written not by the bishops but by Latinists, in good form, so the verb would often be at the end. "You had to wait until the verb to start translating, so with one ear you had to get the sentence and with the other ear the next sentence already, so it was an impossible task for one person to hear Latin and translate it at the same time. There ought to have been two persons. I'm sure Gus Weigel died as a result of Latin!" [GLD, taped interview, April 1987].

43. GLD, 1963:50-51, 177. The minutes of this meeting actually record a series of votes: vernacular concessions, 130 to 5; to authorize preparation of an interim translation, 127 to 7; to work with the International Commission on English in the Liturgy, 126 to 3. (ICEL beginnings will be treated in the next chapter.)

44. Dworschak diary, October 29, 1963.

45. Michael Novak, *The Open Church* (New York: Macmillan, 1964) 201.

46. Dworschak diary, October 29, 1963.

47. GLD, 1963:passim.

48. GLD, 1963:144-145.

49. *Council Daybook:* Vatican II, Sessions 1-2, ed. Floyd Anderson (Washington: National Catholic Welfare Conference, 1965) 293.

50. Desmond Fisher, "The Men Behind the Council," *Sign* (September 1965) 17.

51. Dworschak diary, November 22, 1963.

52. GLD, interview taped in Rome, November 1963.

53. GLD, 1963:186 and taped interviews.

54. GLD, interview taped in Rome, November 1963.

55. GLD, 1963:195.

56. GLD, 1963:218ff. Excerpt from the address of Pope Paul VI is taken from *Documents on the Liturgy,* 27-28.

CHAPTER *9*

THE MONTHS between the second and third sessions of the Council sped by. Godfrey returned to teaching, retreats, editorial work, and now an endless series of talks on the Constitution and the Council:

> Fred and I have been very busy lecturing to groups of priests through-
> out the country ever since returning from Rome. And the list of such
> engagements stretches through the next months, until September. Ac-
> tually, it has been very edifying to discover how willing, and even
> eager, priests of advanced years are to listen and to learn. If only we
> can reach enough of them.[1]

At the same time, the Consilium for the Implementation of the Constitution on the Sacred Liturgy shifted into high gear. As a consultor to the Consilium, Godfrey was assigned as *relator* [literally, the one who makes the report] of Study Group 11, a group charged with the reorganization of the readings for Mass. His participation in the international liturgical study week at Mont César in 1954 stood him in good stead for this new assignment. That meeting ten years earlier had thoroughly reviewed the questions of a several-year cycle of readings, the advisability of *lectio continua* versus discrete selections, the need to honor the weight of tradition in the assignment of readings for major feasts and seasons, and the desire for a more copious presentation of God's word. In addition, Godfrey contributed sensitivity to the ecumenical ramifications of Lectionary preparation as he guided this work in its first months. Most of the Churches issuing from the Reformation used the traditional Lectionary; their counsel had to be sought.

Lectionary reform was one of the most difficult tasks of the entire liturgical renewal, and one of its most urgent. The study group was motivated in its work by the Constitution's strong statement of the need to restore a love for Scripture among the faithful:

> Sacred Scripture is of the greatest importance in the celebration of the liturgy. For it is from Scripture that the readings are given and explained in the homily and that the psalms are sung; the prayers, collects, and liturgical songs are scriptural in their inspiration; it is from the Scriptures that actions and signs derive their meaning. Thus to achieve the reform, progress, and adaptation of the liturgy, it is essential to promote that warm and living love for Scripture to which the venerable tradition of both Eastern and Western rites gives testimony.[2]

Reorganization of the Lectionary had the potential of restoring a deep reverence and love for the word of God in the liturgy, a matter of undoubted neglect in the Catholic Church in recent centuries.[3]

The Constitution furnished the overarching goals of Lectionary reform that would guide the work: "In sacred celebrations there is to be more reading from holy Scripture and it is to be more varied and apposite."[4] In particular: "The treasures of the Bible are to be opened up more lavishly, so that a richer share in God's word may be provided for the faithful. In this way a more representative portion of holy Scripture will be read to the people in the course of a prescribed number of years."[5]

Godfrey, together with Gaston Fontaine, Heinrich Schürmann, Pierre Jounel, Pacifico Massi, Emmanuel Lanne, and Heinrich Kahlefeld, set to work to articulate the principles that would direct their selection of readings.[6] At the second plenary meeting of the Consilium, these specific guidelines were approved:

> 1) On Sundays, first- and second-class feasts of the Lord, and holy days of obligation, the Mass is to have three readings, though it will be permitted to drop the first (prophet) or the second (apostle) depending on the special circumstances of the congregation.

> 2) Even in a system of readings covering a three- or four-year period, there is always to be a one-year cycle of readings for some Sundays and principal feasts, so that the same passages will always be read on these days.

3) The tradition is to be kept of having certain books of Scripture assigned to certain seasons of the year.

4) In distributing the readings from Sacred Scripture, the principal part, both of the Old and the New Testament, is to be looked upon as a kind of complement to the readings in the Missal.[7]

The group next turned their attention to assembling tables of lections used in Eastern and Western liturgies and in the liturgies of the Reformed Churches, comparing the use of lections in liturgies ancient and modern, and selecting passages best suited for liturgical use. Biblical scholars were invited to participate in the selection and division of texts; the advice and critique of catechetical experts and pastors were sought.

Early in the deliberations Godfrey argued for optional use of the first or second reading, a suggestion accepted provisionally until further discussion could take place. In the end, three readings became normative for Sundays and solemnities, but for pastoral reasons and by decree of a conference of bishops the use of only two readings was permitted.[8]

Was the Consilium an independent body, or was it accountable to the Curia, and specifically to the Congregation of Rites [SRC]? Turf questions surfaced at the beginning of the third session of the Council. Godfrey sent an account of the tug of war to Abbot Baldwin:

> Tuesday, rumor spread like wildfire that work of the post-conciliar liturgical commission would have to be channeled in future through SRC—which would have been the death of the hope hitherto alive, that this "international senate of bishops" would henceforth decide in matters liturgical, and thus as it were bypass the Curia instead of fighting it head on—and that this would also set patterns in other areas in the future. Bugnini admitted that until two days ago it had been touch and go. But the Holy Father has now decided, despite high pressure from SRC, to abide by the decision published in *Osservatore Romano,* that implementation of the Liturgy Constitution is to be in the hands exclusively of the post-conciliar liturgical commission. Deo gratias! It was a test case—significant for the entire question of world bishops and Curia.[9]

As it happened, Godfrey was wrong. An unhappy truce was established in which, technically, documents came from SRC after being prepared by "study groups" of the Consilium.

The work of the Consilium kept Godfrey so busy that he was unable to attend as many sessions of the Council as he would have liked. Nor did he have much leisure to spar good-naturedly with the press. In fact, the pace of the third session of the Council had picked up considerably:

> Council is pushing so fast and hard this year that many bishops are beginning to think it is *rushing matters too fast.* Because of pressure and protests from a number of national hierarchies, Felici this morning announced that some discussion of the "Propositione" will be allowed. I suspect that the "Propositione" on Seminaries and Religious will make most lively debate and may need substantial re-editing.[10]

And Godfrey couldn't resist a bit of evaluation in the postscript: "Ritter's intervention on Religious Liberty was disappointing . . . Meyer, first rate. Léger, most outstanding."[11]

Godfrey was delighted to return to the Council in the fall of 1964. He was no longer the newcomer, but a seasoned *peritus* who was among the most respected of the theological experts—and among the most captivating and entertaining as well! In an article for *America,* John Cogley included Godfrey among Council "stars," describing the way he commanded the attention of others by the sheer force of his personality:

> Father Godfrey Diekmann from the Collegeville Benedictines is another kind of star. At a party the other evening he began to talk quietly to a group around him, about theological issues. Little by little others at the party dropped their own conversation and began to listen. Soon he was the only one talking, with an almost boyish enthusiasm for the possibilities open to the Church in our day. This was a tough audience to play to, too. Not at all the Ladies Sodality dutifully shutting up to listen to Father. Among those listening intently were a half dozen international press people, a group of Protestant observers, a couple of young Italians who said that they had left the Church as soon as they grew up and were free to do so, and a number of Fr. Godfrey's theological peers.[12]

Perhaps because he was a seasoned participant, Godfrey's diaries for the third and fourth sessions of the Council are decidedly thin. Again, he attended to the whole scene, the high emotions that accompanied some discussions, the deadly silences or the buzzing (once described as "the buzzing of angry bees") that followed announce-

ment of results of a particular vote. He noticed that some bishops
were so interested in certain discussions that they left their places and
gathered around the confession toward the front of St. Peter's in order
to hear better. He offered his judgment on the Consilium's work in
progress: "De Ordine Missae—disastrous!" and sang an Alleluia
when the vote to restore a functional diaconate was positive. He remained acutely aware of the thinking and the reactions of the Protestant observers, often seeking them out for their opinion on this or
that. The details of the liturgies continued to rankle, for example,
twenty-four concelebrants "forming an episcopal curtain, obstruct-
ing the view of the altar, a lamentable regression to ordination scenes
of years gone by!"[13]

During the third session of the Council, women were admitted
for the first time as *auditrices,* and this posed its own problems of "cultural adaptation": "The big problem of the Council today is to find
a powder room for the auditrices. . . . Also crucial question, whether
auditrices may come to the coffee bars. Men auditors have been
coming—and, especially if auditrices become more numerous, and
they will be denied access, they could voice holy cain about discrimi-
nation.[14]

The most interesting debates of the third session concerned the
Declaration on Religious Liberty, and Godfrey found himself cheering on those bishops to whom he was particularly partial. High on
the list was Cardinal Cushing: "Everybody grinning—he yelled *modo
suo,* wouldn't need a loudspeaker. And after he had expressed his pleasure with the main features [of the Declaration on Religious Liberty],
he got a round of applause."[15] For his efforts Cushing also got im-
mortalized in verse:

> Cardinal Cushing of Boston avows
> He, freedom to all men allows.
>   Though he's no Latin scholar,
>   He knows how to holler.
> At the Council he brought down the house.[16]

Godfrey's fascination with the Declaration on Religious Liberty
turned on its effects on different countries, cultures, churches, and
religions. He also recognized a new maturity in the United States
hierarchy as they dealt with this document. November 19, he claimed,

was a turning point for the Council, and beyond doubt its most exciting day. The vote on the Declaration on Religious Liberty had been postponed, due in great measure to the strong opposition of the Spanish. The United States bishops countered by protesting the postponement:

> Instantaneously some U.S. bishops left their seats. They gathered around Meyer and Ritter. Quinn, Reh, Unterkoefler channeled their anger into concrete action—circulated a petition and got over 800 signatures asking the Holy Father to assure that the Declaration would be brought to the floor for a vote before the end of the session. (Bugnini telephoned—when I told him about Meyer and Ritter et al. he said "Bisogna combattere"—they need to fight!)

> Proud that this was predominantly and overwhelmingly American. In some ways I'm glad it happened. Collegiality came into its own. Some French who had some reservations on the argumentation of the document entered their dining room singing "Dies Irae" but left singing "Te Deum," and when the document passed, they fell all over John Courtney Murray congratulating him. Clearly even more important than the vote was the consciousness of collegiality.[17]

It may have been the whole question of religious liberty, together with some foot-dragging in the liturgical commission and the protracted frustration of the Council liturgies, that prompted a last entry in Godfrey's 1964 diary, an *Oratio Contra Rubricistas* [Prayer Against Rubricists]:

> Deus, qui per rubricistarum ordinem viam caeli impedisti, da nobis, quaesumus, ipsis in mare rubrum detrusis, ut per aliam viam vitam aeternam consequamur.

> O God,
> who through the Order of Rubricists
> has impeded the way to heaven,
> we pray that you give to us
> who have been buried under this sea of red,
> another way to eternal life.[18]

By the time the final session of the Council convened in the fall of 1965, enthusiasm for conciliar *aggiornamento* seemed to be flagging. Dissatisfaction was in the air. One bishop, disgruntled by the Curia, was heard to say, "They are giving us the mushroom treatment: 'Keep 'em in the dark and feed 'em horse manure.' " (An avid fungophile himself, Godfrey filed that simile away for future use.) Another bishop disclosed that two members of the Consilium [Felici and Antonelli] had done an end run on the *Ordo Missae* project by going to the Pope and blocking experimentation. F. X. Murphy reported to Godfrey that the bishops of the United States had lost interest in the Council and wanted to go home. They had convened as a national body only once since returning to Rome, and "that meeting was miserable." Schemas were coming to the floor for final emendations, and some of them—the schema on education, for example—were met with fairly widespread discontent; yet there seemed to be little energy to fight. Because of this climate, the American *periti* were called to a meeting to plan strategy for the implementation of the Council, lest the bishops return home without much enthusiasm and revert to "business as usual."[19]

A highlight of the last session of the Council, as far as Godfrey was concerned, was the day Pope Paul VI met with the observers. It was the Pope himself who first suggested that he and the observers should not merely speak to each other but together they should speak to God. Pope Paul then warmly seconded the suggestion of the Secretariat for the Promotion of Christian Unity that there be a common prayer service but declined the invitation to preside. "No," he said, "we will not have a Catholic service at which others are present, but let this truly be a common effort."

The Pope asked that a certain degree of simplicity surround this event and chose St. Paul's rather than St. Peter's—a monastic setting instead of a highly vested papal court. When the Pope's advance man, John Long, S.J., went out to St. Paul's, he found a big throne and drapes prepared for the Pope. Long insisted that it be dismantled, and so it was.

But perhaps no one communicated this desire for simplicity to the Protestant observers. According to Godfrey, there was a great mix-up. In order not to appear triumphalist (the "in" word at the time), Catholic cardinals and bishops had been instructed not to wear their brilliant red and purple robes, but rather what is known as their domestic garb—black with, of course, a discreet touch of red. Someone had forgotten to inform the Protestants. Most of them arrived in academic garb. "Perhaps it was the one and only occasion in history when Protestant and Anglican divines 'outsplendored' their Catholic counterparts.'' As one embarrassed friend said to Godfrey, "I've never in all my life felt as much like a gamecock in mating season."[20]

Besides delighting in the details of this ecumenical event as it was planned and executed, Godfrey wrote very little about the last session of the Council, though in spurts he jotted down who blocked what, who ghostwrote what, who said what to whom, who wanted, didn't want, or was actually relieved when. . . . While "history with a capital H" continued to be made, Godfrey furnished fewer mosaic pieces for future understanding. In part, this may have been due to the press of work for the Consilium; in part, another work had begun that captured Godfrey's imagination, his energies, and a good portion of his time. This latter was Godfrey's collaboration with a group that would become "The International Commission on English in the Liturgy" (ICEL).[21]

Beginning in a few informal and unplanned meetings in and about the coffee bars toward the end of the first session of the Council, and well before the extent of vernacular use had been determined, a few bishops and *periti* began to discuss how to prepare an English translation of liturgical and scriptural texts. Collaboration across the English-speaking world was essential. As Archbishop Denis Hurley of Durban pointed out to Archbishop Francis Grimshaw of Birmingham: "Like many English-speaking countries around the world, we [South Africa] find ourselves caught in a cross-fire of British and American translations and the missals used by our people manifest a wondrous variety. Something will have to be done about this when the vernacular comes into official use."[22] Moreover, the high rate of travel between countries, the need for standard texts for the composition of liturgical music, the advisability of a common text for quotation, comment, and explanation, and the lack of resources of some national conferences—all were reasons that recommended a collegial approach to translation.

Some persons outside the discussion followed initial developments with a wary eye:

> There were two interesting items in the papers today. The one referred to the fact that Archbishop Grimshaw has organized a group of bishops from English-speaking countries to begin working on the vernacular missal that will be approved without question by the Council. The

initiative in this matter was taken by Grimshaw, which is an interesting fact. He has the reputation of being the most conservative of all English prelates on the matter of the vernacular. Why should he be taking this initiative? Could he be trying to head off any extensive use of the vernacular in all English-speaking countries? This is a development which will bear watching. Hallinan and Griffiths are on his committee to represent the U.S. O'Neill of Regina represents the English-speaking Church in Canada. A name that I was happy to see on the list was that of Archbishop Young from Tasmania. I know he will not be satisfied with a mere minimum use of vernacular.[23]

Godfrey arrived at the Council for the second session just as these first, more formal exploratory meetings began. He and Fred McManus were asked to serve with Archbishop Hallinan to work out a *modus agendi* and plans for an ultimate "common text." Godfrey spoke of this new venture in a letter to Abbot Baldwin:

I'm also on the committee working towards a long-range program of deciding on a common text for all English-speaking countries. And we meet at the English College several evenings a week, under the presidency of Archbishop Grimshaw. . . . Ten bishops, each appointed by his respective national group of bishops. Plus Fr. Fred McManus and myself. Very likely that Archbishop Hallinan of Atlanta, appointed by U.S. bishops, will be named permanent secretary with McManus and me his immediate "committee." This will, very likely, entail a considerable amount of extra work. The whole thing is tentative as yet.[24]

Tentative, but not for long. It was clear that a long-range plan *had* to be in place for the time when the Consilium completed its revisions of the Missal, Ritual, Breviary, etc., a work anticipated to take five years. But in the meantime the group had to hammer out a strategy and appoint a small working group of bishops and experts. This working group would, in turn, establish a permanent body to which bishops could turn for translations, decide the extent of their mandate, and develop a philosophy to guide ICEL's future program. Not the least of the hurdles to be faced was to identify a pool of experts—Latinists, linguists, musicians, poets—who were specialists in English of the simple, beautiful, and dignified variety.

The meetings at the English College were frequent and filled with the by now familiar ups and downs, victories and setbacks:

Meeting at English College with officers of English-speaking Bishops Committee for Common Texts [ICEL's original name]: Archbishop Grimshaw (president), and Archbishops Young and Hallinan. Present: Msgr. Baum (K.C.) and J. B. O'Connell. Big success on main point—Grimshaw all for RSV and for dropping thee's and thou's. *SO* is Archbishop Heenan!! Said that Cardinal Godfrey is still warm in his grave, so we'd have to wait a few weeks—but he definitely assured us of green light![25]

But a few days later: "Fred said Grimshaw, at meeting of textual commission, began to weasel out. Gray of Edinburgh told him the Scot bishops would not feel bound by his example, but would go all out."[26]

Meanwhile, as policy and broad principles were being developed at these meetings, Godfrey and Fred McManus had a first taste of the difficulty of translation—and of pleasing "all of the people all of the time." Clifford Howell had prepared a translation of the Constitution on the Sacred Liturgy, which Godfrey and Fred reworked for

Five founding members of ICEL at Edinburgh (1978): Godfrey, Cardinal Cordeiro of Karachi, Cardinal Gray of Edinburgh, Archbishop Hurley of Durban, Frederick McManus

ICEL board of advisors, Rome, 1967: (front row) Gerald Sigler and Stephen Somerville; (standing, left to right) John Hackett, G. B. Harrison, Godfrey Diekmann, Harold Winstone, Herbert Finberg, Fred McManus, Percy Jones

ICEL meeting, Rome, 1982: (left to right) John Fitzsimmons, Archbishop Hurley, John Page, Godfrey Diekmann, Kathleen Hughes, Christopher Willcock

262

publication in *Worship,* but Howell was unhappy and told them so in no uncertain terms. He did not want his name attached to a text that, in his judgment, was full of Latinisms and slavish interpretation. Among his examples:

> Whatever do you mean by "sobriety" in the rite for nuns' renewal of vows? Does it mean that the sisters mustn't get drunk before Mass? Of course not. Then why put "sobriety?" Just because the Latin is "sobrietas?" Moreover a *"rite of religious profession and renewal . . . "* all those r sounds one on top of another . . . and soon "religious PROFession should PREFerably . . . I can't see that what I have written means anything different . . . and so, wherever I have felt it safe I've stuck to what I wrote myself. But sometimes, without the Latin, I just don't know and am FORCED to accept your version.[27]

[Howell was at a disadvantage in this work, not being present in Rome, where the text of the Constitution was being changed during the waning days of the second session.]

As supplementary instruction, Howell sent Godfrey and Fred a copy of Hilaire Belloc's "Principles of Translating," a text that serves remarkably well to capture ICEL's translation guidelines as they developed in the next few years:

> Transmute boldly; render the sense by the corresponding sense without troubling over the verbal difficulties in the way. Where such rendering of sense by corresponding sense involves considerable amplification, do not hesitate to amplify. . . . Sometimes, even, a whole passage must be thus transmuted, a whole paragraph thrown into a new form, if we would justly and elegantly render the sense of the original: and the rule should stand that, after having grasped as exactly as possible all that the original stands for, with the proportion between its various parts, the distinction between what is emphasized and what is left on a lower plane, we should say to ourselves, not 'How shall I make this foreigner talk in English?' but 'What would an Englishman have said to express this?' THAT is translation. THAT is the very essence of the art—the resurrection of an alien thing in a native body; not the dressing of it up in native clothes but the giving to it of native flesh and blood.[28]

At the end of his letter, Howell reiterated that he wanted nothing to do with the final text and to please remove his name. Then, referring to a check he had enclosed, he invited Fred and Godfrey to go out to dinner on him!

Godfrey responded to Howell, defending their translation as more closely capturing the intent of the original, though conceding that many of his and Fred's phrases were often quite cumbersome and not as felicitous as Howell's clearly superior English style. "In examining your translation, there were literally dozens of times when both of us spontaneously exclaimed about the splendid manner in which you were able to capture the ponderous Latin in attractive, idiomatic English."[29]

But more important than the work was their friendship. Godfrey thanked Howell for the check, which had enabled a pleasant agape "in which we duly included Clifford Howell among the commemorations. For it assured us that, though you were very angry with us, you had not repudiated fellowship. I can only once again express my infinite relief that your annoyance with us has not affected our personal relations of friendship, which I treasure very much indeed."[30]

By the fall of 1964, ICEL's mandate had been developed[31] and a first advisory committee appointed: G. B. Harrison, Harold Winstone, Herbert Finberg, Frederick McManus, Percy Jones, Stephen Somerville, Godfrey, and John McGarry, who resigned early in 1965 and was replaced by John Hackett. Godfrey could not be present at the preliminary organizational meeting in London early in 1965. He wrote to Fred to go on record on some of the most basic questions facing the committee as they began their work:

> There will probably be an impasse at your meeting in regard to the use of "thee" or "you." The chief argument in favor of the former can hardly be "tradition." The Council has made it clear that, for the sake of pastoral aggiornamento, it is imperative to adapt the external expressions of our faith, even in doctrinal pronouncements, in favor of intelligibility and pastoral spiritual gains. The decisive question at issue, therefore, is whether "thee" and "thou" or "you" and "your" suits better the devotional and spiritual needs of your people. Granted that "thee" and "thou" (but not the corresponding verb forms!), precisely because they are not in everyday idiomatic usage, are conducive to instilling a sense of reverence for the Deity. But I am convinced that an even greater need at the present time is to make the Christian religion more *relevant* to the man living in the world today. He must again discover, not merely the transcendent God, but

even more importantly, the God who became flesh and became one of us, including the use of language, in all things except sin. The greatest single advance made by the Council is precisely its determination that the Christian religion may no longer be a beautiful museum piece, but must be the leaven that transforms the world in which we live. . . . It seems to me, moreover, that our own experience here in the U.S. in adopting the "you" form, has not lessened due reverence for God, but has simply been gratefully taken in stride.[32]

In the fall of 1965 the first full, formal meeting of the advisory committee was held in Rome. "Thou" versus "you" was the subject of hot debate. A participant at that meeting, G. B. Harrison, recalled the discussion of this point: "Finberg was firm that in speaking to God one should always say 'Thou,' never 'You,' so strong in fact that he declared that if the committee adopted 'you' he would resign. The debate extended a day and a half; vote was 7 to 1—and Herbert did not resign."[33]

A second issue that Godfrey addressed was style of translation, particularly for the collect:

In regard to the sticky problem of translating the Latin collects, and whether to keep the long, periodic sentence, as does the Latin, or whether to break them up into several sentences, even though this may involve some loss in nuances of meaning and of relationships, I personally strongly favor the shorter sentences. The decisive factor is that these Collects will be read aloud. And modern man's span of attention is such that the shorter sentences are imperative if the total meaning is to have any impact at all. Undoubtedly the long sentence, with one or several dependent clauses, will often sound more dignified and impressive, but again, it is a painful choice between external form and content. Wherever this dilemma occurs, it would be a serious disservice to spirituality to opt for the former. But if, in principle, content is given preference, this makes it all the more important that we discover stylists who can present the content in suitably dignified form.[34]

Again, Godfrey's instincts proved accurate. After other members of the advisory committee tried their hands at translation of collects, Godfrey declared himself "mightily impressed" by the excellent work done by Father Winstone and Dr. Harrison in such a brief period of time. "I am particularly happy that both of them broke up the lengthy collects into shorter sentences. Once our priests learn to read the collects and prayers with due deliberation and dignity, it seems to me that any sentence longer than about a dozen words or so will prove ineffectual.''[35]

Finally, regarding the translation ''And with your spirit,'' Godfrey proposed to the advisory committee that the strongest justification for retention of its usage was the ecumenical one. But, he asked, ''isn't this one of the things that we should be discussing with our Protestant friends? They also are keenly aware of the need of up-dating their translations, and perhaps one of the most important things that your meeting could accomplish is to plan how such collaboration with Protestants can be initiated.''[36] These were the kinds of issues being debated almost daily in the closing days of Vatican Council II while ICEL's episcopal board and a number of their advisory committee had easy access to one another.

There were numerous rites of closure to mark the end of the Council. One day the Pope invited some of the *periti* to concelebrate the Eucharist. John Courtney Murray and Henri De Lubac led the crowd. Afterwards the Pope said slyly to De Lubac, ''I was told it would be all right to concelebrate Mass with you.''[37] Many audiences were granted to individuals and groups, and when it was the turn of the *periti,* the Pope welcomed them and urged them, ''Now that you've learned to talk to the bishops you must continue to do so. It is important for the Church.''[38]

As a parting gift the Pope gave each bishop a simple gold-plated ring. When told this would happen, the bishops applauded, but according to Godfrey, the *periti* in his tribune did not clap. Some groaned. The Church of the poor! Godfrey thought that steel would have been better and that bishops should be weaned from rings altogether. He tried to start a rumor that the gold rings would be handed back at the offertory of the closing Mass and the poor would be fed from the money, but this did not catch on![39]

The last few pages of Godfrey's Council jottings include a lengthy summary of a talk by Hans Küng on the meaning of the Council. Obviously Godfrey agreed with this ''teenage theologian,'' as Küng had dubbed himself in an earlier session. Inspired by Küng's address, Godfrey recorded these highlights of the Council:

> Judgment will differ whether we judge 1) in terms of things achieved or 2) in terms of things whose foundations are laid but need implementation. Documents are of unequal value and not all parts of a single

document have the same value. No use complaining that this or that hasn't been achieved. These are the tasks of the future, for on December 8th the Council is not ending but *starting*. Better things are not enemies of good things, but good things are harbingers of *better* things. Note the open doors to the future. In the big river, don't concentrate on stones and obstacles, but see the great current and even the gold in the sands.

During time of council preparation: need of "realistic pessimism." Now, when it's over, we should have a "realistic optimism."

What is not expressed in the documents but is even more important than any of the formulations is: a new spirit; a new freedom of thinking and a lively experience of how fruitful is discussion; a new attitude of truth; an understanding of the piece-meal character of all documents which also helps in the interpretation of documents from the past. There were no new definitions. There was an absence of scholastic language. There was a new esteem for theology and a new ideal of Church government which is collaborative.[40]

Hans Küng and Godfrey at St. John's in the mid-sixties

Godfrey's few lines about the closing liturgy of the Council included this telling comment: "Six small boys (six continents) receive communion. Sr. Mary Luke: Why not at least one or the other a girl? (and unless she had pointed it out, I would not have adverted to the disparity)."[41] Perhaps Sister Mary Luke's comment helped to sensitize Godfrey to feminist issues. Moments later, when the Pope addressed various categories of persons, he singled out women. Godfrey asked: "Why a special category? Imagine if a special category for males!"[42]

Of the whole experience, Godfrey mused: "This has become, despite all expectations, a Council of the Pope! . . . great popular enthusiasm. During this last session, Paul VI has emerged as a great statesman and leader of a *unified* Church."[43]

And then it was over.

Godfrey remembers returning for a last visit to St. Peter's on December 9, the day after the close of the Council. There were throngs of people milling along the Via della Conciliazione into St. Peter's Square. "They came by the thousands, clapping and shouting for the Pope to appear at his window, joined soon by the honking of taxi, bus and auto horns. He did appear—a mystic figure in white, barely discernible against the lighted background. Fell to my knees. Blessing for journey and for coming work."[44]

And Godfrey's work was blessed. For sure, it multiplied. Again, there was a seemingly endless series of talks to be given, retreats to be preached, colloquia to be prepared. Godfrey was in constant demand in settings large and small, and each time he spoke about the Council his own understanding of its import deepened.

Of particular interest to him was a new ecclesial self-understanding embedded in the Constitution on the Sacred Liturgy and enfleshed and developed in later Council documents. Ecclesiological themes highlighted by the Constitution on the Liturgy included the following:

> The importance of community celebration—the entire body, and each of its members is to be actively engaged. This underscores the dignity of responsible Christian personhood, based on the sacraments of Baptism and Confirmation, whereby the person has a true share in the priesthood of Christ. The liturgy is not the preserve of the clergy, but the action of the whole body to whom the priest *ministers* the mysteries. Christ is present in the worshipping assembly, in the proclaimed

word, in the sacramental action. It is in the liturgy, above all, that the priestly work of Christ is continued, his paschal mysteries become operative. The Eucharist—Bread *and Word*—is the sign of the Church's unity, and effects it: at the tables of the Word and Bread, Christ wills to create his people in a brotherhood of faith and love. The local community gathered around its bishop or his priest-representative for eucharistic worship is, therefore, the preeminent self-manifestation of the Church: diocese and parish are representative of and, pastorally speaking, the most important realization of the universal visible Church. As a consequence, while substantial unity must be maintained, reasonable diversity in rite and adaptation to given cultural structures are imperative. Territorial groups of bishops can best judge about such needs, and therefore some degree of decentralization of liturgical legislative powers is a precondition of meaningful reform.[45]

Ecclesiological themes, particularly the epiphany of Church in the local assembly, the dignity and role of the laity in virtue of their baptism, and the pressing need for a dialogue between liturgy and culture have remained central to Godfrey's theology. To these, in recent addresses, he joins elements of Christology and Pneumatology which he draws out of the Council, but of the latter he laments: "Attention to the role of the Holy Spirit was very limited at the Council. When members of the Eastern Church complained, the Holy Spirit was stuck in a document here and there like raisins in a cake—it simply was not organic. Liturgists should have known better because the liturgy is the place where the Holy Spirit works above all."[46]

Besides countless public presentations, Godfrey's work with the International Commission on English in the Liturgy has remained central to his professional commitments after the Council. It is a work entirely consistent and continuous with his long campaign for the vernacular and for active participation. It has also been a *constant* labor of love. In his correspondence Godfrey has referred to the executive secretary of ICEL as "Dear S. D. (i.e. slave driver)," and added the words of the Apostle, "Day and night I spend in your ministry."[47]

That statement is only a *slight* exaggeration. Over the years Godfrey has translated some non-biblical readings, generally patristic texts, for the Liturgy of the Hours; worked on collects of the Roman Missal and edited the final draft of the alternative opening prayers; collaborated with others in the translation of the Eucharistic Prayers, including the ancient texts of Hippolytus and Basil—the latter a particular favorite because of his fascination with the Coptic Church and because of the frequent acclamations of the community, the "people cheering the priest on by their interventions"; prepared a draft of the consecration prayer in the Rite of Religious Profession; researched the form for Orders, and crafted the form for the Rite of Ordination of a Bishop; edited the addresses and litanies in the Rite of Baptism; attended meetings of the Consultation on Common Texts as ICEL's representative; prepared the form of Confirmation; developed a position paper on the ICEL manner of translation; wrote a lengthy critique of the Prefaces in the *Missale Romanum,* some of which he judged "irrelevant in style and concept" ["At Rome meeting I did point out thinness of content of some of the prayers of Ordinary Time. Can we do anything about it short of rewriting (recreating) the prayers?"]; identified and developed the patristic references in the Our Father; worked on the rubrics for the Funeral Rite; edited a final version of the Solemn Blessings;[48] and *always* weighed in with his considered opinion on work in progress, both his own and others.

Some examples of such opinions: "We've got to avoid translating every generic term of goodness and virtue by the one word 'love.' Why do we avoid so scrupulously the word 'grace'? I'm all for it, used rightly—and discreetly."[49] Or, on the translations of responsories and versicle and responses: "Apt to be too 'cuddly,' too 'sticky'—if not erotic, e.g., in Common of Virgins. Translator loves the 'embrace me' bit, even when text doesn't call for it. All this business of Virgin = Bride of Christ has its own problems. We shouldn't compound them."[50] Regarding Roman collegiality: "Thanks for the Penance text. It's damnably frustrating that translators get the text only a few days before its publication, with its inevitable pressure for the vernacular version quick, quick, quick. (It's even more damnable, however, that bishops don't get to see it, and are not consulted about it. Collegiality? Pfui!)"[51]

When Godfrey believed a particular intervention of the Congregation for the Sacraments and Divine Worship regarding ICEL work was unmerited and/or unjust, he was quick and strong in his reaction. The following letter was sent to the ICEL secretariat after confirmation of the Order of Christian Funerals had been withheld. [Cardinal Augustin Mayer, O.S.B., was prefect of the Congregation at the time; Cuthbert Johnson, O.S.B., is on the staff.]

I wish to go on record to express my *outrage* at the recent maneuver-ings and demands of Gus Mayer (we used to call him that, as stu-dents) re the funeral rites. They simply have no business, no right whatever, to dictate "corrections" or "alternatives" of translation. The very thought of one man, Cuthbert Johnson, presuming to im-pose his views (many of which are palpably nonsense) over against a version arrived at with much labor by many experts, makes me froth at the mouth. . . . Thank God we have a strong man like Archbishop [Denis] Hurley to carry the ball.[52]

In support of his contention that much of the Congregation's letter withholding confirmation of the Order of Christian Funerals was pal-pable nonsense, Godfrey attacked one point for two pages. The Con-gregation for the Sacraments and Divine Worship had criticized the use of the word "tender" in addressing God—"untraditional," they said, and "too sentimental." Those were fighting words for Godfrey. He refuted the Congregation's claim in notes citing, among other authorities, Psalm 33, 1 Peter, Justin, and, naturally, his friend Ter-tullian.[53]

From the very beginning of his ICEL association, Godfrey has been greatly respected. His special gift in ICEL work has been his patristic understanding of liturgy and the wealth of sources he is able to summon in the interpretation of a Latin text. He also brings an enthusiasm for the work, despite the unavoidable frustrations he and his colleagues have faced. At meetings of the advisory committee he is sensitive, especially about social issues. His concern for the role of women in the assembly as well as the question of inclusive lan-guage is always evident. He has very definite opinions but is willing to listen to others—and only occasionally "hijacks" the meeting to pursue a tangent. He has served as a good mediator with some of the more conservative members of the advisory committee such as Herbert Finberg (whom G. B. Harrison, another founding member, characterized as "a very English type of elderly academic, sure of himself, and that all others, especially Americans, were incompetent").

Indeed, Godfrey's diplomatic skills were pressed into service at an early stage of ICEL's work. He was sent to Glenstal Abbey in Ireland to try to negotiate so that there would only be the ICEL Lit-urgy of the Hours rather than two translations. He was not received warmly. England, Ireland, and Australia thought ICEL was dragging its feet in the production of the Liturgy of the Hours. Besides, some didn't like some early sample texts, so they went ahead to produce their own *Divine Office*.[54]

Godfrey now serves as ICEL patriarch, vigorous as ever at meetings of the advisory committee and the subcommittee on translation and revisions. He is able to criticize his own earlier contributions, saying, "I think I have to change my mind," and plunges on.

When ICEL sent a letter of congratulations to Godfrey on his seventieth birthday, he replied: "For my part, I can honestly say that my work for ICEL and the fraternal good fellowships it has entailed through the years rank among the most pleasant and rewarding experiences of my life (Not to speak of the opportunities offered to exercise my vocation of "pilgrim"!).[55]

Godfrey's vocation, pilgrim and otherwise, is the subject of the final chapter.

NOTES TO CHAPTER 9

1. GLD, letter to J. B. O'Connell, March 3, 1964.

2. *Documents on the Liturgy 1963-1979: Conciliar, Papal, and Curial Texts* (Collegeville, Minn.: The Liturgical Press, 1982) 9-10.

3. Annibale Bugnini, *The Reform of the Liturgy (1948-1975)*, trans. Matthew J. O'Connell (Collegeville, Minn.: The Liturgical Press, 1990) 409-410. I have relied on Archbishop Bugnini's book to supply details of Godfrey's work with the Consilium.

4. *Documents on the Liturgy,* 11.

5. Ibid., 14.

6. Cf. Godfrey Diekmann, "De lectionibus in Missa," *Notitiae* 1 (1965) 333-337. The following is a synthesis of Godfrey's presentation to the general meeting of the Consilium in April 1964, as provided by Bugnini, *Reform of the Liturgy,* 410-411:

> The basic principle is that "the mystery of Christ and the history of salvation" must be presented in the readings. Therefore, the new system of readings must contain the whole nucleus of the apostolic preaching about Jesus as "Lord and Christ" (Acts 2:36) who fulfilled the Scriptures by his life, his preaching, and, above all, his paschal mystery and who gives life to the Church until his glorious return.
>
> The new Lectionary must make clear:
> —that the Church is today living out the mystery of salvation in its entirety, the mystery that found its complete form in Christ and that must also be completed in us;
> —the mysteries of faith and the principles governing Christian life, which are then to be explained in the homily;
> —that the entire Old Testament is presupposed in the Lord's preaching, his actions, and his passion;
> —that attention to the central theme, the Lord's Pasch, must not lead to forgetfulness of other themes, for example, the coming of God's reign;
> —finally, that the liturgical year provides the ideal setting for proclaiming the message of salvation to the faithful in an organized way.

7. Bugnini, *Reform of the Liturgy,* 411.

273

8. Cf. The General Instruction of the Roman Missal, no. 318 *(Documents on the Liturgy,* 528). Godfrey oversaw this work of the study group until June 1965, when he asked to be replaced as *relator* because of commitments in the United States and the difficulties of attending frequent meetings abroad. For similar reasons his participation as a member of Study Group 4, which was assigned the choice of Scripture readings for the Office, was also curtailed.

9. GLD, letter to Abbot Baldwin Dworschak, September 17, 1964.

10. GLD, letter to Abbot Baldwin Dworschak, September 25, 1964.

11. Ibid.

12. John Cogley, "Roman Diary," *America* (September 26, 1964).

13. GLD, 1964:17, 3, and passim. While the diary is considerably shorter than that of the previous year, the strength of Godfrey's reactions is unabated. The diary is full of underlines, capitals, exclamation points, and repetition, for example, "Why, why, why, *insist* on this point?"

14. GLD, letter to Abbot Baldwin Dworschak, September 28, 1964.

15. GLD, 1964:21.

16. Dworschak diary, November 1964.

17. GLD, 1964:48–59.

18. GLD, 1964:62.

19. GLD, 1965:1, 2, 5.

20. GLD, 1965:11 and sermon delivered on Reformation Sunday, November 1, 1981.

21. For a history of the International Commission on English in the Liturgy, especially its early years, see Peter C. Finn and James M. Schellman, eds., *Shaping English Liturgy* (Washington: The Pastoral Press, 1990), particularly Frederick R. McManus, "ICEL: The First Years," 433–459; G. B. Harrison and Percy Jones, "Personal Reminiscences of the Early Years of ICEL," 461–472; and John R. Page, "ICEL, 1966–1989," 473–489.

22. Denis Hurley, letter to Francis Grimshaw, February 4, 1963.

23. Dworschak diary, October 19–20, 1963.

24. GLD, letter to Abbot Baldwin Dworschak, November 16, 1963.

25. GLD, 1963:115.

26. GLD, 1963:186.

27. Clifford Howell, letter to GLD, November 27, 1963.

28. Ibid. Belloc's principles contain, in a nutshell, the substance of the Instruction *Comme le prévoit,* on the translation of liturgical texts for celebrations with a congregation, 25 January 1969 *(Notitiae* 5 [1969] 3–12). This Instruction developed principles for liturgical translation to render the original faithfully but not in a slavishly literal style. The Instruction also acknowledged the need to create new texts, since texts translated from another language are not sufficient for the celebration of a fully renewed liturgy.

29. GLD, letter to Clifford Howell, January 6, 1964.

30. Ibid.

31. Mandate of The International Advisory Committee on English in the Liturgy:

The Hierarchies of England and Wales, Scotland, Ireland, the United States of America, Canada, Australia, New Zealand, India, Pakistan and Southern Africa, having agreed to the establishment of an International Advisory Committee on English in the Liturgy with a view to achieving an English version of liturgical texts acceptable to English speaking countries and bearing in mind the ecumenical aspects, entrust this Committee with the following Mandate:

1. To work out a plan for the translation of liturgical texts and the provision of original texts where required in language which would be correct, dignified, intelligible, and suitable for public recitation and singing; to propose the engagement of experts in various fields as translators, composers, and critics and to provide for the exchange of information with the sponsoring Hierarchies and with other interested Hierarchies; and to give special attention, within the scope of this plan, to the question of a single English version of the Bible for liturgical use or at least of common translations of biblical texts used in the liturgy.

2. To submit this plan to the interested Hierarchies with a view to obtaining their consent.

3. To implement the plan.

4. To submit final recommendations to the interested Hierarchies for their approval.

5. To use such funds as shall be made available for these purposes by the Hierarchies, under the general control of the Episcopal Secretary representing them for the time being, the Most Reverend Paul J. Hallinan, Archbishop of Atlanta.

32. GLD, letter to FRM, January 25, 1965.

33. *One Man in His Time: The Memoirs of G. B. Harrison* (Palmerston North, New Zealand: The Dunmore Press Ltd., 1985) 285–286.

34. GLD, letter to FRM, January 25, 1965.

35. GLD to Gerald Sigler, first executive secretary of ICEL, April 18, 1966.

36. GLD, letter to FRM, January 25, 1966. The ecumenical aspect of the ICEL mandate led naturally to ICEL's participation in the North American Consultation on Common Texts, out of which developed the International Consultation on Common Texts (ICET), an ecumenical working group recently revived as the English Language Liturgical Consultation (ELLC). In each of these groups, ICEL has been a contributing presence.

37. GLD, 1965:3.

38. GLD, 1965:29.

39. GLD, 1965:24.

40. GLD, 1965:13–24.

41. GLD, 1965:29.

42. GLD, 1965:30.

43. GLD, 1965:29.

44. GLD, 1965:30.

45. GLD, "Dogmatic Constitution on the Church: A Commentary," *American Participation in the Second Vatican Council,* ed. Vincent A. Yzermans (New York: Sheed and Ward, 1967) 75–76.

46. GLD, taped interview, fall of 1988.

47. GLD, letter to John Rotelle, May 19, 1974.

48. I am indebted to John R. Page, executive director of ICEL since 1980, for acquainting me with the span of Godfrey's work and for giving me access to the ICEL archives.

49. GLD, letter to Ralph Keifer, September 28, 1972.

50. GLD, letter to John Rotelle, May 19, 1974.

51. GLD, letter to John Rotelle, February 9, 1974.

52. GLD, letter to John R. Page, August 21, 1987.

53. Ibid.

54. In order to develop Godfrey's contribution to ICEL, I have relied on interviews with his ICEL colleagues: John Page, December 12, 1987; Gilbert Ostdiek, O.F.M., December 15, 1987; Joseph Cunningham, taped reflections prepared early in 1988.

55. GLD, letter to John R. Page, May 13, 1978.

CHAPTER *10*

IT IS NO EASY TASK to provide a portrait of Godfrey Diekmann, and that for several reasons. His ebullient public personality is matched in private by a sometimes reticent and occasionally withdrawn self. His extraordinary reputation as scholar and teacher contrasts sharply with his great difficulty in putting pen to paper. His praise as "the great communicator" goes unsung in the monastery, where he rarely speaks at chapter meetings. His conviction about liturgy as the source and summit finds easy alliance with some unconventional practices of personal piety. He is by turns jovial and moody, ostentatious and shy, prophetic and wary of controversy. He is, like most of us, a bundle of contradictions.

In this final chapter we will look at the public and the private man through the eyes of his confreres, colleagues, family, and friends, highlighting along the way some of the preoccupations and passions that shaped his life—justice, ecumenism, and the theological enterprise, as well as travel, table fellowship, storytelling, fungophilia, and the many other human *attraits* that make this monk's tale so rich and worth telling.

A primary passion for Godfrey is the relationship of liturgy and justice. In this he simply reiterates a central concern of many of the early liturgical leaders, who believed that there is an intrinsic affinity between liturgy and just living and that one cannot, with integrity, worship different gods on Sunday and during the week. The liturgy itself, they believed, was the preeminent school of justice.

For Godfrey, as for his predecessors, the school of the liturgy was supplemented by encyclicals and conciliar texts—and by the headlines in the daily newspaper. Monsignor John Egan, himself a tireless prophetic voice, characterized Godfrey as a man who, in the quiet of his room, pondered these many signs of the times. "This is a scholarly man and a holy man," said Egan, "because he is a man of prayer, and he cannot help but read those documents and say: 'Yes, not only does the Church need to read the signs of the times, but so do I—and not only read, but act!' "[1]

Those dispositions led to Godfrey's involvement in a variety of marches and protests. In 1963, together with many from the Liturgical Week gathering in Philadelphia, Godfrey participated in the peaceful protest march against racial injustice staged in Washington shortly after the Philadelphia meeting. Gerard Sloyan, president of the Liturgical Conference, had urged all members of the conference to participate:

> In these days of national unrest when brother is set against brother I feel I must appeal to you as members of the Liturgical Conference to give active witness to that truth we all profess as Christians: that all men regardless of race are brothers in Christ. We who partake of the Eucharist are especially obligated and enabled by that Food to fulfill a brother's office.[2]

Once the group arrived in Washington, Godfrey found a spot close to Dr. Martin Luther King, perhaps only fifty yards away, during King's famous speech: "This is no time to engage in the luxury of cooling off or to take the tranquilizing drug of gradualism. . . . But in the process of gaining a rightful peace, we must not be guilty of wrongful deeds. . . . I have a dream . . . I have a dream . . . I have a dream. . . . " Godfrey was magnetized by the extraordinary power that King exercised and by the substance of his message—if my black brother or sister is suffering, Christ is suffering. He described it as "one of the greatest moments of truth in my life."[3]

The following year John Howard Griffin, author of *Black Like Me*, spoke at St. John's. Though Godfrey was in Rome at the time, he heard about Griffin's effect on the abbey and university communities. Twenty-five hundred turned up for the talk. Griffin portrayed in startling detail the radical difference in treatment he received just by changing the pigment of his skin. "The hopelessness of the situation is terrifying," Abbot Baldwin wrote to Godfrey, "and it becomes worse when you hear the indictment against the hierarchy and clergy."[4]

Perhaps it was this experience that prompted Abbot Baldwin to give his permission so readily for Godfrey's participation in the march on Selma in 1965, an experience that Godfrey remembers vividly years later. It was a beautiful day when he arrived in Birmingham. A Catholic doctor and his family met Godfrey's contingent at the airport and took about forty people to their home to sleep on the floor overnight and to prepare together, in conversation and prayer, for the next day's ordeal.

Not everyone supported the presence of the clergy at Selma. The bishop of Birmingham was not happy that there were so many priests there, and he gave orders that no Mass was to be said by priests unless they could show their *celebret,* a now obsolete document which guaranteed that its bearer was a priest in good standing. An Australian priest was able to produce his *celebret,* so the marchers celebrated Mass at their camp on the outskirts of Birmingham. A black preacher gave a marvelous homily on the Exodus theme, "Let my people go!," the justice and rightness of which fired Godfrey with courage for what lay ahead.

He remembers the soldiers lining the way, their backs to the marchers, facing the swamps to protect the marchers from snipers. Godfrey does not remember any fright, just a conviction that this was something that had to be done. He had a sense of doing something worthwhile, a sense that this was a historic occasion, that civil rights were at a turning point, and that the desire in every heart and on most lips—we shall overcome—would triumph. The banner Godfrey carried with him—and continued to display in his room back at St. John's—read: "Selma is in Minnesota, too." It captured his conviction that racism is everywhere and that one's obligation is not fulfilled in a weekend march.

Back home Godfrey was invited to speak to the Minnesota legislature about racial justice. He decided to include "red is a color, too" in order to decry the more subtle forms of racism against Native Americans in his own state. On the day this speech was scheduled, the legislature adjourned to attend the funeral of one of its members. Godfrey's talk was never delivered. But five years later he was back on the steps of the Minnesota capitol, one of several speakers at a rally organized in the wake of the widening war in Indonesia and the shooting deaths of four Kent State college students. Godfrey's ad-

dress centered on "How blessed are the peace*makers,*" with emphasis on the active *doing* of peace. In both substance and rhetorical style, he appeared to be inspired by Dr. King:

> We are here because we feel frustrated, because we feel increasingly helpless to fight the machine of war, because we are being smothered by logical arguments for war—for war just a few more months, a few more months. It is now more than ten years that we have been hearing that refrain: a few more months, and all will be well. And always the refrain is drilled into us by those who claim to know the facts, who ask us to trust them a few more months, because "they know things we don't know."
>
> We are here because we reject that refrain. We reject the logic of risk of continued war in the name of peace just around the corner, if only we are patient for a few more months. We ask only for the right to live human lives, lives in which peace is the norm, and not just a breathing space in which to produce more bodies to be killed.
>
> We plead that risks of peace be sought out, be embraced even in what might seem hope against hope. We ask, that is, our *right* to work for *making* peace without being foreordained to certainty of failure, with-

280

out being damned to cynicism, to despair. We ask for the right to
dream, though we know such dreaming, such working for peace, is
a helluva lot of work. In your making of peace, I pray that you have
good dreams.[5]

Throughout his professional life Godfrey never ceased to under-
score the importance of the Church at worship as having to be socially
conscious and active. After receiving the Berakah award in 1977, he
offered a retrospective appraisal of the liturgical movement in which
he delighted that "every sort of social justice group felt at home"
at the Liturgical Weeks.

At the same time, Godfrey himself is not a social activist. Apart
from his participation in protest marches and these several public
stands, his work for justice is largely Church-related and worship-
centered. Active participation is, for him, an issue of justice, as are
the role of the laity, the place of the divorced and remarried within
the Church, and, more recently, the place of women and their full
inclusion in all ministries of the Roman Catholic Church.[6]

It is not at all surprising, given Godfrey's predilections about the
liturgy itself as the primary school of justice, that he seemed
dismayed—and said so publicly—about the heavy emphasis on *direct*
social action at the Liturgical Week in Milwaukee in 1969.[7] Yet, it
was the very activity of which Godfrey was a part, the march on
Washington, that had provoked participants into considering individual and collective Christian responses to the revolution that the
human family was experiencing. It was the conviction of many of
the leaders of the Liturgical Conference that "somehow these responses
must harmonize that which goes on inside our churches with what
goes on outside their doors."[8]

In 1969, direct involvement in soup kitchens, on skid row, with
migrant workers, in prison ministry, in shelters for the abused and
the homeless was not yet happening broadly in the Roman Catholic
Church in the United States. The Milwaukee conference functioned
as a "curtain raiser" and caused fear in many hearts, confusion in
others. Were some in the liturgical movement deserting liturgy for
social action? Were the pioneers—Godfrey among them—simply naive
about the concrete ramifications of their theoretical positions? Gerard Sloyan offered this analysis of the growing rift between liturgists
and social activists of that time:

I know this much from the past 20 years, that while the committed liturgy people tend invariably to be right on national and international politics and the social order, Catholics deep in social questions often don't give a fig about public worship, thinking it a luxury of the elite. And, in fact, most of the country's oppressed underclass seldom darken a church door, so it's no mystery how the social activists get to thinking that way.[9]

Godfrey was one of a good number of liturgists caught in the crossfire over strategies of justice in the late sixties and early seventies, an inevitable dispute given the early liturgical movement's presumption that a social agenda would be achieved by a *slow* and *organic* development, with the laity gradually becoming empowered through liturgy to assume their position as leaders in the marketplace. This strategy, according to Andrew Greeley, became unsatisfactory to promoters of justice. Instead of waiting for the liturgy to transform the laity, priests took over! Liturgical activists of the fifties promised great results if liturgy were modernized—but no one dreamt how far things would go, and there was no structure in place, in terms of artists, musicians, scholars, resources at every level. "We need to realize," Greeley concluded, "that transformation is going to take a long, long time. Social activists demand short-term results; what Godfrey was predicting is necessarily long-term."[10]

Another of Godfrey's passions—and one also demanding patience for the long haul—is that of ecumenism, an interest supported and sustained in his abbey's pioneering efforts at ecumenical dialogue and collaboration, an interest deepened in Godfrey's daily contact with Protestant observers during Vatican II. Not surprisingly, after the Council he became a participant in a number of bilateral ecumenical dialogues. He also was instrumental in establishing the Ecumenical Institute at Tantur, Jerusalem, in 1971.

Godfrey's appetite for ecumenical dialogue had been whetted in 1963 in Montreal. He and four others served as observers officially appointed by the Holy See to the Faith and Order meeting of the World Council of Churches. When appointed, he confided to Fred McManus both his elation and his nervousness, "for my knowledge of Protestant theology is thin."[11]

Roman Catholic observers in Montreal, while not speaking in the name of the Church or of the Secretariat for the Promotion of Chris-

National Theological Colloquy, December 1–3, 1960: (seated, left to right) The Reverend Luther A. Weigle, Father Gustave Weigel, Monsignor Henry G. Beck, Pastor Berthold von Schenk; (standing, left to right) Bernhard Christensen, Father Godfrey Diekmann, Father Raymond Bosler, Dr. Charles Wesley Lowry

tian Unity, were allowed to speak in their own name—*when asked,* and only in closed session. Godfrey listened and learned as debate ranged across topics such as the implications of recognizing one baptism, the character of the Eucharist, the question of intercommunion, and the wisdom of celebration of the Eucharist at ecumenical conferences. Explored as well were guidelines for the indigenization of worship in cultures old and new, a discussion that coincided with Godfrey's work on inculturation for the preparatory commission of Vatican II. On this issue his knowledge was decidedly *not* thin, and he gave his opinions freely.

According to Godfrey, the Montreal meeting was beyond all his expectations. It proved again to his satisfaction that a common concern with biblical data will result in a remarkable convergence of theological thinking. The statement on baptism, for example, was one that Godfrey would have been pleased to print verbatim in *Worship.* Even the more neuralgic question of the nature of Eucharist found some advance; all participants were willing to explore its sacrificial nature.[12]

Both by personality and theological training Godfrey was an ideal dialogue partner. His presence and his enthusiasm for the task at hand inspired hope and promise. Such had been his reputation among Protestant colleagues at the Council:

> The theological talks that some of us have had with men like Fr. Godfrey Diekmann and Hans Küng have left us so optimistic about the resolution of old differences that we feel the need to guard against euphoria. During the last four years, we have seen the bishops move steadily in the direction of the thought of such men as these, and if the momentum in this direction continues, we are in for a period of restatement and reunderstanding among all Christians. [13]

The momentum *did* continue in a series of bilateral dialogues. As a delegate of the American bishops, Godfrey served as a member of the Lutheran-Catholic dialogues from their inception, an experience he found an honor and "one of the greatest graces of my life." During the dialogues he learned to know and cherish as brothers such men as Jaroslav Pelikan, Warren Quanbeck, George Lindbeck, and "that holy man of God, Carl Piepkorn." In Godfrey's estimation, it was these friendships—"such graced, mutual love"—that made growth in common understanding possible, even inevitable. Years later, Godfrey reminisced about their meetings:

> As an original member of the Lutheran-Catholic dialogue in this country, I can vouch for the fact that it has been accompanied consistently by common prayer, a humble prayerful effort together to seek God's will. In arriving at the knowledge of God's truth, it most certainly also brought us together in Christian love.
>
> We had at one point already made remarkable progress in regard to the Creed, Baptism, Christ's eucharistic body and blood. Then we began studying what we knew was especially critical: the Eucharist as sacrifice. Three times we met, and three times (we now recognize) we talked at cross-purposes. We were ready to give up. Then someone had the bright idea: Let's give the Holy Ghost one more chance. So we met again in St. Louis, and, contrary to all humanly reasonable expectations, we came to a substantive agreement. I think most of us were never so humble before in our entire lives as on that day. We felt we had won out over our own blindness and perhaps unwilling stubbornness. [14]

In the beginning, dialogue had been friendly but very cautious. It was new to be talking, and certainly new to be talking with the blessing of the respective Church bodies. Godfrey took his work as a grave obligation and resented implications in *The Wanderer* that Catholics in such dialogues tended to compromise too easily. According to *The Wanderer*, what dialogue partners said did not represent the whole Church, for some of them were "heretics" and others were "outstanding heretics." On the contrary, Godfrey's experience was just the opposite: he believed that participants in these dialogues were extremely *rigorous* and *orthodox* because they were appointed representatives and could not speak simply for themselves. "We tried," he said, "to be flaming centrists."[15]

In 1968 one of Godfrey's colleagues at St. John's, Kilian McDonnell, O.S.B., joined the Lutheran-Catholic dialogue. He and Godfrey agreed to collaborate in producing a paper on papal primacy, a fatal mistake as far as Kilian is concerned. Kilian and Godfrey had diametrically opposed styles of research and writing. "He lets everything go until the last minute and then becomes positively frantic," said Kilian of "the world's worst procrastinator." Kilian approached Godfrey about a dozen times, but Godfrey kept postponing their collaboration, hoping, according to Kilian, that the latter would eventually produce the paper alone. In the end they each did a section, but "quite rightly, it was never circulated."[16]

Around the same time, Kilian and Godfrey also served together as members of the first national ecumenical dialogue between Southern Baptists and Roman Catholics, a strange dialogue that was official only from the Roman side. No one was permanently on board. For the inaugural session both Kilian and Godfrey were to prepare papers. Kilian slaved over his paper on monasticism and the Southern Baptist ethos, both representing a pietist tradition. He honed it for months both in Europe and at home. On the way to the meeting Godfrey confessed that he hadn't even started his paper! That night he stayed up and made some notes. "Next day he was marvelous," said Kilian. "They gave him a standing ovation. It was really a great talk! I was furious!!!"—the latter added with the rueful chuckle of one who recognizes that Godfrey's metier is not the written word but a public presentation.[17] William Skudlarek, O.S.B., another of Godfrey's confreres, concurs with Kilian's assessment:

> [Godfrey's] personal presence did more to advance ecumenical understanding than his more formal theologizing. Godfrey is a person who comes alive before an audience, and a person who, before speaking,

often goes through sheer agony, and is fit to be tied—and then produces a speech which is not just inspiring but perfectly organized, the kind of thing that is a delight to note-takers, and insightful and original as well. It certainly wasn't that he didn't prepare. He was always preparing. But he needed the deadline—and the adrenalin that comes with live "performance."[18]

An ecumenical contribution of another kind was Godfrey's participation as a founding scholar in residence at the Ecumenical Institute, Tantur, Jerusalem. Much like St. John's own Institute for Ecumenical and Cultural Research, which had been inaugurated in 1967, the Tantur Institute was envisioned as a place of close daily living, praying, working, and dialogue. The institute was born during the third session of the Council, 1964, when a delegation of Protestant and Orthodox observers approached Pope Paul VI about the possibility of founding an ecumenical center for study, prayer, and the seeking of union in Christ. Oscar Cullmann expressed the hope of the group that Catholics and Protestants might pursue theology on a common basis. Pope Paul accepted the idea, and it became one of his pet projects. Several Catholic colleges were asked to oversee its organization; Theodore Hesburgh, C.S.C., of the University of Notre Dame, presided over the planning.

An early decision of the planning group was to attract a group of scholar-monks who would act as a permanent praying presence at Tantur. St. John's Abbey was invited to provide this core community, which would welcome ecumenical scholars and visitors, but the community declined, fearing that sending seven or eight theologians would seriously weaken the theology program of St. John's University. Godfrey suggested the monks of Montserrat, an inspired recommendation. The community at Montserrat accepted the Vatican's offer and appointed a number of its men as "foundation stones" of Tantur. Godfrey accepted an invitation to participate in the inaugural program.

By 1971 all was in readiness—or almost all. For the first three weeks of the program, the building at Tantur was not ready. The fellows lived at St. George's College just outside the Damascus Gate— providential, as far as Godfrey was concerned, because it meant that the group was thrown together into a "common life" that enabled them to get thoroughly acquainted and establish an esprit de corps.

Godfrey (back row, third from left) with the Tantur group

Père Benoit and Dr. Georg Kretschmar at Tantur, where both were scholars in residence during the first year of the institute (1971)

287

It also provided the opportunity to absorb the fantastically diverse and colorful impressions that Jerusalem offers before settling down to their work. Conditions at Tantur were still a bit primitive when the group transferred there. The many hardships with plumbing, heating and so on forged a strong community since, in Godfrey's estimation, "hardship is the necessary cement of community building."

Not surprisingly, Godfrey was put on the committee dealing with common worship. He wrote home frantically to his confrere Daniel Durken, O.S.B., to send a large collection of St. John's resources—melodies, responses, some good hymns—IMMEDIATELY. All the participants felt that common prayer was of the essence in their time together, and soon the question of intercommunion became a focal point. Regularly daily Mass was celebrated in the morning and Vespers each afternoon. On Sundays there was only one Eucharist, celebrated in the tradition of the presider, to which all came. There were no private Masses.

As the group drew closer together, Sunday worship was more and more dreaded as a painful reminder of their divisions. One day, on a trip through the desert on the way to Mount Sinai, the group decided to celebrate Eucharist with Godfrey presiding. He sensed tension, and putting aside his homily, he invited each one to speak from his or her heart. It was a very moving moment for the group; at the exchange of peace some were in tears. Then, wonder of wonders, all communicated. Afterwards the group was shaken by the experience, which had been so palpably of the Spirit.[19]

Godfrey's retrospective on the ecumenical movement was offered on Reformation Sunday, 1981:

> Perhaps, after Vatican Council II, when hopes ran so high, we became victims of what is sometimes called the disease of spiraling expectations. The more we get, the more we want, and we want it at once! A sense of proportion ought to sober us, for there simply is no doubt whatever that in the last twenty years we have traveled further together than in the previous four hundred.
>
> Or perhaps we pinned our initial hopes, unrealistically, on the wrong objectives, on solving before all else, the sticky problems of structure, of hierarchy, of the papacy. But however important these matters are, we should take notice that they receive relatively little attention in the New Testament writings. And, therefore, I believe that in the eyes

of God such questions are of far lesser importance than the unmistakable growth in unity of faith and of love that have happened, a unity which I believe each of us has experienced. The God of unity will not be stopped.[20]

The doing of theology and communication of its fruits is surely one of Godfrey's greatest passions, for he is a theologian of passionate convictions and a marvelously compelling conversationalist, a combination of gifts that stood him in good stead in ecumenical exchange as well as in the classroom and on the lecture circuit. It is not an exaggeration to call Godfrey "the great communicator." Perhaps his extraordinary success may be attributed to his own sense of limits and his absolute reliance on the Spirit of God. His correspondence is filled with urgent requests for prayer for the next talk, always considered "a splendid opportunity" to reach this group or that, but "I really need the help of the Holy Ghost for this one."[21]

Even when Godfrey had written things out or was speaking from notes, his listeners had the sense that it was extemporaneous and from the heart, and often when he spoke it sounded as if it were coming from some kind of oracle. "Perhaps he was a showman," said one of his admirers, "but his showmanship derived from the fact that he was enraptured by the thought and the truth of what he was saying, and he wanted others to be enraptured by it too. He used every device he could in order to get his listeners to understand what he was saying."[22] Another noted: "He is a man so filled with his insights and understandings that he can't keep them to himself, and they just tumble out a bit helter-skelter."[23] A third added, "He was instant charisma. He walked in and began to talk almost as though he were in the middle of the subject. As I got to know him later, I realized he was probably making it up as he went along, but it didn't seem that way and it was just dazzling!"[24]

People remember his words. Years after an address, a class, a quiet conversation, people can quote his words verbatim. This should please a man so given to the collection of apothegms from his own mentors. Furthermore, in a good number of cases his interlocutors report that they have used and built upon his insights in their own work, surely the highest form of praise.[25]

The word "popularizer" sounds too crass for present-day theological sensitivities—and perhaps, ambitions—but not so for Godfrey. Popularization is where he has placed his energies without apology, expressing ideas in a way that people without the linguistic or philosophical background could understand them—and not only understand, but love. Abbot Jerome Theisen noted admiringly: "People went away from a talk with the idea that this is the most important thing in the world. Godfrey may well have been saying things that other people said, but he said them in his own way and with an intensity, enthusiasm, and personal conviction that mesmerized his hearers."[26]

Bishop Charles Buswell summarized Godfrey's charismatic impact with these words: "Godfrey is, first of all, a marvelous Christian; he is a big person, a man of unusually great faith, and because of this, his words, whether in his oral pronouncements or in written form, have a great impact on all those who listen to him or read what he has written."[27]

Though it is no small task to characterize Godfrey's approach to theology, perhaps the words "inspired and original synthesizer" best capture his theological gift.[28] Godfrey is not a man who frequently engaged in primary scholarship, though his work on the topic of the laying on of hands might qualify as such.[29] Yet he is a theologian: he thinks theologically and expresses himself theologically. Indeed, he lives his theology—for theology, according to a definition he proposed more than fifty years ago, is simply a loving probing of the infinite depths of God and of God's merciful relationship with humankind.[30] His theological vision is characteristically monastic, and noteworthy for its biblical-patristic grounding.

While not a typical academic nor engaged in breaking new ground, Godfrey has always had an uncanny way of knowing who *was* breaking new ground, who should be read, who should be taken seriously. He is able to make associations, to assimilate, to relate. He soaks up the ideas of others; his genius is in having so many points of reference. He is both a brilliant synthesizer of the works of others and an unparalleled interpreter of original texts. He has, for example, an incredible gift for opening up the significance of a passage of, say, Irenaeus, and relating both content and provenance to contemporary questions and concerns.

Remarkably, Godfrey has lost neither his theological vision nor his enthusiasm for the things of God, which are so often mediated through all too human structures. It may be his appreciation of history that helps him expect as inevitable the present postconciliar backlash. He is forthright in acknowledging that there have been some setbacks, often taking the opportunity of his annual Christmas letter to assess the state of the Church and its "human structures":

> Yes, I too am deeply disturbed by some of the things that are happening in the Church today: for example, in Seattle which (it seems to me) epitomizes the current problem; or in Vienna, where the new archbishop was appointed without so much as Cardinal Koenig his predecessor being consulted (as the latter has explicitly declared).
>
> It obviously means that collegiality is more important, and neuralgic— and difficult of implementation after 1500 years of contrary momentum, even given the best of intentions on the part of all concerned— than we had anticipated. We were perhaps naive to have thought otherwise.
>
> It all means that we couldn't allow a temporary discouragement to lessen our gratitude to God for what has happened through Vatican II, and *is continuing to happen now.* Collegiality is only one dimension of the far broader and more important principle of co-responsibility: of *all,* of each according to his/her charism and office. Moreover, after Chapter II of the Constitution on the Church was approved by the Council, that principle cannot be canceled. Our painful experiences today are, not least of all, struggles to find "structures" to carry it into effect. On all levels. For both sexes.[31]

Godfrey has neither dismissed the Church nor despaired of its humanity, but has consistently proclaimed as his credo: "I believe in one, holy, catholic, apostolic, and *changing* Church," always under the impulse of the Spirit of God. At the age of eighty-one he addressed the participants of the Virgil Michel Symposium with these hope-filled words:

> Present tensions cannot be allowed to erase the overriding *fact* of what the Holy Spirit managed to get done at Vatican II: give us a radically new and life-transforming understanding of Jesus Christ, of His *redemptive* resurrection, of His full humanity, of His presence and work also in the here and now; and of the Church, too, especially the local church, and the true partnership and co-responsibility of the laity.

And these new (recovered) theological insights were gained, not by juggling concepts at a desk, but by the lived *experience* of the pastoral liturgical movement of the previous 40 years or so. It is, I believe, that most striking (and most weighty) instance in history of the axiom: *"Lex orandi legem statuat credendi*—as you worship, so you believe." It seems to me, therefore, that so long as we keep on worshipping in this renewed manner, and are aware of what we are doing, the theological principles will continue to keep coming alive, and cannot be brushed aside, or wished away. They will relentlessly demand recognition in institutional implementation. Sooner or later. *Fiat!*[32]

One of the great puzzles of Godfrey's professional life has been his diffidence as a writer. Shawn Sheehan recalled trying to get a manuscript from Godfrey, the text of a talk delivered to great accolades, but Godfrey "hated to give the final word to go into print; he wanted everything to be theologically exact. He kept revising."[33] Perhaps, since he pulled talks out of his heart rather than his head, he believed they would not translate into the written word. Indeed, some find that Godfrey's speeches are a disappointment in written form.

Godfrey found this inability to write a cause of frustration. To one request for an article he responded: "If I could write easily, I might still accept. But production is always a case of the mountain laboring and not always being sure even of bringing forth a mouse."[34] To his friend C. J. McNaspy, he confessed: "I envy your facility of writing. It's always an agony for me. And that is why I do so little of it, though I know I should do much more."[35]

Others thought so too. Gerard Sloyan tried to lure Godfrey to a full-time post at Catholic University (before "the troubles") with these words of encouragement: "I want with all my strength to have you on this faculty for a period of real productive scholarship. You have a contribution of a different kind to make than the great one you have already made, and I am convinced that the University is the optimum place to make it. I speak of writing, of course, and the direction of important dissertations at the doctoral level."[36] Whether Godfrey could have made this "contribution of a different kind" at Catholic University was never tested; he could not be spared from his many St. John's commitments to accept Sloyan's offer.

Obviously one reason why Godfrey's corpus of written work, apart from his editorials and reviews in *Worship,* is made up largely of published addresses is that he had little leisure for writing. Yet, there may also be a question of temperament involved, and a certain mental block against writing because of the inevitable judgment to which a writer is subject. A colleague recalled hearing once that someone had criticized Godfrey, and he reacted very noticeably to it. That sensitivity to criticism in the public forum is operative at the level of personal relationships too.

Godfrey's confreres confirm his distaste for controversy of any kind. He has confessed to some of his brothers that confrontation makes him nervous. Indeed, when he is involved in a squabble, he can become both hurt and depressed. He sometimes seems unpredictable, changing his position rather than disagreeing, or choosing not to speak at all rather than confronting a colleague—strategies to dodge a potential conflict.

On the other hand, once a misunderstanding has occurred, Godfrey has been known to harbor a grudge, at least for a time. In her *Private Faces, Public Places,* Abigail McCarthy divulged that the Secret Service had to disarm a monk of St. John's who had concealed a revolver on his person during a visit of the McCarthys to the abbey. Godfrey regarded it a breach of family loyalty for a friend of St. John's to make such an event public. "Godfrey wasn't speaking to me," said the author, recalling the incident, "but I didn't even know it until the day he made a beeline to me during the exchange of peace at Mass to say he had repented."[37]

Ever sensitive, Godfrey can be lavish in his apologies if he thinks he has hurt another person. A story helps to illustrate this trait. Patricia Joyce, longtime friend of Godfrey's, sometimes finds him an incorrigible teacher who is apt to seize the floor and lecture rather than converse, even in the middle of her living room. She remembers a conversation they once had about Romanesque art. She had just written a paper on the subject and found herself in disagreement with the point Godfrey was making. She finally said to him, "Father Godfrey, you know a lot about a lot of things; I know a little about *this* subject, and you're going to listen!" To the end of their talk, Godfrey thought her position wrong. Later, conscious that she may have been hurt, Godfrey brought her flowers, a Coptic cross, and several notes. "Such a sensitive human being, he couldn't bear the misunderstanding."[38]

This story is telling from another point of view as well. Perhaps "seizing the floor" is how a very shy person—Godfrey's description of himself—handles a public role. John Page, executive director of the International Commission on English in the Liturgy, who has had his fair share of dinners with Godfrey over the years, corroborates Patricia Joyce's assessment. Often enough at ICEL dinners of seven or eight, Godfrey is the only one conversing. If he is in an upbeat mood, he can dominate a group of people for a whole evening. He might be absolutely exhausted at the end and look as if he is going to have to totter home, but he will have talked non-stop, and that is when Godfrey is at his most delightful.

At the dinner table Godfrey tells many stories. He often shies away from intellectual or theological issues in favor of stories about a piece of art, a church to visit, a dish to sample, his latest trip, and so on. Does he repeat himself? "Rarely does he ever tell the same story," John Page said appreciatively, "and even on those rare occasions when Godfrey tells the same story, it always has a new ending."[39]

Godfrey delights, for example, in telling the story of the woman near the Red Sea who set her mind on marrying him. She was an Italian who had migrated to the area, and then her husband died. She served Godfrey's meals and paid a lot of attention to him. She was a good cook, he recalls. One day she said to him: "I've been watching you. I love your smile, your white hair, your personality. I am alone and would love to have someone share my life."

Godfrey protested that she did not understand: "I'm a monk, I have vows, I'm committed."

"Ah," she responded, "these things can be arranged." Godfrey described this encounter gleefully to his abbot, concluding, "I have a place to come to if you give me any trouble."[40]

More often than not, Godfrey's stories have been gleaned from his travels, for travel is another of his lifelong passions. In explaining his wanderlust, Godfrey likes to tell friends, "I've never doubted that I have a monastic vocation, but perhaps I'm the reincarnation of a Celtic monk whose ideal is to be a constant pilgrim, in contrast to the Benedictine ideal of stability." Despite this quip, Godfrey is not simply the lighthearted tourist but a man open to new and different experiences that broaden his horizons and deepen his understanding of others and the world. On one occasion he put some of his travel

philosophy in a letter to Franz Mueller, a friend who, because of homesickness, was going to cut a sabbatical short:

> Don't be a fool. You owe it to yourself, and not least of all to St.
> Thomas College, to take full advantage of a year, getting acquainted
> with thought and conditions on the Continent. Moreover, it would
> be a splendid widening of your competence if you could arrange to
> investigate, however cursorily, social and economic conditions in the
> Far East. This is one instance in which you must simply force your
> brain to control your emotions. You are not an adolescent and you
> would never be able to explain it either to yourself or to others in the
> future were you to cut short your wonderful opportunity because of
> homesickness. The latter does you credit, of course. But not enough
> to offset the moral obligation you have to make use of your year's sab-
> batical leave. Don't worry about your family. They are getting along
> splendidly. This, of course, will make you feel worse. What I mean
> to say is that they are worried most of all about your being worried.[41]

Godfrey is a magnificent traveling companion who is never shy
on the road. He gains *entrée* to Sicilian wedding receptions; he charms
proprietors of overbooked hotels to open their doors; he secures the
latest recipes from otherwise secretive chefs. And being with Godfrey is like being with a historical encyclopedia. He knows so many
details about a place, a building, a saint who lived on the spot. He
has a sense of wonder, from which springs poetry, philosophy, all
kinds of thought, and he is guileless and unguarded even in new situations. Everything he thinks and feels surfaces and is available to
people.

Certainly his piety becomes accessible during his travels. In the
ruins of a monastery Godfrey will sing the *Salve Regina* aloud because
the monks for many centuries had kept that tradition within those
walls. While honoring Mary, Godfrey also sings in remembrance of
forgotten brother monks. Sometimes, in similar circumstances, he
has invited a companion to say the rosary in order to reconsecrate
the place. At such times Godfrey's faith and religious intensity are
deep and sincere.

Gilbert Ostdiek, Godfrey's traveling companion on the way to
an ICEL meeting in 1987 (one of Godfrey's famous *"last* tours of
the great cathedrals'') described being with him in Peterborough Cathedral, a simple, uncluttered, Romanesque building. Godfrey kept

Godfrey the traveler in the Theatre of Dionysos in Athens (1964)

Godfrey with Ethiopian monks in front of their hermitages on the roof of the Church of the Holy Sepulcher (1956)

Monks in imperial robes, with crowns and crosses, at the Monastery of Zeghie, Lake Tana, Bahar Dar, Ethiopia (1967)

Godfrey and his confrere Father Sebastian Schramel on a trip to the Canadian Rockies (1985)

doing 360-degree turns throwing out both arms *(and* a cane which could have decapitated a passerby) in joy and wonder, moving in what almost resembled a dance. Finally Godfrey exclaimed: "I really ought to hug someone!"

"Here I am," said Ostdiek.

"Not you!" roared Godfrey, coming to his senses.[42]

Godfrey tends to be a competitive tourist. His friends the Joyces once looked at a book on Burgundy with Godfrey. Subsequently, Godfrey visited the Burgundy region and sent them many postcards. The first said: "I saw this." Subsequent cards each day or so bore simply the message " . . . and this," " . . . and this." On another occasion they gave him a book on the early history of Rome. On his next trip to Rome he walked his way through every page of that history and then mentioned at least fifteen churches the author had missed![43]

Once at the cathedral in Winchester, an old Benedictine foundation in England, a tour guide, a rather proper lady, was explaining that this had been a monastery attached to a cathedral and the monks used to chant Office, etc. Godfrey listened briefly and then took over the tour, describing monastic customs, what stairway would have been used for what, and so on. Godfrey actually hijacked the woman's tour of thirty to forty people, but she took it well![44]

Sometimes Godfrey has been able to combine travel to a meeting of the International Commission on English in the Liturgy with projects for St. John's. One such project very dear to his heart is the preservation of monastic manuscripts on microfilm. After one "fishing expedition for new manuscripts," that project became the subject of his Christmas letter in 1977:

> I did have sixteen wonderful days in late October and early November, for a work session of ICEL at Edinburgh, preceded and followed by several days of visiting some of the English cathedrals and ancient monastic churches, to sound out the possibility of St. John's microfilming their collection of manuscripts, charters, etc., for our Hill Monastic Microfilm Library. Everywhere I met with utmost courtesy, and even with enthusiasm for the project. The great majority of the English cathedrals before the Reformation, as you know, had abbeys and priories of monks instead of canons, responsible for the public divine worship; and hence very many of the MSS of the great libraries of England today are monastic in origin. And the thought of an American Benedic-

tine Abbey interested in ensuring the preservation of this heritage on microfilm, seemed fitting.

And so my journey (and happy "duty") took me to St. David's in Wales (a Norman dream, well preserved), Shrewsbury, Chester, Carlisle, Durham (architecturally, the closest image of heaven that I know), Glasgow, Edinburgh, York, Beverley, Minster, Selby Abbey, and Southwell—fewer than a fifth of the places that need to be contacted![45]

Teaching in St. John's Israel Study Program has periodically provided another justification for travel. Godfrey loved the Holy Land more deeply with each visit. One day he tried to communicate his joy to Abbot Jerome: "Before leaving Ein Karim, I want to express, once again, my deepest gratitude for permission to accompany this semester's St. John's group. Back in 1980 [four years earlier], when I was 72 years old, I was certain it would be my last visit to the Holy Land. So when I did arrive here again, in early January, I cried for joy (after locking myself into my room that first evening)."[46]

Lecturing also provided the occasion for travel. Among the more famous Godfrey stories is the one about the shepherds' crooks, a story that begins in the midst of a lecture tour to Australia and New Zealand. While in New Zealand, Godfrey saw shepherds' crooks for sale in many stores, shipped in from Cooper and Sons, Ltd., of England, a firm that made them by the thousands. Here is the story in his own words:

On my next trip to England I went to Cooper's and told the manager my hopes to obtain crooks for crosiers but that they would have to be somewhat taller than those used by New Zealand shepherds. The manager was high church Anglican and understood at once. He promised that the next time he obtained a good ash or chestnut of sufficient length, he would set it aside and make crosiers for me—as many as I wanted. That's exactly what has happened. In the course of the years I have brought back from England at least twenty-five to thirty crosiers and distributed them among the bishops of the United States and Canada. It is my contribution to the conversion of the hierarchy!

My friend Bishop Topel of Spokane, Washington, who was widely known for embracing apostolic simplicity and poverty, wrote several times expressing his gratitude, saying he took the crosier along on confirmation tours and it was a pleasure to gather the children around and explain the meaning of the staff—which he could not have done if it had been of a gilded metal encrusted with real or spurious stones.

Word got around, so that when Bishop Kelly was appointed to Louisville from his position in the national office in Washington, his staff got together and ordered a crosier for him. This happened to get into the news, and ever since I've been getting letters, much less now (thank God!), saying, "Enclosed seven dollars. Please send shepherd's crook."[47]

There is a sequel to this story. It was not always convenient for Godfrey to pick up the "crosiers" when he was traveling in England. At one point Tom Joyce was commuting between London and New York, opening a new office in London for the Wall Street law firm of Sherman and Sterling. Godfrey decided that Joyce would be a fine courier and had the crooks sent to Joyce's office on his first day in the new building. A puzzled secretary came to announce: "Mr. Joyce, your shepherds' crooks are here!"

"Thank you," replied Joyce, trying not to show any reaction. "Just put them in the closet."[48]

This story helps to explain why a shepherd's crook adorns Godfrey's cell at St. John's. During his travels he has been an inveterate collector, and his room is full of exotica: baroque angels, Ethiopian crosses, a marvelous hat collection, a camel chaser, some specimens found in the woods, a crosier or two, afghans from the abbot of such and such, a dashiki for a new chasuble, zulu cloth, a censor—and each item has a personality of its own, a story told with childlike exuberance.[49] Amid the exotica are piles of papers on the floor, desk, shelves, everywhere—"No wonder he occasionally lost an article submitted for *Worship*"—and hundreds of audio cassettes of music Godfrey has recorded from National Public Radio broadcasts for the monastic infirmary. He now has few books because, to the horror of many in the monastery, he sent his library to Mary Collins, O.S.B., for Holy Wisdom Monastery, a new monastic foundation in North Carolina. He also sent cartons of books to Africa. Some of his confreres found Godfrey's generosity irresponsible and took to hugging their books to themselves when he was near lest he wrest them from their grasp for another worthy cause.

Godfrey gives things away as quickly as he collects them, and he never goes anywhere without taking a gift. "He is generous to a fault," said his friend Emeric Lawrence, O.S.B., who has been the recipient of many gifts: "Twenty years ago he 'lent' me a beautiful primitive Tanzanian crucifix, which I still have. He has also 'lent' me a lovely statue of St. Joseph and the child Jesus, a very old Ethiopian cross, and last but not least, his old Jerusalem Bible, the pages of which are covered with notes and text."[50]

This world-class collector actually lives a very simple life.[51] Those who have traveled with Godfrey commend his frugality and his unpretentious ways. He prefers simple lodging, such as bed and breakfast places, and simple, family-owned restaurants where he can go to the kitchen and talk to the cooks. To share a room with him is another matter altogether. It has been reported that he snores "with a collection of snorts, whistles, and wheezes such as you've never heard," and more than one roommate has moved a mattress into the corridor to get some sleep.

A lovely picture has been painted of Godfrey the traveling *monk:* "While on a journey, he retires for prayer, the Breviary, a rosary, solitude, and quiet. Sometimes he just gazes out the window for long stretches of time. There is a sense about him that he has never left the monastery, but as if the whole world has become his monastery and he is just moving into a different part of it."[52]

True. Wherever he is, Godfrey is first of all a monk. The search for God that is the monastic life is his primary passion. He is a man of the *Opus Dei,* a man of liturgy, not just theoretically but by dedication and choice. He is a man who joined a community to help him in his search for God, a man who has a great love for his monastic community and the priority given to the Liturgy of the Hours and the Eucharist.

One day Godfrey talked of this common pilgrimage: "We walk with God, we walk in the presence of God—we already have God and yet we search for God and help one another, just as we hasten towards the resurrection but it is already there within us." And later he added: "We are on pilgrimage. Now a pilgrimage is not a leisurely stroll. Again and again Benedict uses the word 'hasten.' Our pilgrimage need be characterized by eager joy in the search for God."[53]

He offered a rare glimpse of his understanding of religious life in a letter to his friends Florence and Al Muellerleile when their daughter, Mary, was about to make her religious profession:

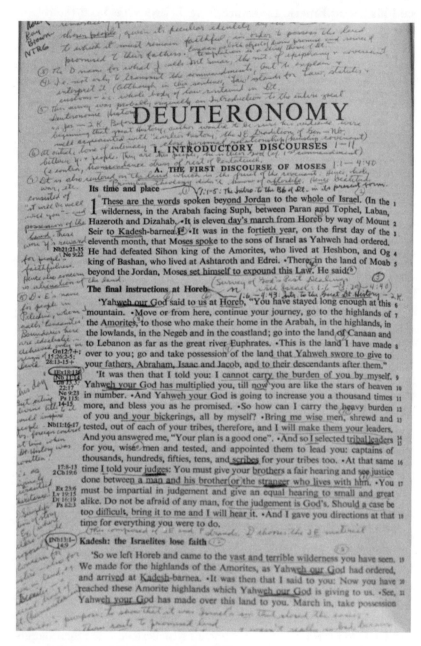

An annotated page of Godfrey's Jerusalem Bible

A vocation to the Religious life is a gift, one of the most precious and certainly one of the most important gifts that God bestows on those of his children whom he especially chooses to be the recipient. God has chosen Mary—and Mary is going to say "Yes" to God next Tuesday with a joyful and generous heart. She was God's gift to you some twenty or more years ago. You were happy about this great gift; but you knew all the time that, in a very real sense, Mary belonged to God even more than she belonged to you. You were taking care of her with parental affection and devotion; but, as good Christian parents, you were at the same time teaching her a growing love for another Parent, God Himself, who had made her His own child in the Mystery of Baptism, and who has really loved her all these years of her growth into young womanhood with a love exceeding even your own, for it is an infinite, divine love.

And now Mary has taken the big step of concentrating her love on God, and of taking vows which will free her to serve God as he deserves to be loved and served—not only for herself, but also for you, her dear parents, for all her loved ones, and for all the world which is so busy with daily concerns that it is apt to neglect responding to God's love. The Religious life is not a selfish life: looking out only for one's own perfection. On the contrary, it is the most unselfish life, for it means carrying the burden of others to God's throne of mercy; it means loving God *really* with one's whole heart, and therefore loving others more than ever before, because now one can love them with the undivided love of God.[54]

Godfrey has little patience with approaches to the spiritual life that seem to smack of self-seeking and self-centeredness. "It is my understanding," he said, "that we develop our personality by other-relatedness." And then, after quoting Augustine, "Christ is a person insofar as he is begotten by the Father," Godfrey pressed his point: "Thinking of God, being God-centered, other-centered, really comes first in the spiritual life and *not* a concern about the degree of wholeness that *I* have attained."[55]

And, on another occasion, he took up the same theme: "Self-realization is not the first concern of the monk, but the seeking of God and service to the community—and in this comes self-realization." After this he paused, and then added with quiet pride, "This giving was my brother Conrad's way."[56]

Conrad Diekmann, O.S.B.,
Godfrey's older brother
and
monk of St. John's
(1904–1974)

Conrad Diekmann, four years older than Godfrey, had been sent as a young monk to Munich to study under Martin Grabmann. He also took art lessons under Sandberger, a portrait artist. Conrad had talent, and his choice would have been the art department. But once back at St. John's, he was asked to devote his life to literature, which he did with great distinction in the classroom after obtaining a master's degree in English literature at the University of Minnesota.

Conrad and Godfrey became companions and friends in the forties and grew quite close as the years progressed despite their different temperaments. Conrad was reticent, slow-speaking, with a dry sense of humor—a very unassuming man. They would walk and talk together on their frequent visits to their mother, who lived in Collegeville until her death in 1955. Rosalie Diekmann is buried next to her husband and her daughters Clara and Julia at St. John's, a place she loved because she was so proud of her two sons who called it home.

The rooms of the brothers Diekmann were opposite each other in the monastery. The two monks would visit back and forth, sometimes suggesting reading to each other from their respective fields. Conrad would say, ''Godfrey, have you read Flannery O'Connor's this or Saul Bellow's that?'' Conrad would keep after Godfrey until the latter had read the book, and this usually resulted in a fairly well-balanced literary fare. They also took walks in the woods and planted black walnuts as they went along, thinking of themselves as latter-day Johnny Appleseeds. Besides their love of nature, they shared a love for music and would sometimes go into the music room and play their instruments together for an hour or so. But about the spiritual life they spoke not at all: "Maybe sometimes we'd speak about a conference or something like that when it was good, but not our own spiritual lives. We spoke of family affairs, of course, about liturgy and literature, but we were both very reticent about ourselves."[57] Perhaps the caution and reserve in matters of the spirit that Godfrey mentioned on another occasion applied equally to Conrad:

> I never had a single person with whom I regularly talked about my spiritual life. I really never made a great distinction between theology and the spiritual life. For me they are tied together—one flows from the other, and insofar as they are bound together, if a question arises, I talk about it. I've never had a spiritual director and am somewhat fearful of that. I always saw it as wet-nursing.[58]

In the summer of 1973 Godfrey was at St. Michael's in Winooski, Vermont, when he received a call that Conrad had terminal cancer in both kidneys and a lung. Godfrey hurried home to be with his brother, who went through cycles of rallying and decline for nearly a year. Godfrey became Conrad's nurse, caring for him, wheeling him around, and Conrad depended on Godfrey's presence and care. Several times as Conrad lingered, the community assembled for the anointing of the sick. The first time the abbot laid hands on Conrad, the second time Godfrey joined the abbot, and after that all the monks who had assembled laid on hands and prayed for healing, the healing power of fraternal love.

Conrad died on April 4, 1974. After his death, about forty large charcoal portraits were discovered in his room, the first-fruits of a talent buried years earlier for the sake of the community's need. As close as they had grown, Godfrey never knew these portraits existed; some he had framed for an exhibit which drew a large and appreciative crowd.

Godfrey missed his brother's company. After Conrad's death Godfrey was more than ever a solitary in the monastery.

In contrast to his reputation and great success beyond the walls of the abbey, Godfrey lives a most ordinary life at home. He speaks almost not at all of his professional life outside the monastery once he comes home, a custom that puzzles some of his confreres and annoys others. Yet St. Benedict says that the returning monk is not to talk about what he has seen, and Godfrey, recognizing the numerous opportunities he has had, chooses not to flaunt them or to inflict on the unwary matters that might not particularly interest them. In a sense, he has lived two very different lives in two very different worlds. For that reason, the Virgil Michel Citation, which he received in 1988 from St. John's Abbey, St. John's University, and the Liturgical Press on the occasion of a symposium marking the fiftieth anniversary of Virgil Michel's death, is a most touching tribute. It represents an affectionate recognition from inside the monastery of what others outside have recognized and revered for many years:

> Others have recognized and cited your far-reaching accomplishments, celebrating your youthful enthusiasm, your vitality, your generosity, and your wisdom. Our experience confirms their judgments. Nevertheless, we choose to add to their tributes our acknowledgment of you as a gifted and faithful confrere, one who has stated that he owes much to "the support of many brethren" (Rule of Benedict, ch. 1).[59]

As the Virgil Michel citation was conferred on Godfrey by his brethren, his "two persons living in two worlds" seemed to converge.

In the monastery Godfrey "comes home to be quiet," to walk in solitude, to live the Rule, and "his stature outside does not prevent him from donning a floppy hat and old jeans and heading for the woods to pick mushrooms for the confreres."[60]

Mushrooms—yet another passion. Fungophilia occupies Godfrey's leisure every fall. He described a particularly rich harvest one year in his Christmas letter:

> For about 3 weeks in October, excursions in the woods easily netted 10 or more gallons of "oak" or "honey" mushrooms daily. The fall growth of watercress, too, seemed inexhaustible: a half-hour picking resulted in a bushel or more of the leafy delicacy (have you ever had cream of watercress soup, chilled?). As for jams: 186 quarts of choke cherry; 85 of wild plum; no wild grapes, sadly. I concur heartily with the author(s) of the *Didache,* (perhaps the earliest Christian non-Scriptural writing): "You (God) have given us food and drink to enjoy, that we may thank You" (10:1).[61]

This letter elicited the following response from Godfrey's good friend Albert Outler: "Your claim to having poisoned so few guests with mushrooms (yet) put me in mind of a sly comment of Fr. Georges Florovsky's to a horrified Anglican that, in their practice of triune immersion of infants, the Orthodox had a *very low* incidence of 'deaths by drowning'!"[62]

From Godfrey's description of his mushroom excursions—not to mention his international meetings, teaching, speeches, retreats, and so on—one might presume that his energy knows no bounds and that his health is robust. True, to a point. But over the years he has had so many brushes with death that he seems to be the epitome of Benedict's monk, who "has death daily before his eyes."[63] His childhood nickname, "Pechvogel" (the bad-luck bird), suggests a history of accidents that continued even in his adult years: falling through the ice while skating in his cassock and having great difficulty getting out; being swept under the waves and pulled to safety by friends; losing his way in a snowstorm while mountain climbing and by some miracle discovering footprints nearly obliterated but pointing the way; being discovered alone and paralyzed after eating bad mushrooms and having his stomach pumped; preparing for a crash landing on a plane ("I had previously pronounced absolution quietly at least five times—to be sure I included all the laggards"), and then the wheels remained firm and the landing was normal.

Serious illnesses have been interspersed with Godfrey's accidents. A pulmonary embolism in December, 1962, was followed by a lengthy recovery *and* a new appreciation of life:

> I was indeed quite seriously ill. A pulmonary embolism, which usually proves fatal, with additional complications of pneumonia. This put me out of commission for several months, and it is only now that I am beginning to catch up with the work that accumulated, including correspondence. But I have never before been filled with such an overwhelming joy in just being alive. No doubt the Lord wanted to give me further opportunity for doing penance. Any suggestions?[64]

In 1969 a stroke paralyzed Godfrey, and for several months he was unable to speak, and that bothered him very much. He retired within himself and spent great portions of time engaged in Scripture study, which had been quite secondary in the years of his education

Godfrey holding a giant puffball mushroom

Thomas Wahl, O.S.B., and Godfrey compare mushroom finds

309

Godfrey making chokecherry jam in the monastery kitchen

Godfrey collecting sap for St. John's maple syrup operation

310

1) Cream of watercress soup.

Chicken stock, 1 pint — bring to boil.

Watercress: 2-3 cups very finely chopped. Add to above.

Butter: 1/3 cup. Add to above; allow to simmer 10 min.

Flour, all purpose — 1/3 cup   (recommended: some finely
Salt ——————— 1/2 tbs   chopped celery and
Pepper, ground ——— 1/8 tsp.   onions)

Milk (with some cream added, if desired: 1 1/2 pints. Heat. Add to flour, salt + pepper, whip smooth. Then add to chicken stock, cress + butter, and heat for a few min. (Do not boil.) — Serves 6.

Some prefer the soup chilled.

This

2) Dressing for watercress salad.

Chop watercress into pieces @ 1 inch long. Pour on oil, and toss, to coat each piece generously. Add cider vinegar, and toss again. (Because of the oil, little of the vinegar will stick to the cress, and it is impossible to get the salad too sour: excess vinegar will sink to the bottom.)

You may want to add chopped onions and salt and crumbled bacon

3) Watercress sandwich. Spread mayonnaise on 2 thin slices of St. John's Bread — or any dark bread. Cram as much watercress as you can between the 2 slices. (Two slices of crisp bacon will add the crowning touch!)

4) Potato and watercress soup. Add finely chopped watercress to a potato soup, made with chicken base. (Also add chopped celery, if you wish.

5) Pasta with fried watercress

1 lb. cooked spaghettini or other slender pasta./4-6 tbsp olive oil/1 tbsp sesame oil/ 1 bunch watercress, minced — which makes about 1 cup — be sure to remove coarse stems! 6 tbsp toasted pine nuts/lots of freshly ground pepper/salt to taste /a few dashes chili oil, or Tabasco.

Add olive oil to pasta while pasta is still warm + will readily absorb it. In wok or skillet, heat sesame oil + stir-fry watercress 1 or 2 min, or until wilted. Combine watercress + pine nuts, pepper, salt and chili oil (or Tabasco) with pasta, mixing well so that the strands imbibe the herb and spices. (Serves 4 as main course)

A few of Godfrey's watercress recipes

and formation. During the months of recuperation he read and studied the Bible six to eight hours a day; sometimes it was two in the morning before he realized it, so absorbed had he become in his study. His main tools were Anderson for the Hebrew Scriptures and the Collegeville Bible commentaries for the Christian Scriptures. During these days he resolved to read the Christian Scriptures in Greek every year and, if possible, the Hebrew Scriptures as well. Godfrey finds time for this by rising at 5 A.M. (he cannot sleep after that hour) and doing his study before the day begins. In any case, after about six months of intensive "Scripture therapy," his speech began to come back. He snapped out of withdrawal and got back to his regular duties.

But "The Perils of Pauline" continued. In September 1984 Godfrey was looking for watercress and sank up to his hips in a swamp. Much to his embarrassment, he had to be pulled out by a truck hoist! His hip boots remain, to this day, at the bottom of the slough. He told the story in his Christmas letter of 1984 with this addendum: "What now bothers me is that during the entire ordeal of about twenty-five minutes I didn't have a single pious thought! What does that say of my more than fifty years of monastic life? Do I have to start all over again?"[65]

Once more, the following year, he had another brush with death, and this time his fifty years of monastic life did not fail him. In December, while out walking in a fairly remote area of St. John's property, Godfrey slipped on ice and fell, breaking his hip and lying immobile for over an hour in below zero weather. Without reasonable hope of being discovered, and thinking he would die in the cold, he experienced euphoria at the prospect of meeting Christ:

> I knew this was the end but it didn't bother me. I just thought: this means I'm going to meet Christ. This was the opposite of what had happened when I was mired in the watercress swamp. I didn't think of sin or judgment but simply of how wonderful it all would be, unalloyed peace and serenity and happiness, just waiting for Christ. It was a state of euphoria. I'd say it was a mystic state but I wasn't "out of body" or anything like that. When I heard the sound of a car coming down the road, I was really sorry because I thought: I'll never be so near death again and so well prepared.[66]

Godfrey did not recover full mobility after breaking his hip. Walking was reduced to a few hundred yards, with sudden jabs of arthritic pain virtually immobilizing him. Constantly favoring the other leg, he was off balance and in danger of another serious fall, so in January 1988 he had a hip replacement. This put him in mind of the psalmist's phrase: "The days of our life are seventy years, or perhaps eighty, if we are strong" (Ps 90:10). Godfrey adds, "After seventy, it's all patchwork." His recovery was swift and nearly complete. He called a friend to report on his progress: "I feel like Godfrey Jr.!"

Godfrey has also undergone two rather serious cancer operations and the radiation of a basal cell cancer. Early in 1989 he wrote to family and friends: "The doctor assures me that I'm now free of cancer. God be praised! I can now better empathize with the leper in the Gospel story, when he was declared 'clean.' It's a great feeling. And each day becomes a new *Amen, Alleluia.* Love life!"[67]

While Godfrey treasures life he has contemplated death: "I believe that because of so many brushes with death I have lost my fear of it. I have gone through the valley and now am quite indifferent about whether I shall die sooner or later. My thoughts are turning more and more frequently to the meeting with Christ, to the fulfillment of my destiny in love."[68]

And what of heaven? "Heaven," mused Godfrey, "is like a honeymoon." And then he elaborated on this theme:

> Jesus spoke of heaven as a marriage feast. The theology of the covenant is pertinent here; Israel is the spouse of God. The idea of marriage brings up the honeymoon period and love that characterizes the honeymoon. We make heaven difficult for ourselves because we speak of the "beatific vision." It means much but it is not inspiring to most. Yet "beatific" is "making happy," an awareness that makes us totally happy. Heaven is an awareness that makes us totally happy. If we start from that premise and then go on to the marriage feast, we come to the love of the honeymoon period, a love that is fresh, exciting, always open to new vistas, and add to that the concept of permanence, since this is the case of heaven. . . . This gives some faint idea of what heavenly love might be, though way beyond our comprehension.[69]

Beyond comprehension, perhaps, but not beyond imagination or faith.

Godfrey Diekmann is a man of deep faith whose enthusiasm for the Gospel and the Church touches all whom he meets. He is a large personality, a man of stature and vision, who perceives where the

Spirit is blowing and acts as a kind of magnet for others. He has an incredible appetite for experience, whether that be for new Palestinian cuisine or the study of Eastern anaphoras. He has a remarkable ability to blend past and future without fear, for his historical roots give him a security about the substance of the faith, which may be embodied in ever new forms.

Godfrey Diekmann is a free spirit, a childlike man who has never stopped growing, whose mind is inquisitive, whose curiosity is insatiable, who has "read and digested *L'Osservatore Romano* before breakfast"—or so some surmise. Though always enthusiastic about new ideas, he has rarely been swept away by fads. As a liturgical pioneer who was there from the beginning, he has combined love of the liturgy, deep spirituality, and old-fashioned common sense. He has thrown in his lot for the long haul, recognizing that if something is not finished in his lifetime, it doesn't mean it wasn't addressed or wasn't worth it. And when the hearts of others have been overshadowed by the anxieties and uncertainties of our times, he has maintained a spirit of joy and high humor.

Godfrey Diekmann's priorities have been clear and reassuring. He has always put scholarship at the service of the pastoral life of the Church. Though trained in patristics, adept in the arts, and skilled in historical criticism, he blended these with American pragmatism: the liturgy should work, and work better. It should foster full, conscious, and active participation. It should be the celebration of the whole community, the Body of Christ, *all* called to stand in God's presence, *all* counted worthy to give thanks and praise.

One final metaphor captivates Godfrey. This one captures his experience of God:

> I've come to the conclusion in recent months that God is *beautiful music;* more concretely, God is *melody.* (An exhilarating thought. I hope it's not too unorthodox!). . . . Is that what Clement of Alexandria had in mind when he wrote that the Word, the Logos, is not just a prose word, but the New Song; and we and all redeemed creation find the very meaning of our existence in being able now to be a part of that new song. God is Beauty, and music through the ages has consistently been called the most "spiritual" or "divine" of the arts.[70]

If God is melody, Godfrey Leo Diekmann has been one of God's most supple instruments.

NOTES TO CHAPTER 10

1. John Egan, taped interview, November 17, 1987.
2. Gerard S. Sloyan, letter to members of the Liturgical Conference, August 6, 1963. Coincidentally, at the same Week Godfrey was recognized and applauded for the recent publication of his Liturgical Week speeches, *Come, Let Us Worship*.
3. GLD, taped interview, summer 1988.
4. Abbot Baldwin Dworschak, letter to GLD, September 23, 1964.
5. GLD, speech delivered May 9, 1970, at the Minnesota Capitol on the occasion of a rally against the war in Indonesia.
6. Godfrey, once he is converted to a position, tends to acknowledge with a *"mea culpa"* that he has not always seen the light. Occasionally his apologies are misinterpreted, however, as was the case when the *National Catholic Reporter* (November 16, 1990) stated: "The Benedictine monk, an advocate of women's ordination, apologized for his role in helping prepare the council's liturgy document. . . . " Actually, Godfrey did not apologize for his work but rather for the fact that women were not also part of the process of liturgical reform at the Council, as members or consultors to the liturgical commission and the Consilium, and that, at the time, he did not note and protest their absence.
7. Others, reportedly, had similar misgivings. Rabbi Abraham Heschel, one of the speakers at the Milwaukee Liturgical Week, is said to have wondered aloud: "Isn't this a liturgy conference? I thought this was to do with the worship of God."
8. Joseph M. Connolly, *Liturgy* 14:4 (May, 1969) 1.
9. Gerard Sloyan, letter to KH, October 7, 1987. Sloyan suggested another explanation of Godfrey's unease with the direction of the Liturgical Conference, namely, that he may have felt rather abruptly excluded from decision-making when he retired from the board of the conference after serving a number of consecutive terms.
10. Andrew Greeley, taped interview, November 24, 1987.
11. GLD, letter to FRM, April 30, 1963. Other Roman Catholic representatives included Gregory Baum and George Tavard of the United States, Bernard Lambert of France and Jan C. Groot, of the Netherlands.
12. GLD, letter to FRM, August 6, 1963.

13. Douglas Horton, *Vatican Diary 1965* (Philadelphia: United Church Press, 1966) 164.

14. GLD, sermon on Reformation Sunday, 1981.

15. GLD, taped interview, fall 1987.

16. Kilian McDonnell, taped interview, October 13, 1987.

17. Ibid.

18. William Skudlarek, letter to KH, November 22, 1987.

19. GLD, taped interview, fall 1987.

20. GLD, sermon on Reformation Sunday, 1981.

21. GLD, letter to FRM, August 14, 1961.

22. John Egan, taped interview, November 17, 1987.

23. Gilbert Ostdiek, taped interview, December 15, 1987.

24. Andrew Greeley, taped interview, November 24, 1987.

25. Ibid.

26. Abbot Jerome Theisen, taped interview, October 13, 1987.

27. Bishop Charles Buswell, letter to KH, October 21, 1987.

28. I have relied on the very helpful assessments of Abbot Jerome Theisen, Kilian McDonnell, Allan Bouley, Alberic Culhane, Hilary Thimmesh, Vincent Yzermans, and William Skudlarek in order to describe Godfrey the theologian.

29. See, for example, "The Laying on of Hands: The Basic Sacramental Rite," in *Proceedings of the 29th Annual Convention of the Catholic Theological Society of America,* June 10–13, 1974 (New York: Manhattan College, 1974) 339–351.

30. GLD, letter to Philip Kaufman, November 13, 1938.

31. GLD, Christmas letter, 1986.

32. GLD, Christmas letter, 1988.

33. Shawn Sheehan, taped interview, December 4, 1987.

34. GLD, letter to Robert Lechner, May 8, 1963.

35. GLD, letter to Clement McNaspy, May 17, 1965.

36. Gerard Sloyan, letter to GLD, January 13, 1957.

37. Abigail McCarthy, phone interview, January 25, 1988. See her *Private Faces, Public Places* (New York: Doubleday, 1972) 420.

38. Patricia Joyce, taped interview, October 23, 1987.

39. John R. Page, taped interview, December 8, 1987.

40. GLD, taped interview, spring 1988.

41. GLD, letter to Franz Mueller, October 25, 1957. A number of years later Godfrey admitted to some homesickness himself. On October 4, 1976, he wrote to Abbot John Eidenschink: "I'm sincerely grateful for your letter of a few days ago. Strange: when I was quite young, a student in Europe for 5 years, I felt almost no homesickness. But it seems that the older I get, the more dependent I am, for my happiness and interior feeling of well-being, on news from the abbey and confreres.

42. Gilbert Ostdiek, taped interview, December 15, 1987.

43. Patricia and Thomas Joyce, taped interview, October 23, 1987.

44. John R. Page, taped interview, December 8, 1987.

45. GLD, Christmas letter, 1977. Ethiopia is another important and, from

a scholarly perspective, even more urgent site for this microfilm work, as the following letter from Godfrey to his abbot attests:

> The stay in Ethiopia was as "successful" as anyone could have hoped for. Situation very complex. 1400 monasteries and convents, all quite independent, and suspicious of anything modern or foreign. Not one of them, I was told, has a "library" in our sense of the word; but most have old MSS lying in corners or "attics," exposed to rodents—and to dangers of tourists: latter get monks drunk, pay a token price for MSS, and cart them away, and perhaps tear out "illuminations" and throw the rest away. But it *is* certain that there are very many old MSS. So I saw nearly everyone of importance in Addis Ababa, both in government and Church. No definite "yes" or "no" (and Canadian Jesuits, teaching in the University, with whom I stayed, assured me, that is last thing one could expect in Ethiopia). But I'm quite sure I got their interest and good will (spectacularly so in case of the acting Patriarch). Contacts now have to be kept alive, and then the follow-up. Am writing to Fr. Oliver in detail. Also—I think it would help our hopes much, if St. John's could accept one or two Ethiopian students on scholarship basis. It would create much good will [GLD, letter to Abbot Baldwin Dworschak, December 17, 1966].

46. GLD, letter to Abbot Jerome Theisen, April 25, 1984.

47. GLD, taped interview, fall 1987.

48. Patricia and Thomas Joyce, taped interview, October 23, 1987.

49. The late Alfred Deutsch, O.S.B., provided me with this "glimpse" of Godfrey's room.

50. Emeric Lawrence, O.S.B., taped interview, November 4, 1987 .

51. Gordon Tavis, O.S.B., prior at St. John's in 1975, wrote to Godfrey after reviewing his annual budget. After a long preamble about the relationship of one's budget to one's lifestyle, values, and goals, Father Gordon continued: "Having said that, let me indicate that I judge your lifestyle, from indications of your budget, to be one of obvious self-abnegation and solitude. I commend you and ask God's blessings on your efforts" [July 18, 1975].

52. Gilbert Ostdiek, taped interview, December 15, 1987.

53. GLD, taped interview, fall 1987.

54. GLD, letter to Florence and Al Muellerleile, August 3, 1963.

55. GLD, taped interview, summer 1988.

56. Ibid.

57. Ibid.

58. Ibid. These sentiments also explain Godfrey's approach when he has been asked to be a spiritual director: "A number of people came to me and asked me to direct them—and I tried to keep this as minimal as possible and never interfered with them. I said as little as possible because I wanted them to mature." One person who approached Godfrey for direction corroborated this "minimal" approach, saying Godfrey appeared "uninterested."

59. The complete citation may be found in the Appendix.

60. Vincent Yzermans, taped interview, October 23, 1987.

61. GLD, Christmas letter, 1982.

62. Albert Outler, letter to GLD, January 19, 1983.

63. See *The Rule of St. Benedict,* ch. 4.

64. GLD, letter to J. B. O'Connell, May 10, 1963.

65. GLD, Christmas letter, 1984.

66. GLD, Christmas letter, 1985 and taped interview, fall 1987.

67. GLD, After Christmas letter, 1988.

68. GLD, taped interview, spring 1988.

69. GLD, taped interview, spring 1988.

70. GLD, Christmas letter, 1985. In the same letter Godfrey mentions the glorious time he has had in building up a modest library of cassettes, mentioned earlier. His taste is catholic:

> I've gone overboard on Bach—and to a lesser degree on Mozart. (Am I wrong in thinking that Bach's cantatas are the sacred, and uncluttered, forerunner of our opera?) Then recordings of Masses. Among them: some in Gregorian chant; by the Renaissance greats, especially Palestrina, Vittoria, Byrd; Bach's Mass in B-minor, Beethoven's Missa Solemnis, and (yes, it really deserves to rank with them) Bruckner's Mass no. 3; the two "moderns," Faure's *Requiem,* and the *Requiem* of Andrew Lloyd Webber (who wrote the music also for "Jesus Christ Superstar"). And what a pleasure to discover Charpentier.

Father Godfrey Diekmann OSB of Collegeville Minn.   Frederick Franck
                                                          Rome 1962   With warmest greetings
                                                                             to Father Godfrey
                                                                             Frederick Franck 1980

APPENDIX

HONORS RECEIVED

LIST OF DOCUMENTS

Gift for Father Godfrey Diekmann on His Jubilee as Editor of *Worship*, 1963

Saint Vincent College, Latrobe, Pennsylvania, 1963

St. Anselm's College, Manchester, New Hampshire, 1963

St. Benedict's College, Atchison, Kansas, 1964

St. Bernard College, Cullman, Alabama, 1964

Cardinal Spellman Award, 1965

The Church Architectural Guild of America, 1965

St. Procopius College, Lisle, Illinois, 1966

University of Notre Dame, Notre Dame, Indiana, 1966

Christian Service Award, Minnesota Council of Churches, 1967

Gerald Ellard Award, 1972

Catholic University of America, 1976

Conover Award, 1976

Berakah Award, North American Academy of Liturgy, 1977

College of St. Thomas, St. Paul, Minnesota, 1978

Michael Mathis Award, Center for Pastoral Liturgy, University of Notre Dame, 1981

International Commission on English in the Liturgy, 1981

University of San Francisco, 1982

Regents Professor, St. John's University, Collegeville, Minnesota, 1984

Domino Servientes, Presbytery of the Church of St. Cloud, 1985

Virgil Michel Citation, St. John's Abbey, St. John's University, and the Liturgical Press, Collegeville, Minnesota, 1988

Catholic Theological Union, Chicago, Illinois, 1990

GIFT FOR FATHER GODFREY DIEKMANN
ON HIS JUBILEE AS EDITOR OF
WORSHIP

Hans A. Reinhold

(Chapter 1 of *The Revival of the Liturgy,* a Festschrift presented during the 1963 North American Liturgical Week held in Philadelphia. The dedication reads: TO GODFREY DIEKMANN IN GRATITUDE FOR TWENTY-FIVE YEARS OF *WORSHIP*)

At first nothing seems easier than my task: to write about a beloved and loyal friend, Godfrey Diekmann, the monk from St. John's Abbey and professor of dogmatic theology at St. John's University, on the occasion of his twenty-fifth anniversary as editor of the monthly, *Worship.* Fortunately, we too now have this custom of collecting articles and essays into a book for a man we want to honor. . . . Because this tribute lasts and is flattering: Everyone can see how much love, affection, esteem, and work went into it. It is also useful and appropriate, because it advances knowledge, often in a recondite field. What could be more appropriate than to see your friends busy writing for you. This is the truest gift for the academician: to be recognized as a master and to be rewarded with the crown of achievement in a field of common endeavor. I am sure that all will agree with me that Godfrey Diekmann, in all his modesty, deserves this gracious gift. I should know, because I am one of the older contributors to his magazine, and was for fifteen years a monthly contributor. I say this less in vainglory, than to establish myself as among the generation for whom all this is a thing of the past, the dark ages of the Liturgical Movement.

The very size of our country is a reason why something like the Liturgical Movement has had such a hard time in getting a foothold and in bearing fruit. How can a Catholic in Oregon know what has been done in Vermont or Massachusetts? To this we must add the different "national" backgrounds and traditions of the faithful in this country. The Germans and Slavs have a tradition of singing in their churches, while the Celts follow the Mass with silent reverence in order to let the "hedge priest" escape from his pursuers as fast as he can. The Romance-language peoples act differently again, which becomes nowhere as evident as in the "Italian Mission" at Brompton Oratory, where the liturgy is embalmed by the will of the priests who run the church according to Father Faber's infatuation with post-baroque Rome. These differences are easily multiplied and the poverty and far separation of Catholics from each other add yet other reasons for the slower development and thus the uniform growth of the Catholic parish and religious life in this country. In view of these facts, the general remedy for all cases in doubt has been to stay as close to Trent as possible: It was safe and prudent. No sooner had the Catholic put foot on American shore than he took refuge under the umbrella of Trent, and the United States became the most Tridentine country on earth. What was apparently settled by the council of Trent was with great fidelity observed. The great trees in the Church were Trent and Canon Law and the underbrush covering the space between these trees was the growth of the "Old Country" tradition.

Godfrey Diekmann is of German, to come closer, Westphalian stock. His own sense of humor attests that without doubt; it is not Irish anyway. It is true of other apostles of the liturgical renewal in the Midwest. To mention only a few, there are Martin Hellriegel, Reynold Hillenbrand, William Busch. These are only the "post-apostolic fathers"—there are probably a hundred more by now. They differ in one aspect from what we might call the New England school, or more closely circumscribed, the Boston group: Fathers Shawn Sheehan, McManus, Leonard, and a score more in the different seminaries and places of learning.

If one could differentiate these two groups, one might say with a certain justification that the Boston group is the learned one, and that the Midwest represents applied learning. Boston's background is Irish. The immense territory of the Far West, the Southwest, and the South, have partially followed these two dominant groups. In any case these two great liturgical regions are hardly topped now.

The names of Bishops Buswell, Reed and many a still silent worker hold great promise for the future, for they are hardly bound by Old Country nostalgia, they object less to genuine change than the more hidebound East and the more advanced Midwest. The latter suffers from repristination of the "good old days" in Europe, while the East resents anyone who touches even the most encrusted, and in itself hardly meaningful, usage.

On this turbulent sea appeared the good ship *Worship,* or as it was then a bit incongruously entitled, *Orate Fratres.* Like all things done by Virgil Michel, it was a daring piece and he was not afraid of the billows of adversity. He died much too early, if I may be permitted a correction of Providence, and left the monthly to Godfrey Diekmann, who with great *pietas* conserved its outward form. Father Godfrey steered the vessel through plenty or scarcity unafraid, and with a conscience filled with trust and optimism.　　•

Apart from his knowledge and experience, Godfrey Diekmann has in twenty-five years given shelter to the ideas of many an author of bold vision: the evening Mass, the use of modern languages in the liturgy, the restored diaconate, the coming theology of the layman, the thorough reform of the liturgy, the ecumenical movement, the social demands on the Christian of our day, the new kerygmatic attitude in teaching and Scripture, all of these and many more found their expression first of all, or at least in the beginning of their struggle, in the magazine edited by Godfrey Diekmann, with his kind approval, and with a word of commendation.

In reality this relatively small and not too much read monthly contributed a great deal to changing the face of the American Church, and often was the only link with Europe, especially during the war years. Many a European Catholic, who had weird notions about American Catholicism as an externalized, obedient, and spineless brand of the Universal Church, woke up to another reality when he saw *Worship* and in it the report on life and applied faith on these shores.

Not that Godfrey Diekmann's influence was limited to his magazine and its few thousand readers; it evoked parallel movements, like a mystical awakening: it influenced the social apostolate, it gave Christian art a steadier course, and housed for several years the biblical renewal, which it kept under its shelter in the days when its survival was seriously threatened. This is what a single man with devoted collaborators is able to do and to do well, when he is unafraid, convinced, and has that amount of charity with which Godfrey Diekmann is so richly endowed.

Father Godfrey used to make me angry, when he disclaimed having a talent or two as an English writer. And this at a time when he used to correct my own contributions. I know that he not only corrected them, he improved them, and retyped them, and thus I acknowledge gladly and publicly a private debt.

If I am not misinformed, it is the task of *Worship* to inform its readers of the latest developments here and abroad, at the center of the Church and at the periphery, to explain the liturgy, to point to those explanations which are above the average, and to provide prudent leadership for its readers. Who will doubt that Godfrey Diekmann has done this with a rare degree of perfection and often under adverse circumstances? And who will wonder that his fame as a theologian, retreat-master, and spiritual director has crossed the borders of our nation? Bubbling with enthusiasm, with an optimism that sometimes seemed to be sheer madness, he has a calmness when flattered that shows his self-control.

The great thing is not that the magazine *Worship* did not founder but kept afloat so many years, although that is achievement in itself, but that it is lively and interesting. . . .

The greatest thing is the power of rejuvenation Father Godfrey has always shown. . . . There is only one wish: may he stay with us many years yet in ineluctable courage and bold vision.

SAINT VINCENT COLLEGE

Doctor of Letters

June 2, 1963

CITATION

It seems fitting on this Pentecost Sunday, the anniversary of the Commence-ment of the Church, that we honor a man whose career for twenty-five years has been dedicated to the Liturgical Apostolate. In him we find a conserva-tive who treasures the spirit and central tradition of Christ's Church. In him we find a Christian liberal who is willing to shed those institutional forms that impede the growth of Christ among men. For leadership that keeps fellowship with his followers, for his contribution to the Liturgical Apostolate which has effected a renaissance in Christendom, for his witness to the prowess of the Holy Spirit that possesses the penchant to renew the face of the earth, St. Vincent College confers on Godfrey Leo Diekmann, of the Order of Saint Benedict, the Degree of

DOCTOR OF LETTERS

SAINT ANSELM'S COLLEGE

Doctor of Laws

June 13, 1963

CITATION

Service to the Church has long been a characteristic of a fully matured monasticism. In all ages and under every condition monasticism has con-sistently spoken to men of the things of God, repeating to them the word of salvation which it has received in the quiet of the monastic life.

The Benedictine monks of St. John's Abbey and, in particular, Father God-frey Diekmann have long carried on the traditional apostolate of the word of salvation through the publications of a religious press directed towards a deeper understanding of God's word in Sacred Scripture and a more meaningful participation in the worship of the Church.

During the twenty-five years in which he has served as editor of the review which today enjoys international reputation under the title, *Worship,* Father Godfrey has consistently directed attention to the riches of the Church's inner spiritual realities, presenting the timeless truths of the Gospel and the traditional teaching of God's Church in ways intelligible to modern man.

Prominent in all of the movements which define the Church's vitality in the twentieth century, he has powerfully promoted the popularization of modern scriptural scholarship and has personally participated in the movement towards fuller understanding and eventual unity amongst all those who own Christ as their Lord and Savior.

In recognition of his contribution to the vitality of American Catholicism and of his fidelity to the best traditions of Benedictine monasticism, I request, in the name of the Trustees of St. Anselm's College that the degree of Doctor of Laws, Honoris Causa, be conferred upon the Reverend Godfrey Diekmann.

Given This Thirteenth Day of June
In The Year of Our Lord, 1963

(Signature)

✝ BERTRAND C. DOLAN, o.s.b.
Chancellor

SAINT BENEDICT'S COLLEGE

Doctor of Letters

May 7, 1964

CITATION
The Reverend Godfrey Diekmann, O.S.B.

Right Reverend Chancellor, it gives me pleasure, both personally and as president of St. Benedict's College, to present to you this evening our candidate for the Honorary Degree of Doctor of Letters.

This candidate is Father Godfrey Diekmann of the Order of St. Benedict, internationally famous liturgist. He was educated at St. John's University, Collegeville, Minnesota, and in Rome, where he earned a doctorate in Sacred Theology, and he pursued graduate studies in Liturgy at the Abbey of Maria Laach in Germany. A priest two years, in 1933 Father Godfrey became assistant editor of *Orate Fratres,*, now *Worship,* and began teaching Theology, Patrology and Church History in the college and seminary at St. John's. During the summer months he gave lectures, conducted retreats, and also did some teaching.

In 1956 he helped organize the American delegation to the International Pastoral Liturgical congress at Assisi. He has served as vice president of the National Liturgical Conference, as consultant to the Pontifical Liturgical Commission preparing for the Second Vatican Council, and also as a theological expert at the Council.

Since the adjournment of the Council he has been appointed a consultor to the Post-Conciliar Commission on Liturgy. This is a role which will give him much influence in shaping the various aspects of Catholic worship, i.e., in the sacraments, in the Mass, and in the divine office.

His distinguished editorship of *Worship* extends from 1938 to the present and has inspired, pioneered and popularized many of the concepts basic to the Liturgical Movement. In addition to his many articles in *Worship,* Father Godfrey has contributed substantially to the *Encyclopedia Britanica* and is author of an unusual book, *Come, Let Us Worship.*

Because of his career of illustrious service to our Holy Mother Church—because of his distinctive record of leadership in this career—and because of his unselfish work for our Venerable Order, I am privileged and happy to present to you, Right Reverend Chancellor, as candidate for an honorary degree, the Reverend Godfrey L. Diekmann.

(Signature)

Rev. Alcuin Hemmen, o.s.b.
President

SAINT BERNARD COLLEGE

Doctor of Letters

1964

SAINT BERNARD COLLEGE

Acclaims today a leading Roman Catholic theologian whose ecumenical efforts on the world stage have so profoundly promoted interfaith dialogue and understanding for contemporary man that all religious communities are deeply aware of the restorative power of the Word of God. He is the editor of *Worship* Magazine, perhaps the single most influential publication in effecting liturgical reformation in the United States. He is a prolific author of liturgical and theological articles that draw all men of faith to a common love of their possession of God's truths. He is a leading liturgical theologian at Vatican Council II in Rome. From this lofty station he has kept in touch with the ministry of the people by "opening windows," in Pope John XXIII's memorable phrase, for the enrichment of human society and the increase of the effective grace of the Divine Mysteries through social worship, use of the vernacular of the people and fuller participation of the laity. In this world of great and revolutionary transitions, he has fostered a concept of dialogue and worship that directs the souls of all mankind toward a vast common adoration of the God that is our common Father. St. Bernard College takes pride in conferring the degree of Doctor of Letters, *honoris causa,* on this quintessential monk of modern times—Father Godfrey Diekmann, O.S.B.

CATHOLIC THEOLOGICAL SOCIETY OF AMERICA

Cardinal Spellman Award

1965

The theologian chosen for the Cardinal Spellman Award this year has made memorable contributions in two areas of theology, both of which are of historic significance.

With the permission of the Holy Office he pioneered in intercredal dialogue when he brought eminent Protestant theologians to St. John's University,

Collegeville, Minnesota, where he is professor of theology. In January, 1959, he was the first Catholic to address Minnesota's State Pastors' Conference.

It is in the area of liturgical renewal, however, that he is best known. For 25 years he has given leadership to the Liturgical Movement as editor of WORSHIP magazine.

He was one of the founders of the National Liturgical Conference and to-day is a member of its executive board.

He was one of five Americans asked to prepare the liturgical agenda for the Second Vatican Council.

He is a Council *peritus* and a consultor for the post-conciliar Commission on Sacred Liturgy.

The Catholic Theological Society of America has the honor to announce that Father Godfrey Diekmann, of the Order of St. Benedict, is the 1965 Cardinal Spellman Award winner.

THE CHURCH ARCHITECTURAL GUILD OF AMERICA

April 27, 1965

THE CHURCH ARCHITECTURAL GUILD OF AMERICA

is honored to present to

THE REVEREND GODFREY DIEKMANN, O.S.B.

HONORARY MEMBERSHIP

In recognition of outstanding service as a teacher and editor, and his con-structive influence on architecture as an interpreter of the forces of Renewal.

April 27, 1965 (Signature)

President

SAINT PROCOPIUS COLLEGE

Doctor of Humane Letters

1966

CITATION OF

THE REVEREND GODFREY L. DIEKMANN, O.S.B.

The very first of all the historic documents promulgated by the Second Vatican Ecumenical Council was the Constitution on the Sacred Liturgy. It is a document which can truly be called great and significant. As good Pope John so eloquently pointed out, it was eminently fitting that the great Council, convoked in the Holy Spirit for the purpose of renewing the Church of God, should before anything else direct its attention to that work of the people of God which, in a way, constitutes its principal *raison d'être:* the solemn, public worship of God, which we call the Sacred Liturgy.

That the Constitution on the Sacred Liturgy is epoch-making in the Church's history is hardly debatable, but it must be remembered always that it was not something that was born full-grown from the minds of the Council Fathers. Like most other profoundly significant documents which have influenced history, both in the Church and out of it, it has a long and not always tranquil history. The constitution is the culmination of a movement that was initiated by educated men who are long since dead. Pioneers like Dom Prosper Guéranger and Dom Maurus and Dom Placid Wolter, and so many others whose patient work of scholarship is known only to fellow-scholars.

It was a long time before what we now refer to as the Liturgical Movement crossed the Atlantic. Many would agree that it is not too much to say that Father Virgil Michel brought it back in his luggage when he came home to St. John's Abbey in Collegeville, Minnesota from his studies in Europe. Father Virgil had that rare talent which is able to communicate enthusiasm to others. The number of those, here in America, who were won over to the cause by Father Virgil, directly or indirectly, by personal contact or by his writings is incalculable, but it is certainly no exaggeration to say that more than any other man he *was* the Liturgical Movement in the United States.

When we say that the man whom we are about to present to you is the worthy successor of Father Virgil Michel we mean just that. He has not merely received the torch from his master and predecessor, he has carried it further. Building solidly on the firm foundations laid by others he, together with a host of like mind and similar dedication, has helped to place the capstone on the glorious structure which is the Liturgical Movement. As a member of the Liturgical Commission of the Council and as a Council *peritus* he had a significant part to play in the drafting and final polishing of the Constitution on the Sacred Liturgy. The whole Church will forever be in debt to men like this, who, in spite of all difficulties and obstacles, have persevered in their labors to bring to realization what was once no more than a dream.

Saint Procopius College deems it an honor and a privilege to single out publicly for recognition one who has deserved so well of the People of God. The College takes particular satisfaction in the fact that the recipient of this honor—the highest within its power to bestow—is not only a brother in the great Benedictine family but a distinguished member of an Abbey closely bound to St. Procopius by many ties of fraternal affection and gratitude.

It is with great pleasure, therefore, Right Reverend Father Chancellor, that I have the privilege of presenting to you the Reverend Godfrey Diekmann, Monk of St. John's Abbey, and of asking, in the name of the faculty of this College, that he be awarded the honorary degree of Doctor of Humane Letters.

UNIVERSITY OF NOTRE DAME DU LAC

Doctor of Laws

June 5, 1966

At
The One Hundred Twenty-first Commencement
The June Exercises
The University of Notre Dame confers the degree of
Doctor of Laws, *honoris causa,*
on

a worthy son of St. Benedict, who, faithful to his Order's mission of service to the Church, has spent himself tirelessly on behalf of the authenticity of divine worship. A student of the Fathers and professor of Theology at St. John's University, Collegeville, Minnesota, he has for more than twenty-five years directed the endeavors of the editorial staff of *Worship,* formerly called *Orate Fratres* in the old vernacular. With the sharp foresight of a prophet and the easy balance of one steeped in theological tradition, he anticipated the liturgical program of the Second Vatican Council and taught the American Church to prize meaningfulness in worship. Gifted lecturer and ardent apostle, he has traveled from coast to coast zealously instructing, cajoling, rousing both clergy and laity to the full commitment to Christ encountered in the Church's sacramental life. These talents and this zeal were summoned to the service of the Church on a grander scale when he was appointed consultor for both the Conciliar and Post-Conciliar Liturgical Commissions. Earlier this year on this campus, he made a notable contribution to the success of our international conference exploring the main theological issues of the Council. On

REVEREND GODFREY DIEKMANN, O.S.B.,
COLLEGEVILLE, MINNESOTA.

CHRISTIAN SERVICE AWARD FOR DISTINGUISHED ECUMENICAL LEADERSHIP

Minnesota Council of Churches

February 14, 1967

THE REV. GODFREY DIEKMANN, O.S.B., St. John's Seminary, Collegeville, "For his contributions to the Second Vatican Council and for the many ways he has exemplified the spirit of ecumenism in Minnesota."

In presenting the award to Father Godfrey, Dr. Motter recalled that in January, 1962, Father Godfrey was the first Catholic to address the Minnesota State Pastors Conference and that his address and liturgical studies helped to pave the way not only for changes which were to be approved by Vatican II but also for Protestant understanding and appreciation of that event.

THE GERALD ELLARD AWARD

1972

GODFREY DIEKMANN, O.S.B.

For Singular Contribution to American Liturgical Life

by

THE NEW ENGLAND LITURGICAL COMMITTEE

CATHOLIC UNIVERSITY OF AMERICA

Doctor of Humane Letters

May 8, 1976

With scholarly diligence and youthful enthusiasm, Father Godfrey Diekmann meets the challenge of each fresh lecture, article, retreat, or liturgical translation. Along with the rest of the Catholic community, this University has often benefited from his work, as lecturer in the summer session and most recently as distinguished Visiting Professor in the liturgical program of the School of Religious Studies. To us he represents the Benedictine liturgical inheritance of Maria Laach, San Anselmo, and his own Saint John's Abbey, as well as the honored liberal arts tradition of our sister institution, Saint John's University of Collegeville, where he serves as Professor of Patristics.

Godfrey Diekmann's impact upon Christian spirituality and liturgy has been massive and pervasive ever since he joined and then succeeded the pioneer Virgil Michel in the editorship of *Worship,* the principal liturgical journal in the English-language world. For forty-three of its fifty years he has served as managing editor and editor-in-chief of *Worship.* He has been a wise guide and leader as mainstay of the Liturgical Conference of the 1940's and 1950's, as expert at the Second Vatican Council in the 1960's, as consultant to national and international bodies, and for the past decade as a major participant in the International Commission on English in the Liturgy. At the same time he has had a full career as an outstanding college professor and as preacher of retreats, especially retreats directed to the spiritual and liturgical growth of priests.

For several decades Father Godfrey has called the Christian people to a celebration of the liturgy that has greater meaning and beauty, reflective of his own warm appreciation of God's creation and human art. His work and message are summed up in the title of a collection of his writings: *Come, Let Us Worship.* With deep affection for him as a priest and monk, scholar and teacher, The Catholic University of America is happy to award to the Reverend Father Godfrey Diekmann of the Order of Saint Benedict the degree of Doctor of Humane Letters, *honoris causa.*

CONOVER AWARD

July 7, 1976

GRA
Affiliate of the American
Institute of Architects

THE GUILD FOR RELIGIOUS ARCHITECTURE
presents
THE REV. GODFREY DIEKMANN, O.S.B.
with the Elbert M. Conover Memorial Award
in recognition of his contribution
to religious architecture

Elbert M. Conover was director of the Methodist Bureau of Architecture from 1924 to 1936. He was also the first director and moving spirit of the Bureau of Church Building and Architecture from 1936 until his death in 1952.

He was instrumental in organizing the North American Conference of Architecture and the Church Architectural Guild of America.

In all his life, he was an ardent crusader on behalf of those who labored to adorn the house of God with beauty and strength.

President (signature)   Date: July 7, 1976

NORTH AMERICAN ACADEMY OF LITURGY

Berakah Award

1977

INTRODUCTION:

Our humanity seems to come in different concentrations and different size bundles. I suppose that, in some philosophical way, maybe all human beings are human, but it seems that the thing in which we live and participate concentrates more in some people than in others and Godfrey Diekmann certainly is a vital, colorful person. He has been such an important voice in the liturgical renewal for a very long time and I think it is hard to measure how important to the movement it is to have the leadership carried by incredible people. The movement has to win its way, to be persuasive. It wields no power except such convincing power as its own face can make for it. In the hands or through the voice of someone who is not represented well it will not prevail. And so we will never know, I am sure, how important it is that Godfrey and people like Godfrey have been the voice.

Godfrey is a modest person. When I first talked to him about the award he said, "How nice for the magazine!" I do not think he realizes how large a place he occupies in the hearts of many of us and how we appreciate the understanding we have gained of the field in which we work and the leadership he gave us, the things he has said and which we all have learned. Our Award will not change his mind and make him less modest but it will be for us at least a gesture to let him know the regard in which he is held by many of his associates and colleagues. And so the Award will be presented and is printed as follows:

"In recognition of his achievement in behalf of the renewal of worship as writer, scholar, teacher and advisor and of his editorial encouragement and dissemination of the achievement of others, in appreciation of his own unfailing vitality of mind, breadth of interests, generosity of spirit and love for what he is doing, and as an expression of gratitude for the joy of his friendship, the wisdom of his counsel and inspiration of his leadership, the North American Academy of Liturgy presents its Berakah Award to Godfrey Diekmann, O.S.B. in this the jubilee of the journal with which he so long has been associated and of his own profession in the Order of Saint Benedict."

DANIEL B. STEVICK, President

COLLEGE OF ST. THOMAS

Doctor of Letters

Twentieth Day of May, 1978

Citation to accompany the conferring of the degree of Doctor of Letters given at the College of St. Thomas the twentieth day of May, 1978

THE REVEREND GODFREY DIEKMANN, O.S.B.

Godfrey Diekmann, monk of Saint Benedict of the Abbey of Saint John, throughout your life as priest, scholar, educator, and writer, you have delved into the history and traditions of Christianity and have illuminated its values and truths for generations of enthusiastic students.

Through your life-long example of worship and work, you have demonstrated the richness and variety of the religious life.

As Professor of Patristic Theology you have drawn from the treasures of the Fathers of the Church and have given them meaning and relevance for a questioning and restless people.

As a Consultant of the Second Vatican Council you assisted in drafting the Constitution on the Sacred Liturgy.

As Editor-in-chief of the influential journal, *Worship,* for nearly forty years of its fifty-year existence, you have disseminated the most incisive writing produced concerning sacred liturgy and have contributed significantly to the building of the climate of acceptance in which our renewed liturgy has come to be appreciated and reverenced by scholars and pastors, by students and parishioners.

As promoter of religious unity you fostered the ecumenical spirit prior to the Second Vatican Council. Since then you have enlightened and nourished that spirit by your active service with the official Lutheran-Catholic Dialogue and through your prolific writing as well as your teaching at many distinguished universities and seminaries throughout the nation.

Truly a Man For All Seasons, you are as much at ease and at home traversing the hills and vales of Stearns County in search of the elusive mushroom or in a rural kitchen preparing a supply of choke cherry preserves as you are in the lecture halls of great universities or in the sanctuary of God's house.

Wherever your inspiring presence abides, you remain always and firmly the "good and faithful servant," an exemplar of what Irenaeus of Lyons meant when he wrote that "man fully alive is the glory of God."

Grateful for the gifts of your learning and leadership, your teaching and humility, the College of St. Thomas fondly salutes you, Godfrey Diekmann, and proudly confers upon you the degree of Doctor of Letters, *honoris causa*.

THE MICHAEL MATHIS AWARD

June, 1981

THE
MICHAEL MATHIS AWARD

is presented to

REV. GODFREY DIEKMANN O.S.B.

Monk, Professor, Pastor, Liturgical Pioneer

in recognition
of his outstanding contribution
to the renewal of pastoral liturgy
in the United States.

Given on the occasion
of the Tenth Annual Conference
Notre Dame Center for Pastoral Liturgy
June, 1981

(Signature)
JOHN ALLYN MELLOH, S.M.
Director

INTERNATIONAL COMMISSION ON ENGLISH IN THE LITURGY

1981

It is with great joy that we acknowledge that Father Godfrey Diekmann, O.S.B. is celebrating the fiftieth anniversary of his ordination to the priesthood. We need not recall in any detail the immense and lasting contributions which he has made to the work of liturgical renewal from his earliest years as a priest. To say that he has been editor-in-chief of *Worship* since 1938, was a peritus at the Second Vatican Council, and a consultant to the Consilium is to mention just some of the high points of his career. We are deeply conscious that within the world of ICEL he has done invaluable work as a member of the Advisory Committee, has served on a number of special subcommittees, and has won the respect and affection of many devoted friends.

May the Lord give to you, Father Godfrey, long years to continue your wholehearted, generous, and joyful service to your Benedictine community and to the wider Church.

The present members of the Advisory Committee and their guests take this opportunity to express their good wishes in song:

> This day God give you
> Strength of high heaven,
> Sun and moon shining,
> Flame in his hearth,
> Flashing of lightning,
> Wind in its swiftness,
> Deeps of the ocean,
> Firmness of earth.
>
> This day God send you
> Strength as your steersman,
> Might to uphold you,
> Wisdom as guide.
> Angels of heaven.
> Drive from you always,
> All that would harm you,
> Stand by your side.

(Signatures)

D. S. Amalorpavadass
Anscar J. Chupungco O.S.B.
Joseph Cunningham
J. Frank Henderson
William Jordan
Edward Matthews
Marjorie Moffatt S.N.J.M.
Christopher Willcock S.J.

Anthony B. Boylan
Daniel Coughlin
John H. Fitzsimmons
Kathleen Hughes R.S.C.J.
Thomas Krosnicki S.V.D.
Frederick R. McManus
John R. Page

UNIVERSITY OF SAN FRANCISCO

Doctor of Sacred Theology in Liturgy

May 23, 1982

UNIVERSITY OF SAN FRANCISCO

The Board of Trustees

CITATION

THE REVEREND GODFREY DIEKMANN, O.S.B.

One of the most dramatic movements in the Roman Catholic Church during the past decades has been the renewal and reinvigoration of the prayer of the Church, the Sacred Liturgy. Not without nostalgia for the past, not without many tentative and sometimes awkward sorties into the future, the Liturgy of the Church now becomes each day a richer prayer of the People of God—more catholic, more universal in the eloquence of its statement and the depths of its understanding.

A voice of suasive reason in this evolution, a voice of creative innovation, all the while imbued with respect for authentic tradition, was and remains the quiet and learned voice of Father Godfrey Diekmann. Father Godfrey, perhaps more than any other, has plunged the American Church into the mainstream of liturgical renewal, even as he and his colleagues have endeavored to light the way of the Catholic world toward the future directions of worship.

Long-time and beloved professor at Saint John's University in Minnesota, Father Godfrey participated, before the Second Vatican Council, in five International Liturgical Study Weeks whose task it was to prepare the way for the liturgical reforms of the Council. His acknowledged expertise in liturgy, patristic theology, early Christianity and liturgical history won for him the role of *peritus,* or expert, in service to the Vatican Council itself.

Father Godfrey celebrates this year fifty years as a priest in the Order of Saint Benedict, whose arms are emblazoned with the motto, *Ora et labora*—Work and pray! Central to the Benedictine charism has always been prayer, the prayer of the Church. The Benedictines have been the zealous custodians of our prayer, and of our civilization, through eras of decline as well as the new spring of liturgical renaissance. Father Godfrey has incarnated in his own life the Benedictine motto—indeed, his work *is* prayer. And there is no more zealous or articulate advocate of genuine liturgy than he, no more loyal son of Saint Benedict and of the Church than he.

In recognition of his immeasurable and devoted contributions to the life and prayer of the Church, and of his selfless and dedicated years of teaching and research with which he has personally enriched the theology programs and life of our University, the University of San Francisco salutes him and confers upon Father Godfrey Diekmann, of the Order of Saint Benedict, the degree of Doctor of Sacred Theology in Liturgy, *honoris causa,* with all the rights, privileges and honors pertaining thereto.

Given at San Francisco in the State of California this Twenty-third day of May in the year of Our Lord Nineteen hundred and eighty-two, and of the University the One hundred and twenty-seventh.

NEWS RELEASE FROM ST. JOHN'S UNIVERSITY

May 3, 1984

TWO SAINT JOHN'S TEACHERS NAMED
REGENTS PROFESSORS

Collegeville, Minn.—Two long-time Saint John's University teachers have been named Regents Professors by the Board of Regents, the University's governing body. The Rev. Godfrey Diekmann, OSB, and the Rev. Alfred Deutsch, OSB, have received the appointments, which acknowledge distinguished careers in the arts, education, business or professional fields.

Fr. Diekmann is an internationally-respected theologian who served as a liturgy expert to the Second Vatican Council. He has been active in the movement for liturgical reform as a member of and advisor to numerous committees, and as editor of *Worship* magazine. Fr. Diekmann has been a member of the theology faculty at Saint John's since 1933, specializing in liturgy and patristic theology.

(The second paragraph is dedicated to Fr. Deutsch)

PRESBYTERY OF THE CHURCH OF SAINT CLOUD

Presentation

8th day of October, 1985

Godfrey Leo Diekmann, you were born a child of the Church of Saint Cloud on April 7, 1908, chosen a son of Saint Benedict of Saint John's Abbey on July 11, 1926, and ordained a priest of Christ Jesus on June 28, 1931. Your family had deep roots in the rich, religious ground of Stearns County, living under the shadow of the abbey church, with your father serving for many years as a schoolmaster. You and your brother, Conrad, also a son of Saint Benedict, followed in your father's steps as teachers.

You returned to your abbey in 1933, receiving your doctorate in patristic theology after completing your studies at the College of Saint Anselm in the Eternal City. Year after year, from then until the present, you have shared your scholarship and learning with thousands of students of Saint John's University and Saint John's Seminary. Your reputation as a learned teacher spread far and wide. Thus you were called to teach during summer sessions in places as distant and varied as The Catholic University of America in Washington, D.C., The University of Notre Dame in South Bend, Indiana, the University of San Francisco in San Francisco, California, and— among many others—Lutheran Theological Seminary in Saint Paul, Minnesota. We apply to you the words of Scripture: "Those who instruct others in holiness shall shine as the stars."

Your charism as a teacher embraced both the spoken and written word. Since 1938 you have served as editor-in-chief of *Worship;* under your direction it became a leading publication in the service of the liturgical apostolate. Through its pages you continued to teach thousands throughout the world. Among your other numerous writings two works have influenced many of us in our ministry as priests among God's people. These are *Come, Let Us Worship,* published in 1961 and *Personal Prayer and the Liturgy,* published in 1971.

In God's Providence your wisdom and experience reached their finest hour when you were named a consultant to the Second Vatican Council and appointed to serve on the committee that drafted the "Constitution on the Sacred Liturgy." In helping to shape this document you served again as a teacher of all God's people on earth through the acceptance and approbation of all the bishops of the Church of many of the liturgical and patristic insights you had advanced for many years among your students in the classroom.

Hundreds of thousands of people know you as a brilliant lecturer and thoughtful teacher. We especially have been enriched for many years by your presence among us and with us as a brother and a friend. You willingly and eagerly arrived on a Saturday afternoon to assist in one or other of the parishes. You moved among us during both joyful and sorrowful events that have marked the life of the Church of Saint Cloud. We marveled how such a man could be so childlike in his enthusiasm for digging mushrooms in the woods of Indianbush; at stirring up a batch of currant preserves in the monastic kitchen; and—yes, indeed,—even risking life for a handful of water cress in a pond behind the Sagatagan.

Most of all, your warmth flooded us by your smile, instilling in all of us a ray of your own serenity that emanated from a heart and soul filled with optimism because it was grounded in a deep Christian realism. You expressed it yourself in a recent address when you said: "I for one refuse to be part of the faintheartedness, the pessimism, the fear, that seems currently to have infected so many." We are grateful, to be sure, for your teachings; most of all we are grateful for your example of Christian joy.

The Presbytery of the Church of Saint Cloud is honored by honoring you this day. We know of your great love for Justin Martyr, Ignatius of Antioch, Clement of Rome and all the apostolic fathers of the Church. We know how you await to be joined with them before the throne of the Risen Christ. We know also how much we need you among us and with us to guide and direct us in the paths of holy hope and peace. For these reasons we pray that before God calls you home to shine with the apostolic fathers of the Church in heaven He will permit you to remain among us a long time to shine among us as a father of the Church on earth.

Presented by the Presbytery of the Church of Saint Cloud
In General Assembly at Alexandria, Minnesota
On the 8th day of October, 1985
By Bishop George H. Speltz

ST. JOHN'S ABBEY, ST. JOHN'S UNIVERSITY
THE LITURGICAL PRESS

Virgil Michel Citation

July 14, 1988

(Presented on the occasion of the Virgil Michel Symposium, July 11–14, 1988, the year of the fiftieth anniversary of the death of Virgil Michel.)

GODFREY DIEKMANN: monk, teacher, editor, scholar. You are, in our day, one of our Holy Father Benedict's most distinguished sons.

When many hear the name of St. John's, they think of you, for you have been an ambassador of this community for half a century. The message you have borne from us is captured in the title of your book, *Come, Let Us Worship.*

Pre-eminently, you are a patristic teacher of distinction. Fortunate are the students of St. John's and other distinguished universities who have experienced your professorial charism. Fortunate, too, are those clergy who have been formed and enlivened by your message in retreats you have given.

In the decades that preceded the Second Vatican Council, you nurtured and held high the flame of liturgical renewal, and made your own the mission of your predecessor, Virgil Michel. As editor of *Worship* from 1939 to 1964, you sensed the major currents of American and European liturgical thought and directed them to readers here and abroad. You helped draft the Constitution on the Sacred Liturgy and served as a *peritus* at the Council. And, bearing witness to the profound bond between worship and social regeneration, you were present when Martin Luther King, Jr., proclaimed to all Americans, "I have a dream."

Others have recognized and cited your far-reaching accomplishments, celebrating your youthful enthusiasm, your vitality, your generosity, and your wisdom. Our experience confirms their judgments. Nevertheless, we choose to add to their tributes our acknowledgment of you as a gifted and faithful confrere, one who has stated that he owes much to "the support of many brethren" *(Rule of Benedict, ch. 1).*

You have quipped that as a young monk you confused the Benedictine vows, promising stability of morals and conversion of place. Well, we have come to value your early confusion; for, while your copy of the *Holy Rule* may contain a worn passport tucked inside its cover, you have produced lasting and nourishing fruit not only for this monastery and this university, but for scholars and pastors, and worshippers worldwide. Therefore, on this fourteenth day of July in this nineteen-hundred-and-eighty-eighth year of the Christian era, on the occasion of a symposium honoring the work of Virgil Michel, we confreres, colleagues, and friends bestow on you this citation.

CATHOLIC THEOLOGICAL UNION

CHICAGO, ILLINOIS

In its commitment to training men and women for the ministry, Catholic Theological Union recognizes the profound significance of liturgical studies. In this twenty-fifth anniversary year of the closing of the Second Vatican Council, we are eager to honor a priest and scholar who has made a pre-eminent contribution to the renewal of the church's worship in the spirit of the Council.

Father Godfrey Diekmann, O.S.B. has taught and lived what *Amen* means— that word which he has said is "the most wonderful word invented." He has taught Christ as the *Amen of* God; he has taught theology as a way of knowing God's *Amen* to us as church and our participation in the *Amen* of Christ. As editor of *Orate Fratres/Worship;* organizer and participant in national and international liturgical weeks; popular and gifted speaker; consultant to the Pontifical Liturgical Commission which prepared for the Second Vatican Council; Council *peritus* from 1963 to 1965; member, from its founding of the International Commission on English in the Liturgy; consultor to the Post-conciliar Commission on Liturgy, he has enriched the word *Amen* by the Alleluia of his own life.

As a Benedictine monk Father Diekmann has lived the life of a priest and a scholar with contagious effervescence and rock-solid faith. He has understood his task of teaching, speaking and preaching as an obligation to share not only his knowledge and interest but also his love of Christ, his enthusiasm. He has said that from the teacher of theology sparks must fly. The fire of his own enthusiasm and love of God have warmed the hearts of his hearers when, as a preeminent teacher of patristics and theology, as one of our country's most sought-after retreat directors he has taught God, not merely truths about God, and inspired others with the vision of liturgy as a way of life.

Therefore, for his outstanding contribution to the liturgical renewal of the church in our times, I am honored to present to Father Godfrey Diekmann, O.S.B., the Degree of Doctor of Theology, *honoris causa,* on this 31st day of May, 1990.

Signed: DONALD SENIOR, C.P.
President

BIBLIOGRAPHY OF
GODFREY DIEKMANN, O.S.B.

BOOKS AND MONOGRAPHS

Mass Symbols. Illustrated by Joachim Watrin. Collegeville, Minn.: The Liturgical Press, 1947.

The Easter Vigil: Arranged for Use in Parishes. Collegeville, Minn.: The Liturgical Press, 1953.

The Masses of Holy Week and the Easter Vigil: Arranged for Use in Parishes. Collegeville, Minn.: The Liturgical Press, 1956 [2nd revised edition, 1957].

Editor, *The Assisi Papers.* Collegeville, Minn.: The Liturgical Press, 1957.

Come, Let Us Worship. Benedictine Studies 12. Baltimore: Helicon Press, 1961.

Editor, *The Book of Catholic Worship.* Washington, D. C.: The Liturgical Conference, 1966.

Personal Prayer and the Liturgy. London: Geoffrey Chapman, 1971.

Associate Editor, *Concilium,* vols. 1–42, 1965–69.

CHAPTERS IN BOOKS

"Lay Participation in the Liturgy of the Church." In *A Symposium on the Life of Pope Pius X,* 137–158. Washington: Confraternity of Christian Doctrine, 1946.

"The Primary Apostolate." In *The American Apostolate,* 29–46. Edited by Leo R. Ward. Westminster, Md.: The Newman Press, 1952.

"The Church-Related College and the Parish." In *Association of American Colleges Bulletin* 41, no. 2 (May 1955): 246–256. See *Come, Let Us Worship,* 163–175.

"The Chief and Indispensable Source." In *Participation of the Laity in the Liturgy of the Mass,* 5–11. Washington: National Council of Catholic Men, 1955.

"Living with the Church in Prayer and Reading." In *1955 Proceedings of the Sisters' Institute of Spirituality,* 159–243. Edited by A. Leonard Collins. Notre Dame, Ind.: Univ. of Notre Dame Press, 1956.

"Worship." In *Catholics in Conversation,* 137–153. Interview with Donald McDonald. New York: J. P. Lippincott Co., 1960.

"Liturgy in the Life and Apostolate of the Religious." In *Religious Life in the Church Today: Prospect and Retrospect,* 131–151. Proceedings of the Second National Congress of Religious in the United States, August 16–19. Edited by Mother Mary Florence. Notre Dame, Ind.: Univ. of Notre Dame Press, 1962.

"Liturgy." In *The Catholic Bookman's Guide: A Critical Evaluation of Catholic Literature,* 153–171. Edited by Sister M. Regis. New York: Hawthorne Books, Inc., 1962.

"Factors That Unite Us." In *Christians in Conversation,* 81–112. Westminster: The Newman Press, 1962.

"Two Approaches to Understanding the Sacraments." In *Readings in Sacramental Theology,* 1–17. Edited by C. Stephen Sullivan. Englewood Cliffs, N.J.: Prentice Hall, Inc., 1964. See *Come, Let Us Worship,* 23–40; *Education and the Liturgy,* 12–27. Eighteenth North American Liturgical Week 1957; and *Worship* 31 (October 1957): 504–520.

"The James A. Gray Lectures on The Second Vatican Council." In *The Duke Divinity School Review* 30, no. 1 (Winter 1965): 9–41. Durham, N.C.: Divinity School of Duke Univ., 1965.

"The Place of Liturgical Worship." In *The Church and the Liturgy.* Concilium 2:67–107. Edited by Johannes Wagner and Helmut Hucke. New York: Paulist Press, 1965.

"The Reformed Liturgy and the Eucharist." In *Church Architecture: The Shape of Reform,* 35–51. Proceedings of a Meeting on Church Architecture Conducted by the Liturgical Conference, Cleveland, February 23–25. Washington: The Liturgical Conference, 1965.

Foreword to *Our Changing Liturgy,* by Clement J. McNaspy. New York: Hawthorn Books, 1966.

ARTICLES IN *LITURGICAL WEEK PROCEEDINGS*

"Initiation into Christian Life and Worship Through Baptism." National Liturgical Week 1940, Chicago. Newark, N.J.: Benedictine Liturgical Conference, 1941: 54–63. See *Come, Let Us Worship,* 55–64.

"The Liturgy and Orthodox Belief." National Liturgical Week 1944, New York. Chicago: The Liturgical Conference, 1945: 114–118.

"The Marriage of Christ and the Church." In *The Family in Christ*, 34–43. National Liturgical Week 1946, Denver. Elsberry, Mo.: The Liturgical Conference, 1947. See *Come, Let Us Worship*, 95–107.

"With Christ at Mass." In *Christ's Sacrifice and Ours*, 42–48. National Liturgical Week 1947, Portland. Boston: The Liturgical Conference, 1948. See *Come, Let Us Worship*, 87–95.

"Unto Full Stature." In *The New Man in Christ*, 139–151. National Liturgical Week 1948, Boston. Conception, Mo.: The Liturgical Conference, 1949. See *Come, Let Us Worship*, 74–86; and *Worship* 23 (February 1949): 161–168.

"The Lord's Day in the Old and New Testament." In *Sanctification of Sunday*, 52–61. National Liturgical Week 1949, St. Louis. Conception, Mo.: The Liturgical Conference, 1949. See *Come, Let Us Worship*, 107–117.

"Christ in the Liturgy." In *For Pastors and People*, 62–81. National Liturgical Week 1950, Conception. Conception, Mo: The Liturgical Conference, 1950. See *Come, Let Us Worship*, 40–55.

"The High Priesthood of the Bishop." In *The Priesthood of Christ*, 32–43. National Liturgical Week 1951, Dubuque. Conception, Mo.: The Liturgical Conference, 1951. See *Come, Let Us Worship*, 143–155.

"The Fast Ought Not Prevent Communion." In *St. Pius X and Social Worship*, 72–79. National Liturgical Week 1953, Grand Rapids. Elsberry, Mo.: The Liturgical Conference, 1954. See *Come, Let Us Worship*, 155–163; and *Worship* 27 (October 1953): 516–523.

"Rebirth in Christ." In *The New Ritual—Liturgy and Social Order*, 20–29. National Liturgical Week 1955, Worcester. Elsberry, Mo.: The Liturgical Conference, 1956. See *Come, Let Us Worship*, 64–74.

"The Sacrament of Confirmation." In *The New Ritual—Liturgy and Social Order*, 38–39. National Liturgical Week 1955, Worcester. Elsberry, Mo.: The Liturgical Conference, 1956.

"Report on Efforts to Improve Liturgically the Prayer Life of a Novitiate in the Communities of Both Men and Women." In *The New Ritual—Liturgy and Social Order*, 76–81. National Liturgical Week 1955, Worcester. Elsberry, Mo.: The Liturgical Conference, 1956.

"Two Approaches to Understanding the Sacraments." In *Education and the Liturgy*, 12–27. North American Liturgical Week 1957, Collegeville. Elsberry, Mo.: The Liturgical Conference, 1958. See *Come, Let Us Worship*, 23–40; *Readings in Sacramental Theology*, 1–17; and *Worship* 31, (October 1957): 504–520.

"The Church Year in Action." In *The Church Year*, 14–28. North American Liturgical Week 1958, Cincinnati. n.p: The Liturgical Conference, 1959. See *Come, Let Us Worship*, 117–134.

"Popular Participation and the History of Christian Piety." In *Participation in the Mass*, 52–63. North American Liturgical Week 1959, Notre Dame. Washington: The Liturgical Conference, 1960. See *Come, Let Us Worship*, 7–22.

"The Constitution on the Sacred Liturgy." In *Vatican II: An Interfaith Appraisal*, 17–40. International Theological Conference, University of Notre Dame, March 20–26. Edited by John H. Miller. Notre Dame, Ind.: Univ. of Notre Dame Press, 1966. See *Worship*, 40 (August–September 1966): 408–423.

"Liturgical Practice in the United States and Canada." In *The Church Worships*. Concilium 12:157–166. Edited by Johannes Wagner and Helmut Hucke. New York: Paulist Press, 1966.

"Some Observations on the Teaching of Trent Concerning Baptism." In *Lutherans and Catholics in Dialogue, 2: One Baptism for the Remission of Sins*, 61–70. Edited by Paul C. Empic and William W. Baum. Washington: Bishops' Commission for Ecumenical Affairs, 1966.

"Dogmatic Constitution on the Church." In *American Participation in the Second Vatican Council*, 73–91. Edited by Vincent A. Yzermans. New York: Sheed and Ward, 1967.

"The Theology of Liturgy According to Vatican II." In *Crisis in Church Music*, 27–39. Proceedings of a Meeting on Church Music Conducted by the Liturgical Conference and the Church Music Association of America. Washington: The Liturgical Conference, 1967.

"Worship." In *Theology of Renewal, 2*, 88–99. Proceedings of the Congress on the Theology of the Renewal of the Church: Centenary of Canada, 1867–1967. Edited by L. K. Shook. Montreal: Palm Publishers, 1968. See *Worship* 41 (March 1967): 142–151.

Discussion after this paper reported in *Discussions*, 51–54. Congress on the Theology of Renewal of the Church, August 20–25. Toronto: Pontifical Institute of Mediaeval Studies, 1968.

"Liturgy: Shaped by and the Shaper of the Ongoing Christian Community." In *Christian Action and Openness to the World*, 23–35. The Villanova University Symposia 2–3. Edited by Joseph Papin. Villanova: The Villanova Univ. Press, 1970.

"Is There a Distinct American Contribution to the Development of Liturgy?" In *Proceedings of the 26th Annual Convention of the Catholic Theological Society of America*, June 14–17, 1971, 26:200–210. New York: Manhattan College, 1972. See *Worship* 45 (December 1971): 578–587.

"The Laying on of Hands: The Basic Sacramental Rite." In *Proceedings of the 29th Annual Convention of the Catholic Theological Society of America,* June 10–13, 1974, 29:339-351. New York: Manhattan College, 1974. See *Liturgy* 21 (January 1976): 22–27.

Foreword to *Strong, Loving and Wise,* by Robert Hovda. Washington: The Liturgical Conference, 1976.

"Celebrating the Word." In *Celebrating the Word,* 1–22. The Third Symposium of the Canadian Liturgical Society. Edited by James Schmeiser. Toronto: The Anglican Book Center, 1977.

"The New Rite of Penance: A Theological Evaluation." In *The Rite of Penance: Commentaries,* 3: *Background and Directions,* 82–91. Edited by Nathan Mitchell. Washington: The Liturgical Conference, 1978.

"Reconciliation Through the Prayer of the Community." In *The Rite of Penance: Commentaries,* 3: *Background and Directions,* 38–49. Edited by Nathan Mitchell. Washington: The Liturgical Conference, 1978.

"The Church as a Community of Prayer." In *Pastoral Music in Practice,* 43–54. Edited by Virgil C. Funk and Gabe Huck. Washington: National Association of Pastoral Musicians, 1981. See *Pastoral Music* 3, no. 4 (June–July 1979): 16–21.

"The Eucharist Builds Up the Building." In *The Environment for Worship,* 43–51. Edited by Bishops' Committee on the Liturgy and The Center for Pastoral Liturgy at Catholic University. Washington: USCC, 1980.

"Mathis Award: Response." In *Sunday Morning: A Time for Worship,* 189–191. Edited by Mark Searle. Collegeville, Minn.: The Liturgical Press, 1982.

"Sunday Morning: Retrospect and Prospect." In *Sunday Morning: A Time for Worship,* 173–187. Edited by Mark Searle. Collegeville, Minn.: The Liturgical Press, 1982. See *Sunday Morning: A Time for Worship.* Audio tape.

"Mary, the Model of Our Worship." In *The Liturgy and Unity in Christ,* 61–66. North American Liturgical Week 1960, Pittsburgh. Washington: The Liturgical Conference, 1961. See *Come, Let Us Worship,* 135–143; *Worship* 34 (October 1960): 579–586; and *Our Lady's Digest* 15 (February 1961): 238–245.

"Feast of the Immaculate Heart of Mary." Homily. In *Bible, Life, and Worship,* 91–92. North American Liturgical Week 1961, Oklahoma City. Washington: The Liturgical Conference, 1962.

"Retreats to Priests and Religious." In *Bible, Life, and Worship,* 204–205. North American Liturgical Week 1961, Oklahoma City. Washington: The Liturgical Conference, 1962.

"First-Born from the Dead." In *Thy Kingdom Come,* 16–28. North American Liturgical Week 1962, Seattle. Washington: The Liturgical Conference, 1963.

"Sacramental Life—The Mystery Shared." In *The Renewal of Christian Education,* 35–43. North American Liturgical Week 1963, Philadelphia. Washington: The Liturgical Conference, 1964. See *Worship* 37 (October 1963): 589–598.

"The Full Sign of the Eucharist." In *Challenge of the Council: Person, Parish, World,* 86–94. North American Liturgical Week 1964, St. Louis. Washington: The Liturgical Conference, 1964.

"Feast of St. Zephyrinus, Pope and Martyr." Homily. In *The Challenge of the Council: Person, Parish, World,* 267–270. North American Liturgical Week 1964, St. Louis. Washington: The Liturgical Conference, 1964.

"The Eucharist Makes the People of God." In *Jesus Christ Reforms His Church,* 102–113. North American Liturgical Week 1965, Baltimore, Portland, and Chicago. Washington: The Liturgical Conference, 1966. See *Worship* 39 (October 1965): 458–468.

ARTICLES AND NOTES IN *ORATE FRATRES/WORSHIP*

Vol. 10 (1935–1936)
  "Light and Life," 98–101
  "The Lord Has Truly Arisen," 194–197
  "Veni Sancte Spiritus," 290–292

Vol. 23 (1948–1949)
  "Unto Full Stature," 161–168. See *Come, Let Us Worship,* 74–86; and National Liturgical Week 1948, 139–151.
  "Movement in Germany," 471–474. See *Caecilia* 77 (March 1950): 111–112.

Vol. 24 (1949–1950)
  "Candlemas," 228–229

Vol. 25 (1950–1951)
  "For the Tre Ore or a Holy Hour," 173–176
  "Easter-eve Celebration," 278–283
  "Abbot Alcuin Deutsch," 290–294. See *Commonweal* 54 (July 13, 1951): 335.

Vol. 26 (1951–1952)
  "What Is a Bishop?" 238–247. See *Come, Let Us Worship,* 143–155; and National Liturgical Week 1951, 32–43.
  "To Our Readers," 497

Vol. 27 (1952–1953)
"Objections to the Easter Vigil," 204–205
"Some Reflections on the Eucharistic Fast," 205–208
"Easter Vigil Questionnaire," 416–420
"Fast Ought Not Prevent Communion," 516–523. See *Come, Let Us Worship*, 155–163; and National Liturgical Week 1953, 72–79.

Vol. 28 (1953–1954)
"Louvain and Versailles," 537–545. Reprinted: "Louvain-Versailles," *Heiliger-Dienst* 8 (1954) 129–132.

Vol. 29 (1954–1955)
"Father Jungmann, Associate Editor," 475

Vol. 30 (1956)
"A Report on Holy Week," 399–406
"A Good Mass Program," 656–657

Vol. 31 (1957)
"Assisi in Retrospect," 48–51
"The New Regulations Governing Holy Week," 296–299
"Two Approaches to Understanding the Sacraments," 504–520. See *Come, Let Us Worship*, 23–40; *Readings in Sacramental Theology*, 1–17; and North American Liturgical Week 1957, 12–27.
"Diocesan Commission at Work," 299–302

Vol. 32 (1958)
"Una Cum Papa Nostro," 638–639

Vol. 33 (1959)
"Liturgical Week, 1959," 442
"Mass Commentary," 56–66
"Mass Commentary," 111–115
"Mass Commentary," 185–188
"A Papal Letter," 650–653

Vol. 34 (1960)
"Dom Ermin Vitry, R.I.P.," 470–471
"Mary, Model of Our Worship," 579–585. See *Come, Let Us Worship*, 135–143; North American Liturgical Week 1960, 61–66; and *Our Lady's Digest* 15 (February 1961): 238–245.
"Welcome, Fr. Barnabas," 604–606

Vol. 35 (1961)
"Liturgical Week, 1961," 456–457
"Looking Ahead," 2–3

Vol. 36 (1962)
"Looking Ahead," 2–3

"The New Bible Magazine," 484–485

"Looking Ahead," 624–625

Vol. 37 (1963)

"Sacramental Life—The Mystery Shared," 589–598. See North American Liturgical Week 1963, 35–43.

Vol. 38 (1964)

"Monsignor Martin B. Hellriegel," 497–498

Vol. 39 (1965)

"The Eucharist Makes the People of God," 458–468. See North American Liturgical Week 1965, 102–113.

Vol. 40 (1966)

"Altar and Tabernacle," 490–509; reprinted: "Autel et tabernacle," Secretariat National de Pastorale Liturgique, Montreal (February 1967)

"The Constitution on the Sacred Liturgy in Retrospect," 408–423. See *Vatican II: An Interfaith Appraisal,* 17–40.

Vol. 41 (1967)

"The Reform of Catholic Liturgy: Are We Too Late?" 142–151. See *Theology of Renewal 2,* 88–99.

Vol. 45 (1971)

"In Memoriam: Frs. Carroll and Damasus Winzen," 441–442

"In Memoriam: Msgr. William Busch," 179–180

"Is There a Distinct American Contribution to the Liturgical Renewal?" 578–587. See *Proceedings of the 26th Annual Convention of the Catholic Theological Society of America,* 26:200-210.

Vol. 51 (1977)

"Response to the Presentation of the Berakah Award: Some Memories," 361–372. See *A Time for Worship,* 173–187.

In addition, Godfrey Diekmann wrote all the editorial material in *Orate Fratres/Worship* from 1938 to 1962 and much of 1937 to 1938.

ARTICLES IN VARIOUS PERIODICALS

"Baptism: Its Significance for Teacher and Pupil: Summary." *Liturgical Arts* 8 (January 1940): 35–36.

"Movement in Germany." *Caecilia* 77 (March 1950): 111–112. See *Orate Fratres* 23 (September 1949): 471–474.

"Some Outstanding Catholic Books." *Action* 4 (February 1951): 23–24.

"Abbot Alcuin Deutsch, O.S.B." *Commonweal* 54 (July 13, 1951): 335. See *Orate Fratres* 25 (June 1951): 290–294.

"Witness to the Truth." *Catholic School Educator* 21 (January 1952): 3–5.

"Why We Fast Before Communion." *Catholic Digest* 18 (December 1953): 114–115.

"Journalist's Responsibility to the Word." *The Catholic School Editor* 25 (January 1956): 2–5.

"Liturgy of Holy Week: Palm Sunday, Holy Thursday, Good Friday, Easter Vigil, and Easter Mass." *Jubilee* 3 (April 1956): 2–24.

"Liturgy for the Laity." *St. Joseph Magazine* 60 (November 1959): 12–16.

"Mary Our Model of Worship." *Our Lady's Digest* 15 (February 1961): 238–245. See *Come, Let Us Worship,* 135–143; North American Liturgical Week 1960, 61–66; and *Worship* 34 (October 1960): 579–586.

"The Mass and Its Meaning in the Daily Lives of Catholics." *New City* 1 (December 15, 1962): 8–9.

"Can We Neglect the Redemptive Character of Our Lord's Death and Resurrection?" *Catholic Messenger* 80 (September 13, 1962): 5–6.

"The Unity of the Mass." *Motive* 23 (February 1963) 2–6.

"The Theology of Worship." *Theology Digest* 10 (September 1962): 131–134.

"Christians in Conversation." *Catholic Digest* 27 (November 1962): 36–44.

"Vernacular Is Keystone: Excerpts." *Catholic Messenger* 81 (August 29, 1963): 1.

"Today and Tomorrow: Conversation at the Council." Interview by Vincent Yzermans. *American Benedictine Review* 15 (September 1964): 341–351.

"Council Conversation." Interview by Vincent Yzermans. *Ave Maria* 100 (October 3, 1964): 10–11.

"The Parish Dinosaur." Summary of a conversation with Godfrey Diekmann by Robert Hoyt. *Way* (U.S.) 20 (January–February 1964): 50–52.

"The Eucharist as Center." *Sister Formation Bulletin* 11 (Spring 1965): 2–8.

"Liturgical Renewal and the Student Mass." *National Catholic Education Association Bulletin* 62 (August 1965): 290–300.

"The Church of the Future: An Interview with Godfrey Diekmann." By Dennis Howard. *U.S. Catholic* 31 (August 1965): 6–16.

"Some Thoughts on the Relevance of Church Architecture." *Journal of the American Society for Christian Architecture* 8 (February 1967) 24–39.

"Vatican II and the Catholic Layman." *The Procopian: A Quarterly* 10 (July 1966): 1, 2, 15.

"De lectionibus in Missa." *Notitiae* 1 (November 1965): 333–337. See *Orien-*

tations Pastorales 18 (1966): 188–190; *Ora et Labora* 13 (1966): 298–302; *Documents Catholiques* 48 (1966): 797–800.

"Inter-Communion: Its Ecumenical Dimensions and Problems." *IDO-C (Information Documentation on the Conciliar Church)* 68-38 (September 22, 1968): 1–11. See *Christian Unity 68*, 34–48.

"Inter-Communion—Its Ecumenical Dimensions and Problems." In *Christian Unity 68*. The Fifth National Workshop for Christian Unity, June 16–20, 1968, Detroit. See *IDO-C* 68-38: 1–11.

"H. A. Reinhold 1897–1968: in Memoriam." *Jubilee* 15 (March 1968): 30–32.

"The Liturgy and Personal Piety." *The Priest* 25 (January 1969): 25–35. See *Personal Prayer and the Liturgy*, 20–30.

"Theological Reorientations in the Liturgical Constitution." *Liturgy* 18 (January 1973): 18–21.

"Sermon for the Mass Celebrating the Centennial of the Parish of St. John the Baptist, Collegeville." Brochure for the celebration, 1975. 1–10.

"The Laying on of Hands." *Liturgy* 21 (January 1976): 22–27. See *Proceedings of the 29th Annual Convention of the Catholic Theological Society of America*, 1974. 29:339–351.

"The Church as a Community of Prayer." *Pastoral Music* 3 (June–July 1979): 16–21. See *Pastoral Music in Practice*, 43–54.

"A Confession of Christ the King." *Occasional Papers* 4 (January 1979). Institute for Ecumenical and Cultural Research, Collegeville, Minn.

"Perspectives on American Liturgical Renewal." *Aids in Ministry* 7 (Fall 1979): 4–9.

"The Laying On of Hands in Healing." *Liturgy* 25 (March–April 1980): 7–10. See *Payton Lectures* #1 (tape) 1979.

"Pioneer Liturgist Dies." (Tribute to Martin B. Hellriegel) *The National Catholic Reporter* 17 (May 8, 1981): 15.

"Saint John's and the Ecumenical Movement 1962." *Scriptorium* 24 (1985): 107–119.

ENCYCLOPAEDIA BRITANNICA

"Abbot"; "Acolyte"; "All Souls' Day"; "Angels"; "Archdeacon"; "Ascension, Feast of"; "Censer"; "Chrism"; "Confession"; "Crosier."

TAPES

"Study the Liturgy." *The Living Voices of Renewal.* Chicago: Argus Communications, 1971.

"A Theological History of Penance." Kansas City: National Catholic Reporter Publishing Co., 1975.

"The Abba Prayer of Jesus." Lecture presented at University of San Francisco. Kansas City: National Catholic Reporter Publishing Co., 1976.

"Reconciliation Through the Prayer of the Community." Lecture presented at the Baltimore Liturgical Congress. Severna Park, Md.: Time Consultants, 1975.

"The Influence of the *Lectio Divina* on Prayer." Lecture presented at the Baltimore Liturgical Congress. Severna Park, Md.: Time Consultants, 1976.

"The Meaning of Worship." Lecture presented at the Baltimore Liturgical Congress. Severna Park, Md.: Time Consultants, 1977.

"Let Us Pray, Let Us Kneel, Let Us Stand." Lecture presented at the Spiritual Institute meeting, March 3, 1978, St. John's University, Collegeville, Minn.

"To Worship in Spirit and Truth." 6 cassette tapes. Collegeville, Minn.: St. John's University, 1978.

"Posture and Gesture." Payton Lecture 1, Ministers' Week, Southern Methodist University. Dallas: Perkins Audio-Visual Service, 1979. See *Liturgy* 25 (March–April 1980): 7–10.

"Our Father." Payton Lecture 2, Ministers' Week, Southern Methodist University. Dallas: Perkins Audio-Visual Service, 1979.

"Vatican II: Hopes Dashed or Fulfilled." Lecture presented to Church Goods Dealers Convention, Collegeville, Minn., 1979.

"The Place of the Eucharist in Western Monasticism." Lecture presented at the Benedictine Congress. Collegeville, Minn.: The Liturgical Press, 1980.

"Sunday Morning: Retrospect and Prospect." *Sunday Morning: A Time for Worship.* Notre Dame Liturgical Institute, June 15, 1981. Kansas City: National Catholic Reporter Publishing Co. See *Sunday Morning: A Time for Worship*, 173–187.

"An Overview of Twenty Years of Liturgical Renewal. Have the Hopes Been Fulfilled?" Opening lecture at Notre Dame Liturgical Institute, June 13, 1983. Notre Dame: Notre Dame Liturgical Institute.

RADIO TALKS

"O Come, O Come, Emmanuel." Radio talk for "Church of the Air" (December 2, 1956).

"Holy Week and After." Four radio talks on ABC's "Christian in Action" (April 1957), Washington, sponsored by the National Council of Catholic Men, 1957.

BOOK REVIEWS

Callan, Charles J., and McHugh, John. *The Catholic Sunday Missal.* In *Orate Fratres* 9 (March 1935): 235–236.

Kavanagh, William. *Lay Participation in Christ's Priesthood.* In *Orate Fratres* 10 (December 1935): 94–96.

Vonier, Anscar. *The Spirit and the Bride.* In *Orate Fratres* 10 (May 1936): 333–335.

Puetter, William. *The Christian Life Calendar.* Monks of St. John's Abbey. *The Christ-Life Liturgical Calendar.* In *Orate Fratres* 11 (November 1936): 44–45.

Gordon, W. *The Liturgy and Its Meaning.* In *Orate Fratres* 11 (December 1936): 94–95.

Abbaye du Mont-César, Belgium. *La Vie Eucharistique de L'Eglise.* In *Orate Fratres* 11 (December 1936): 95.

Nuns of St. Hildegard's Abbey, Eibingen. *Die Väterlesungen des Breviers.* In *Orate Fratres* 11 (December 1936): 96.

Jungmann, Josef A. *Die Frohbotschaft und Unsere Glaubensverkündigung.* In *Orate Fratres* 11 (January 1937): 142–144.

Parsch, Pius. *The Liturgy of the Mass.* In *Orate Fratres* 11 (March 1937): 235–236.

The Roman Breviary. An English Version. In *Orate Fratres* 11 (March 1937): 237–238.

Casel, Odo, ed. *Jahrbuch für Liturgiewissenschaft.* In *Orate Fratres* 11 (May 1937): 333–334.

Löhr, Emiliana. *The Year of Our Lord.* In *Orate Fratres* 11 (May 1937): 335–336.

Michel, Virgil. *Christian Social Reconstruction.* In *Orate Fratres* 11 (June 1937): 377–378.

Willging, Eugene. *The Index to American Catholic Pamphlets.* In *Orate Fratres* 11 (June 1937): 379.

Gruden, John. *The Mystical Christ.* In *Orate Fratres* 11 (June 1937): 380–383.

Ambruzzi, Aloysius. *The Newman Book of Religion.* In *Orate Fratres* 11 (June 1937): 383.

Robertson, Alec. *The Interpretation of Plainchant.* In *Orate Fratres* 11 (October 1937): 525–526.

Deutsch, Alcuin. *Manual for Oblates of St. Benedict.* In *Orate Fratres* 12 (November 1937): 44–45.

Lefebvre, Gaspar. *Catholic Liturgy.* In *Orate Fratres* 12 (November 1937): 45.

Cabrol, Fernand. *The Holy Sacrifice.* In *Orate Fratres* 12 (November 1937): 46.

De Angelis, Michael. *The Correct Pronunciation of Latin According to Roman Usage.* In *Orate Fratres* 12 (May 1938): 333.

Gunn, William W. *A Double-Faced 12 Inch Recording of the Latin Versicles and Responses of the Mass for Altar Boys According to the Traditional Roman Pronunciation.* In *Orate Fratres* 12 (May 1938): 333.

Quasten, Johann. *Monumenta Eucharistica et Liturgica Vetustissima.* In *Orate Fratres* 12 (June 1938): 380.

Vonier, Anscar. *The People of God.* In *Orate Fratres* 12 (June 1938): 380–381.

Casel, Odo. *Jahrbuch für Liturgiewissenschaft. Vol. XIV.* In *Orate Fratres* 12 (June 1938): 381–382.

Lortz, Joseph. *History of the Church.* In *Orate Fratres* 12 (June 1938): 382–383.

Cicognani, Amleto Giovanni. *Addresses and Sermons.* In *Orate Fratres* 12 (July 1938): 428.

Parsch, Pius. *Jahr des Heiles. Klosterneuburger Liturgiekalender.* In *Orate Fratres* 12 (July 1938): 431.

Martindale, C. C. *The Prayers of the Missal. II: The Offertory Prayers and the Post Communions.* In *Orate Fratres* 12 (July 1938): 432.

Attwater, Donald. *The Eastern Branches of the Catholic Church.* In *Orate Fratres* 12 (September 1938): 475.

Ettensperger, Hariolf. *Das Ministrantenbuch.* In *Orate Fratres* 12 (September 1938): 478–479.

Paredi, Angelo. *Prefazi Ambrosiani.* In *Orate Fratres* 12 (September 1938): 479.

St. Thomas, Mary. *Sayings of Dom Marmion.* In *Orate Fratres* 12 (September 1938): 479.

Lefebvre, Gaspar. *How to Understand the Mass.* In *Orate Fratres* 13 (November 1938): 45–46.

Dix, Gregory. *The Treatise on the Apostolic Tradition of St. Hippolytus of Rome.* In *Orate Fratres* 13 (December 1938): 94–95.

Stedman, Joseph F. *My Sunday Missal.* In *Orate Fratres* 13 (February 1939): 186-187.

Franke, Hermann. *Lent and Easter: The Church's Spring.* In *Orate Fratres* 13 (March 1939): 236.

Leen, Edward. *The True Vine and Its Branches.* In *Orate Fratres* 13 (May 1939): 335-336.

Bussard, Paul. *The Sacrifice.* In *Orate Fratres* 13 (June 1939): 383-384.

Saint Augustine. *The Happy Life.* In *Orate Fratres* 13 (July 1939): 427-428.

Hymns for Children. In *Orate Fratres* 13 (July 1939): 428.

Webb, Geoffrey. *The Liturgical Altar.* In *Orate Fratres* 13 (September 1939): 479.

Adam, A. *Der Primat der Liebe.* In *Orate Fratres* 13 (September 1939): 479-480.

Maraschi, Vincenzo. *Le Particolarita del Rito Ambrosiano.* In *Orate Fratres* 13 (September 1939): 480.

Deus Meus et Omnia. St. Bonaventure Seminary Year Book, Vol. 22: *Patristic Catechesis*; Vol. 23: *Fathers of the Church in the Breviary.* In *Orate Fratres* 13 (October 1939): 523.

The White List of the Society of St. Gregory of America. In *Orate Fratres* 13 (October 1939): 526-527.

Cabrol, Fernand. *The Year's Liturgy.* In *Orate Fratres* 13 (October 1939): 527.

Calkins, Hugh. *It's Your Mass Too.* In *Orate Fratres* 13 (October 1939): 574.

Hausmann, Bernard A. *Let Us Pray for Our Dead.* In *Orate Fratres* 14 (January 1940): 140.

Noppel, Constantine. *The Shepherd of Souls.* In *Orate Fratres* 14 (January 1940): 141-42.

Furfey, Paul Hanly. *This Way to Heaven.* In *Orate Fratres* 14 (January 1940): 142-143.

Russell, William H. *What Catholics Do at Mass.* In *Orate Fratres* 14 (January 1940): 143.

Underhill, Evelyn. *Eucharistic Prayers from the Ancient Liturgies.* In *Orate Fratres* 14 (March 1940): 236-237.

St. Michael's Guild. *The Eastern Churches.* In *Orate Fratres* 14 (April 1940): 285.

Ellard, Gerald. *Men at Work and Worship.* In *Orate Fratres* 14 (July 1940): 431-432.

Graham, E. P. *The Saints in the Canon of the Mass.* In *Orate Fratres* 14 (September 1940): 480.

Marmion, Columba. *Words of Life on the Margin of the Missal.* In *Orate Fratres* 14 (September 1940): 480.

Stedman, Joseph F. *My Sunday Missal.* In *Orate Fratres* 15 (December 1940): 47–48.

Bell, Bernard Iddings. *Religion for Living.* In *Orate Fratres* 15 (December 1940): 48.

Vonier, Anscar. *Sketches and Studies in Theology.* In *Orate Fratres* 15 (December 1940): 92–93.

Beebe, Catherine. *We Know the Mass.* In *Orate Fratres* 15 (December 1940): 94.

De la Taille, Maurice. *The Mystery of Faith.* In *Orate Fratres* 15 (January 1941): 140–141.

Frank, Henry. *Holy Hour.* In *Orate Fratres* 15 (February 1941): 188–189.

Frank, Henry. *The Fourteen Stations of the Cross.* In *Orate Fratres* 15 (February 1941): 188–189.

Hintgen, Victor J. *What the Mass Means.* In *Orate Fratres* 15 (February 1941): 191.

Stedman, Joseph F. *My Lenten Missal.* In *Orate Fratres* 15 (March 1941): 238–239.

National Catholic Library Association. *A Reading List for Catholics.* In *Orate Fratres* 15 (March 1941): 239–240.

McCloud, Henry J. *The Sacramentals of the Catholic Church.* In *Orate Fratres* 15 (July 1941): 432.

The Imitation of Christ. In *Orate Fratres* 15 (October 1941): 526–527.

Lindemann, Herbert. *The Psalter.* In *Orate Fratres* 16 (November 1941): 46–47.

Puetter, William H. *The Christian Life Calendar.* In *Orate Fratres* 16 (December 1941): 95.

Frank, Henry. *A Guide for Confession.* In *Orate Fratres* 16 (December 1941): 96.

Harney, Martin P. *The Jesuits in History.* In *Orate Fratres* 16 (March 1942): 239.

Bussard, Paul. *The Meaning of the Mass.* In *Orate Fratres* 16 (May 1942): 335–336.

National Liturgical Week 1941. In *Orate Fratres* 16 (May 1942): 336.

Von Hildebrand, Dietrich. *Marriage.* In *Orate Fratres* 16 (June 1942): 382.

Larsson, Raymond E. *Saints at Prayer.* In *Orate Fratres* 16 (June 1942): 382–383.

Watkin, E. I. *The Praise of Glory.* In *Orate Fratres* 16 (June 1942): 383–384.

Hart, Elizabeth. *Mary of the Magnificat.* In *Orate Fratres* 16 (November 1942): 575–576.

Rossini, Carlo. *The Priest's Chants and Recitatives at the Altar.* In *Orate Fratres* 16 (November 1942): 576.

Stedman, Joseph F. *My Sunday Missal.* In *Orate Fratres* 17 (November 1942): 46.

St. Paul, Mother. *Spiritual Readings.* In *Orate Fratres* 17 (November 1942): 47–48.

Wilmot, Christopher J. *The Priest's Prayer Book.* In *Orate Fratres* 17 (December 1942): 95–96.

Hurrell, Grace. *The Church's Play.* In *Orate Fratres* 17 (January 1943): 141.

Hugo, John. *In the Vineyard.* In *Orate Fratres* 17 (January 1943): 142.

Sherman, James Edward. *The Nature of Martyrdom.* In *Orate Fratres* 17 (January 1943): 144.

Toth, Tihamer. *The Our Father.* In *Orate Fratres* 17 (February 1943): 190.

Grigassy, Julius. *The Epistles and Gospels.* In *Orate Fratres* 17 (February 1943): 190–191.

The National Catholic Almanac 1943. In *Orate Fratres* 17 (March 1943): 240.

Anderl, Stephen, and M. Ruth. *The Technique of the Catholic Action Cell Meeting.* In *Orate Fratres* 17 (April 1943): 288.

Moore, Verner. *Prayer.* In *Orate Fratres* 17 (May 1943): 334–335.

Byrnes, Aquinas. *Hymns of the Dominican Missal and Breviary.* In *Orate Fratres* 17 (May 1943): 336.

Lowrie, Walter. *The Lord's Supper and the Liturgy.* In *Orate Fratres* 17 (August 1943): 432.

Kelly, Bernard J. *The Sacraments of Daily Life.* In *Orate Fratres* 18 (November 1943): 43.

Morrison, Bakewell. *In Touch with God.* In *Orate Fratres* 18 (November 1943): 44.

Pax Aeterna. In *Orate Fratres* 18 (January 1944): 144.

Blunt, Hugh Francis. *Life with the Holy Ghost.* In *Orate Fratres* 18 (February 1944): 191.

Jarrett, Bede. *The Abiding Presence of the Holy Ghost.* In *Orate Fratres* 18 (February 1944): 191.

Broderick, Robert C. *Concise Catholic Dictionary.* In *Orate Fratres* 18 (March 1944): 240.

National Liturgical Week 1943. In *Orate Fratres* 18 (May 1944): 333.

Winzen, Damasus. *Symbols of Christ.* In *Orate Fratres* 18 (October 1944): 526-527.

Morison, Stanley. *English Prayer Books.* In *Orate Fratres* 18 (October 1944): 527-528.

Cirrincione, Joseph A. *Church Year Projects.* In *Orate Fratres* 18 (October 1944): 528-529.

The Order for the Dedication or Consecration of a Church. The Consecration of a Bishop. Order for the Laying of the Corner-Stone of a New Church. The Blessing of a Bell. In *Orate Fratres* 18 (November 1944): 576.

Reinhold, H. A. *The Soul Afire.* In *Orate Fratres* 19 (March 1945): 237-239.

Hall, A. W. *The Layman's Ritual.* In *Orate Fratres* 19 (March 1945): 239.

Beck, Berenice. *The Nurse, Handmaid of the Divine Physician.* In *Orate Fratres* 19 (May 1945): 335.

Monro, Margaret T. *Enjoying the New Testament.* In *Orate Fratres* 19 (May 1945): 335-336.

Brown, Stephen J., and Thomas McDermott. *A Survey of Catholic Literature.* In *Orate Fratres* 19 (May 1945): 336.

Green, Andrew. *A Retreat for Religious.* In *Orate Fratres* 19 (June 1945): 384.

The Psalms. In *Orate Fratres* 19 (October 1945): 528.

Bourke, Vernon J. *Augustine's Quest for Wisdom.* In *Orate Fratres* 19 (November 1945): 575-576.

Maynard, Theodore. *Pillars of the Church.* In *Orate Fratres* 19 (November 1945): 576.

Attwater, Donald. *Modern Christian Revolutionaries.* In *Orate Fratres* 21 (April 1947): 285-287.

Sheed, F. J. *Theology and Sanity.* In *Orate Fratres* 21 (May 1947): 332-334.

Ryan, Mary. *Our Lady's Hours.* In *Orate Fratres* 21 (June 1947): 382.

The White List of the Society of St. Gregory of America. In *Orate Fratres* 21 (June 1947): 382-383.

Frey, Joseph. *My Daily Psalm Book.* In *Orate Fratres* 22 (December 1947): 95.

Schlarman, J. H. *With the Blessing of the Church.* In *Orate Fratres* 22 (December 1947): 96.

Murray, Jane Marie, O.P. *Teacher's Manual for Living in Christ.* In *Orate Fratres* 22 (April 1948): 286-287.

Windeatt, Mary Fabyan. *David and His Songs.* In *Orate Fratres* 22 (May 1948): 336.

Attwater, Donald. *The Christian Churches of the East.* In *Orate Fratres* 22 (June 1948): 383-384.

Hoehn, Matthew. *Catholic Authors.* In *Orate Fratres* 22 (October 1948): 574-575.

Strittmatter, Blase. *Sacred Latin Hymns.* In *Orate Fratres* 23 (November 1948): 47-48.

Drinkwater, F. H. *Readings and Addresses.* In *Orate Fratres* 23 (December 1948): 96.

Achievement of a Century. In *Orate Fratres* 23 (February 1949): 186.

Burton, Katherine. *The Next Thing.* In *Orate Fratres* 23 (June 1949): 384.

Attwater, Donald. *A Catholic Dictionary.* In *Orate Fratres* 23 (September 1949): 480.

Martyrologium Romanum. In *Orate Fratres* 23 (September 1949): 480.

The Missal. In Latin and English. Being the Text of the *Missale Romanum.* In *Orate Fratres* 24 (December 1949): 39-41.

Berger, Florence. *Cooking for Christ.* In *Orate Fratres* 24 (January 1950): 91-92.

Lebbe, Bede. *The Mass: A Historical Commentary.* In *Orate Fratres* 24 (March 1950): 187.

Thurston, Herbert. *The Holy Year of Jubilee.* In *Orate Fratres* 24 (March 1950): 189.

De Sales, St. Francis. *Introduction to the Devout Life.* Newly Translated and Edited by John K. Ryan. In *Orate Fratres* 24 (March 1950): 190-191.

Daniélou, Jean. *The Salvation of Nations.* In *Orate Fratres* 24 (April 1950): 238-239.

Wilmot, Christopher. *The Priest's Prayer Book.* In *Orate Fratres* 24 (May 1950): 288.

Burton, Katherine. *The Great Mantle: The Life of Pope Pius X.* In *Orate Fratres* 24 (June 1950): 336.

Merton, Thomas. *What Are These Wounds?* In *Orate Fratres* 24 (July 1950): 382-383.

The Spirit of Unity. Daily lectures given at Blackfriars, Oxford, during the Church Unity Octave. In *Orate Fratres* 24 (August 1950): 427-429.

The Roman Ritual. In *Orate Fratres* 24 (August 1950): 430.

King, Archdale. *The Rites of Eastern Christendom*. In *Orate Fratres* 24 (September 1950): 474.

De Coninck, L. *Problèmes de l'adaptation en apostolat*. In *Orate Fratres* 24 (September 1950): 476.

The Holy Sacrifice of the Mass. Gateway to the Faith. Two films. In *Orate Fratres* 24 (September 1950): 476–479.

Woodgate, M. V. *Charles de Condren*. In *Orate Fratres* 24 (September 1950): 479.

Ansdrucksformen der lateinischen Liturgiesprache bis ins Elfte Jahrhundert. In *Orate Fratres* 24 (November 1950): 575–576.

Brodrick, James. *St. Peter Canisius*. In *Orate Fratres* 25 (March 1951): 189.

Kempf, Placidus. *The Mass Year*. In *Orate Fratres* 25 (March 1951) 191. Walker, William. *Lenten Vignettes from the Masses of Lent*. In *Orate Fratres* 25 (March 1951) 191–192. Monks of St. Meinrad's Abbey. *Prayers for Lent from the Psalms*. In *Orate Fratres* 25 (March 1951) 192. Mary John Berchmans, B.V.M. *The Three Hours of Good Friday*. In *Orate Fratres* 25 (March 1951) 192.

Graef, Hilda. *The Case of Theresa Neumann*. In *Orate Fratres* 25 (June 1951) 329–330. Siwek, Paul. *Une stigmatisee de nos jours*. In *Orate Fratres* 25 (June 1951) 330. Martindale, C. C. *The Meaning of Fatima*. In *Orate Fratres* 25 (June 1951) 330. Petitot, Henri. *The True Story of Saint Bernadette*. In *Orate Fratres* 25 (June 1951) 330–331.

Heckenlively, Lura. *The Fundamentals of Gregorian Chant*. In *Orate Fratres* 25 (June 1951): 331.

The Confessions of Saint Augustine. Books 1–9. In *Orate Fratres* 25 (June 1951): 332.

Van Straelen, H. *Through Eastern Eyes*. In *Orate Fratres* 25 (June 1951): 334–335.

Mersch, Emile. *The Theology of the Mystical Body*. In *Worship* 26 (December 1951): 46–47.

Pieper, Josef, and Heinz Raskop. *What Catholics Believe*. In *Worship* 26 (January 1952): 108–109.

Hynek, R. W. *The True Likeness*. In *Worship* 26 (January 1952): 109–110.

Thompson, T. *St. Ambrose "On the Sacraments" and "On the Mysteries."* In *Worship* 26 (March 1952): 219–220.

Doncoeur, Paul. *La naissance, le mariage, la mort*. In *Worship* 26 (November 1952): 590–591.

Ryelandt, I. *Mass and the Interior Life*. In *Worship* 27 (December 1952): 60–61.

Van der Meer de Walcheren, Peter. *The White Fathers.* In *Worship* 27 (December 1952): 61–62. *The Carthusian Foundation in America.* In *Worship* 27 (December 1952): 61–62. *The Carthusians.* In *Worship* 27 (December 1952): 61–62.

The Monastic Diurnal Noted: Music of Vespers, the Little Hours and Lauds of Greater Feasts. In *Worship* 27 (July 1953): 401–402. *Antiphons of the Blessed Virgin Mary.* In *Worship* 27 (July 1953): 401–402.

Bauer, Benedict. *The Light of the World.* In *Worship* 27 (August 1953): 433–434.

Kempis, Thomas à. *The Imitation of Christ.* In *Worship* 27 (August 1953): 436.

McSorley, Joseph. *Father Hecker and His Friends.* In *Worship* 27 (September 1953): 481–482.

Quasten, Johannes. *Patrology.* In *Worship* 27 (November 1953): 574.

Pezeril, Daniel. *Rue Notre Dame.* In *Worship* 27 (November 1953): 578.

Barbet, Pierre. *A Doctor at Calvary.* In *Worship* 28 (April 1954): 266–267.

Guilday, Peter. *The Life and Times of John Carroll.* In *Worship* 28 (October 1954): 501.

Ehrhardt, Arnold. *The Apostolic Succession in the First Two Centuries of the Church.* In *The Catholic Historical Review* 40 (November 1954): 287–288.

Kleist, James A., and Joseph L. Lilly. *The New Testament.* In *Worship* 29 (December 1954): 60–61.

Henry, A. M. *Introduction to Theology.* In *Worship* 29 (March 1955): 237–238.

The Gregorian Institute of America. *Liber Brevior.* In *Worship* 29 (September 1955): 500.

Palmer, Paul F. *Sources of Christian Theology.* In *Worship* 29 (November 1955): 618–620.

Ladner, Gerhart B. *The Idea of Reform.* In *The Catholic Historical Review* 46 (October 1960): 329–331.

Oesterreicher, John M. *The Bridge: A Yearbook of Judaeo-Christian Studies.* Vol. 1. In *Worship* 30 (February 1956): 230–231.

Oesterreicher, John M. *The Bridge: A Yearbook of Judaeo-Christian Studies.* Vol. 2. In *Worship* 31 (December 1956): 59–60.

Henry, A. M. *Man and His Happiness.* Theology Library, Vol. 3.

Putz, Louis J. *The Virtues and States of Life.* Theology Library, Vol. 4. In *Worship* 31 (July–August 1957): 423–426.

Deferrari, Roy J. *Denzinger's Sources of Catholic Dogma.* In *Worship* 31 (September 1957): 499–500.

Bauer, Benedict. *Saints of the Missal.* In *Worship* 32 (July–August 1958): 442–443.

Parsch, Pius. *The Liturgy of the Mass.* In *Worship* 32 (July–August): 443.

Hitchcock, James. *The Recovery of the Sacred.* In *The Critic* 168 (October–December 1974): 77–81.

Reinhold, Hans Anscar. *H.A.R.: The Autobiography of Father Reinhold.* NC News Service (September 30, 1977).

ARTICLES/TRIBUTES TO GODFREY DIEKMANN

McManus, Frederick R., ed. *The Revival of the Liturgy.* New York: Herder and Herder, 1963. [To Godfrey Diekmann in Gratitude for Twenty-five Years of *Worship*].

Stevick, D. "Presentation of the Berakah Award." *Worship* 51 (July 1977): 361–372.

Tegels, A. "Fifty Years of *Worship.*" *Worship* 50 (July 1977): 466–471.

INDEX

Numbers in italics refer to photographs.

Adam, Karl 51, 56, *57*-59, 64, 81, 116, 153
Addams, Jane 104
Agagianian, Cardinal Gregorio P. 222
Agustoni, Msgr. Gilberto 168
Agustoni, Luigi 168
Ahern, Barnabas M., C.P. *120*-121, 239, 240
Aids in Ministry 147
Albers, Joseph 174
Altar 115, 172
  facing the congregation 236
  tabernacle 172
Altar and Home 136
Alter, Archbishop Karl 131, 187, 194-195
Ambrose, St. 151
  De Sacramentis 151
Amen 140
America 144, 219, 255
American Ecclesiastical Review 199
American Participation in the Second Vatican Council 276
Anderson, Bernhard W. 312
Anderson, Floyd 251
Anger, Joseph 19
  The Doctrine of the Mystical Body According to the Principles of St. Thomas 19
Anne Catherine, C.S.J. 145
Anselm, St. 54
  Proslogion 54
Anti-Semitism 113
Antonelli, Ferdinando, O.F.M. 167-168, 189, 202-205, 207, 219, 258
Antonianum 88
Apologetics 87

Architecture 115, 169-171, 173
Aristides 93
Assisi Congress xx, 161-*163*, 165-167, 172, 181, 233
Assisi Papers, The 181, 215
Association of Theological Schools xvi
Attwater, Donald 131, 134, 138-139, 144
Augustine, St., Bishop of Hippo 39, 52, 72, 89-90, 164, 303

Bahamas 72
Bak, Bruno 172
Ball Club, Minnesota 141-142
Baptism 56-57, 63, 99-100, 126, 150, 167-168, 171-172, 215, 268, 283-284, 303
  baptistry 172, 174
  fonts 150
  immersion 150
  rite 270
Barrett, Noel Hackmann 84
  Martin B. Hellriegel: Pastoral Liturgist 84
Barry, Colman, O.S.B. 182
Bartholome, Bishop Peter 135, 208, 211, 227
Basilica of St. John Lateran 40
Basilica of St. Paul Outside the Walls 78
Basilica of St. Peter 152, 268
Baum, Gregory 249, 315
Baum, Msgr. William 261
Baumstark, Anton 58-59
Bea, Cardinal Augustin, S.J. 116, 224
Beauduin, Lambert, O.S.B. 18, 56, 116, 148
Bechtold, LeMay xviii
Beck, Msgr. Henry C. *283*

Being at Ease with the Liber Usualis 130
Bekkers, Bishop Willem M. 231
Belgium 68, 168–169
Belloc, Hilaire 263, 274
Bellow, Saul 305
Benedict, St. 307
  fourteen hundredth anniversary 44
  The Rule of St. Benedict 318
  Solemnity of 44
  tomb 43, 46
Benedictine Liturgical Conference
  123–*125,* 132–133, 146
  laity 132
  See also Liturgical Conference.
Benedictines 15, 90, 123, 132–134,
  141, 235, 301, 308
  American 123–124
  Bahamas 72
  China 72–73
  Liturgical Week 132, 133–134
  spirituality 90, 301
Bennett, Clifford 136
Benoit, Pierre, O.P. *287*
Berakah Award 281
Berger, Dr. and Mrs. Alfred 131
Bethlehem 72
Bethune, Ade xviii, 131
Bible 10, 89, 99, 113, 115, 119, 158,
  178–179, 215, 253–254, 275,
  290, 308
  and the *Didache* 93
  biblical movement 123
  Christian Scriptures (N.T.) 312
  Hebrew Scriptures (O.T.) 93, 119,
  159
  Lectionary 159
  Revised Standard Version 261
Bible Today, The 121
Bilheimer, Robert xviii
Bishop, Edmund
  Liturgica Historica 59
Bishops 119, 121, 152, 177–178,
  183–184, 186, 190, 195,
  199–200, 202–206, 210,
  216–217, 224–227, 230, 238,
  240, 245, 254, 256–259, 266,
  269, 278–279, 284, 291, 299
  American 135, 169, 199–200, 206,
  238, 240–241, 256–259, 299
  Canadian 299
  collegiality 210, 257, 291
  conferences 186, 195, 216, 230,
  233–234, 241, 245, 254, 269
  Dutch 152
  French 152, 195, 202, 203, 224, 257

  German 195, 202–203
  Latin American 240
  missionary 183
  power 193
  Protestant observers 227
  Scottish 261
  Spanish 230, 257
  Swiss 152
  West African 224
Bishops' Committee on the Liturgical
  Apostolate. *See* Bishops' Com-
  mittee on the Liturgy.
Bishops' Committee on the Liturgy
  177–178
Black Like Me 278
Blackfriars 149, 170, 174
Blanchard, Paul 224
Bloy, Léon 55
Bonet, Msgr. Emmanuel 205
Borella, Msgr. Pietro 189
Bosler, Raymond *283*
Boston 130, 182
Boston College xix, 181
  Social Worship School 139
Botte, Bernard, O.S.B. 122, 160, 236
Botz, Paschal, O.S.B. xviii, 24–25,
  27–28, *29,* 30–35, 39–40, 43,
  45, 47, 49, 57, 64, 69–70,
  74–75, *77,* 78, 85, 133, 153
Bouley, Allan, O.S.B. xviii, 316
Bouyer, Louis, C.O. 116, 122,
  138–139, 151, 160
Boylan, Eugene, O.C.S.O. 116
Brady, Archbishop William O. 178
Braga, Carlo, C.M. 205
Breuer, Marcel 170–*171,* 174
Breviary 260, 269
Brinkhoff, Lucas, O.F.M. 167
Brunner, August, S.J. 168
Buckley, Francis J., S.J. xx
Bugnini, Archbishop Annibale, C.M.
  116, 183, *188,* 192–193, 201–204,
  206, 218–219, 241, 254, 257, 273
Busch, William 16, 84, *125,* 127,
  128, 129–130, 134, 136, 144–146
Buswell, Bishop Charles xx, 131,
  206, 290, 316
Bussard, Paul C. 102, 146
  Small Catechism of the Mass 102
Butler, Edward C., O.S.B. 249

Caecilia 146
Caesar, Doris 92
Canon law 112, 118, 224

Capelle, Abbot Bernard, O.S.B. 122, 148, 167
Carroll, Thomas xi, *125,* 131, 134–135, 146
Casel, Odo, O.S.B. 51, 59, 62
Cass Lake, Minnesota 102
Catacombs 36
Catechetics 104, 115, 121, 151
  liturgy 121, 151, 246
  method 104
Catechumenate 168
Catholic Art Quarterly 136
Catholic Choirmasters' Correspondence Course 136. *See also* Gregorian Institute.
Catholic press 107
Catholic Rural Life Movement 107
Catholic Song and Prayer Book 9
Catholic Theological Union xvii, xx
Catholic University of America xii, xv, 22, 96–97, 121, 136, 140, 162, 190, 196–201, 219, 231, 236, 250, 292
Catholic Worker 104, 131
Catholicism 103, 107, 112
  American 102–103, 107, 112, 115
  Celtic 112
  German 58, 112
  Italian 112
  Slavic 112
Celebration of the Eucharist, The 159–160
Celibacy 225–226, 241
Censorship 67
Centre de Pastorale Liturgique 155
Chalice 74, 232
Charity 90, 93, 100, 134, 225–226, 269–270, 303
Chavasse, Msgr. Antoine 160, 167
Chenu, Marie Dominique 210
Chicago ix, 28, 32, 124, 131
  Holy Name Cathedral 124, 131
China 72–73
Chippewa Indians 102
Christ-Life Series 103, 139
Christ Our Brother 58
Christensen, Bernhard *283*
Christian Life and Worship 139
Christian Religion Series 139
Christianity 57, 63
  deification 57
  integral 56
  message 57
  tranfiguration 63
Christians in Conversation 182
Christmas 9, 34, 72

Christology 51, 58, 104, 111, 245, 269
  Recapitulation theory 111
Christ's Sacrifice and Ours 25
Church x–xii, 9–10, 26, 63, 81, 90, 100, 103, 112–113, 121, 123, 126, 149, 164, 176, 187, 191, 193, 199, 210, 213–217, 239, 245–246, 249, 255, 266–269, 272, 278, 291, 313
  collaboration 267
  East German 191
  inculturation 187, 215
  Irish 9
  local 63
  mission xii, 72
  prayer life 103, 123, 164, 246, 269
  Reformation 252
  rites 215
  Russian: music 40
  social-political-economic doctrine 81
  United States 111–113, 123, 199
Church and state 38
Church year 103, 115, 158–159, 216, 253
  Lectionary 158–159, 181, 253
  prayers 270
Church's Year of Grace 9, 150
Cicognani, Cardinal Amleto 193, 202
Cicognani, Cardinal Gaetano 183, *188,* 189–190, 193–194, 208–211, 235, 242
Cincinnati 124, 131
Civil rights 279
Clinical pastoral education 175
Coddington, Dorothy and Thomas 135–136
Cofell, William xxi, 109
Cogley, John *229,* 255, 274
Collectio Rituum 162
College of St. Benedict, St. Joseph, Minnesota 91
Collins, Mary, O.S.B. 300
Come, Let Us Worship 201, 315
Commitment 99–100, 111, 143, 191, 269
Commonweal 113, 219
Communism 68, 187
Community 100, 235, 268–269, 288, 301, 303
Concelebration 151, 158–160, 169, 173–174, 181, 185, 226, 232, 256, 266
  "ceremonial" 150
  monasteries 160
  pilgrimages 160

Concelebration *(cont.)*
  synchronized Masses 160
  Vatican II 185
Conception Abbey, Conception, Missouri 144
Confession 11, 149
Confirmation 99, 167, 215, 268, 270
Confraternity of Christian Doctrine 162
  Cincinnati Conference 124
Congar, Yves, O.P. 116, 203, 210, 224
Congregation for the Eastern
  Churches 193
Connolly, Joseph M. 315
Convent of the Sacred Heart,
  Grosse Pointe, Michigan 124
Conway, Bertrand, C.S.P. 87
Cordeiro, Cardinal Joseph M. *261*
*Corporation Sole: Cardinal Mundelein and
  Chicago Catholicism* 146
Cotton, Francis R. 109
Cotting, Helen 182
Council Daybook 242, 251
Coyle, William, C.SS.R. 139
Crahan, Marietta, O.S.B. xxi
Creed 100, 126, 247, 284
Culhane, Alberic, O.S.B. xviii, 316
Cullmann, Oscar 286
Cummins, Patrick, O.S.B. 144
Cunningham, Joseph xix, 31, 49, 176
Cushing, Cardinal Richard J. 138, 256
Cushman, Robert xxi, 230
Cyril of Alexandria, St. 126

Daniélou, Jean, S.J. 116, 138, 210
Dante, Archbishop Enrico 222, 241
Day, Dorothy 104, 111, 131
Dearden, Cardinal John 203, 219
Death 312–313
De Hueck Doherty, Catherine 104
*De Imagine Dei in Homine Secundum
  Tertulliani Scripta* 54, 82
Dell'Acqua, Msgr. Angelo 235
De Lubac, Henri 203, 210, 266
De Roo, Bishop Remi xxi
Deshayes, Henri 160
Deutsch, Abbot Alcuin 13, 15,
  21–*23*, 24–26, 30, 33–35, 40–41,
  43, 46–*47*, 49–50, 53–54, 58–62,
  66, 68–70, 72–74, 76, 78–81,
  83–86, 97, 101–102, 105–107,
  109–110, 118, 132, 136,
  140–141, 145–147, 196
Deutsch, Alfred, O.S.B. xix, 95, 317
Devout Instructions 9

Diaconate 225–226, 256
Didache 93, 307
Dialogue Mass, The 139
Diekmann, Boniface 2, *5*, 7, *8, 17,*
  43, 76
Diekmann, Clara 2, *5*, 7, 42–43, 50,
  53, 70, 74–76, 83, 85–86, 304
Diekmann, Conrad, O.S.B. 2, *5,*
  7–*8,* 15–16, 32, 34, 69, 76, 249,
  303, *304,* 305
Diekmann, Doris xviii, 50
Diekmann, Godfrey, O.S.B.
  Catholic University of America
    196–201
  chaplain to prisoners 141–143
  childhood 1–12
  college 15–25
  correspondent 117–118
  ecumenist xvii, 175–176, 209, 227,
    232
  editor *(Worship)* 111–122
  educator xvii, 87
  formation director 86–87, 96
  high school 12–15
  hobbies xviii, 4, 34, 37, 40, 67,
    308–311
  humorist 222–224
  International Commission on English in the Liturgy 251–298
  missionary 27–28
  monk xvii, 72–73, 90, 204, 290,
    294, 301
    budget 33–34, 80, 161, 223, 317
    spirituality 42, 45–47, 52–53,
      70, 75–76, 78–79, 99, 102,
      106, 140, 202, 206, 277
  nicknames 5–6, 118, 308
  novitiate 10, 13, 15–16, 72
  patrologist xvii, 88–89
  peritus at Vatican II xviii, 182–275
  photos *5, 8, 14, 17, 29, 36–37, 45,
    47, 55, 77, 92, 125, 142, 154,
    158, 159, 163, 173, 188, 199,
    228, 229, 261, 262, 267, 280,
    283, 287, 296–297, 306, 309,
    310*
  priest 73–75, 78, 81, 96–97
  retreat master xvii, 86, 97–101,
    233, 234, 252, 268
  scholar 277
  social activist xvii, 278–282
  solemn profession 26, 43–*45*
  student in Rome 13, 32, 34, 49–85
  teacher 86–95, 252, 277
  theologian 289–293, 316

Diekmann, Godfrey, O.S.B. *(cont.)*
  traveler 294–301
  writer 292–293
Diekmann, Hubert 2, *5*, *7–8*, 76
Diekmann, John Conrad 1–4, *5–8*,
  12–13, 15, 27, 43, 69–70, 72,
  74–76, 81, 304
Diekmann, Julia 2, 4–*5*, 7, 76, 304
Diekmann, Marie xvi, xviii, 2, 7,
  43, 74, 76, 85–86, 109, 148,
  154, 223
Diekmann, Paul xvii, 2, 6–8, 12, *17*,
  40, 43, 50, 69, 74, 76, 84
Diekmann, Rosalie Loxterkamp 1–*5*,
  7, 13, 15, *17*, 27, 43, 53, 74–76,
  83, 85, 304
Divine Office 96, 99, 103, 115, 137,
  162, 164, 166, 174–175, 181,
  184–186, 191–194, 215–216,
  218, 223, 226, 233–235, 238,
  245, 272, 274, 301
  Commission on the Liturgy 184
  Roman Breviary 216, 225, 245
  priests 162
  reform 164, 166, 181, 184–185,
    225, 233–234
  religious and laity 115, 132, 137,
    216, 234–235
  vernacular 185, 193, 235, 238
Doctrine. *See* Theology.
The Doctrine of Spiritual Perfection 83
Documents on the Liturgy 1963–1979:
  Conciliar, Papal, and Curial Texts
  250–251, 273–274
Doepfner, Cardinal Julius 222
Dominicans, Marywood, Grand
  Rapids, Michigan 103, 139
  Christ-Life Series 103, 139
  Christian Religion Series 139
Doncoeur, Paul 160
Donohue, James, C.R. xxiv
Dowling, Mary Dolores, O.S.B. xxi
Downside Abbey, England 39
Ducey, Michael, O.S.B. 132–133, 146
Durken, Daniel, O.S.B. 288
Dworschak, Abbot Baldwin, O.S.B.
  xix, 121, 135, 146–147, 167,
  170–*171*, 180–182, 196–197,
  211, 219, *228*, 235, 250, 254,
  260, 274, 278–279, 315, 317
Dworschak, Bishop Leo 131, 203,
  207–209, 211, 220, *228*, 231,
  239, 243, 249–251

Easter Vigil 153, 157–158
Eastern Churches 63–64, 72, 95,
  131, 144, 164, 214, 269
  Armenian 95
  Chaldean 95
  Ethiopian 95
  Orthodox Church 237
Ecclesia Orans 62, 84
Ecclesiology 26. *See also* Church.
Economics 81
Ecumenical (Spiritual) Institute xxii,
  282, 286, *287–288*
Ecumenism 95, 107, 175–176, 179,
  192, 199–200, 209, 226–230,
  232, 237–238, 240–241, 258,
  266, 275, 277, 282–284, 286,
  288–289
  clergy retreats 209
  liturgy 226, 275
  Lutheran-Catholic Dialogue 284
  observers at Vatican II 223–224,
    227, 239, 255–259, 282
  prayer 175
  Presbyterians 237
  Southern Baptist-Catholic Dialogue
    285
  Tantur 286, 288
  World Council of Churches
    282–283
Education 90, 107
  Catholic 107
  methodology 60–61, 88, 90
Egan, Msgr. John xix, 178, 182,
  277–278, 315–316
Eichhorst, Jack xxi, 175
Eidenschink, Abbot John, O.S.B.
  xix, *171*, *228*, 316
Ellard, Gerald, S.J. 84, 127–*128*,
  130–131, 136–137, 144–147,
  155, 167, 169, 181
  Christian Life and Worship 139
  The Dialogue Mass 139
  Men at Work and Worship 139
  St. Mary's Seminary, Kansas 144
Ellerker, Mary, O.S.D. 144
Ellis, Msgr. John Tracy xix, 198, 219
Encyclicals 113, 127, 129
Engelberg 54, 84, 151
English College (Rome) 260–261
English Language Liturgical Consul-
  tation (ELLC) 275
English-Speaking Bishops' Commit-
  tee for Common Texts. *See* In-
  ternational Commission on
  English in the Liturgy.

Epiphany, feast of 113
Ethiopia 297, 316-317
Eucharist 56, 100, 122, 136, 149, 155, 166, 171-172, 214, 235, 241, 269, 278, 283-284, 288, 301
  Communion rail 171-172
  intercommunion 283, 288
  reform 166, 171
  rite 155
  Sunday 191, 288
Eucharistic Prayers 155, 169, 269
  Basil, St. 169
  Hippolytus 169
  Orient 169
Europe 26-27, 31, 81, 101, 148-152, 161
  Austria 31
  Catholic thinkers 81
  England 31
    Oxford 152
  France 27, 31
    dechristianized 161
    Lourdes 152
    Mont St. Michel 152
    Poitiers 152
  Germany 27
  liturgical leaders 148
European relief 22
Evangelization 72
Evans, Illtud, O.P. 170, 174, 182
  Blackfriars 170, 174
Exorcisms 168
Externals of the Catholic Church 87

Faber, Frederick William 112
Faith 52, 69-70, 89-90, 99, 157, 169, 174, 187, 191, 214, 237, 248, 269, 290, 292, 313, 314
Family Life in Christ 131
Fasting 40, 93, 142-143
  Didache 93
  Eucharistic 142
  Stewardship 93
Felici, Archbishop Pericle 219, 239, 247, 255, 258
Fenton, Msgr. Joseph 200, 221, 240
Finberg, Herbert 150, *262*, 264-265, 270
Finn, Daniel xix
Finn, Peter C. 274
Fischer, Balthasar xxi, 116, 167, 190, 232
Fisher, Desmond 220, 251
Fitzsimmons, John *262*

Florovsky, Georges 308
Following of Christ, The 10
Fontaine, Gaston 253
Fortescue, Adrian 59
  Ceremonies of the Roman Rite 59
  Mass: a Study of the Roman Liturgy 59
France 168-169
Franck, Frederick xxiii
Franquesa, Adalberto, O.S.B. 232
Franklin, R. William 145
  Virgil Michel: American Catholic 145
Friends of Friends 178, 182
Friendship 117-118, 126, 134-135, 139, 264, 284
Friendship House 104
Die Frohbotschaft und Unsere Glaubensverkündigung 104
Fulbright Scholarship 27
Fullness of Christ, The 105

Garofalo, Msgr. Salvatore 168
German 9, 68
  culture 10, 88
  language 3, 10, 68
  literature 3, 88
  theologians 58
Germany 58, 66-68
  bishops 58
  Catholicism 58
  Nazism 58, 66-68
  Westphalia 51
Gifts of the Holy Spirit 90
Gelineau, Joseph, S.J. 160
Gnosticism 54
God 11-13, 26, 52, 56-57, 76, 89-90, 93, 99, 122, 215, 247, 264-265, 270, 289-290, 301, 303, 314-315
  presence of 56, 90, 93
  providence 70-71
  transcendence 71, 264
Godfrey, Cardinal William 261
Goethe, Johann Wolfgang 88
Goffine, Leonard 9
Good News and Our Proclamation of the Faith, The 104
Gordon, Paul, O.S.B. 105, 151, 232
Grabmann, Martin 304
Grace 56-57, 70, 76, 78-79, 174-175, 270
  priesthood 75-79
  sacramental 56
  St. Paul 56-57
Grailville, Loveland, Ohio 137

Gray, Cardinal Gordon Joseph xxi, 237–238, *261*
Greek 195, 236, 312
Greeley, Andrew xix, 114, 172–173, 182, 282, 315–316
"Timely Tracts" 114
Gregorian chant 193, 235, 247
Gregorian Institute 136. *See also* Catholic Choirmasters' Correspondence Course.
Gregorian University 52
Gregory, St. 164
Gremillion, Joseph 178
Griffiths, Bede, O.S.B. 116, 260
Griffiths, Bishop James H. 260
Griffiths, John Howard 278
Grimshaw, Archbishop Francis J. 237, 259–261, 274
Groot, Jan C. 315
Grosse Pointe, Michigan 124
Convent of the Sacred Heart 124
Guardini, Romano 16, 62
The Spirit of the Liturgy 16, 62
Gy, Pierre-Marie, O.P. 116, 149, 167, 171, 182, 205, 232

Hackett, John *262,* 264
Hagen, Christopher, O.S.B. 109
Hallinan, Archbishop Paul J. x, 131, 203–204, 206, *208*–209, 211–212, 220, 225, 230–231, 237–238, 251, 260–261, 275
Hamer, Jerome, O.P. 166
Hammenstede, Albert, O.S.B. 60, 84, 116
Hänggi, Anton 232
Häring, Bernard, C.SS.R. 116, 203, 249
Harrison, G. B. xxi, *262,* 264–265, 270, 274–275
Harvard University 113
Hebrew 70–71, 312
Heenan, Bishop John C. 261
Hellriegel, Msgr. Martin x, 84, 118, *125,* 127, *128*–129, 136, 144–146, 155, 166, 180
Holy Cross Parish, St. Louis, Missouri 127
International Congress of Liturgical Studies 155
Precious Blood Sisters, O'Fallon, Missouri 127, 144
Herder-Korrespondenz 157

Herwegen, Abbot Ildefons 51, 60, 63–64, 68, 81, 84, 129
Hesburgh, Theodore, C.S.C. 286
Heschel, Rabbi Abraham 315
Higgins, Msgr. George 100, 110
The National Catholic Welfare Conference 100
Hillenbrand, Msgr. Reynold xxii, *125,* 127, *128*–129, 134, 136–137, 146, 155, 177–178, 182
International Congress of Liturgical Studies 155
St. Mary of the Lake Seminary 127–129
Hitler, Adolph 64–66, 142, 153
Hofinger, Johannes, S.J. 116, 138, 186, 215, 217
Holiness 46–47, 63, 99–100, 115, 122, 226
Holy Cross Parish, St. Louis, Missouri 127
Holy Land 162, 299
Franciscan Biblical House of Studies in Jerusalem 162
Holy Name Cathedral, Chicago 124, 131
Holy Office 157, 203, 210, 241
Holy Spirit 51, 56, 90, 93, 99, 165, 176, 247–248, 269, 284, 289, 291
Holy Week 113, 157
Horton, Douglas 316
Houselander, Caryll 116
Hovda, Robert xi, xxi
How Firm a Foundation x
Howell, Clifford, S.J. 116, 138–139, 204–205, 219, 232, 261, 263–264, 274
Hughes, Kathleen xi, 181, *262*
Hull House 104
Humility 53, 73, 78, 89–90, 138
Hunthausen, Archbishop Raymond 291
Hurley, Archbishop Denis 259, *261–262,* 270, 274

Ignatius Loyola, St. 100
Ignatius of Antioch, St. 89–90
Immaculate Conception Seminary (New Jersey) 123
Inculturation xiii, 165, 186–187, 194, 215–218, 233, 269, 283
Initiation 167. *See also* Baptism; Confirmation.

Institute for Ecumenical and Cultural
  Research 175, 286
International Commission on English
  in the Liturgy (ICEL) xi, xv,
  xvii, 31, 251, 259, 261–262,
  263–266, 269–276, 294–295, 298
International Congress on the Lit-
  urgy 153, 155–158, 160–169,
  180–181, 184, 189
  Maria Laach 153
  Strasbourg 155
  Lugano 155, 180
  Mont César 158, 252
  Assisi 161–166, 179, 181
  Montserrat 167
  Munich 169
  Vatican II. Commission on the
    Liturgy 184
International Consultation on Com-
  mon Texts. *See also* English Lan-
  guage Liturgical Consultation.
Irenaeus, St. 89, 149, 290
Irenikon 149
Isaiah the Prophet 121
Islam 95
Italy 38–39, 67–68
  Fascism 67

Jane Marie, O.P. 103, 139
Jenny, Archbishop Henri 231–232
Jerusalem
  Church of the Holy Sepulcher *296*
Jesuits
  Canadians in Ethiopia 317
  Salzburg 104
Jesus Christ 56, 58, 73, 79, 90, 93,
  213, 239, 245, 268–269, 273,
  291, 312–313
  humanity 58
  Infant 72, 94
  sacrifice 79
Jews 153
John XXIII, Pope 176, 183, 187,
  189, 191–193, 200, 204–205,
  207, 219, 232–235
John Cassian, St. 119
John Chrysostom, St. 89
Johnson, Cuthbert, O.S.B. 270
Jones, Audrey, O.S.B. xxi
Jones, Percy *262*, 264, 274
Jordan, Placid 240
Jounel, Pierre 253
Joyce, Patricia xix, 293–294, 298,
  316–317

Joyce, Thomas xix, 298, 300,
  316–317
Judaism 95
Jungmann, Josef A., S.J., 104, 116,
  138, 165, 167, 194, 203
  *The Good News and Our Proclamation
    of the Faith* 104
  The Mass of the Roman Rite 104
Justice 68, 277–279, 280–282
  and the liturgy 277–278
  divorce and remarriage 281
  Indonesia 279
  Kent State College 279
  Native Americans 279
  racism 279
  Selma, Alabama 279–*280*
  women 281
Justin Martyr, St. 126

Kacmarcik, Frank, Obl.S.B. xix,
  121, 145
Kahlefeld, Heinrich 253
Kantowicz, Edward R. 146
  *Corporation Sole: Cardinal Mundelein
    and Chicago Catholicism* 146
Kapsner, Oliver, O.S.B. 60, *229*
Kaufman, Philip, O.S.B. 316
Keifer, Ralph 276
Keillor, Garrison 1
Kelly, Bishop Thomas C. 300
Kennedy, President John F. 19, 245
Kennedy, Vincent, C.S.B. 116, 146
  Institute of Medieval Studies,
    Toronto 146
Kilzer, Ernest, O.S.B. 81
King, Martin Luther 278, 280
Klauser, Theodore 116, 129
Klosterneuburg, Austria 16
Knowledge (gift of the Holy Spirit) 90
Koenig, Cardinal Francis 291
Kramp, Joseph, S.J. 129
Kretschmar, Georg *287*
Kritzeck, James *228*
Krol, Cardinal John 203, 226
Krumpelman, Frances, S.C.N. xxiv
Küng, Hans 198–*199*, 200–201, 210,
  224, 241, 250, 266–*267*, 284

Labor 80
Ladies of the Grail 136–137
Laity 99, 115, 131–132, 165, 185,
  210, 226, 238, 241, 246, 269,
  281–282

Laity *(cont.)*
  liturgical movement 131-132
  marriage 226, 281
  participation 115, 165, 269
  priesthood 210
  spirituality 115, 246
  Vatican II 185
Lambert, Bernard 315
Landersdorfer, Bishop Simon 157
Lanne, Emmanuel, O.S.B. 253
Larraona, Cardinal Arcadio 194,
  203-204, 207-209, 212, 230,
  232-233, 241-242
Latin 187-190, 193-195, 230,
  233-238, 251, 263-264, 270
Laukemper, Bernard *125,* 131, 137
Lavanoux, Maurice 131, 182
  Liturgical Arts Society 131
Lawrence, Emeric, O.S.B. xix, 25,
  113, 301, 317
Leadership 96, 108, 117, 210
Leaflet Missal 139, 146
Lechner, Robert 316
Lectionary 158-159, 252-254, 259
  Church year 158-159, 252
  reform 252-253
  Liturgies: Eastern, Reformed,
    Western 154
Léger, Cardinal Paul Emile 255
Lenin, Vladimir 113
Lent 99
Leo XIII, Pope 18
Leonard, William, S.J. xi, xix, 131,
  146-147, 165-166, 181-182
Lercaro, Cardinal Giacomo 116,
  156-157, 164, 181, 222, 243
Lessing, Gotthold 88
Liberalism 81
Liberty, religious 255-257
Lichten, Joseph *229*
Liénart, Cardinal Achille 202
Life of the Spirit 149
Ligutti, Msgr. Luigi G. 240
Lindbeck, George 230, 246, 284
Liturgical adaptation. *See* Inculturation.
Liturgical apostolate 102-103, 105
Liturgical Arts 136, 182
Liturgical Arts Society 131
Liturgical Commission of Spain 168
Liturgical Conference 127, 131,
  133-135, 156, 162, 166,
  176-179, 181, 278, 281, 315
  by-laws 133
  secretariate (Washington) 177
Liturgical Days 101

Liturgical Institute (Maria Laach)
  51, 60
Liturgical Institute (Paris) 171
Liturgical Institute (Trier) 155
Liturgical legislation 117-118
Liturgical movement xvi-xvii, 16,
  18, 21, 98, 101-105, 107-108,
  111-112, 115-117, 121-126,
  129-132, 134-135, 137, 140-141,
  148, 150-151, 155-158, 161-162,
  165-167, 177, 181, 184-185,
  194, 207, 243-244, 246, 253,
  281-282, 292, 314
  apostolate 102-103, 156, 167-177
  catechetics 121, 150
  Europe 16, 63, 105, 111-112, 116,
    148, 150-151, 167
  Germany 59, 112
  laity 131-132
  leadership 117, 148, 184
  pastoral 18, 62-63, 165-166, 291
  reform 242, 246, 253
  scholarship 122
  social justice 18, 111-115, 150
  United States xvi, 16, 51, 86, 98,
    101, 103-104, 107, 111-116,
    121-124
  vernacular 140, 157, 165-166, 185,
    195
Liturgical Press 19, 84, 101, 103-104,
  130, 145, 148, 150, 307
  Popular Liturgical Library 19, 84,
    130
Liturgical Summer School 137
Liturgical Week Bulletin 146
Liturgical Weeks ix-x, 25, 123,
  125-127, 129-134, 146, 160,
  176-179, 278, 281, 315
  Chicago 126-127
  Milwaukee 281, 315
  New York 145-146
  Philadelphia 278
  Pittsburgh 176, 182
  Worcester 182
Liturgical year. *See* Church year.
Liturgie et Paroisse 149
Liturgy 113-115, 119, 121, 123,
  129-132, 134, 136-137, 141,
  149, 152, 157-158, 161, 171,
  186-187, 191, 207, 216, 222,
  226, 236-238, 241, 245-246,
  253, 269, 270-271, 277, 305,
  314
  bishops 152
  catechetics 121, 246

Liturgy *(cont.)*
  ecumenism 226
  Europe 148–152
  history 130
  inculturation 186–187, 283
  justice 277
  lay spirituality 137, 246
  Patristics 271
  prayer 132
  Scriptures 119, 253
  Theology for Catholic Action 129
  vernacular 113–115, 119, 186–187,
    283
Liturgy 149, 315
Liturgy and Mission 215
Liturgy and Sociology 135
Liturgy Training Publications x
Living Light, The 121
Living Parish 136
Loew, Joseph, C.SS.R. 189, 203
Long, John, S.J. 258
Lord, Daniel, S.J. 131
Louvain, Belgium 124, 145, 180, 181
Lowry, Charles Wesley *283*
Loxterkamp, Georgetta, O.S.B. xxi
Luther, Martin 87
Lutheran-Catholic Dialogue 284–285
Lutheranism 87
Luykx, Boniface, O. Praem. 138,
    186, *188,* 241

McAllister, Msgr. Joseph 198, 200
McCarthy, Abigail xx, 219, 293, 316
McCarthy, Senator Eugene xx, 205,
    219, 293
McDonald, Msgr. William 196–200,
    219
McDonnell, Kilian, O.S.B. xx, 121,
    285, 316
McEneaney, Msgr. John xxi, 145
McGarry, John 264
McIntyre, Cardinal James F. 187,
    223, 241
McManus, Frederick ix, 118–119,
    120–121, 135, 144–145, 169,
    176, 178, 181, 183–185, 190,
    192–194, 201–203, 205–209,
    211–213, 218–221, 224, 230–231,
    237–238, 241–243, 246, 249,
    252, 260, *261, 262,* 263, 264,
    274, 282, 315–316
  "Responses" in *Worship* 118
  The Revival of Liturgy 144
  The Rites of Holy Week 118

McNaspy, Clement J., S.J. xxi, 292,
    316
McQuade, Archbishop John C. 223
Madeleva, Mary, C.S.C. 136
  School of Sacred Theology for
    Women, St. Mary's, Notre
    Dame 136
Maison-Dieu, La 149, 168–169
Malula, Bishop Joseph 183, 185
Maly, Eugene 239
Marella, Cardinal Paolo 206
Maria Laach xvi, 16, 19, 25, 51–68,
    81, 83–86, 101–102, 110, 116, 123,
    146, 149, 153, 155–156, 180
  Nazism 65–66
  "Presence" 50–63
  See also Liturgical Institute.
Marriage 225–226
Marshall, Bruce 149
Martimort, Aimé-Georges 149, 160,
    167, 203, 205–206, 231–232, 237
Martin, Bishop Joseph M. 231, 249
Martin B. Hellriegel: Pastoral Liturgist 84
Martindale, C. C., S.J. 116, 150
Marty, Martin xix, 227, 230, 251
Marx, Karl 113
Marx, Michael, O.S.B. xix
Marx, Paul, O.S.B. 25, 110, 145
  *Virgil Michel and the Liturgical Move-
    ment* 25, 145
Mary, Blessed Virgin 92, 192, 224,
    239–240, 293
  Latin America 240
  sculpture by Doris Caesar *92*
  Vatican II 239–240
Mass 76, 99–100, 115, 137, 140,
    150, 153, 160, 171, 184–186,
    191, 202–203, 218, 223, 233,
    235–238, 245, 254, 256, 288
  concelebration 160
  evening 115
  Latin 185–186
  Missa recitata 150
  of the Catechumens 99
  synchronized 160
  vernacular 185–186, 191, 202, 235,
    238
Mass of the Roman Rite, The 104
Massi, Pacifico 253
Mathis, Michael, C.S.C. 127–*128,*
    130, 137–138, 147, 155, *159,*
    161–162
  International Congress of Liturgi-
    cal Studies 155
  Liturgical Summer School 137

Maurin, Peter 104
Mayer, Cardinal Augustin, O.S.B. 149, 270
Mediator Dei 127
Melrose, Minnesota 9
Men at Work and Worship 139
Merton, Thomas 204
Meyer, Athanasius, O.S.B. 15–16, 19–20, 26, 76
Meyer, Cardinal Albert 194–195, 218, 222, 255, 257
Michel, Virgil, O.S.B. xi, xviii, 15–16, 18–21, *23*, 26, 48, 81, 84–86, 101–108, 111–112, 115, 117, 122, 126, 129, 131, 139, 143–146, 148, 170, 243–244, 307
  and Alcuin Deutsch 105
  Chippewa Indians, Cass Lake, Minnesota 102
  dean of St. John's University 102, 104
  death 106–108
  junior prefect 20–21
  as a monk 104
  Orate Fratres 101–108
  Virgil Michel Citation 307
Milan 71, 162
Military Ordinariate 142
Miller, Leo 144
Miranda Vincente, Bishop Francesco 168
Missal 260, 269–270, 273–274
  Lectionary 273
  Prefaces 270
Missarum Sollemnia 104
Missions 72, 158, 162, 164–165, 215, 217–218
  liturgy 162
Mohrmann, Christine 236, 251
Monaghan, John P. 145–146
Monasticism 235, 285
Monopoli, Peter xxi
Monte Cassino 26, 43–44, 46, 153
Montini, Msgr. Giovanni 159. *See also* Paul VI, Pope.
Montreal 227, 232
Moore, Sebastian, O.S.B. 149
Moral theology 80
Morgan, Josephine, R.S.C.J. xxi
Morrison, Msgr. Joseph P. 131, 140, 146, 155
Moslems. *See* Muslims.
Moslems: religion. *See* Islam.
Motu Proprio on Sacred Music 141

Mount St. Scholastica, Atchison, Kansas 140
Mount Saviour Monastery, New York 146
Mueller, Franz xxi, 295, 316
Mueller, Therese xxi, 131
  Family Life in Christ 131
  Our Children's Year of Grace 131–132
Muellerleile, Al and Florence 301, 317
Muellerleile, Mary 301
Mundelein Seminary 127, 136
Munich 31–32, 34, 51, 64–66, 81, 84
Murphy, Francis X. 258
Murphy, Terence *229*
Murray, John Courtney, S.J. 137, 198–*199*, 200–201, 211, 250, 257, 266
Music 259, 305, 318
Muslims 95
Mussolini, Benito 38–39, 66–67
Muthappa, Bishop Francis 185
My Sunday Missal 139
The Mysteries of Christianity 52, 59
Mystery 52
Mystery cults 54
Mystical Body of Christ 19–20, 51, 56, 63–64, 75–76, 105, 115, 123, 146, 172, 244, 246, 314
The Mystical Body of Christ 105
Mystici Corporis 127
Mysticism 56

Nabuco, Msgr. Joaquim, 219
Nassau 167
National Catholic Reporter 315
National Catholic Rural Life Conference 162
National Catholic Welfare Conference 100, 181, 206
National Center of the Confraternity of Christian Doctrine 140
National Conference of Catholic Bishops 197
National Liturgical Week 146
National Liturgical Weeks. *See* Liturgical Weeks.
National Theological Colloquy 283
Nazism 58, 65–66
  German bishops 58
  German theologians 58
  prisoners of war 141–143
Nelson, Gertrud Mueller 132
Neo-scholasticism 52, 107

Neunheuser, Burkhard, O.S.B. xxii, 83–84
New York City 28, 30, 32
Newman, Cardinal John Henry 152
North American College 224, 226
Notitiae 273–274
Novak, Michael 249, 251
Nuremberg Trials 65–66

Obedience 73, 79
O'Connell, J. B. *125,* 185, 201, 208, 213, 220, 250–251, 261, 273
O'Connell, Matthew J. 272
O'Connor, Flannery 304
O'Hara, Archbishop Edwin 131, 162, 166
  Collectio Rituum 162
  Confraternity of Christian Doctrine 162
  National Catholic Rural Life Conference 162
Old Sources of New Power 62
O'Mahoney, James, O.F.M. Cap. 145
O'Malley, Kenneth, C.P. xxiv
One Man in His Times: The Memoirs of G. B. Harrison 275
O'Neill, Bishop Michael C. 260–261
O'Neill, Sara 144
Open Church, The 249, 251
Opera 32, 40
Orate Fratres. See *Worship.*
L'Osservatore Romano 183, 193, 207, 243, 254, 314
Ostdiek, Gilbert, O.F.M. xx, 276, 295, 298, 316–317
Ottaviani, Cardinal Alfredo 155–157, 168, 202, 204, 206, 240–241
Our Children's Year of Grace 131–132
Our Sunday Visitor 220
Our Father 126, 270
Outler, Albert C. 227, 230, 246, 248, 308, 318
Oxfam 94

Pacelli, Cardinal Eugenio 75. See also Pius XII, Pope.
Page, John xx, *262,* 274, 276, 294, 316
Papal primacy. See Popes: primacy.
Paris 31, 32, 151
Parish Kyriale 103
Parish mission 11–12
Paroisse et Liturgie 168

Parsch, Pius 116, 127, 129, 150
  The Church's Year of Grace 150
Pascher, Msgr. Joseph 189
Patristics 52–54, 57, 88–*92,* 94, 109, 115, 126, 164, 227, 270, 290, 314
  methodology 89–91
Paul VI, Pope 235, 238, 240, 246–247, 251, 254, 257–258, 266, 268, 286. *See also* Montini, Msgr. Giovanni
Paul, St. 36, 56–57, 78, 126, 246
Paulists 227
Paulo, Don, O.S.B. *45*
Peace xii, 113, 280–281
Pelagianism 22
Pelikan, Jaroslav 284
Pelton, Robert D. xxii
Periti 209–211, 226–227, 241, 258, 266
Peter Canisius, St. 104
Philosophy 52
Pieper, Josef 94, 116
Piepkorn, Carl 284
Pinsk, Johannes 129
Pius X School of Liturgical Music 131, 136, 140, 145
  Stevens, Georgia, R.S.C.J. 136
  Ward, Justine 131, 145
Pius X, Pope 18, 140–141, 244
  beatification and canonization 140
  Motu Proprio on Sacred Music 140, 244
Pius XI, Pope 38
Pius XII, Pope 153, 161, 165–166, 172, 181
  Assisi Congress 161
  eightieth birthday 161
  See also Pacelli, Cardinal Eugenio.
Pizzardo, Cardinal Giuseppi 206
Politics 81
Pontifical Institute on Music 193
Popes, primacy 284, 288
Popular Liturgical Library 19, 84, 130
Potkovsky, Benno, O.S.B. 28
Power, Richard 145
Prayer 10, 52, 69, 90, 99, 103, 115, 132, 151, 175, 191–192, 233–234, 237–238, 247, 289, 292, 301
  community 115
  ecumenical 175, 288–289
  family 132
  priests 233–234
The Praying Church 62
Press 199, 224–226, 243, 249, 255
Priesthood 15, 73, 76, 96, 99, 113
  leadership 96

Priests 97–98, 100, 113, 129, 136, 149, 151, 160, 162, 168–169, 178, 185, 191, 201, 222, 233–234, 241, 243, 246, 252, 265, 268, 278–279, 282
Belgium 168–169
Breviary 162, 233
celibacy 241
clericalism 246
concelebration 151, 160
Congo 241
continuing education 149
France 160–161, 168–169
Germany 168
Latin 185, 233
Liturgical Summer School 136
retreats 97–100, 151, 201, 233–234
spiritual life 162, 191
Princeton, Minnesota 141
Prisoners of war 141–142
Private Faces, Public Places 293, 316
Protestants 10, 119, 209, 224, 227, 232, 239, 255–256, 259, 266, 282
clergy retreats 209
Vatican II observers 223–224, 227, 239, 255–256, 258–259, 282
Putz, Louis, C.S.C. 178

Quanbeck, Warren 284
Quasten, Johannes xii, 185, 203, 218, 251
Question Box, The 87
Quinn, John S. 257

Racial question 107, 278, 281
Selma 279–280
Washington 278
Raes, Alphonse, S.J. 160, 167, 169
La Maison-Dieu 160
Rahner, Karl, S.J. 52, 159–160, 203, 210, 224
The Celebration of the Eucharist 159–160
Ratzinger, Cardinal Josef 116
Reed, Bishop Victor 131
The Reform of the Liturgy 218, 273
Reh, Bishop Francis I. 257
Reinhold, Hans A. xi, 18, 25, 112–115, 126–*128*, 129, 134–137, 140, 146–147, 155, 157–*159*, 178, 180, 185, 187, 213, 236
International Congress of Liturgical Studies 155
"Timely Tracts" 113–115
Vernacular Society 139–140

Religious life 113, 225, 255, 270, 302–303
Common of Virgins 270
Rite of Religious Profession 270
Women 97–98, 113
Rerum Novarum 18
"Responses" in *Worship* 118
Restoring the Sunday 137
Retreats 89, 97–101, 107, 151
liturgical 97–98
movement 107
priests 97–100, 151
Revista Liturgica 149
Revival of Liturgy, The 144
Revue des Sciences Philosophiques et Théologiques 149
Richter, Msgr. Bernard 9
Rites 215–216, 270
Funeral Rite 270
Rite of Baptism 270
Rite of Ordination of a Bishop 270
Rite of Religious Profession 270
Rites of Holy Week 118
Solemn Blessings 270
Ritter, Cardinal Joseph 199–201, 219, 255, 257
Ritual 241, 245, 260
Robyns, Anselme, O.S.B. 157
Roguet, Aimon-Marie, O.P. 116, 149, 167
Roman Question, The 39
Rome (City) 13, 26–27, 33, 36, 38, 47, 56, 60, 66, 68–69, 72, 75, 84–85, 96, 103, 112, 185–186, 208, 211, 238, 265, 298
Rome (Vatican) 58, 63, 157, 165–166, 172–173, 193–194, 201, 206, 210, 217, 241, 244, 254, 257
Curia 206, 210, 217, 231, 241, 254, 257
politics 231, 244
Theological Commission 241
Rosary 9, 11, 293, 301
Roscoe, Minnesota 1
Ross-Duggan, Colonel John K. 140, 155, *159*, 165–166, 237, 251
Amen 140
Rotelle, John, O.S.A. 276
Rouault, Georges 153
Rousseau, Olivier, O.S.B. 148
Rubrics 224
Ruffini, Cardinal Ernesto 204, 222, 249
Rule of St. Benedict, The 318
Russell, William H. 147

Ryan, John 181
Ryan, Mary Perkins xi, xx, 132, 146
Rynne, Xavier 231, 250

Sacraments 56, 64, 76, 90, 103, 116,
   122, 126, 136, 145, 149, 214–216,
   218, 235, 237, 245
   spiritual life 53, 103
   theology 53, 90, 149
Sacred Congregation for the Sacraments and Divine Worship 270
Sacred Congregation of Religious
   133, 194
Sacred Congregation of Rites 152,
   157, 172–173, 189, 194, 203,
   211, 218, 230, 232, 241, 254,
   270–271
   collegiality 270
Sacred Heart Messenger 116
Sacrosanctum Concilium xii–xiii
St. André (Belgium) 16, 18
St. Boniface Abbey (Munich) 64
St. Cloud, Minnesota 4, 123
St. George's College 286
St. John's Abbey, Collegeville, Minnesota xv, 9, 16, 19, 22, 26, 43,
   48, 53, 64, 72, 86, 96–97, 101–102,
   104, 107, 123, 133, 145, 169,
   172–173, 205, 211, 221, 255,
   278–279, 282, 286, 292, 293,
   298, 301, 303–304, 307, 316–317
   Bahamas 72
   China 72
   church 169–*173*, 174, *182*
   college 15
   community 104, 107, 169–173,
      197, 211, 301, 303, 316
   ecumenism 282
   Hill Monastic Microfilm Library
      298–299, 317
   Liturgical Days 101
   Mental Health Institute 175
   novitiate 15, 104, 204
   Orate Fratres 102
St. John's Seminary (Collegeville)
   15, 22, 53, 86–88, 94–95, 101, 304
   curriculum 94, 175
   ecumenism 175
   Israel Program 95, 299
St. John's Seminary, Boston 116,
   118
St. John's University, Collegeville
   xv, 22, 53, 86, 94, 101–102,

   104, 109, 121, 250, 278, 286,
      304, 317
   African American students 104
   Ethiopian students 317
   Liturgical Days 101
   Scripture Institute 175–176
St. Joseph of Gerlève Abbey, West-
   phalia 51, 62
St. Joseph's Abbey, St. Benedict,
   Louisiana 132
St. Louis, Missouri 127
St. Martin, Minnesota 10, 12
St. Mary of the Lake Seminary. *See*
   Mundelein Seminary.
St. Michael's College, Winooski,
   Vermont 305
St. Paul Seminary, St. Paul, Min-
   nesota 129, 144
St. Procopius Abbey, Lisle, Illinois 28
St. Thomas College, St. Paul, Min-
   nesota 295
Sainte Odile 156, 180
Saints 115, 159, 164
Salveggiani, Cardinal Francesco 75
Salzburg 81, 103–104, 154
Sammon, Peter xxii
Sant' Anselmo, Rome xvi, 24, 27,
   29, 31, 33–34, 36, 39–40, 46,
   49, 51–53, 56, 59–61, 67–68, 72,
   75–76, 82, 84, 97, 102, 144, 153
   Americans 102
   educational method 60
S. Maria sopra Minerva 75
Sause, Bernard A., O.S.B. *125*
Schachleiter, Abbot Alban, O.S.B. 58
Scheeben, Matthias 52, 59, 94
   The Mysteries of Christianity 52, 59
Schellman, James M. 274
Schillebeeckx, Edward 210
Schiller, Johann 88
Schmidt, Austin *125*
Schneider, John xxiv
Schnitzler, Msgr. Theodor 168
Scholastica, St. 44
School of Sacred Theology for
   Women, St. Mary's, Notre
   Dame 136
Schramel, Sebastian, O.S.B. *297*
Schürmann, Heinrich 253
Scrupulosity 11–13
Seasoltz, Kevin, O.S.B. xx
Sebastian, St. 13
*Second Session: The Debates and Decrees
   of Vatican Council II, September 29
   to December 4, 1963* 250

Secretariat for Promoting Christian Unity 230, 258, 282-283
Selma, Alabama xvi, *279*-280
Semaines Liturgiques (Louvain, Belgium) 124
Seminaries 116, 255
Shannon, James 220
Shaping English Liturgy 274
Sheen, Bishop Fulton J. 105
  The Mystical Body of Christ 105
  The Fullness of Christ 105
Sheehan, Shawn xi, *125*, 131, 133-135, 146-147, 164, 181-182, 292, 316
Shepherd of Hermas, The 93
Short Breviary 174
Sigler, Gerald *262*, 275
Sign 220, 251
Sisters of the Precious Blood (O'Fallon, Missouri) 127, 144-145
Skillin, Edward 145
Skudlarek, William, O.S.B. xxii, 285, 316
Skydsgaard, Kristen E. 246
Sloyan, Gerard S. xi, xxii, *120*-121, 145, 196-197, 219, 236, 251, 278, 281-282, 292, 315-316
Small Catechism of the Mass 102
Smith, Alfred 67
Smith, Hamilton *171*
Social justice 18, 107, 111, 113, 115, 122, 127, 150
  liturgy 111, 113, 115, 122
Somerville, Stephen *262*, 264-265
Southern Baptist-Roman Catholic Dialogue 285
Spaeth, Robert xx, 145
  Virgil Michel: American Catholic 145
Speaking of How to Pray 132
Spellman, Cardinal Francis J. 161, 187, 222, 240, 244
Speltz, Bishop George H. xxii, *229*
Spirit of Catholicism, The 58
Spirituality 18, 56-57, 90, 99-100, 102, 113, 115, 122, 134, 137-138, 140, 245, 247, 303, 305, 312-314, 317
  lay 137, 140
  liturgical 102, 115, 138
  Patristics 90
  sacraments 53, 56, 90
  social justice 18, 113
  spiritual direction 305, 317
Spülbeck, Bishop Otto 190-191
Stack, Gilbert, O.S.B. *125*

Stanley, David, S.J. 116
Stearns County, Minnesota 1-2, 4, 9, 27
Stedman, Msgr. Joseph 130, 139
Steere, Douglas xxii, 230
Stenzel, Aloysius 168
Stevens, Georgia, R.S.C.J. 136
Stohr, Bishop Albert 156-157
Stolz, Anselm, O.S.B. 35, 51-54, 56, 62, 81, 83
Stransky, Thomas 219
Stritch, Archbishop Samuel 124, 146
Stuckenschneider, Placid, O.S.B. xx
Suenens, Cardinal Leo Josef 222
Sullivan, John F. 87
Sullivan, Kathryn, R.S.C.J. xxii, 119, *120*-121
Summa Theologica 52, 79
Summer School of Catholic Action 131, 137-139
Symbolism 121, 216
Symposium on the Life of Pope Pius X 147

Tabernacle 172
Tantur, Jerusalem 94-95, 109, 282, 286-287, 288. See also Ecumenical Institute.
Tape-of-the-Month-Club 131
Tashiro, Augustine *55*
Tavard, George 219, 315
Tavis, Gordon, O.S.B. 317
Teaching. See Education.
Teaching of the Twelve Apostles, The. See *Didache.*
Tegels, Aelred, O.S.B. 122
Tertullian 54-55, 88-89, 91, 126, 139, 270
Theisen, Abbot Jerome, O.S.B. xx, 95, 109, 290, 299, 316-317
Theisen, Sylvester xxii
Theological Studies 137
Théologie de la Mystique 83
Theology 51-52, 72, 88-90, 93-94, 116, 134, 199, 277, 289-290, 305
  definition 290
  humility 89-90
  laity 94
  sacramentals 115-116
  spirituality 305
  teaching 89-90, 93
  theologians 199
  "theology of the heart" 35, 52-53
  "theology of the knees" 89-90
Thimmesh, Hilary, O.S.B. xx, 316

Thomas Aquinas, St. 80, 126
Thompson, Mary Paula, O.S.B.
  xxii, 109
Thorkelson, Willmar xxii
Thuis, Abbot Columban 132
"Timely Tracts" 113–115, 118
Tisserant, Cardinal Eugene 219,
  241–242
Titlis Mountain *37*
Tobin, Mary Luke, S.L. 268
Topel, Bishop Bernard J. 299–300
Translating 263–265, 270, 275
  International Commission on English
    in the Liturgy 270, 275
  Sacred Congregation for the Sacra-
    ments and Divine Worship 270
Trent, Council of 112, 204, 216
Tromp, Sebastian, S.J. 240
Truland, Maureen, O.S.B. xxii, 109
Truth 267, 278
Tübingen 56, 198
Tuzik, Robert x, xxii

Ullathorne, Archbishop William,
  O.S.B. 221, 249
Umberto II, King of Italy, 66–67
Understanding (gift of the Spirit) 90
United States 39, 86, 94, 112
  Catholicism 112
  Great Depression 86
  elections 67
  flag 39
University of Munich 60
University of Minnesota 52, 304
University of Notre Dame xv, 130,
  137, 140, 147, 177, 286
University of San Francisco 55, *92*
Unterkoefler, Bishop Ernest L. 257
Ursuline College, Louisville, Ken-
  tucky 140

Vagaggini, Cipriano, O.S.B.
  185–186, 207, 219
Vagnozzi, Cardinal Egidio 197–198,
  203, 206, 241
Van Bekkum, Bishop Wilhelm,
  S.V.D. 165, 215, 232, 237
Van Zeller, Hubert, O.S.B. 116
Vann, Gerald, O.P. 116
Vatican I, Council 221, 249
Vatican II, Council xii, xv–xvii, 58,
  100, 122, 140, 153, 165, 170,
  172, 174–176, 178–179, 181,

186, 198–206, 208–210, 221,
  252, 263–264, 282–284, 288, 291
  horarium 222–223
  liturgies 233
  observers 223–224, 227, 239,
    255–256, 258–259, 282, 284
  periti 210, 241, 255
  translating 238
  women 256, 315
_____. Central Commission
  193–195, 202–206
_____. Commission on the Liturgy
  183–190, 192–195, 198,
  201–209, 218, 224, 230–233,
  237, 241–246
_____. Consilium 252–255, 259–260
_____. *Constitution on the Church* 241,
  249, 291
  Schema on the Blessed Virgin
    Mary 239–240
_____. *Constitution on the Liturgy* ix,
  122, 185, 194, 202–217, 219,
  224, 225, 230, 241–249,
  252–254, 261–263, 268, 315
  Schema 213–217, 224–225, 230,
    241–243, 246–249
_____. *Declaration on Christian Educa-*
  tion 258
_____. *Decree on Communication* 241, 247
_____. *Decree on Ecumenism* 230
_____. *Decree on Religious Liberty*
  255–257
Vatican Council (1867–1870) Based on
  Bishop Ullathorne's Letters, The 249
Vatican Diary 316
Vatican Radio 226
Velasquez, Diego Rodríguez de Silva y,
  13
Vernacular 140, 157, 165–166, 185,
  187–190, 193–195, 202–204,
  207, 225, 232–238, 241, 245,
  251, 259–260, 269
  Veterum Sapientia 197
Vernacular Society 114, 139–140,
  236, 251
Versailles 31, 160, 180–181
Vespers 9
Veterum Sapientia 197
Vettero, Augustin 59
Vie Spirituelle, La 149
Vielen Messen und das eine Opfer, Die
  159–160
Virgil Michel: American Catholic 145
Virgil Michel and the Liturgical Movement
  110, 145

Vitry, Ermin, O.S.B. 130, 146
Von Papen, Franz 66
Von Schenk, Berthold, *283*
Vonier, Anscar 64

Wagner, Mary Anthony, O.S.B. xx, 109
Wagner, Msgr. Johannes 155, 167–169, 180, 185, 202–203, 213, 231–232, 237, 241, 246
Wahl, Thomas, O.S.B. *309*
Walsh, Archbishop Joseph 184
Walsh, Eugene, S.S. 98, 110
Wanderer, The 285
War 280
Ward, Justine 131, 136, 145–146
Waters, Bishop Vincent 131, 206
Watrin, Joachim, O.S.B. 102
Way, The 202
Weigel, Gustave, S.J. 198–*199*, 200–201, 250–251, *283*
Weigle, Luther A. *283*
Willcock, Christopher, S.J. *262*
Wilmes, Msgr. Aloysius xxii, 166, 181
Winkelmann, Bishop Christian 98, 109–110
Winstone, Harold *262*, 264–265
Winter, Leo, O.S.B. 9
Winzen, Damasus, O.S.B. 123–124, 137, 146
Wisdom (gift of the Spirit) 69, 90

Women 119, 256, 268, 270, 281, 292, 315
  auditrices at Vatican II 256
  ordination 315
World Council of Churches (Montreal) 282–283
World War II 22, 25, 67–68, 94, 152–153
Worship. *See* Liturgy.
Worship/Orate Fratres ix–x, xii, xvii, 19, 25, 48, 84, 101–108, 110, 113–119, 121–123, 127, 130–131, 135–136, 144–149, 156, 161, 169, 179–182, 201, 207, 263, 283, 292, 300
  catechetics 121
  editorial board 116
  name change from *Orate Fratres* 119
  "Responses" 118
  subscriptions 116, 119
  "Timely Tracts" 113–115
Worship and Work 182
Wright, Bishop John 114, 178

Young, Archbishop Guilford xxiii, 225, 260–261
Yzermans, Msgr. Vincent A. xx, 109, *199*, 207–208, 210–211, 220, *229*, 276, 316, 318

Zeal 93
Zurich 69